W9-BTC-389

The
Rhode Island
Guide

The
Rhode Island
Guide

Barbara Radcliffe Rogers
Stillman D. Rogers

Fulcrum Publishing
Golden, Colorado

To Rose Island Lighthouse, where this book began,

and to all those who have relit its beacon

and kept it shining into the Narragansett night.

Copyright © 1998 Barbara Radcliffe Rogers and Stillman D. Rogers
Cover image of Rocks at Beavertail Lighthouse State Park copyright © 1998 Tom Till
All interior photographs copyright © 1998 Stillman D. Rogers, except for
    Brown and Hopkins Store, page 63 copyright © Blackstone Valley Tourism Council
Back cover images © 1998 Stillman D. Rogers
Maps copyright © 1998 XNR Productions
Book design by Deborah Rich

All rights reserved. No part of this book may be reproduced or transmitted in any form or by any means, electronic or mechanical, including photocopying, recording or by any information storage and retrieval system, without permission in writing from the publisher.

The information in *The Rhode Island Guide* is accurate as of this writing. However, prices, hours of operation, phone numbers and other items change rapidly. If something in this book is incorrect, or if you have ideas for the next edition, please write to the authors at Fulcrum Publishing, 350 Indiana Street, Suite 350, Golden, Colorado 80401-50931.

Library of Congress Cataloging-in-Publication Data
Rogers, Barbara Radcliffe.
    The Rhode Island guide / Barbara Radcliffe Rogers, Stillman D. Rogers.
        p.   cm.
    Includes bibliographical references and index.
    ISBN 1-55591-300-8 (pbk.)
    1. Rhode Island—Guidebooks.   I. Rogers, Stillman, 1939–.   II. Title.
    F77.3.R65   1998
    917.4504'43—dc21   97–42548
                                                                                        CIP
Printed in the United States of America

0 9 8 7 6 5 4 3 2 1

Fulcrum Publishing
350 Indiana Street, Suite 350
Golden, Colorado 80401-5093
(800) 992-2908 • (303) 277-1623
e-mail: fulcrum@fulcrum-books.com
website: www.fulcrum-books.com

Contents

Acknowledgments

Authors serve only as catalysts and scribes for a book; it is created by many more people. So many in this case that we can't even name them all. But many we can name, and will.

Two stand out in particular for their early enthusiasm and long-standing continuing help: Barbara Barnes and Charlotte Johnson. Barbara is with Providence Preservation Society, and it was in her company that we first looked up as we walked along Weybosset Street to see the wonderful architectural details of its facades and inspected the elevator doors in banking buildings and learned why the two fronts of the Arcade don't match. Charlotte is the director of the Rose Island Lighthouse Foundation, and although she didn't establish it alone, her vision and drive have made it work. Her stories and the lighthouse itself started us on this long trail through a short state.

Bob Billington of the Blackstone Valley Tourism Council also shared our enthusiasm from the start and led us to corners of the valley we most certainly would have missed. Evan Smith of Newport County Convention and Visitors Bureau, along with Brian Whiting and Nici Lanowy of his capable staff, made sure no detail of Newport escaped our scrutiny. Becky Bovill, Coleen Carson, Martha Sheridan, Kate McCauley and Ann O'Neil were equally helpful in their respective areas, adding place names to our growing lists, helping us track down obscure stories and generally encouraging us in our search. Anita Raphael shared her exhaustive knowledge of Newport history with us, as she does with guests on her Newport on Foot walking tours, and Karen Taylor of Taylor Made Reservations found us lodging when every room in Newport was filled.

We are firm believers in talking with innkeepers, whether the inn is the gleaming Biltmore in Providence or a tiny B&B in South County. Marlene Scalzi, of the former, shared her wealth of knowledge about Providence;

Jan and Will Pinckard at Willingham Manor in Chepachet led us to almost forgotten mill villages; Michael Fayerweather of Country Acres B&B told us of trails his Narragansett ancestors used. Patricia Watkins of Old Clerk House in Narragansett Pier, Leigh Anne Mosko of Villa Liberte in Newport and Pat Grand of Grand View in Westerly shared their boundless knowledge of their towns; owners and innkeepers of The Victorian Ladies, The Francis Malbone House, Pilgrim Inn, Mill Street Inn and Admiral Benbow Inn, all of Newport, added detailed information to the warm hospitality they offer all their guests. Jan Abrams and her family made sure we didn't miss anything on Block Island, although we were so pampered at the Manisses Hotel that we hated to leave it for a minute.

Writing a book is like a great never-ending treasure hunt with too many clues. These have often come from unexpected sources, people we met quite by chance as we sat next to them at dinner or they struck up a conversation while we all were listening to a calliope at Slater's Mill. The Cardi family, whom we met in L'Osteria in Cranston, told us of restaurants we otherwise would certainly have missed. Art Blackman and the Stevenses (Peter Stevens of Olneyville New York System) were drawn into the same inter-table conversation—do these happen anywhere but Rhode Island?—and added their own favorites (and we have remembered them all gratefully as we enjoyed meals in the places they suggested). It was that evening that first drew our attention to Raphael's Bar Ristro, which we think joins Al Forno to form the brightest pair of jewels in the Providence diadem. Closer to home, our thanks to our daughter, Juliette, who keeps us constantly up-to-date on doings on College Hill and the East Side.

Although she's never been to Rhode Island, this book could not have happened without patient, good-humored encouragement and help from Carmel Sferrazza Huestis, our editor in Colorado. She was the first to take us seriously when we suggested a complete guide to the state, and she quickly realized that square miles could not determine the number of its pages. With her help, we've followed Rhode Island's own example to pack a lot into a manageable-sized package.

Introduction

Background Information

Rhode Island's size is a magnet for cliché and for comparison: Every introduction to the state begins with a quip, a snipe or a square-mile analogy with some other place. Far more interesting—and important to the traveler—is the measurement of its coastline.

No nickname could fit Rhode Island better than The Ocean State, since the ocean has shaped its past and defines its present. Four hundred miles of coast stretch like a series of semaphore signals, alternating dots and dashes of white-sand beaches and wild coastal marshes. The former makes it a foremost beach destination in the East, the latter provides habitat for migrating and resident birds, and for the birders who follow them. Divided almost in half by the Narragansett Bay and further separated by the baylike Sakonnet River, the state's low rolling landscape is never more than 30 minutes from salt water. Cool sea breezes fan it in the summer and warming ocean currents protect it from winter's worst weather.

Almost every sort of shore scenery and environment is found somewhere in Rhode Island. Low rocky shores, steep rock cliffs, soaring sand bluffs, extensive tidal marshes, quiet estuaries, salt ponds and harbors—small coves with a few fishing boats at wooden piers, the bustling commercial fisheries at Galilee, the pleasure-craft marina of East Greenwich and the great yacht "fleet" at Newport. No one who loves the sea and ships could fail to love Rhode Island.

It was Rhode Island's shore and its sea breezes that brought the first summer visitors in early colonial times, when aristocratic southern families sailed north to summer in Newport. The wealthy continued to come,

Quick Facts about Rhode Island

Capital: Providence
Square miles: 1,545
Length: 48 miles
Width: 37 miles
Population: 1,000,012 (1993 census)
Full name: Rhode Island and the Providence Plantations

eventually building the astonishing row of palaces that line Bellevue Avenue. While Newport became the summer playground of New York's high society, miles of other beaches attracted everyone else, and resort towns from the modest cabins of Jerusalem to the grander hotels of Narragansett Pier began to grow.

Architecture from every period of the state's long history—which covers the entire span since European settlement, are not only preserved as museums but line the streets and roads as everyday homes. Providence is a standing museum of architectural styles, with entire blocks of eighteenth-century buildings, fine Victorian neighborhoods and imposing structures in Empire, Art Deco and Beaux-Arts styles. Late-nineteenth and early-twentieth-century commercial buildings, sadly lost in the urban renewal craze of so many other cities, are elegantly preserved in its downtown streets.

Ethnic diversity is a way of life in Rhode Island, whose very foundation was based on the live-and-let-think principles of Roger Williams. Free thought and a healthy respect for differences in religion, culture and color have made the state a rich tapestry of influences from all over the world. This goes deeper than a calendar of made-for-tourist festivals. In Rhode Island these boisterous, spontaneous events would be much the same if they were not even mentioned by the tourist office. They are part of the social patterns of real people and provide not only color but dimension and depth—and a richly varied cuisine.

Wherever two or more Rhode Islanders gather, the talk will turn to food. If the state has any obsession, it is with eating well. This translates into a world-class restaurant scene but also into a land of neighborhood restaurants dedicated to every sort of soul food. Only Rhode Island has its own vocabulary of foods, and no other state has so many national dishes. From jonnycakes to the distinctive way Rhode Islanders prepare snails and calamari, from coffee cabinets to quahogs, even to a distinctive style of chowder not found outside its borders, Rhode Island has its own culinary world. If you are judged at all in Rhode Island, it will be by where you eat.

No place loves a festival as much as Rhode Island, so something is always happening there. Newport's calendar is so full that it's hard to find a weekend at any time of year that the city isn't celebrating something. But it is not alone. The celebration may be as big and flashy as a yachting race, or as homegrown as a local May jonnycake breakfast. It may celebrate a holiday, as they do in Bristol every July 4, or a historic event such as the burning of the British ship *Gaspee*, or it may be a whole way of life, such as the Slater's Mill Labor and Ethnic Festival. Likely as not it will celebrate food: a chowder cook-off, a pasta challenge or the state's official mollusk, the quahog. Whatever the event, it will be filled with friendly, upbeat people who will strike up a conversation with you at the slightest excuse—or none at all. At the least, they will tell you about their favorite restaurant.

Once you turn off the interstate, from which so many people get their only view of the state, you are almost certain to find a reason to linger. When you do, you may never drive back up the ramp.

History

Rhode Island's history was shaped by two factors: cussedness—or at least a fierce sense of individuality—and water. Cussedness came first. The earliest settlers arrived by land. They arrived in the dead of winter, fugitives from Puritan Boston, escaping before they could be deported back to England for their seditious views. Their leader, Roger Williams, and a few followers made their way to the head of Narragansett Bay, where Williams founded Providence in 1636 as a haven for those who did not agree with the strict religious conformity required by the Massachusetts Bay Colony.

These free-thinking intellectuals created a society where all beliefs could be practiced openly, in contrast to the other New England settlements, which adhered to particular religious tenets.

From this earliest settlement, the church was completely separate from the civil government. Even today, Rhode Island towns do not cluster around their churches as towns do throughout the rest of New England. Elsewhere the church was the first, and for a long time the only, public building, where town meetings were held, disputes settled and justice dispensed. Not so in Rhode Island, where all religions were tolerated but none held ultimate authority.

Attracted by the colony's independent attitude, other dissenters arrived. Anne Hutchinson, another radical Boston theologian, founded Portsmouth in 1638 with William Coddington. They disagreed so vehemently, however, that Coddington and his followers moved on to found Newport. In 1643, Samuel Gorton was banished from Boston because of his antisocial behavior (he was not only a dissident theologian but a very difficult man), and he founded Warwick. Such a collection of freethinkers this was that the Puritan leader Cotton Mather called the whole lot of them "sewer of New England."

Rhode Island's history differed from neighboring New England states in another major way: It was the only one settled under the

x

Cuisine

Jonnycakes, made from stone-ground cornmeal, are a Rhode Island specialty, but don't expect menus to be filled with traditional old-fashioned Yankee dishes. Restaurants offer ethnic foods, particularly Italian and Portuguese. For the latter, go to Pawtucket or to Valley Falls, at Pawtucket's northern edge. The best selection of restaurants is in Providence and Newport and ranges from modest family and ethnic places to stylish and trendy spots. The Visitor's Bureau in Providence publishes a dining guide with a map. The following glossary of Rhode Island foods and food terms may be helpful in translating menus.

Awful Awful: An ice cream sundae served by Newport Creameries throughout the state.

Chicken Family Style: Found mostly in the Blackstone Valley and in the northern part of the state. Traditionally it is chicken, vegetables and pasta served at communal tables. In restaurants, it is sometimes all-you-can-eat chicken served with all the fixings. You can find it at Wrights Chicken Farm in Burrillville or the Bocce Club in Woonsocket.

Coffee Cabinet: The state drink. A cabinet is a milkshake, or, elsewhere in New England, a frappe. It includes milk, ice cream and coffee syrup. Even in the winter you'll see people lined up to get their cabinets.

Dynamite: A highly seasoned sloppy joe draped over a roll; found on Woonsocket menus.

Jonnycakes: Small griddle cakes made of cornmeal that has been stone ground at Gray's or Kenyon's original water-powered

mills. Some people substitute commercial cornmeal, which makes a tasty griddle cake, but it isn't really a jonnycake. These are served at May Breakfasts, usually at local churches and fire stations.

New York System Wieners: Only in Rhode Island can you find these hot dogs, which are steamed and covered with onions that have been blanched very briefly and mixed with each purveyor's special blend of seasonings. They are rarely found south of Providence. Our favorite place to sample these—and we know this may lead to mass ritual burnings of our book, since everyone staunchly defends their own favorite place—is in Olneyville.

Quahogs: While some might be tempted to suggest that this is any clam that swims through Rhode Island waters and is caught in passing, the quahog is actually an indigenous hardshell clam variety peculiar to eastern waters and particularly plentiful here.

R.I. Clam Chowder: While the rest of New England uses cream and battles it out with southerners who insist on adding tomatoes, Rhode Islanders do neither, serving the chowder as a clear, rich broth. (You can get other styles here, but when you see it labeled R.I., you're getting the local style.)

Rhode Island Greening: A variety of apple developed on an early farm in Newport. By state law, all apple pies served in the state are made from these. (OK, so we made that up. It *ought* to be a law.)

Stuffies: Quahog shells filled with a mixture of ground quahogs and seasoned bread stuffing, then baked.

plantation system used so widely in the South. Instead of in village settlements, much of the land was organized into large estates that were the fiefdom of one family or a small group of families. This system led to the use of slaves as field labor, and although slaves were not uncommon in any of the New England colonies, they were elsewhere used mostly as domestic servants.

Long before Europeans established their plantations and trading posts here, nations of the native Algonquin had roamed the land and fished its waters. On the west side of the bay were the Narragansetts, on the east their rivals the Wampanoags. The few Nipmucks were dominated by these two, and the Manisses had Block Island entirely to themselves. All were undisturbed by outsiders, apart from some early explorers—the Portuguese Miguel Corte-Real may have been here, and Verrazzano certainly was—until the 1600s. (Unless, of course, those who claim early Viking voyages here are correct. There is little definitive proof, and it is quite certain that Rhode Island was not the Vinland of Leif Ericson's sagas, which is now accepted to have been in northern Newfoundland.)

Roger Williams was a friend to the Narragansetts, who had helped him and his followers in their flight from Massachusetts. It was Williams's insistence that the Crown had no right to usurp Native lands as much as his religious unorthodoxy that caused his final banishment from the Bay Colony. He traded with the Narragansett from his trading post in Wickford and studied their language and religion.

Cotton Mather was not the only New Englander who didn't like Rhode Island. Its colonies never became members of the United Colonies of New England, and Connecticut and Massachusetts colonies persistently tried to annex its lands. To protect the Rhode Island settlements from these attempts, as well as to cement them together in the face of the constant bickering among themselves, Roger Williams and a Dr. Clarke of Newport returned to England and implored the Crown for a charter encompassing all the Rhode Island colonies.

This Charter of 1663 not only unified and protected Rhode Island but codified the principles of religious freedom and an independent civil authority. This document (which you can see in the Rhode Island State House) was so forward-looking in its provisions that it was used in place of a state constitution until 1842.

Although the charter protected Rhode Island from a hostile takeover by Massachusetts and Connecticut, it didn't save it from another threat. Colonists from those two areas had different relationships with the Indians than did their Rhode Island neighbors, and their constant attacks led to King Philip's War in 1675. Although Rhode Islanders neither supported nor joined the attacks on the Narragansetts, the bloodiest battle of that war took place in Rhode Island's Great Swamp, and in reprisal Providence and many other settlements were attacked and burned. The home of Roger Williams remained unharmed. Even in the bitterest hours, the Narragansetts remembered that he was their friend.

While Providence rebuilt, focus shifted to Newport. Its protected harbor provided a fine home for a fleet of merchant ships, and farming soon gave way to shipping as the mainstay of the Rhode Island economy. Narragansett Bay became the center of a thriving shipbuilding industry. Newport and, later, Providence ships and sailors roamed the world, trading in Europe, the West Indies, China and other Far East ports. The profitable Triangle Trade began with New England (mostly Rhode Island) ships trading rum for slaves in West Africa and taking the slaves to the Caribbean and southern ports, where they were traded for molasses. The barrels of molasses were brought home to New England and distilled into rum, which was carried to Africa to complete the triangle.

The Sugar Act of 1764 stopped the importation of molasses, or sought to, so Rhode Island shipowners continued their lucrative business by smuggling. It was in an effort to curb this activity that the British custom ship *Gaspee* was dispatched to Narragansett Bay, where it was burned by a group of Providence men. This was the first act of open aggression against the Crown in the years leading to the American Revolution. There would be more.

Whether based on idealism or economics, independence continued to be at the heart of Rhode Island's public and private agenda: It was the first colony to declare its separation from Britain, two months before the Declaration of Independence was signed in Philadelphia. Just as King Philip's War had destroyed Providence, the American Revolution took its worst toll on Newport, which was occupied by British troops. Although it enjoyed a brief resurgence before the War of 1812, it never fully recovered.

Meanwhile, Providence had been busy with other developments. Along with shipping, it had been developing its manufacturing. While much of Rhode Island's early history was shaped by the sea, it was a relatively modest river in northern Rhode Island that gave birth to the American Industrial Revolution. The Blackstone River drops over 400 feet in less than 40 miles, providing enough force to power mills along its entire length. In 1793, Samuel Slater, a Scottish textile-mill worker, arrived in America with an understanding of the workings of spinning mills. With the financial help of Providence's leading commercial family, the Browns, he established a water-powered cotton mill at the falls of the Blackstone, founding New England's textile industry and a whole new way of manufacturing.

With the beginning of the mill system, the American Industrial Revolution was on its way. Soon the entire Blackstone Valley hummed with shuttles and looms. Mills lined the river, surrounded by villages built by the manufacturers to house their workers. So much labor was needed to support the rising textile industry that workers were recruited from the crowded and impoverished countries of Europe and from French-speaking Canada. Italians, Irish, Canadians and other immigrants soon outnumbered the Yankees in the northeast corner of the state and along its southern rivers near Westerly.

As farming diminished and the workforce became more industrial, there was rising pressure to change the provisions of the Charter of

Forts to Explore

Defensive fortifications line the Rhode Island coast, remaining from wars since the Revolution. In Newport, prerevolutionary barracks are well preserved on Rose Island, and Fort Adams remains intact with its nineteenth-century renovations. At Brenton Point are the gun mounts from its days as a World War II coastal defense. In nearby Jamestown are the remains of Fort Wetherill. In Watch Hill, at the end of a long sand spit, are the ruins of a Spanish-American War installation. At Ninigret Point, you can see the overgrown runways of the Naval Air Training Station, and at Quonset the only remaining brick Quonset hut in the East. The oldest remaining fort in the state is one built in Exeter by the Narragansetts as a defensive position during King Philip's War.

1663, which gave the vote only to male landowners and their eldest sons. Efforts to adopt a new state constitution led to the armed insurrection known as Dorr's Rebellion in 1843, but the measures were eventually passed.

When wooden boats were replaced by metal hulled ships for commerce, the ship and boat building that began in colonial times turned to the production of pleasure and racing craft. Successful America's Cup defenders were built in Bristol—you can learn their history at the Herreshoff Marine Museum there—and a number of boat building firms still operate today. One of these is actively involved in building nuclear-powered undersea craft.

Rhode Island was the birthplace of the U.S. Navy in 1775, when Newport's deep, ice-free waters made its harbor an ideal base. That affinity with the Navy has continued, and today Newport is the site of the Navy's Education and Training Center, as well as several other commands. A destroyer, several frigates and other ships are based in Newport. At Quonset Point, south of Providence, the Seabees began in 1942; it is still home to the Naval Construction Force, the famous Construction Battalion's modern counterpart.

Lyme Disease

This infection, resulting from the bite of a deer tick, although it's not common, is present in all areas of Rhode Island and throughout southern New England. Deer ticks live in woods and grasslands and can attach themselves unnoticed, for they are very tiny—about the size of the period at the end of this sentence. If you are hiking or walking in wooded or grassy areas, tuck your pant legs into your socks, wear shoes instead of sandals and use a commercial tick repellent on your clothing. Examine yourself after hiking, and if you find a tick, call a medical center for directions on its safe removal. Symptoms of the disease itself include a slowly developing red rash around the bite area. If you plan to do a lot of hiking, pick up the informational leaflet available at parks and tourist information offices throughout the state. Detected, Lyme disease can be treated with antibiotics, but if it's left untreated it can lead to severe arthritis or worse. As we write, a new vaccine is being tested, so check with a physician for the latest news.

For the traveler, perhaps the most significant fact about Rhode Island's history, apart from its serving as a capsule history of the nation's early years, is that this history is everywhere as you travel. You can visit Roger Williams's trading post at Wickford and watch vintage planes being restored inside a rare brick Quonset hut at the old Naval Air Station nearby. You can tour the homes of the most important colonial families of Providence and Newport, or that of a governor of the Victorian era. Still standing are the rare brick enders of the early settlers and the earliest works of America's first architects and cabinetmakers. You can explore ruined forts from nearly every period of our history, including prerevolutionary barracks on Rose Island. You can stand in the forgotten tower of a fort built by the Narragansetts during King Philip's War or fish above the wreck of the *Andrea Doria*. You can time-travel back to the Gilded Age during a tour of a Newport mansion.

For more details on the state's history, see the beginning of each chapter and the sites where specific events took place. King Philip's War, for example, is discussed with the Great Swamp Fight Monument, and the origins of the Industrial Revolution appear with Blackstone Valley. For details on the early years of Providence or Newport, see those cities.

Geography and Geology

Narragansett Bay and the wide mouth of the Seekonk River, which flows into it, cut Rhode Island in two. Rhode Islanders refer to the two sides quite logically as East Bay and West Bay, with the mainland west of the Seekonk River constituting West Bay, and everything else, including East Providence, in East Bay. This area is further divided by water. Newport, Middletown and Portsmouth are on a separate island connected to the mainland, via the smaller Conanicut Island, by two long bridges over the bay. At the eastern border, the Sakonnet River and Mount Hope Bay cut off another section, leaving two towns glued to the state of Massachusetts by land and to the rest of Rhode Island by bridges. Block Island lies off the southern shore, separated from it by Block Island Sound. The waters south of Newport are in Rhode Island Sound.

The coastal area around the bay and its islands is fairly flat, rising to cliffs in Newport and dramatic bluffs on Block Island but elsewhere lined alternately by beaches, low rocky shores and tidal marshlands. Inland, toward the Connecticut border, the land rises to low rolling hills, the highest of which is Jerimoth Hill in North Foster, with an 812-foot altitude. Lakes and ponds dot the map, and long river mouths, bays and salt ponds mark the entire coast. The smallest state in the United States, Rhode Island measures 48 miles north to south and 37 miles east to west, and has more than 400 miles of shoreline.

The entire state, including Block Island, is a prime example of glacial moraine, which accounts for the rocks you will see scattered through its fields and woodlands. You would see even more but for the miles and miles of stone walls built by early farmers to clear the fields for planting. Especially in the Tiverton and Little Compton area on the east, now covered in large cultivated fields, the stone walls are a noticeable feature of the state's landscape.

Glacial moraine is land created by a glacier as it moves and melts away. The debris it collects as it scours the land comes to rest wherever the glacial sheet stops moving. During the last Ice Age, the sheet that stretched for 2,000 miles to the north stopped moving over what is now Rhode Island, dropping tons of rock, sand, gravel and clay as it dwindled in the warmer southern latitude. An interesting feature of this moraine occurs at the final line of forward advance. At that point, the front of the ice sheet no longer moved, but the glacier behind it continued to advance, bringing more debris with it. This reached the forward edge in a never-ending process, depositing more and more, and creating a long mound that rose above the surrounding area.

The terminal moraine of the glacier that covered New England reached far out into what is now sea, but its top can be seen as the islands of Nantucket, Martha's Vineyard, Block Island and the eastern end of Long Island. For a time the glacier stagnated at this outer point, but as the climate warmed its melting rate increased and a new line was formed some miles behind the first. This second line accounts for the low ridge that runs just north of Rhode Island's south coast, known to geologists as the Watch Hill Moraine.

In the western part of the state, where the underlying bedrock rose higher and was scraped bare by the glacier as it moved south, you can see bare-rock exposures, often with a tumble of large boulders lying to one side. This debris is known as *talus,* and it is formed of pieces that broke off under the abrasive weight of the ice and were pushed off as the ice moved. Bedrock of fine-quality building granite underlies several areas of the state, with major quarries, now largely exhausted, in Westerly and Graniteville (northwest of Providence).

The most outstanding geological features in the state are Block Island's Monhegan Bluffs, which rise abruptly above the crashing waves that constantly erode them, and the rocky sea cliffs overlooking Rhode Island Sound in Newport. Not far from the Cliff Walk along these cliffs, Purgatory Chasm is a narrow cleft in the rock shore, located just west of Sachuest Point in Middletown. A large area of

Public Gardens

One of the best-known topiary gardens in America is at Green Animals in Portsmouth, where shrubs and trees are trained and clipped into animal and other shapes. The extensive gardens at nearby Blithewold Mansion, in Bristol, include a Japanese garden, a stand of bamboo and both formal and cutting beds. Just up the road is Coggeshall Farm Museum, with historical herb and vegetable gardens. Newport has a number of fine gardens associated with its mansions, especially Rosecliff, The Elms and Hammersmith Farm. Westerly has a Victorian strolling park with plantings of flowers and exotic trees, and the University of Rhode Island has an arboretum and medicinal herb garden at its Kingston campus. Although Providence has no major public gardens in the city, several small gardens on Benefit St. are worth seeing. On the outskirts of town, Roger Williams Park has extensive plantings and a greenhouse with collections of exotics. Throughout the state, several restored historic homes have gardens typical of their period.

glacial boulders is in the Parker Woodland at Coventry, and another interesting bedrock formation is at Long Pond in Hopkinton, near the Connecticut border. Queen's Fort, at the eastern boundary of Exeter, is built on an entire hill of glacial stones lying in a jumbled pile.

Flora and Fauna

A paradise for birders, Rhode Island has more than 150 nesting avian species and a hundred more are regularly sighted. Migratory birds pass through during their spring and fall mi-

State Parks

Haines Memorial, East Providence, 253-7482

Colt State Park, Bristol, 253-7482

Breachway, Charlestown (campground), 364-7000

Burlingame, Charlestown (campground), 322-7337

Pulaski Memorial, Glocester, 568-2013

Beavertail, Jamestown, 884-2010

Fort Wetherill, Jamestown, 423-1771

Lincoln Woods, Lincoln, 723-7892

Fishermen's Memorial Campground, Narragansett, 789-8374

Salty Brine Beach, Narragansett, 789-3563

Scarborough State Beach, Narragansett, 789-2324

Wheeler State Beach, Narragansett, 789-3563

Block Island State Beach, Shoreham, 466-2611

Brenton Point, Newport, 847-2400

Fort Adams, Newport, 847-2400

East Matunuck State Beach, S. Kingston, 783-2058

Goddard, Warwick, 884-2010

Misquamicut State Beach, Westerly, 596-9077

World War II Memorial, Woonsocket, 762-9717

grations. Waterfowl, both freshwater and ocean birds, winter in the salt marshes and inland ponds. May is the best month for migrating songbirds as well as for shorebirds, including the piping plover. Fall migrations are heaviest in late September and early October. This is also the best time to see the songbirds as they stop on Block Island. Trustom Pond and Ninigret Wildlife Refuges, both on the south coast, offer excellent birding, and near Newport the Norman Bird Sanctuary has a variety of habitats on its 450-acre site. The Audubon Society maintains several fine reserves, some with blinds and all with interpretive trails. The Society offers guided walks, programs and literature, including bird lists, for its refuges. The **Rhode Island Audubon Society, 12 Sanderson Rd., Smithfield, RI 02917; (401) 949-5454.**

Climates suitable for both northern and southern wildflowers overlap in the state, giving it tremendous variety: Nearly 2,000 species of wildflower have been recorded here. A wide variety of habitats contribute to the numbers, too, from marshy shorelands and beaches to the alkaline cliffs and soils of Lime Rock Preserve. The best source of information on wildflowers, as well as information on its scheduled wildflower walks, is the **Rhode Island Wild Plant Society, 12 Sanderson Rd., Smithfield, RI 02917; (401) 949-0195.**

Climate

Rhode Island has the same well-defined seasons as the rest of New England, but without the extremes. Summer heat is usually moderated by a pleasant breeze off Narragansett Bay, and the same ocean air keeps winter milder, without the intense cold spells known farther north and inland. Occasional heavy snowfalls usually melt away within a day or so, or turn to rain before the storm is over. The northwestern towns have the most snow, but even there the ground rarely stays snow-covered throughout the winter. Summer weather can easily reach the 90s, especially in

August, which is the warmest month, but seldom feels that hot because of the pleasant sea breeze. Late August and September occasionally have hurricane warnings, but only rarely does one actually hit the state. Spring comes earlier than elsewhere in New England, and fall lingers later, with mild days as late as November. Newport has the mildest weather of all, except during a storm, and you'll find Cliff Walk a pleasant excursion on all but the most blustery winter days.

Temperatures in Providence are usually between 20–40°F in the winter and between 60–80°F in the summer, with a fairly even rainfall of about three inches a month year-round. Plan your daytime dress around the weather, especially if you plan outdoor activities. Remember that on the coast, summer evenings can be quite cool if a breeze blows off the water, which it often does. (That's why so many people come here in the summer.) If you plan to do any hiking, bring long pants and heavy socks into which you can tuck your pant legs, since deer ticks are prevalent in some areas and present all over the state. Sunscreen and sunglasses are helpful, especially on the beaches.

Suggested Reading

Walks and Rambles in Rhode Island and *More Walks and Rambles in Rhode Island,* by Ken Weber (Backcountry Publications, updated regularly) are simply musts for anyone who likes to hike or walk. Directions and maps are clear, information is accurate and the places are well chosen. Our copies are dog-eared.

The Newport and Narragansett Bay Book, by Pamela Petro (Berkshire House Publishers, 1994) is useful for the area immediately around the bay, especially its shopping section. It's also nice to get a second opinion on restaurants. The series organizes subjects topically instead of geographically, which is not too useful on the road, but the information is good.

AMC River Guide, Volume 2 (Appalachian Mountain Club, updated regularly). If you plan to canoe on the Chipuxet (through the Great Swamp), Pawcatuck or Wood Rivers, this book is essential.

Rhode Island Adventure Diving I and *II,* by Marlene and Don Snyder (199 Steiger Dr., Westfield, MA 01085; (413) 568-1083) describes 40 dive sites in volume I and 44 in volume II. It includes historic places from the time of the Revolution.

Old Rhode Island, P.O. Box 999 Davisville Branch, North Kingstown, RI 02854; (401) 884-5542. This monthly magazine features little-known stories about the state's history, its characters and way of life. You may read about the Blackstone Canal's passenger packet, about Narragansett Bay in World War II, about the scandalous doings of Newport's four hundred or about jonnycakes.

Rhode Island Monthly, 95 Chestnut St., Providence, RI 02903; (401) 421-2552, is irreverent, pointing its insolent finger at just about everything, but with a style that's pure Rhode Island. Although much of its focus is on people and politics, it is well worth perusing for its calendar of events and restaurant information, not to mention Don Bousquet's cartoons. In August it publishes the results of its annual readers' poll, an oft-quoted assessment of everything from the best doughnuts to the best place to take the kids.

Visitor Information

General Information

To obtain copies of the compact *Rhode Island Visitor's Guide,* as well as a state map, directories of lodging, events and individual activities and other material, contact the **Rhode Island Tourism Division, 7 Jackson Walkway, Providence, RI 02903; (800) 556-2484 or (401) 277-2601.**

These guides and racks full of brochures for individual services and attractions are

The Rhode Island Guide

available at the **Welcome Center** on I-95 between Exits 2 and 3 in Richmond, at the Connecticut border. The hours are 8:30 A.M.–4:30 P.M. daily, year-round; it remains open until 6:30 P.M. between Memorial Day and Labor Day. A visitor's center is also located at the airport in Warwick.

Dollar signs indicate the cost of a double room for one night. Variations in the price range may be seasonal or include rooms of different size or with different facilities.

$—Under $50
$$—$50–$75
$$$—$75–$100
$$$$—Over $100

Getting There

Interstate 95, the main north-south corridor for traffic into the Northeast, passes through the center of downtown Providence, having entered the state in its southwestern corner from Connecticut. This highway cuts the state almost in half diagonally, providing access to routes that reach all corners. Nowhere except Block Island are you more than half an hour from I-95. US Rtes. 6, 44 and 1 cross in Providence, and RI Rtes. 7, 146, 117, 103 and 126 all end there. Rte. 6 enters from central Connecticut, and Rtes. 100, 146, 114 and US Rte. 1 all cross the northern border from Massachusetts. I-195 connects Providence to Cape Cod, New Bedford and Fall River, all in Massachusetts.

Once a major rail center for the entire Northeast, Providence is still easy to reach by train. Amtrak connects it with New York and Boston on about ten trains a day, including the reservations-only express runs. The station is close to the center of the city, convenient to downtown hotels. For **Amtrak** schedules and reservations, call **(800) 872-7245.**

Bonanza Bus Lines connects Providence to Boston (from both the South Station Bus Terminal and Logan Airport) and to New York City, as well as to Newport and points closer in. The station is not as close to the city center

as the train station is, but it's right off I-95 at Exit 25, on Smithfield Ave. Parking at the station is free. The Boston–New York express buses will stop on request at the Rhode Island Public Transit Authority (RIPTA) terminal at Kennedy Plaza. Buses leave every two hours and the trip takes about an hour and 15 minutes to Boston, about four hours to New York. Bonanza also connects Boston to Newport via Fall River, a 90-minute trip. Buses connecting Providence to Albany, New York, stop en route at several towns in the Berkshires and in Springfield, Massachusetts; **(401) 751-8800** or **(800) 556-3815.**

The least expensive way to get to Providence from Boston is via the **T Commuter Rail** from South Station. The trip takes just over an hour and costs $4.75. Trains run on weekdays only, leaving Providence between 6 and 8 A.M. and leaving Boston once in the morning at about 6:45 and between 4:30 and 6:30 in the afternoon. Designed for the many people who live in Providence and work in Boston, the T is a good way for Boston residents to spend a weekend in Providence—or even to connect with a RIPTA bus for Newport or to the ferry for Block Island. These trains also stop at Boston's Back Bay Station; **(617) 722-3200.**

Travelers arriving by air will appreciate the sparkling new facility at **T. F. Green Airport,** in Warwick, which is close to Providence. It's served by the following airlines:

Northwest: (800) 225-2525
American: (800) 433-7300
Continental: (800) 525-0280
Delta: (800) 221-1212
USAir: (800) 428-4322
United: (800) 241-6522
Midway: (800) 446-4392

RIPTA buses connect Providence to T. F. Green Airport, a 15-minute trip, with buses leaving hourly or more frequently. The fare is $1.40, and buses arrive in Kennedy Plaza. Taxi fares to the city are about $20 to $22. For information on airport parking, call **(401) 737-1220.**

Getting Around

RIPTA buses connect Providence to Newport, Narragansett, Wickford, Kingston, Jamestown, Bristol, Warren and other points in the state on a regular schedule at fares ranging from $.85 to $2.50. A RIPTA bus leaves each major city at least once an hour on weekdays, every two hours on weekends. The trip from Providence to Newport takes 55 minutes, with stops in Bristol and other towns along the way. The fare is $2.50. Hourly RIPTA service connects the Wakefield Mall and University of Rhode Island campuses with Newport via the bridges, a 50-minute ride. The fare is $2.50, and all buses on that line are lift-equipped. The central station is in Kennedy Plaza, in the heart of the downtown area. (For information on facilities and fares for handicapped passengers with disabilities, and for special fares for seniors, see **Travelers with Special Needs,** below.) For RIPTA schedules and information call **(401) 781-9400** or **(800) 244-0444.**

For information on getting to Block Island, see the **Getting There** section of that chapter (see page **153**).

In the summer, RIPTA runs a special **Beach Express,** picking up passengers in Providence, Woonsocket, Pawtucket, Central Falls and Warwick, and taking them to the Scarborough, Salty Brine and Roger Wheeler State Beaches. The fare is $2 round-trip for passengers over age five, and because they arrive by bus, there is no entrance fee to the beaches (fees are for parking, not for use of the beaches); **(800) 244-0444** or **(401) 781-9400.**

Travelers with Special Needs

Several RIPTA buses each day on each route are equipped with wheelchair lifts; all weekend and holiday buses are so equipped, and all buses on the Newport-Kingston and Providence-Kingston routes are. The elderly, the disabled or those with a Medicare card can ride free before 7 A.M., between 9 A.M. and 3 P.M. and after 6 P.M. on weekdays and all day on

Dollar sign symbols indicate the price range of most of the dinner entrees (or other meal entrees if dinner is not served) on the menu as follows:

$—$5–$10
$$—$10–$15
$$$—$15–$20
$$$$—$20–$25
$$$$$—$25 and up

weekends and holidays, but they must first get a RIPTA photo identification card. To do this, call **(401) 784-9524.** For RIPTA schedules and information call **(401) 781-9400** or **(800) 244-0444; hearing impaired call (401) 784-9599.**

Tips for Visitors

Driving Distances

Providence is 60 miles south of Boston, 95 miles east of Hartford, 103 miles northeast of New Haven and 180 miles northeast of New York City. It is 40 miles south of Worcester and 80 miles east of Springfield, both in Massachusetts.

Driving Rules

Speed limits are 25 mph in business and residential districts, 50 mph in the daytime and 45 mph at night in other areas. On interstate highways the limit is 55 mph. All other speed limits are posted. All traffic, in both directions, must stop for a school bus flashing red lights. Accidents causing damage of more than $200 must be reported to the Registry of Motor Vehicles. A right turn is permitted at a red light after a full stop, unless signs indicate otherwise. Rhode Islanders are renowned for neglecting to use directional signals, so watch for other telltale indications of an imminent turn, such as slowing down near an intersection. One of our favorite cartoons by Don Bousquet, the state's Cartoonist Laureate, shows a used-car salesman describing a well-worn car with Rhode Island plates to a prospective buyer: "The directional signals are like new!"

Liquor Laws

The legal drinking age is 21. Wine may be purchased in grocery stores, but beer and other alcoholic beverages must be purchased in liquor stores, which are privately owned, not state stores. In some restaurants without liquor licenses, you may bring your own wine; it is wise to inquire about this when you make reservations. In this event, a corkage fee rarely is charged.

Road Conditions

To learn about possible traffic slowdowns caused by construction, call **(800) 354-9595.**

The Usual Caveat

Though we'd like to believe that years from now your grandchildren will be able to eat in the restaurants we've mentioned, the facts of life, and of the restaurant business, are less optimistic. Restaurants come and go, as do chefs, and the place we loved yesterday may not be at all what we've described by tomorrow. We've tried to choose places with a bit of longevity or a good ownership track record. But we have bet on some new places, too. *So please don't blame us if you are disappointed to find a restaurant closed or changed.* Your best bet is to ask around, because chances are good that the chef has left to open his own place just around the corner. The nice thing about Rhode Island is that good chefs have a following here, and people will know where they've gone.

Prices also change, so it is always wise to ask the rate when you call a hotel or B&B. And again, new owners may have made major changes since we stayed there. This book will be revised and updated regularly, so be sure you are using the most recent edition in order to know the latest news.

Smoking Laws

Smoking is allowed in public places unless signs indicate otherwise. Most restaurants have separate areas designated for smokers, although some ban smoking entirely. Newport Creamery restaurants, located throughout the state, have a no-smoking policy.

Taxes

A sales tax of 7% is levied on retail purchases as well as on lodging and restaurant meals. Clothing, medicines, groceries and gasoline are exempt from the sales tax.

Telephones

The area code for the entire state is 401. **Rhode Island Information** is **(401) 555-1212.** Because of Rhode Island's size, you can often find businesses in all parts of the state included in the Providence Yellow Pages. For emergencies, dial 911 from anywhere in the state.

Time Zone

Rhode Island is in the eastern time zone, and it switches to daylight saving time in the summer.

Rhode Island for Kids

A number of child-friendly hotels and restaurants offer special prices, menus and facilities for children. There is plenty to do, even on days when beaches are not a good choice. **Roger Williams Park,** close to downtown Providence, has New England's best zoo, a natural history museum with planetarium shows and interactive exhibits and a carousel; **Watch Hill** has a rare flying-horse carousel suitable for small children. **Crescent Park** in East Providence has a century-old carousel, and Pawtucket's **Slater Memorial Park** has another, as well as pony rides, picnic facilities and playgrounds. **Adventureland** in Narragansett has miniature golf, go-carts, bumper boats and other activities. The ***Blackstone Valley Explorer*** is a riverboat that tours a variety of places along the Blackstone River and other rivers and harbors; call **(401) 334-0837** for a schedule. In Newport, the **Fisherman and Whale Museum** is a favorite for its hands-on exhibits of live sea life. Several theaters throughout the state offer children's performances, including **Theater by the Sea** in Kingstown and the **Providence theaters.**

Rhode Island

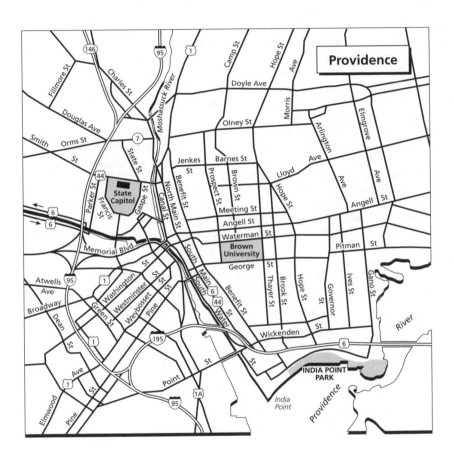

Providence

Providence

Providence

Few cities of Providence's size and importance are so compact: You can see its entire downtown area, from hill to hill to water, as you pass through on I-95. What you can't see, of course, are the row on row of fine homes built before 1800, the wonderfully preserved Art Deco and Beaux-Arts downtown buildings, the tree-lined neighborhoods of distinguished Victorian homes, the lively restaurants and clubs. You do get a glimpse of the green and blue swath of Waterplace Park and a good view of the statehouse dome and a quick look at some of the other landmarks, but you don't hear the lyrical conversations of Atwells Avenue, which seem at any moment ready to break into an aria, or the voices of the wobbly rows of little angels singing in a saint's day procession in East Providence. But the city is so compact that you're almost within earshot of one or the other.

Its two hills seem to scoop the city toward the Providence River, which was its original center and is once again its focal point. This has not been the case for very long. Little more than a decade ago the entire river was invisible, buried beneath a solid bridge of roadways, its waters so nasty that no one wanted to uncover them. No more. The river is clean enough to kayak and to enjoy a picnic beside.

The streets now run beside the river, not over it, and the bridges form graceful arches from one park-lined bank to the other.

The buildings on either side of the river seem to have thrown back their shoulders to stand taller, and the lines of their varied styles reflect in one another's gleaming glass. If ever a city has been reborn it is Providence, and its new look is matched by a vibrant new spirit. It had a lot to work with: Over 5,000 of the city's buildings are on the National Register of Historic Places. Entire neighborhoods are designated historic districts. The city could have saved tons of metal by simply erecting a giant bronze sign on I-95 reading "Providence is on The National Register of Historic Places."

Restoration shows everywhere, not just in the prerevolutionary and Federal homes of College Hill, but in the gleaming facades of mercantile buildings and the soaring vaulted ceilings of the banking halls. Spared the ravages of urban renewal that stripped so many cities of their architectural heritage, Providence was too poor to tear down block after block. Instead, it "modernized" by covering the facades with wood to simulate the bland new streets of wealthier cities. Now these midcentury masks have been torn away to reveal astonishingly preserved decorative detail. This benign neglect saved priceless architecture, which now beams out over the downtown streets.

There's a lot more to see and admire in Providence than its world-class art museums

Providence (Sur)Prizes

"Congratulations! You have been chosen to participate in our New England promotion... . You are guaranteed to receive one of the above fabulous prizes." The letter detailed an assortment ranging from television sets to camcorders, and there was no fine print, just a time and date to pick up the prize. Nearly 100 of the lucky recipients of the letter arrived as instructed.

They were met by Detective Robert Lauro of the Providence Police Department, and by warrants for their arrest. The suspects assembled in this clever sting were wanted on charges as serious as rape but had hitherto evaded police. They did, evidently, read their mail.

and priceless antiquities. Its Mile of History is only the first you'll want to walk.

History

It's hard to imagine, as you walk down Weybosset Street between its richly ornamented buildings, under the marquis of Beaux-Arts Loew's Theater, past the little kiosk, alongside the classical facade of the Arcade and into the canyon of banking and commercial buildings with their carved stone flourishes, that you are walking the Pequot Trail, where generations of Native Americans walked silently through the forests to the bluff that once overlooked the Providence River. The very word "Webbosset" comes from their word for the narrows, where they were able to cross the river and continue into what is now Massachusetts. Only the irregular curving route the street still follows testifies to its origins as a footpath.

Banished to England from the Massachusetts Bay Colony for holding "newe and dangerous opinions" (along with believing in freedom of conscience, he opposed the taking of Indian lands), Roger Williams and a few of his followers escaped in the dead of winter across a wilderness. With the help of the Wampanoags, they reached the shores of the Mohassuck River in 1636 to found a place they named "God's gift": Providence Plantation. It was the vision of Roger Williams and his belief that people of differing views should live together in mutual respect—indeed that they must—that formed the basis of Rhode Island thinking.

Although Williams established the strong spiritual and political base that shaped the city for the centuries ahead, it was the Brown brothers who built its firm commercial and economic footing. This remarkable quartet, whose ancestors were among the earliest settlers, used their considerable talents to amass a fortune, the largess of which they shared with their native city. Each had his own talents, and together they formed Nicholas Brown and Company. Nicholas and John were

3

merchants; John founded Providence's profitable China trade, and his ships traded throughout Europe and the East and West Indies. But he also saw that trade alone was not enough, and he became active in manufacturing. A staunch patriot, he was a leader in the Revolution. Joseph was the architect of some of the city's finest colonial buildings, and Moses helped William Slater establish the nation's first cotton mills in Pawtucket. He gave land for schools, his son endowed a school and Nicholas Jr. would become the main financial supporter of Brown University.

It was manufacturing that saved Providence from the fate of Newport after the War of 1812, when shipping was severely curtailed. Moving away from the economics of the sea, Providence built factories and became a center for textiles, jewelry, tools and silver. The need for labor in these mills brought waves of immigration, adding new dimensions to the city's cultural life. Education, manufacturing and commerce, all legacies of the Browns, continue to support Providence today.

From Roger Williams's first settlement to the present, Providence has remained flexible enough to change with the times, moving from farming to sea trade to manufacturing. Each has brought a new diversity of people and ideas that have further enriched the city.

4 Suggested Reading

Those with an interest in architecture or historic preservation should contact **Providence Preservation Society** for a list of its superb neighborhood guides. These well-illustrated and intelligently written booklets cover several neighborhoods of particular architectural interest, with maps and descriptions. They identify styles and point out details that few travelers would find on their own and that, in

The Old Stone Bank will someday be the home of Brown University's Haffenreffer Museum.

parts of the city, the casual traveler would never find. Broadway, Elmwood and the Armory District are three of these hidden enclaves of fine architecture in the process of restoration. The Benefit Street booklet is $2, all others are $1 each; **(401) 831-7440.**

Getting There

All roads lead to Providence—or at least all major highways do. Interstates 95 and 195 intersect there, and I-295 curls around its northern and western perimeters. US Rtes. 6, 44 and 1 cross in its center, and RI Rtes. 7, 146, 117, 103 and 126 all end there. With all these roads converging and passing through, you might picture a tangled web of traffic too horrible to imagine. But they do it with such ease that you can be through Providence almost before you know it. The interstates sail overhead—providing fine views of the city—and other routes merge in and out of them so smoothly that local traffic uses the interstate to cross town. Yes, it gets a little backed up during rush hour, but drivers used to trying to get out of New York or Boston will compare it to Sunday morning traffic. For a city at the intersection of traffic moving from New York and New Haven to Cape Cod, and the main artery between New York and Boston, traffic is amazingly unsnarled. Providence residents complain about the delays, but that's because they are used to so few of them. From either north or south, an interstate exit brings you directly into the heart of the city, literally to the doors of the Biltmore and Westin Hotels and into the central Kennedy Plaza.

Getting there by public transportation is almost as easy. **Amtrak** connects Providence with New York and Boston on about ten trains a day, including the reservations-only express runs. The station is close to the center of the city, on Gaspee St. opposite the statehouse grounds and overlooking the new Waterplace Park. For Amtrak schedules and reservations, call **(800) 872-7245.**

Bonanza Bus Lines connects the city to Boston (from both the South Station Bus Terminal and Logan Airport) and to New York City, as well as to Newport and points closer in. The station is not as close to the center of town as the train is, but it is right off I-95 at Exit 25, on Smithfield Ave. Parking at the station is free. Buses leave every two hours, and the trip takes about an hour and fifteen minutes to Boston, about four hours to New York; **(401) 751-8800** or **(800) 556-3815.**

RIPTA (Rhode Island Public Transit Authority) buses connect Providence to Newport, Wakefield and other points in the state on a regular schedule at fares ranging from $.85 to $2.50. The station is in Kennedy Plaza, in the very center of the downtown area. Several buses each day are equipped with wheelchair lifts; all weekend and holiday buses are. (See page **xix** for information on discounted fares for seniors and handicapped passengers.) For RIPTA schedules and information, call **(401) 781-9400** or **(800) 244-0444.**

The least expensive way to get to Providence from Boston is via the **T Commuter Rail** from South Station, which takes just over an hour and costs $4.75. Trains run only on weekdays, leaving Providence between 6 and 8 A.M. and leaving Boston once in the morning at about 6:45 and again between 4:30 and 6:30 in the afternoon. Designed for the many people who live in Providence and work in Boston, the T is a good way for Boston residents to spend a weekend in Providence—or even to connect with a RIPTA bus for Newport. These trains also stop at Boston's Back Bay Station; **(617) 722-3200.**

Travelers arriving by air will appreciate the new facility at **T. F. Green Airport,** in nearby Warwick, which is served by the following airlines: Northwest (800) 225-2525; American (800) 433-7300; Continental (800) 525-0280; Delta (800) 221-1212; USAir (800) 428-4322; United (800) 241-6522; Midway (800) 446-4392.

RIPTA buses connect Providence to T. F. Green Airport, a 15-minute trip, with buses leaving hourly or more frequently. The fare is $1.40, and buses arrive in Kennedy Plaza. Taxi fares to the city are about $20 to $22. For information on airport parking, call **(401) 737-1220.**

Getting Around

RIPTA buses provide a transit system for the city as well as for the entire state—a model other states could wisely follow. You can get almost anywhere on them, and the in-city fare is $.80. This makes the bus terminal on **Kennedy Plaza** a good first stop, where you can pick up a bus plan and schedules. Weekend visitors will find that they can easily drive to most attractions—or to each part of the city, where it will probably take only a few minutes to find a parking space. But so much of Providence is within walking distance that it often makes more sense to leave the car at your hotel or in a centrally located lot. (For a list of Providence parking lots and garages, see the Services section at the end of this chapter.)

Taxi fares in Providence are $1.25 for getting into the cab, plus $2 a mile. Taxis can be found in Kennedy Plaza and in front of all the downtown hotels. Some of the major cab companies are **Arrow (401) 946-5333; Red & White (401) 941-9888;** and **Economy (401) 944-6700.**

Festivals and Events

Chinese New Year Celebration
February

With folk dances, music, martial arts and a movie, this celebration is at the **Beneficent Congregational Church, Weybosset St.; (401) 277-2669.**

Rhode Island Spring Flower and Garden Show
February

The show features gardens of southern New England with landscape and floral displays, a trade show and marketplace of garden-related goods, workshops, demonstrations and competitions; **(401) 272-4441.**

Brown Commencement
May

The last weekend of May is a good time to avoid Providence, since every available hotel room, restaurant reservation and parking space will be filled. Prior to that are the graduations of Providence College and Rhode Island College, making this the tightest month in which to find lodging.

The Festival of Historic Houses
June

The festival is sponsored by the **Providence Preservation Society,** the organization responsible for the continued presence of much of the magnificent historic architecture you see in the city today. At this weekend event (for which tickets are often sold out), restored private homes of various eras are opened to view, as are the gardens, at their peak in mid-June; **(401) 831-7440.**

Independence Day
July

The Fourth of July is celebrated in East Providence with an outdoor evening concert at **Pierce Memorial Stadium on Mercer St.** and a fireworks display; **(401) 345-7511.**

Cape Verdean Independence Day
July

This holiday is celebrated, with art displays and cultural events for the whole family, at **India Point Park on India St.; (401) 277-2669.**

The Annual East Providence Heritage Festival
July

The festival includes foods, crafts, music and family activities. At **Pierce Memorial Field in East Providence; (401) 435-7511.**

The Best of Rhode Island Party
August

A gala evening when *Rhode Island Monthly* magazine honors those businesses that have been voted top honors by the magazine's readers. Restaurants (which make up a number of the award categories) bring their winning dishes for sampling at the **Rhode Island Convention Center, 1 Sabin St.; (401) 781-1611.**

The Pasta Challenge
September

The challenge is an all-you-can-eat competition among area restaurants for the best pasta dishes, and since Providence has a plethora of Italian eateries, it's not a matter to be taken lightly; **(401) 351-6440.**

Providence Waterfront Festival
September

The Waterfront Festival celebrates the city's historic and ongoing relationship with the sea with sailboat rides, harbor cruises, historic ships, exhibits of sea life, regattas, fireworks, seafood, ethnic foods, crafts, sea kayak instruction and tours, plus entertainment on five stages at and around **India Point Park.** Admission is $3; **(401) 785-9450, (401) 274-1636** or **(800) 233-1636; (401) 453-1633 to arrange canoe and kayaking lessons and tours.**

Heritage Day Festival
September

Heritage Day draws 30 different ethnic groups to the statehouse lawn for song, dance, foods, crafts demonstrations and other activities celebrating the state's wide range of cultural influences, from China to Ukraine. Rhode Island has a lot of cultural diversity to celebrate; **(401) 277-2669.**

Rhode Island Food and Wine Experience
October

A two-day festival with wine competitions and plenty of opportunity to sample fine food and wines. As may be becoming clear, Rhode Island welcomes any excuse to celebrate food and drink. It's at the **Convention Center, 1 Sabin St.; (401) 272-4441.**

Columbus Weekend Festival
October

This weekend festival brings the already lively **Federal Hill** neighborhood to the streets, as sidewalk stalls along Atwells Ave. sell Italian foods and street musicians and other entertainers perform. A Sunday parade brings 14 divisions and lively crowds; **(401) 351-2415.**

Montgolfier Day Balloon Regatta
November

Beginning at dawn, 15 to 20 hot-air balloons rise from the **state house lawn** in celebration of the anniversary of the first manned hot-air balloon's ascent in 1783. Hope for a clear morning and bring plenty of film; **(401) 253-0111.**

The Annual Chrysanthemum Show
November

Held in the greenhouse at **Roger Williams Park,** the show is an extravaganza of brilliant autumn bloom. Free admission; **(401) 785-9450.**

The Annual International Holiday Sale
December

Features foods and crafts from all over the world. Held at **International House of Rhode Island, 8 Stimson St.; (401) 421-7181.**

A Latin Christmas Carol Celebration
December

A celebration featuring carols in Latin, classical readings, instrumental and a capella music. In **Sayles Hall, on the Brown campus; (401) 863-2123.**

Buy Rhode Island Festival
December

This festival provides a showcase of and opportunity to buy locally made gifts, foods and services ideal for the holidays. It's held at the **Rhode Island Convention Center, 1 Sabin St.; (800) WE-BUY-RI.**

Poinsettia Display
December

Open daily during the middle two weeks of the month at the **Charles H. Smith Greenhouse at Roger Williams Park; (401) 785-9450, ext. 250.**

A New Year's Eve Paddle
December

A celebration bringing kayak and canoe enthusiasts to the river for an afternoon trip through **Waterplace Park and the Hurricane Barrier; (401) 453-1633.**

First Night
December

First Night turns downtown Providence into one big festival of the arts with more than 40 venues for performers, music, art, food and children's entertainment on New Year's Eve, ending with a midnight fireworks display; **(401) 521-1166.**

Outdoor Activities

Parks and Recreation Areas
Waterplace Park

A four-acre public park bordering the river in the center of the city, Waterplace is clean, open and well lighted for nighttime strolling. Its granite walls are made from the blocks of the former city railroad abutment, and panels show and explain the history of the area. Landscaping includes lawns, a pond with a fountain, benches, walking and bicycling paths, and an amphitheater provides a place for concerts and performances. An information center, bike racks and telephones make it handy for visitors as well as a favorite place for downtown workers to bring their lunches.

India Point Park

Formerly the site of John Brown's piers and warehouses, which made Providence a major port in the China Trade, the waterfront is now a small park with sailing access and a children's playground. Each summer it is the site of the Providence Waterfront Festival (see page **6**).

Fox Point Hurricane Barrier, which protects the downtown area from devastating floods brought on by hurricanes, such as those of 1938 and 1954, begins just a block from the park, on Tockwotton St. From here it extends across the mouth of the river and overland to US Rte. Alt. 1. Small craft can easily pass through, but it is closed when storms threaten to cut off the flow of water from the bay during abnormally high tides. It is open for tours during the Providence Waterfront Festival (see page **6**).

Prospect Park

Located atop College Hill, this is the burial place of Roger Williams, and his statue gazes out over one of the best views of the city he founded. The land drops sharply away for a prospect of the entire downtown area. Climb the hill on Meeting St. then turn left onto Congdon. The park is opposite the intersection with Cushing St.

Roger Williams Park

Small lakes, gardens and landscaped grounds, exotic trees, walking paths and roads, plus a variety of recreation areas, fill 435 rolling acres in the southwest corner of the city. It is a charming classically Victorian park, even to its sometimes fanciful buildings and the statu-

ary appearing throughout. Within its bounds are enough activities to keep a family busy for at least a weekend. The third zoo ever constructed in America (in 1872) and now considered the finest in New England is here and could occupy the better part of a day. We include here all but the park's two entirely indoor attractions, the Natural History Museum and Planetarium, and the Betsey Williams Cottage, both discussed in the Museums and Historic and Sites section later in this chapter (see page **19**). A trolley shuttles between park attractions; $1 buys an all-day ticket.

Rhode Island Zoological Society

This organization has come a long way from the Victorian zoo of its origin. It now incorporates the most modern thinking in zoo design, offering few cages or fences but a chance to learn about the animals, not just look at them. And a chance to learn about other subjects as well, in biopark exhibits that involve not only an animal but the world it comes from—its history, geography and people. Innovative graphics tell the story of endangered domestic breeds in the farmyard. Rare animals, including snow leopards and the Arabian oryx, join the always popular African plains animals and the polar bears. And don't be surprised as you drive down I-95 to see zebra grazing beside the road. Open daily, Apr.–Oct. from 9 A.M.–5 P.M., Nov.–Mar. from 9 A.M.–4 P.M. Take Exit 17 from I-95 south, Exit 16 from I-95 north. Admission is $4; **(401) 785-3510.**

Charles H. Smith Greenhouse

Really several greenhouses that bloom all year with flower displays, including a fine collection of orchids. In the summer the adjoining outdoor beds are filled with solid color; seasonal shows display poinsettias, spring flowering bulbs and chrysanthemums. The greenhouses are free and open daily from 11 A.M.–4 P.M.; **(401) 785-9450.**

Carousel Village

The village features, in addition to a newly built carousel, pony rides, a Japanese garden, miniature train rides, performers, a large playground filled with climbing structures and a miniature golf course of Rhode Island landmarks. Carousel rides at $1 or 6 for $5; **(401) 781-8008.**

Dalrymple Boathouse

Here you can rent paddleboats (some in the shape of hippos) from 11 A.M.–5 P.M. weekdays and from 10:30 A.M.–6:30 P.M. weekends. The boathouse itself is half-timbered Queen Anne style with a round tower.

The Mounted Command Building

The building houses the stables for the city horses and offers free stable tours. For a current schedule, call **(401) 785-9450.**

Todd Marsilli Tennis Center

The center has the state's only public clay courts. It is open daily in the summer from 9 A.M. (7 A.M. on weekends) until dusk. Court fees are $3 to $4 a person for 90 minutes; **(401) 785-9450.**

The Casino

Housed in the large porticoed building, and surrounded by flower beds in the summer, it stands on the banks of the lake. It is used for private receptions, but if it is not open you can easily admire its elegant decoration through the large windows on the porch. The interior woodwork is hand finished, and the original maple floors are still intact; **(401) 785-9450.**

Biking

A bike path along the river and through **India Point Park** connects Providence to the **East Bay Bike Path** (see page 8). It goes right past the Days Inn Hotel on India Point, making this a convenient place to stay for those who plan to explore the city on two wheels. Roger Williams Park offers miles of shaded paved roadways and paths.

Boating

The **Community Boating Center** at India Point provides recreational boating and lessons. Boating hours are from noon–6 P.M. weekdays and from 10 A.M.–6 P.M. on weekends.

Canoeing and Kayaking

The river that winds so picturesquely beneath its arched bridges is a new feature of Providence. It is perfect for kayaking, and **Baer's River Workshop** is there, May through October, to teach you how and to rent kayaks and canoes. Mini kayaks are $19 a day, canoes and sea kayaks are $29 a day, and both canoes and minis are available for half-hour rental at $5. Walk-ins are welcome, or you can reserve a craft. Baer's also teaches the use of both canoes and kayaks through **The Learning Connection** and leads tours of local rivers and Providence Harbor. **222 South Water St.; (401) 453-1633.** For **Learning Connection classes,** call **(401) 274-9330** or **(800) 432-5520.**

Golf

Triggs Memorial Golf Course has 18 holes with carts available and a restaurant. It is open year-round, located at **1533 Chalkstone Ave.; (401) 521-8460. Cranston Country Club** has 18 holes, carts available and a snack bar and bar, as well as reduced rates for senior players. It's on **Burlingame Rd. in Cranston; (401) 826-1683. Silver Spring Golf Course** is a small, six-hole, facility without carts, located on **Pawtucket Ave. in East Providence; (401) 434-9697.** See the chapters covering the surrounding towns of Warwick and Lincoln for other nearby courses.

Ice Skating

Two indoor skating rinks are open to the public; neither of them offers skate rental. Public hours vary, so you should call before going to either. They are Brown University's **Meehan Auditorium,** at **Hope and Lloyd Sts.; (401) 863-2236,** and the **Schneider Arena** at **Providence College** on **Huxley Ave.; (401) 865-2168.** In the winter, the ponds at Roger

9

Downcity buildings are visible through the gardens of Benefit Street.

Williams Park become skating rinks, and the Dalrymple boathouse a warming shelter.

Jogging

The river, with the new parks and greenways that now line its banks, provides a pleasant route for joggers, who can vary their routines a bit by taking any street uphill on the East side to **Benefit Street.** From its beginning on Wickenden St. to its end at North Main St., Benefit is lined with trees and fine restored homes and public buildings. Automobile traffic is one-way, going north.

Blackstone Boulevard, at the far northeast edge of the city, past the Brown University campus, is another favorite for joggers, who enjoy its landscaped parklike center strip designed by Frederick Law Olmsted. Beautifully maintained and landscaped mansions and fashionable Victorian homes line both sides of the street.

Tennis

The Todd Marsilli Tennis Center at **Roger Williams Park,** has the state's only public clay courts (see page **9**); **(401) 785-9450. Tennis Rhode Island** has indoor courts open daily

from September–Memorial Day. You can reserve courts until 11 P.M. They are located at **70 Boyd Ave. in East Providence; (401) 434-5550.** Another facility is in Warwick at **636 Centerville Rd.; (401) 828-4450.**

Activities for Kids

Roger Williams Park is the first place that comes to mind, with its planetarium, natural history museum, zoo, paddleboats and Carousel Village. The latter, along with the carousel, has a miniature train to ride, a playground filled with giant jungle gyms and entertainments all summer long. Storytelling in the park is featured periodically in the summer. For more information on the park's attractions, see page **8**, and for a current schedule of park activities, call **(401) 785-9450. Children's Programs at the Providence Athenaeum** include films and storytelling, nearly all of which are free, with a $.50 snack fee (see page **17**). **India Point Park,** south of Wickenden St., has a playground, and the entire riverfront is ideal for bicycling. Providence's many theater and performance venues frequently have events designed for children; see the individual theaters in the Nightlife section (see page **19**). Festivals, especially ethnic celebrations, always have a lot of family-oriented activities. Try the day-long **Heritage Day Festival** in September on the state capitol grounds (see page **6**). **First Night** events begin in the afternoon on December 31, with activities designed for children.

Seeing and Doing

The Lay of the Land

The topography of Providence is easy to find your way around in, because you can almost always see where you are. Except from the few deep canyons between Weybosset and Washington Sts. (known as Downcity), College Hill always provides a backdrop and a westward beacon. Head toward it from any part of Downcity and you will find the river. Federal Hill is on the west, on the other side of I-95, and the state capitol building marks the north, its dome visible from nearly anywhere. On the east side of the river (not to be confused with East Providence, which is across the much wider Seekonk River and approached only by two bridges), you can always tell where you are by the slant of the hill. Head downhill and you'll find Main St. and the river. Head uphill and you'll find Brown University. Go over the crest of the hill and you'll meet Hope St., which goes right to Wickenden St. or left into another business neighborhood (with some restaurants). Wickenden St. borders College Hill on the south—it's a busy street of cafes and restaurants in a neighborhood known as Fox Point. Beyond that is India Point Park and the bay.

Kennedy Plaza is a one-block walk from either the Downcity theater district or the river. It is easy to spot because the handsome profile of the Westin Hotel's green roof and brick walls mark it like a giant exclamation point. The plaza is surrounded by impressive buildings: The elegant Biltmore Hotel and City Hall on one end, the Courthouse on the other and the unmistakable Union Station stretching along its entire north side. Kennedy Plaza is where all the RIPTA bus lines meet, and the Amtrak rail station is across the river, toward the capitol building.

The city publishes an excellent street map of the central city that is large enough to read by a street light and shows major attractions, restaurants and hotels in a color-coded format. We've seen and used a lot of city maps all over the world and have never seen a better one. Call ahead to get one to use in your trip planning; **(800) 233-1636.** Or pick one up at the Visitors Center in the old Union Station.

For planning purposes, Downcity is the theater district, with five major venues within a few blocks. The convention center is here, as is the main campus of Johnson and Wales University. Shops, major banks and restaurants fill in the spaces. The heaviest concentration of restaurants is along the opposite (east) bank of the river on Main St. and on Wickenden Street, which runs at right angles to Main on the southernmost end. Most of the historical sites, along with the art museums, are on College Hill. Federal Hill, beside the state capitol, is the lively Italian section, with another heavy restaurant concentration. Rhode Island College and Providence College lie north of this area.

You can walk to every major site in the city or take a bus when your feet get tired of the brick sidewalks. And although you should take the same safety precautions you would in any city, Providence has been named the safest city in the continental United States by *Livable Cities Almanac.* Be warned, however, that it leads the known universe in car thefts.

Museums and Historic Buildings and Sites

The Banner Trail

Throughout the city you will see colorful flags marking theaters, historic places, museums, noteworthy churches, art galleries, parks and information centers. Each type of attraction has a flag of a different color. These destinations are part of the Banner Trail, and you can get a map of their locations, as well as a brief description and hours of operation, from any information center, or from the Visitors Bureau; **(800) 233-1636** or **(401) 274-1636.**

THE WEST SIDE

The Arcade

The oldest indoor marketplace in the United States, the Arcade was built in 1828 by two owners who could agree on everything except what the pediments of the facades should look like. Fortunately, the building had two ends, so they hired different architects who designed facades to suit each. The 22-foot columns were cut from single pieces of granite, and each took a month to complete before it was dragged to Providence by ox teams of 12 to 18 yokes. At the time they were put in place they were the largest monolithic columns in the

United States. Inside are three stepped-back tiers bordered by the original iron railings. On the first floor are food courts selling everything from ice cream to egg rolls. On the upper floors are boutiques and shops selling clothing, accessories, crafts and antiques. It's a bright, lively place, especially at lunchtime. Open Mon.–Sat. from 10 A.M.–6 P.M., at **65 Weybosset St.; (401) 272-2340.**

Atwells Avenue/Federal Hill

Enter through an arch over the street with a giant pine cone. Cafes, shops, food stores, restaurants, even a piazza right out of Italy with a three-tiered fountain, Piazza Pasquale, create the atmosphere of a street market, especially during the Columbus Day weekend festival; **(401) 831-7440.**

Banking Halls

Some of the most impressive interior architecture in Providence is in its banking halls, several of which are still in use for the everyday business of making deposits and cashing checks. The **Rhode Island Trust** has bronze elevator doors designed by the sculptor Daniel Chester French. Inside the main hall, a soaring coffered ceiling with medallions is supported on mammoth marble columns. You can walk right through these halls during banking hours. One is no longer a bank but is still in original condition and houses a restaurant named, appropriately, **Federal Reserve**. Its coffered ceiling is decorated with 3,000 plaster roses and its windows have stained glass crests representing the world's major banking houses. It is on **Westminster St., between Dorance and Orange.**

Beneficent Congregational Church

The oldest building in the downtown area. The basic church was built in 1808 and was a major inducement for people to build homes in this then undeveloped area across the river. In 1836 the portico and dome were added. The chandeliers, particularly the ornate central one, are striking. Empire St., which runs into Weybosset, was home to the Chinese community in the late nineteenth century, and many

became part of the congregation there. This ministry remains strong, and the church is the scene of the annual Chinese New Year's festival. Services are at 10:30 A.M. on Sunday, but the church is open Mon.–Fri from 9 A.M.–4 P.M., and Sat. 9–noon, and Sun. from 9 A.M.–1:30 P.M. **300 Weybosset St.; (401) 331-9844.**

City Hall

A rare Second Empire–style building that is often compared to the Louvre in Paris, the City Hall was in such bad condition that it was almost torn down—its demolition was proposed in the 1959 Master Plan—before its restoration. Climb the impressive marble staircase to see the rooms on the upper floors, especially the ornate Council Chamber and the Aldermen's Chamber, with gold stars on its blue ceiling. Open Mon.–Fri. from 8:30 A.M.–4:30 P.M. (4 P.M. in July and August). If the chambers are locked, ask at the city clerk's office for a custodian to let you in. This building shares the **west end of Kennedy Plaza** with the Biltmore Hotel; **(401) 421-7740.**

Johnson and Wales Culinary Museum

If it concerns cooking or food service, it's most likely here, from a three-tier Tunisian lunch pail to the first electric stove or a brick of tea once used as currency. Follow the evolution of the food processor or of chef's uniforms (and find out why the chef's jacket is double-breasted). With honey pots, lemon squeezers and a Roman wine vessel from the time of Christ, this collection cries out for a permanent home where it can be fully displayed and interpreted, but the warehouse that currently houses it is at least roomy. Unfortunately, you can't just wander and read labels, and the student-led individual tours vary greatly in quality. Quirky as it is, we love it, as will any foodie. Open Mon.–Fri. from 9 A.M.–4:00 P.M., Sat. from 10 A.M.–3 P.M., with a $3 admission fee. It's a bit tricky to find, at **315 Harborside Blvd.** It is off Allen's Ave., close to I-95 Exit 18. Turn onto Northrup St., beside the Shell service station, then left into the first parking lot; **(401) JWU-2805.**

Rhode Island Black Heritage Society

The museum has displays and exhibitions on Black history and culture. "Creative Survival" has been heralded as one of the finest exhibits on Black history in America. The collections spotlight Rhode Island, which figures more prominently in Black history than any other place in the Northeast (Rhode Island was the only northern colony with a plantation system, although all the colonies held slaves). Along with the museum are extensive historical archives. Ask for the brochure listing important Rhode Island sites in Black history. The museum is handicapped-accessible. **46 Aborn St.** (opposite Providence Public Library), open Mon.–Fri. from 9 A.M.– 4:30 P.M.; **(401) 751-3490.**

State House

Designed by the architectural firm of McKim, Mead and White, the monumental marble building stands on a hill close to the center of the city. Its huge dome is variously considered to be the second, third or fourth largest unsupported dome in the world. Everyone seems to agree that Saint Peter's in Rome is the largest; those who say the Rhode Island state capitol is third cite the Taj Mahal as second; those who say it's fourth place the Minnesota capitol third (and the most authoritative sources agree on this one). Whatever its rank, it's big. Inside, in the elaborate Governor's Reception Room, is a full-length portrait of George Washington by Gilbert Stuart and Rhode Island's original charter, issued in 1663 by Charles II. All manner of treasures are tucked away in the building: needlepoint tapestries in the House of Representatives chamber; the carved and gold leaf ceiling of the library; a cannon in the lobby, which has had the cannonball stuck in it since misfiring during the Battle of Gettysburg; and a silver service from the *USS Rhode Island.* Open Mon.–Fri. from 8:30 A.M.– 4:30 P.M., guided tours are by appointment. The building is handicapped-accessible; **(401) 277-2357.**

Brown University crowns College Hill; its oldest building was used as a barracks hospital during the Revolutionary War.

THE EAST SIDE

Annmary Brown Memorial

This small art museum has, among its other works, an interesting collection of "problem" paintings. These, expertly labeled by scholarly curators, include many that have previously been attributed to well-known artists but that are now thought to have been works by their students or others. A visit here will make you look at the collections of other art museums with a sharper eye. We consider this to be Providence's most overlooked gem of a museum. It is free and open Mon.–Fri. from 9 A.M.–5 P.M. **17 Brown St.,** just south of the campus green; **(401) 863-2429.**

Bayard Ewing Building

This outstanding example of nineteenth-century commercial architecture has been restored and adapted for use by Rhode Island School of Design's various architecture departments. Changing exhibits and lectures on architectural subjects are open to the public. It is open Mon.–Fri. from 9 A.M.–5 P.M. at **231 South Main St.; (401) 454-6280.**

Brown University Campus

The campus centers around **University Hall**, which originally housed the entire school

The Rhode Island Guide

(explaining something about the tradition of graduation in the Baptist Church). If you plan to take the free campus tour, go directly to the **Corliss-Brackett House**, the ornate Italianate villa at **45 Prospect St.**, where it begins; **(401) 863-2378.** But if you plan to explore the campus on your own, begin at its historic and geographic center, University Hall, which was used as a military barracks and hospital during the Revolution.

To its right (left as you face it) is **Manning Hall**, a replica of a Greek temple. Beyond, at the corner of Prospect and Waterman Sts., is the ornate stone and brick **Carrie Tower**. Continue along Prospect St. to the **Corliss-Brackett House**, on your right, which is open during business hours as the administrative offices of the college (if you change your mind about taking a tour, inquire here for times). This was the home of George Corliss, inventor of the Corliss steam engine (an original example of which you can see at the **Wireless and Steam Museum** in East Greenwich; see page **91**) and of several climate control methods with which he kept this home at a temperature that never varied more than one degree year-round. The woodwork is richly carved. Call **(401) 863-2378.**

Although it is part of Rhode Island School of Design, not Brown, the grand Italianate **Woods-Gerry Mansion** is just up **Prospect St. at # 62,** and well worth a detour (see page **19**). Return on Prospect St. and across Waterman to College St. On your left are the ornate iron **Van Wickle Gates**, which open only twice each year: on the first day of classes and for the commencement procession to First Baptist Church. On your right is the **John Hay Library,** built by Andrew Carnegie for his friend, who was Secretary of State under two presidents. It houses a complete collection of U.S. postage stamps in uncancelled blocks. It is open Mon.–Fri. 9 A.M.–5 P.M.; **(401) 863-2146.** A few steps down (literally) College St., in the **List Art Building**, is the **David Winton Bell Gallery**, with excellent changing exhibits of contemporary and historic art. Admission is free, and the gallery is open Mon.–Fri from 11 A.M.–4 P.M., Sat.–Sun. from 1–4 P.M.; **(401) 863-2932.**

Returning to continue along Prospect St., the **John D. Rockefeller Library** is on the right, often with special exhibits on book-related subjects in its foyer and adjoining gallery; **(401) 863-2167.** Turn left at George St., and go through the gate into the campus grounds. Past the flagpole, once the mast of a yacht, is the **John Carter Brown Library** of rare books, a classic Beaux-Arts limestone building housing, among other collections, rare early maps. It is open, free, Mon.–Fri. from 8:30 A.M.–5 P.M., Sat. from 9 A.M.–noon; **(401) 863-2725.**

Cathedral of St. John

The altar table of this Georgian-cum-gothic-revival church is reputed to be from Durham Cathedral in England, and from the dome ceiling hangs a Waterford crystal chandelier with a gold reflector above it. Separating the sanctuary from the nave is a fine oak screen. Several other interesting details are described in a flyer that you will find near the front door as you enter the cathedral. Those interested in organs should also look for a folder describing the 1851 Hook organ and its later restoration. Selections from 1939 vestry minutes mention that, prior to restoration, its bellows were patched with chewing gum, Band-Aids and tongue depressors! A nice bookshop located in the cathedral close is open Mon.–Sat. from 9 A.M.–5 P.M. Sunday services are at 8:30 and 10:30 A.M. Opposite Roger Williams National Memorial at **271 North Main St.; (401) 331-4622.**

First Baptist Meeting House

Roger Williams founded the Baptist Society in Providence in 1638, and this Georgian building was designed by Joseph Brown in 1775. It houses not only the oldest congregation but is the oldest surviving meeting house as well, considered the "Mother Church" by Baptists all over the world. Its 185-foot steeple, rising in five stages, was built on the grounds by shipwrights in a telescoping system. The tower took three days to build, the entire church a year, during the blockade of the harbor during the Revolutionary War, when Providence had a ready labor force. The interior is one of the best examples of Georgian architecture in America. Brown University confers its degrees here, although the church is not large enough to hold parents or faculty, who wait at the campus above. A brochure is available for a self-guided tour of the building that details its history and architecture and points out displays, which include Roger Williams's tea-kettle. Mon.–Fri. from 9:30 A.M.–3:30 P.M. The Sunday worship service at 11 A.M. is followed by a guided tour at 12:15 P.M. **75 North Main St.; (401) 454-3418.**

First Unitarian Church

A masterpiece of federal architecture with re-fined gothic touches, the soaring steeple holds the largest bell ever cast by Paul Revere. Open by appointment only; Sunday worship service is at 10:30 A.M. **Benefit and Benevolent Sts.; (401) 421-7970.**

Governor Henry Lippitt House

Beyond Brown University, in a neighborhood filled with fine and grand old homes, this renaissance revival mansion stands out above the rest. The inside is spectacular for its stenciled ceilings and trim, its stained and etched glass, and for faux marble and false-grained woods. This is among New England's finest interiors, a museum of Victorian decorative styles. Just as important as the artistic quality of the house is the skill of the curatorial staff, not only in overseeing a careful restoration but also in interpreting the house to visitors. This is done through the usual tours and also in Victorian entertainments, dinners and events that show the house in use as it was during Governor Lippitt's era. Authentic Victorian dinners and teas are served to guests, many of whom wear period costumes for the occasion, and workshops are offered in Victorian arts. Set apart geographically and historically, this house is to Victorian Providence what the John Brown House is to colonial Providence. **199 Hope St.** Open Tues.–Fri. from 10 A.M.–4 P.M., Sat. from 1–4 P.M. From Memorial Day to Labor Day, Tues.–Sat. from 1–4 P.M. A fee is charged; **(401) 453-0688.**

The First Unitarian Church, built in 1816, is a fine example of the federal style in church architecture.

John Brown House

John Quincy Adams described Brown's home as "the most magnificent and elegant mansion that I have ever seen on this continent." John Brown, who was the first man of importance to build a home outside the narrow confines of the riverfront town, chose a prospect from which he could see his busy wharves at India Point, whence his vessels sailed in their profitable China trade. The house, designed by Brown's brother Joseph, shows that the owner was a man of good taste as well as prominence in commerce and politics. The home remains elegant today, with its French wallpapers, fine moldings and original Brown family furnishings. It contains some of the finest examples of Rhode Island decorative arts and of the work of its cabinetmakers. If you can see only one colonial home in Providence, it should be this one, not only for its own grace, but for the view of eighteenth-century life you will gain from the tour. Access to the gardens is separate from the house, and free. Open Tues.–Sat. from 10 A.M.–4:30 P.M., Sun. from noon–4:30 P.M. In Jan.–Feb., Sat. from 10 A.M.–4:30 P.M., Sun. from noon–4:30, and weekdays by appointment only. The 45-minute tours begin every half hour. Admission is $5, which includes on-

The Athenaeum is a private library where Edgar Allen Poe once read.

site parking. Although the **address is on Power St., the property adjoins Benefit St.;** (401) 331-8575.

Market House

What tales this place could tell. Providence's first marketplace, built where the Pequot and Wampanoag Trails crossed, the building was originally two stories, and its lower arches were open to permit goods to be brought in on wagons. It was the city's commercial center, civic center and meeting place. Talk of revolt turned to action here as tea was burned in 1775 to protest taxes. Local government met here, and in 1797 a Masonic lodge was added by building a third floor. Read the marker on the outside that describes the high tides that covered this area periodically before the building of the Fox Point Hurricane Barrier.

Museum of Art of the Rhode Island School of Design

One of New England's finest art museums, the school's permanent collections include more than 75,000 works. Not only are pieces characteristic of most of the world's art styles and periods, but most often they are outstanding examples. They are arranged chronologically, even though this may mean combining works of different nations and media. An outstanding collection of eighteenth-century furniture is shown in an adjoining house. Among the American antiques is another of the rare Newport secretaries like the one sold to rebuild the Nightingale House (see **below**). Classical art, nineteenth-century French paintings and art from the Far East are particularly well represented, with fine Greek bronzes, Roman marble and mosaics, and well-known works of Cezanne, Degas and Manet. Allow plenty of time here, these are works to be savored. The museum is accessible to wheelchairs. Summer hours (June 30–Labor Day) are Wed.–Sat. from noon–5 P.M.; winter hours are Tues., Wed., Fri. and Sat. from 10:30 A.M.–5 P.M., Thur. from noon–8 P.M., Sun. and holidays from 2–5 P.M. Admission is $2, free on Saturdays; **(401) 454-6500.**

Nelson Winthrop Aldrich House

Built in 1822, this was the home of the Rhode Island senator known as the father of the Federal Reserve system. Its exhibits on the state's history cover subjects such as architecture and decorative arts; it is now the home of the Rhode Island Historical Society. A modest fee is charged. Open Tues.–Fri. from 9 A.M.–5 P.M. **110 Benevolent St., just east of Hope St.; (401) 331-8575.**

Nightingale-Brown House

Legend has it that Colonel Joseph Nightingale, a business rival of John Brown, had his house built to block Brown's fine view of his India Point Wharves. If so, the Browns had the last laugh, because this house soon passed into Brown family ownership and stayed there for nearly two centuries before the family donated it to Brown University. It is the largest wooden-frame house from the eighteenth century to survive in America and is restored in painstaking detail. Each step in the restoration turned up more problems, from termite and water damage to underlying structural deficiencies. When the job seemed impossible, the Brown family offered to auction a priceless Newport-built secretary desk, one of only 12 known to exist. The $12.1 million raised by the sale of that single piece allowed them to save the house. Frederick Law Olmsted designed the gardens, and throughout the restorations on

Dark Tales: Edgar Allen Poe and H. P. Lovecraft in Providence

Before Edgar Allen Poe came to Providence to lecture at the Franklin Lyceum, he had corresponded with a widow, Sarah Whitman, an admirer of his work. She was herself a poet of note and had attracted his attention by writing a poem to him, which was published in a national magazine. He fell in love with her, and she promised to marry him if he would stop drinking. The garden at her home at 88 Benefit St. and the alcoves of the Providence Athenaeum are often cited as the scenes of their short courtship; they are reputed to have at least once chosen a cemetery for an assignation. She was the inspiration for his poem "To Helen" but soon broke off their engagement because he continued to drink. Poe left Providence with a broken heart and died less than a year later, in 1849.

H. P. Lovecraft, who was hailed as the greatest master of the horror tale since Poe, was born in Providence, where he set many of his stories: A vampirelike creature lives in a house on Benefit St., the steeple of an abandoned Federal Hill church holds a mysterious winged monster, a Brown professor dies ... all chilling tales of the dark side. A bookish boy (and, like Poe, a member of the Athenaeum), Lovecraft was kept isolated by an overprotective mother. He grew up on the gothic genre, and when he made it his own, he found homes for his unearthly creatures in the neighborhoods he knew best. His tombstone, erected in the 1980s, fifty years after his death, reads simply "I am Providence." The John Hay Library at Brown has a collection of his works and papers. For a good selection of his books, visit **Cellar Stories Books, 190 Mathewson St.** in Providence.

the house, the gardens and trees were carefully protected. Now a university center for American studies, tours are given of its first-floor rooms. Open Fridays from 1–4 P.M. Admission is $3. **357 Benefit St.; (401) 272-0357.**

Providence Art Club

The two unmistakable buildings on Thomas St. beside the First Baptist Meeting House, one pink and the other looking as though it had fallen out of a medieval English city, are the Providence Art Club. Built in 1789 and 1791, respectively, the pink building was raised and a ground floor added to it to provide commercial space, which accounts for the suspended doorway. This was the home of the jeweler who perfected gold plating and founded the costume jewelry industry. The galleries featuring both collection shows and works of contemporary artists are open free to the public Mon.–Fri. from 10 A.M.–4 P.M., Sat. from noon–3 P.M., Sun. from 3–5 P.M. **10 and 11 Thomas St.; (401) 331-1114.**

The Providence Athenaeum

One of the oldest libraries in America, **the Athenaeum** houses rare books in an atmosphere that can only be described as bookish. Edgar Allen Poe courted Sarah Whitman in its recessed alcoves. Changing exhibits from the rare book collections are on display: These collections include two medieval manuscripts from the 1300s, the works of Robert Burns, a complete original set of Audubon's *Birds of America*, old juvenile books, erotica and more than 300 items from the presses of the Roycrofters. The "occasionally annual" book sale offers quality books donated for the occasion, not discards from the Athenaeum's own shelves. A lively arts schedule may include music, dance, children's story hours, films and literary events. Although only members can withdraw books, membership is open to anyone, and the public is welcome to use books in the library, where comfortable reading space is provided. Mon.–Fri. from 8:30 A.M.–5:30 P.M.,

The Rhode Island Guide

Sat. from 9:30 A.M.–5:30 P.M. **251 Benefit St. (401) 421-6970.**

Rhode Island Historical Society Library

Along with its library of genealogies, histories, newspapers and significant documents (among them the personal papers of Roger Williams), the society houses exhibits of artifacts, photos, paintings and other collections. Use of the library and access to its exhibits is free, and it is open Sept.–May on Wed.–Sat. from 10 A.M.–5 P.M.; June–Aug. on Tues. from noon–8 P.M. and Wed.–Fri. from 10 A.M.–5 P.M. **121 Hope St.; (401) 331-8575.**

Roger Williams National Memorial

A small open park beside the river marks the spot where Williams and his followers settled and the spring they used for their water sup-

The Governor Stephen Hopkins House has a terraced period garden.

ply. The Visitor Center has displays and a brief slide show on Williams, the early settlement and the beliefs that led Williams and his followers to begin anew here. Williams's vision for Providence is commemorated by the fact that land for the park was given in memory of the first Jewish citizen of Providence to be elected to public office. Open daily from 8 A.M.–4 P.M. **282 North Main St.; (401) 521-7266.**

Shakespeare's Head and Gardens

The odd name refers to a sign that, in the late 1700s, identified this building as a bookstore and printery for the *Providence Gazette.* It was one of the few three-story wooden homes in colonial Providence. The restored terraced garden behind the house is open to the public; it's a pleasant shaded place for a picnic lunch. At night it is charming, with very delicate lighting from no apparent source. The plan follows a 1930s perception of what a colonial garden might have been, with separate herb beds, abundant lilacs and an umbrella-shaped apple tree. The garden is now under renovation to make it more authentic to the house's period. The building is headquarters for Providence Preservation Society, which publishes architectural guides to the city. **21 Meeting St.; (401) 831-7440.**

Stephen Hopkins House

The nine-term colonial governor, signer of the Declaration of Independence and Chief Justice of the Rhode Island Superior Court, bought this house in 1743 and added a new two-story front section to the original, which is now the rear ell. It has been restored to his period. George Washington stayed here. The parterre garden, which is open even when the house is not (although the gate latch sticks—keep jiggling it to open), is built in terraces. One of the best views of the gold dome of the Old Stone Bank, with modern high-rise buildings as a backdrop, is from the garden in the late-afternoon sunlight Admission is free, although donations are welcome. Open Apr.–mid-Dec. on Wed. and Sat. from 1–4 P.M. **Benefit and Hopkins Sts.; (401) 751-1758 or (401) 884-8337.**

Woods-Gerry Mansion

Used as the admissions office of Rhode Island School of Design, this is a grand Italianate brick and sandstone building with an arched porte cochere and a terrace with French windows. The largest house of its time in the city, it is built on the site of an alarm beacon that was set on an 85-foot mast to warn colonists of approaching British during the Revolution. Inside are galleries with changing exhibits, and the gardens are decorated with sculpture. It is open Mon.–Sat. from 10 A.M.–4 P.M., Sun. from 2–5 P.M. At **62 Prospect St.; (401) 454-6140.**

ROGER WILLIAMS PARK

Betsey Williams Cottage

This gambrel-roofed cottage was the home of the descendant of Roger Williams who donated the first 100 acres of land for Roger Williams Park. It dates from 1785 and is furnished in pieces from that period. Open mid-April–mid-June and mid-Sept.–October on Sun. from 1:30–4 P.M. It is inside the park, close to the Elmwood Ave. gate, but signs throughout the park point the way; **(401) 785-9457.**

Museum of Natural History

The French chateau–style museum contains permanent exhibits focusing on the relationship of Native Americans with the natural world, on the many facets of Narragansett Bay (this one uses interactive computers) and on a look at the world of the Victorian collectors whose treasures were the foundations of so many natural history museums. Also in the museum is the **Cormack Planetarium,** with changing shows. (If you want to get married under the stars but in the daytime, you can have your wedding inside the planetarium.) Open daily from 10 A.M.–5 P.M., admission is $2. Planetarium admission is $3. Located **in Roger Williams Park; (401) 785-9457.**

Nightlife

Between the active schedule of theaters in the new Downtown Arts and Entertainment District

The Betsey Williams Cottage is at the center of Roger Williams State Park.

and the offerings of the city's several colleges, there is almost always something happening. *The Providence Journal* and *Rhode Island Monthly* are good sources of the latest listings, although you might be wise to call a venue ahead if you are interested in any particular type of performance.

Providence Performing Arts Center

Located at **220 Weybosset St.** in the 1928 Loew's Movie Palace, the Beaux-Arts Center has been completely restored to its glittering original condition. It hosts full Broadway stage productions, opera and internationally heralded performers and has a large restored movie screen. Call **(401) 421-ARTS.**

Trinity Repertory Company

The Trinity is known for its Tony Award–winning, innovative productions of both classic and contemporary works. It is New England's oldest resident theater company. **201 Washington St.; (401) 521-1100.**

Rhode Island College

The college presents both student theater and major guest artists and groups. **Roberts Auditorium** is at **600 Mt. Pleasant Ave.; (401) 456-8060.**

The Rhode Island Philharmonic

For more than 50 years, this orchestra has brought serious music to the city. Its seven principal performances are on Saturday evenings in October through May in the **Veterans Memorial Auditorium.** Ticket prices range from $18 to $32, with $3 discounts for students and seniors. Friday lunchtime concerts are $10, and Sunday-afternoon family concerts are $8 for adults and $4 for children. Three chamber concerts are held at **Grace Episcopal Church** on Wednesday evenings for $15; **(401) 831-3123.**

Veterans Memorial Auditorium

This year-round venue for the performing arts offers over 70 events each year. Wynton Marsalis, the Moscow Ballet and the Boston Handel and Haydn Society have performed here recently; **(401) 277-3150.**

Brown University's Stuart Theater

Offering a variety of performances, Brown's main stage is a venue for visiting artists and student productions; **(401) 863-2838.**

Perishable Theater

Alternative plays and a variety of other works highlight the schedule at **95 Empire St.; (401) 331-2695.**

Alias Stage

This small theater specializes in classics and original contemporary works of drama and comedy at **36 Elbow St.; (401) 831-2919.**

Lupo's Heartbreak Hotel

At **239 Westminster St.** in Downcity, Lupo's has top-name rock and rhythm and blues musicians; **(401) 272-5876.**

The Strand

Top alternative rock and hip-hop acts are brought to its gigantic stage; it is probably the city's wildest club. Anyone over 30 will feel ancient here. **79 Washington St.; (401) 272-8900.**

The Living Room

There's a full house here almost every night and a variety of performers and groups from all over the world. Top names perform here: You may find punk rock, alternative or blues, with crowds to match. Depending on the show, this club appeals to all ages. **23 Rathbone St.; (401) 521-5200.**

Brewpubs and Cafes

Providence has two brewpubs: **Union Station Brewery** attracts a young, lively crowd at **36 Exchange Ter.; (401) 274-BREW. Trinity Brew House** is nearby at **186 Fountain St.; (401) 453-2337.** Both brewpubs are handicapped-accessible and each has both smoking and nonsmoking sections.

Several cafes and coffee houses in the city have live music on some or all evenings. See **Sweet Retreat** and **Cafe Zog** in the Cafes section and **829 Hope** in the Restaurants sections later in this chapter.

The Irish Ceilidhe Club of Rhode Island

In Cranston. The Club holds dances every month that are open to the public. On Friday evenings members teach jigs, reels and Irish set dancing. Lessons are open to the public. **50 America St.; (401) 944-3233.**

Shopping

COLLEGE HILL

Wickenden Street, at the southern end of College Hill, is a center for shops, featuring antiques and collectibles and funky boutiques and new age emporia mixed with coffeehouses. **Thayer St.,** which runs along the hill behind the Brown campus, has a lot of bookstores.

Sarah Doyle Gallery

Featuring the works of local and other artists, the gallery is in the Sarah Doyle Women's Center at Brown. **185 Meeting St.; (401) 863-2189.**

College Hill Bookstore

This is the state's oldest bookstore, and no wonder, with its location and hours. It's open every day until midnight at **252 Thayer St.; (401) 751-6404.**

Brown Bookstore

Along with a tremendous selection of books, it houses the Campus Shop, a source of Brown insignia items from sweatshirts to pencils. **244 Thayer St.; (401) 863-3168.**

Camden Passage

Estate jewelry, antique glass and furnishings and vintage decorative items fill a highly eclectic, tasteful shop at **359 S. Main St.; (401) 453-0770.**

WAYLAND SQUARE

This area, in the historic streets just east of Brown University and beyond Hope St., has a pleasant neighborhood quality and is especially rich in bookshops.

Books on the Square

A friendly, relaxed shop with an "if we don't have it, we'll get it for you" policy. Browsers are always welcome (and seldom leave without a book). **471 Angell St.; (401) 331-9097.**

Myopic Books

New and used books in a low-key, old-fashioned bookshop setting on **Angell St.; (401) 521-5533.**

Providence Bookstore Cafe

Not as many books as they once had, but a nice selection of gifts and a comfortable place to rest in the company of lively jazz and art. **500 Angell St.; (401) 521-5533.**

The Opulent Owl

Well-chosen gifts, stationery, linens, jewelry and high-taste crafts fill this attractive shop at **195 Wayland Ave.; (401) 521-6698.**

FEDERAL HILL

Atwells Avenue is the heart and soul of Providence's Italian quarter—lively by day, lighted in a festive atmosphere at night, lined with eateries in all price ranges, as well as bakeries and food shops.

Venda Ravioli

For over 70 years, this Italian grocery shop has been selling fresh pasta, sausage and a wide variety of Italian foods, including their own mozzarella. Open Mon. from 9 A.M.–6 P.M., Tues–Sat. from 8:30 A.M.–6 P.M., Sun. from 8:30 A.M.–1 P.M. **265 Atwells Ave.; (401) 421-9105.**

The Mayor's Own Marinara Sauce

Look in any of the Federal Hill food emporia for The Mayor's Own Marinara Sauce by Providence's colorful live-wire mayor, Buddy Cianci (who has been voted the man most Rhode Island women would like to have a date with). It all started when the mayor was looking for a favor to give guests at his annual birthday party. His favorite recipe for marinara sauce had just been published in a local cookbook, so someone said, "Why not bottle it with your own label and give everybody a jar?" But one jar wasn't enough, and people kept asking for more. From that original 30 cases, more than 700 cases a month are now sold, with the profits going to the Mayor's Scholarship Fund. Everybody's a winner: Providence gets a good marinara, worthy kids get an education and the mayor gets some publicity. You won't find a more appropriate souvenir of Federal Hill (the sauce, not the mayor, who would never leave Providence).

The Rhode Island Guide

Tony's Colonial

Italian foods, cheese, homemade breadsticks, calzones and fine oils are displayed amid the colorful dishes to serve them on. A lively, stylish shop with a top line of Italian imports. Open Mon.–Sat. from 8:30 A.M.–6 P.M., Sun. from 8:30 A.M.–1 P.M. at **311 Atwells Ave.; (401) 621-8675.**

Gasboro's

You can have your wine delivered anywhere in Rhode Island by this well-stocked wine shop. Open Mon.–Sat. from 9 A.M.–6 P.M. **361 Atwells Ave.; (401) 421-4170.**

DOWNCITY

Tilden-Thurber Co.

We considered listing this as a museum, since it has more treasures of art and antiques than many museums do. But here they are for sale. One of the nation's finest collections of American furniture from the neoclassical period, which corresponds to the Federal period in architecture, is displayed along with furniture of other periods and smaller items, including estate jewelry. **292 Westminster St.; (401) 272-3200.**

City Center Artisans

An art gallery, gift shop and school, City Center shows and promotes the work of Rhode Island artists. **59 Eddy St.; (401) 521-2990.**

AS220

Combining many arts, AS220 has a gallery and a performance space with a cafe. **115 Empire St.; (401) 831-9327.**

Spectator Sports

Basketball

The Providence College Friars is one of the most successful teams in the Big East Basketball Conference, and their home games are played in the **Providence Civic Center; (401) 331-0700** or **(401) 865-1000.**

Football

Brown University is a member of the Ivy League, and during the fall home games you may see the football team take on Harvard, Yale, Princeton, Dartmouth or other colleges; **(401) 863-1000.**

Hockey

The Providence Bruins are an affiliate of the Boston Bruins, playing hockey in the Providence Civic Center usually on Friday evenings and Sunday afternoons between late September and early April. For ticket information call **(401) 273-5000.** Providence College hockey games are played in the **Schneider Arena; (401) 865-2168.**

Tours

Providence Preservation Society

Offers rentals of audio walking tours for $5 that cover both College Hill (including Benefit St.) and the downtown areas. These point out historic landmarks and are particularly helpful about the city's many architectural highlights. Cassette rentals are available Mon.–Fri. from 9 A.M.–3 P.M. In July, August and September the society offers conducted walking tours of Benefit St. and downtown at 10 a.m. every morning. These are 90 minutes long and cost $10 ($5 under age 12). Reservations for these walks should be made by calling **(401) 831-8586.** Excellent illustrated booklets for self-guided tours are also available for $1 each and cover several other neighborhoods of particular architectural interest. These are available Mon.–Fri. from 9 A.M.–5 P.M. at the society's offices at **21 Meeting St.; (401) 831-7440.**

Festival of Historic Houses

In June, the society offers candlelight and afternoon tours of historic private homes and gardens as well as a bus tour of downtown buildings. This is a rare chance to see the interiors of homes that are not otherwise open to the public and is of special interest to anyone considering restoring or preserving a historic home. The "secret" gardens of many of the historic homes are also open. Tickets for the bus tour are $14, for the house tours $24. These are azlways a sell-out, so you will need to get tickets in advance; **(401) 831-7440.**

Providence Banner Trail Trolley

Operating a continuous circuit through the downtown, College Hill, Federal Hill and capitol areas, the trolley stops at landmarks and at major hotels. You can take the complete one-hour circle to get an overview or you can get off and back on anytime during the day at any point. The cost is $14 for adults, $9 for children, and the trolley operates Wed.–Sat. from 9:30 A.M.–4:30 P.M.; **(401) 934-8687.**

Historic Providence

This Gray Line tour includes visits to the John Brown House, the First Baptist Church and the State House. They operate on Tuesdays and Fridays, picking up passengers at major area hotels. The charge is $23, and you must make a reservation; **(401) 658-3408** or **(800) 934-8687.**

Providence Harbor Cruises

Serenity, a 65-foot gaff-rigged schooner, leaves three times daily from **Shooters Yacht Club Marina** at **25 India St.** and at 6:30 P.M. for a dinner cruise. On Fridays the schedule changes, with one morning cruise, a lunch cruise and a happy-hour cruise lasting from 5:30 P.M. until 9 P.M. The sailing excursions, which are those without meals or bar service, cost $20. Lunch is $28 and dinner is $37; **(401) 454-0348.** During the **Providence Waterfront Festival, Baer's River Workshops** conducts one-hour harbor tours by canoe or kayak, for only $3 per boat. It is wise to reserve ahead; **(401) 453-1633.**

The Art Trolley

The third Thursday of each month is Gallery Night, when the trolley shuttles between 12 or so art events, galleries, antiques shops and museums. It makes a continuous circuit from 5–9 P.M., and you can get on or off at any or all stops. To catch the first run, be at **Freeman** Park, at the corner of Westminster and Mathewson Sts., at 5 P.M. Best of all, it's free; **(401) 274-9120** or **(401) 751-2628.**

Neighborhood Walks

The best companion to the city (apart from Barbara Barnes of the Providence Preservation Society, who occasionally escorts groups through the city) is the excellent *Directory Map,* with most landmarks shown in a color-coded format. It is easy to read and more complete than the smaller, also free, *A Stroll through Providence,* although the latter has more detailed text. Get both at the **Visitor's Center** at **30 Exchange Terrace (off Kennedy Square); (800) 233-1636** or **(401) 274-1636.**

For architectural tours of other neighborhoods, contact the **Providence Preservation Society** for its excellent booklets. Although these cover Benefit St., downtown and Brown University in great detail, we have provided the following brief descriptions for those who arrive in Providence on a weekend or evening, when the society is not open, or for those who want to see the city's highlights in a more limited time. The society is at **21 Meeting St.; (401) 831-7440.** (See also Brown University Campus, page **13.**)

A Mile of History

Benefit Street was the social, cultural, artistic, civic and intellectual heart of Providence during the late colonial and early federal periods, and to stroll along its brick sidewalk and through a few of its gardens is to immerse yourself in the aura of that exiting time in Providence's history. A vital, living neighborhood today, it is not a period piece frozen in time. Later buildings, including some distinguished Victorians and relatively modern additions, give it variety and life.

To understand the sometimes puzzling layout of College Hill, it is helpful to know the history of the early land division. The city's first buildings all stretched along the riverbank on Towne St., now Main. The steep pitch of the hill behind made building difficult, so the back

23

land was divided into long narrow plots that ran uphill behind the Towne St. homes. On this land were orchards and pastures. By the 1760s, Towne St. was so congested that a second street was laid out along the hillside behind it, cutting across these back lands. It became a mix of fine homes—the finest in the city—and the more modest homes of artisans.

Other streets were later laid out up the hill, but its slope created problems that remain today, as a look at the map, or the hill itself, shows. Streets have unaccountable gaps, then resume farther on under the same names. These gaps are the steep drop-offs where even Providence planners could not build a street. After you've climbed a few where they were able to build streets, you'll realize just how steep these gaps must be.

Like inner city neighborhoods everywhere, after more than a century of use, this one became old, an undesirable quarter of rundown multifamily houses. It has been a long, slow

climb to the street we see today, but the spirit of restoration is strong in Providence, and the result is so fine that it is hard to remember what this area looked like in the middle of the twentieth century, when children were too embarrassed to give a Benefit address at school.

The **Jenckes House** at **43 Benefit St.** is one of the rare early gambrel-roofed houses to survive in Providence (you will see a number of these in Newport).

The **Barnes House**, at **#49,** with its original 1798 porch, has an interesting siding of wooden blocks cut to simulate stone, again rare in Providence but often seen in Newport. Opposite, **#52** and **#56** are nearly identical and also from the 1790s. Number 56 is known as the childhood home of the founder of Gorham Corporation, the silver company. He was born at **#88,** but its fame is as the home of Sarah Whitman, the widow courted by Edgar Allen Poe (they met frequently in the garden at #88).

101 Benefit St. represents another era. It's built of brick and brownstone in the Italian palazzo style. The **Sullivan Dorr** house at 109 stands on part of Roger Williams's original property and is one of the city's outstanding federal homes. Even its original outbuildings are preserved. Dorr was U.S. consul to China, where he made a fortune in the early days of the China trade.

The **Old State House,** one of several buildings that served as the seat of government before the present capitol building, is one of the street's oldest buildings, dating from 1762. The central portion is original, both facades having been added later. Rhode Island declared independence from Britain here in May 1776, two months before the signing of the Declaration of Independence. The houses beginning with **#149** are a rarity for Providence, which has very few row houses. One of three sets on **Benefit St.,** this one is a classic of the Civil War era.

Here you should make a brief detour downhill on Meeting St. to see the 1769 **Brick Schoolhouse,** a Georgian building that once housed Brown University, and Shakespeare's Head, now home of the Providence Preserva-

Victorian architects dealt with the sharp pitch of College Hill in some creative ways.

tion Society (see page **22**). Be sure to see the garden of the latter. Back on Benefit St., you will pass the Gothic-style **Marine Corps Arsenal** (1840) and the back of the **First Baptist Meeting House** (see page **14**). The medieval-looking building down Thomas St. is the **Providence Art Club. The Truman Beckwith House** is on the corner of College St. A distinguished home of the 1820s, it has a fine hillside garden rising in terraces behind it.

Opposite the large courthouse complex is the **Athenaeum,** a Greek revival library built in 1836 (see page **17**), and beyond it Athenaeum Row, the second set of row houses on the street. At the corner of Hopkins St. is the **Governor Stephen Hopkins House,** the rear ell of which was built in 1707; the front was added in 1743 (see page **18**). You can wander through its garden even when the house is not open.

Beyond is the street's third and oldest set of row houses, built in 1814–1819 in the federal style. At the corner of Benevolent St. is the **First Unitarian Church,** built in 1816, and one of the finest examples of Federal church architecture (see page **15**). The unusual Second Empire house with the ornate iron railings at **#314** was the home of Civil War General Ambrose Burnside, whose peculiar whiskers became known as sideburns, in a reversal of his name. The 1864 house at **#336,** the only Gothic-style Victorian house on the street, is particularly noticeable for the unique way it deals with the steep drop in the street level along its north side.

Two of the five grand mansions built on College Hill in the late 1700s, the **John Brown House** (see page **15**), which faces onto Power St., and the wooden **Nightingale-Brown House** (see page **16**), follow on the left. Farther along, still on the left, another pair of houses share the same architectural style, at **#383** and **#389.** The first is brick with brownstone trim, the second entirely of brownstone. Both are in the Italian palazzo style, and both were built in 1853. Opposite, beside the Barker St. Playhouse, is the **Tillinghast Family Cemetery,** dating from the 1600s. It's the only one remaining of the many family burial

Benefit Street, now Prividence's "Mile of History," was a slum only two decades ago.

plots that once sat on the hill behind the Towne St. houses.

25

Weybosset Street

Unlike the other streets of downtown Providence, which proceed in straight lines, Weybosset follows the irregular route of the old Pequot Trail, which came across Rhode Island from the Connecticut border. The first buildings on this bank of the river grew up along this trail, which eventually became the busy street it remains today. Some of the most interesting Downcity buildings are along it.

Begin at the **Providence Performing Arts Center,** at the corner of Richmond St., originally Loew's State Theater. Its Beaux-Arts exterior is decorated in brick and terra-cotta, and inside, its domed auditorium is ornately decorated with rococo sculpture. On the opposite side of the street, between Mathewson and Clemence Sts., is one of the few original residence blocks built on this side of the river. They were remodeled in the 1880s to add some Second Empire ornament. In the center of the street you will see the very ornate **Weybosset Information Center,** built in 1914 as a comfort station and recently renovated as a police substation and information center (but it no longer houses restrooms).

Learning in Providence

One-day cooking classes are offered at Pot au Feu Restaurant, and the cost includes a chef's coat and toque, recipe book, and knives, as well as lunch and dinner at the restaurant and a wine seminar and tasting. **44 Custom House St.;** call **(401) 273-8953** for a brochure.

Johnson and Wales Department of Continuing Education occasionally offers classes with local chefs, usually in the $25 price range; **(401) 598-1085.**

The Learning Connection offers classes by local experts on everything from herb gardening to traveling solo, as well as tours by bicycle, canoe, bus and on foot. Many of these are one-session classes, but you should reserve ahead; **(401) 274-9330.**

Look above the street level on some of the buildings as you continue along Weybosset to see a variety of late-nineteenth-century architectural features. **The Arcade** (see page **11**) will be on your left, and just past it a high-Victorian building at #45. Opposite, at **#50**, is the former **Bank of North America,** built in 1856 and a rare example of an Italian palazzo–style commercial building (the storefronts were added later). Next to it (and appearing again around the corner next to Pot au Feu Restaurant) is the real architectural treasure of the entire street, the **Wilcox Building.** Built in 1875, it was one of the most expensive buildings of its time. The facade and columns are decorated with carved animal and plant themes. On the corner, with the Wilcox Building wrapped around it in an L shape, is a Victorian gothic building with a cast-iron facade, which was constructed at a local foundry. Weybosset ends here, at the **Customs House** and the **Turk's Head Building,** with its modern replica of the Turk's-head sign that marked a colonial house on the same corner.

Where to Stay

Lodging is abundant in Providence, with several large modern hotels but very few small inns or B&Bs. If you can, avoid Memorial Day weekend, which is Brown University's commencement weekend, as well as the second weekend in May, which is when almost everyone else in the city graduates. In general, April, May, September and October are the most crowded months and have the highest rates. The most centrally located hotels are the Biltmore, The Westin and Holiday Inn; the most conveniently located inn is The Old Court, on the East Side.

Lodging is also abundant in Warwick at the T. F. Green Airport, where Rte. 1 is lined with hotels in all price ranges (see page 93). Remember also that the state is small, and you can easily stay in a rural western community or south along the shore and still be able to tour Providence. We frequently drive into the city from Chepachet just for dinner.

Biltmore Hotel—$$$$

Rescued from destruction and restored by the *Providence Journal* and its co-owners, the Biltmore is a classic of turn-of-the-century elegance, its lobby aswirl with gilt and crystal. Continuing the work is a new ownership group that specializes in historic downtown properties, so the Biltmore's future looks secure as the city's premier historic hotel. The grace and luxury goes beyond the lobby, however, with many rooms large enough to have full-sized sitting areas, dressing-room closets and separate vanity areas in the bathrooms—with television sets. The new owners have just added a fitness center and concierge level, the twelfth-floor Heritage Club, which includes complimentary breakfast and cocktails for a flat per-room add-on of $20. Voice-mail, a complete business center and electronic checkout, as well as full-sized desks in rooms and its near-perfect location next to the Providence Convention Center make the Biltmore popular with business travelers, although its location is just as good for theatergoers. Rates here, although in the $100-plus range, are lower than either the Westin or the Marriott. The new **Waterplace Park** is a block away, and the I-95 exit ramp leads straight to the door. Don't leave here without taking a ride in the glass elevator for views of the city. The Biltmore is **next to City Hall, on Kennedy Plaza; (401) 421-0700** or **(800) 294-7709.**

Westin Hotel—$$$$

From nearly anywhere in the city the green gabled roof and stylish neoclassical brick lines of the Westin dominate and enhance the skyline. It's a triumph of modern design that reminds us of Quebec's venerable Hotel Frontenac. Inside, the surprising proportions of its rotunda—several stories of polished marble, an ornate dome and giant windows—dwarf the comfortable sitting area, from which you can get the city's best view of the State House. The hotel is connected to the Providence Convention Center next door by a covered walkway. Throughout the entire hotel are fine architectural details, reminding you that although this is a new and thoroughly modern building, it is a traditional grand hotel at heart. Rooms are large and nicely decorated in the same upscale tone and with extra amenities, such as irons and ironing boards, in all rooms. It has an Executive Club floor and a complete health center with an enclosed pool, plus modern conveniences of voice-mail and electronic checkout. Indoor parking is $6 a day for guests. The hotel is located in the center of downtown, just off Kennedy Plaza at **One West Exchange St.; (401) 598-8200,** or for reservations, **(800) 228-3000.**

Providence Marriott—$$$$

Close to the capitol building, and a 10-minute walk through the new **Waterplace Park** from the business district, the Marriott is a favorite for meetings and conferences, its clientele mainly business travelers. However, its excellent recreational facilities and family plans make it a good choice for those traveling with children. The patio is beautifully landscaped, with a bar and umbrella-covered cafe tables overlooking the outdoor pool. Inside, beyond a glass wall that can be removed in warm weather, is the large, bright indoor swimming area and fitness facility, which has a sauna and whirlpool. Parking is free. Unlike many

large hotels, the Marriott has a long-term staff largely made up of people who've been at the hotel for more than ten years and take a real personal interest in the guests. At **Charles and Orms Sts., near Exit 23 of I-95; (401) 272-2400** or **(800) 937-PROV.**

Holiday Inn—$$$$

An attractive modern property, this hotel offers few surprises but a reliable standard of service and facilities. Rooms are good-sized, with "Feature Rooms" adding amenities such as hair dryers, padded hangers, terry robes and coffeemakers. Children under 18 stay free in rooms with parents. The hotel has an indoor pool, whirlpool and exercise room. Transportation to and from T. F. Green Airport is free to guests. Rates are at the low end of the $$$$ category, beginning at $105, and they do not increase seasonally or for special events. Between the Providence Convention Center and the beginning of the colorful Italian section on Federal Hill, Holiday Inn is convenient to the theater district as well. It is almost directly on I-95, at **Atwells Ave.; (401) 831-3900** or, for reservations, **(800) HOLIDAY.**

Day's Hotel—$$ to $$$

Few frills distinguish this hotel, but very well maintained and nicely furnished rooms make up for it. Nearly half the rooms have harbor views. "Club Rooms" (deluxe) have Jacuzzis, coffeemakers and hair dryers. The building is new and bright, and the attractive coffeeshop in the lobby serves as a cafe gathering place for guests as well as a full-service restaurant with reasonably priced meals. An easy, friendly rapport is evident between staff and guests. One drawback here is that the harbor location, while quiet and pleasant, is not within walking distance of downtown or restaurants. It's a good choice for those who plan to tour the city by bicycle, however, because the bicycle path along the river begins here. Handicapped-access rooms are available. The hotel is close to Exit 3 off I-95, at **220 India Point, Providence 02903; (800) 325-2525** or **(401) 272-5577.**

State House Inn—$$ to $$$

In a neighborhood of homes in the process of restoration, the State House Inn is itself a restored turn-of-the-century home. The neighborhood is under review for a National Historic District and is close to both Rhode Island College and Providence College. Light pine and Shaker reproduction furnishings and American primitive art decorate rooms painted in restful colors. Some rooms have king, others queensized beds, some with canopies. The simplicity of the decor and the well-chosen colors give rooms a subtle elegance. Unlike most B&Bs, the rooms here have telephones, television sets and clock radios. A full breakfast includes a hot-dish specialty each morning along with fresh fruit and baked goodies. It's worth planning your trip around the mornings when scones are served. The genial hosts keep a file of menus sorted by cuisine. It's as close to a country B&B as you're likely to find in a city setting. Business and corporate rates are available on weeknights. Just behind the State House at **43 Jewett St., Providence, RI 02908; (401) 785-1235.**

The Old Court—$$$$

The Italianate Victorian mansion housing this inn is the only one on Benefit Street's Mile of History that has become an inn, creating this a rare opportunity to stay in a historic in-town neighborhood. Rooms have high ceilings, often ornate decorative trim and are decorated to suit their era. Nearly all have fine antiques and carpets. Two of the rooms have television, all have air-conditioning. Along with a guest lounge, there is a washer and dryer for guest use. Espresso and cappuccino are served at breakfast. The inn is not suitable for children under 12. **144 Benefit St., Providence 02903; (401) 751-2002.**

Where to Eat

Dining out is serious business in Providence. Good restaurants abound and are well sup-

ported by loyal followers. Although there is some of the usual city turnover, Providence does not have the sort of fashion-based restaurant scene where good restaurants languish when a new hot spot becomes Place of the Month. Menus are posted, so you can browse. Many, especially the trendier restaurants, do not accept reservations (unless you "know somebody"). Go to the restaurant and have your name put on the list. You will be given an idea of how long the wait will be, then you can go for a walk or for a glass of wine while you wait. Most, if not all, Federal Hill establishments take reservations. Smoking is neither universally accepted nor forbidden; each restaurant has its own policy ranging from smoke anywhere to smoke nowhere.

BREAKFAST

See entries below for Pastiche, La Campagnola, Rue De L'Espoir, 729 Hope, Downcity Diner, Davio's, Cafe Zog, Sweet Retreat and Cafe Verde, all of which serve breakfast.

CAFES

L'Elizabeth—$

A genteel place for afternoon tea, espresso and pastries, with a tea shop atmosphere, fine china and parlor armchairs. It's open all evening, a nice place to stop for a late dessert or brandy after the theater. L'Elizabeth also has a bar. Daily from 3 P.M.–12:45 A.M. On the East Side, at **285 South Main St.; (401) 864-1974.**

Pastiche—$

Desserts are the specialty—a torte of dark Belgian chocolate and almond butter, toffee walnut torte and seasonal fruit tarts, with espresso, of course. Look here, too, for a Continental breakfast that's really Continental, with Euro-style pastries and rich, jump-start-your-day coffees. The surroundings are as elegant as the coffees are good. Open Tues.–Fri. from 8:30 A.M.–11 P.M., Sat. from 8:30 A.M.–

11:30 P.M., Sun. from 8:30 A.M.–9 P.M. On Federal Hill at **92 Spruce St.; (401) 861-5190.**

Sweet Retreat—$

Ice cream, espresso and cappuccino are the best sellers at this relaxed coffeehouse, highly reminiscent of the sixties. An early opening makes it a good choice for breakfast before other places have the coffee going. Good biscotti. On Wednesday nights you can listen to gospel music and on Fridays an acoustic jam session. Open Mon.–Fri. from 6 A.M.–11 P.M., Sat. from 6 A.M.–8 P.M., Sun. from 6 A.M.–2 P.M. **426 Atwells Ave.; (401) 621-7213.**

Cafe Zog—$

Regulars begin their day here with coffee (plain or otherwise) and a bagel, scone or croissant while they read the morning paper or one of the books Zog keeps on hand. Sandwiches—chicken salad with apples and walnuts, hummus and tabouli, provolone and veggies, BLT and turkey—are served until closing. Apple pie, carrot cake, fruit tarts, brownies and huge cookies go with the espresso, mocha, latte or cappuccino. On Tues. and Wed. evenings from 8–11 you'll hear live jazz, and Saturday is ragtime night. Open Mon.–Fri. from 7 A.M.–11 P.M., Sat. from 8 A.M.–11 P.M., Sun. 8 A.M.–10 P.M. **239 Wickenden St.; (401) 421-2213.**

Meeting Street Cafe—$

From the breakfast omelets to the late evening desserts, Meeting Street Cafe serves generous portions in a casual College Hill environment. The cookies are enormous. Open daily from 8 A.M.–11 P.M. **220 Meeting St.; (401) 273-1066.**

RESTAURANTS: DOWNCITY

Agora—$$$$ to $$$$$

The grand rotunda entrance to The Westin hotel and the long scenic ride up the escalator are simply a prelude to the hotel's premier restaurant. The dining room is elegant in dark paneled wood and features original artwork, crisp linens and the aura that precedes a fine meal. Fortunately, the food lives up to the setting (which is, happily, becoming more frequent in hotel restaurants, which for many years had lost their luster as bastions of fine dining). Seafood is the focus—only three or four menu items are not seafood. But don't look here for a plain baked haddock or grilled salmon. The seafood is only a point of departure, a showcase for cuisines as diverse as Thai (mahimahi served in a fumet redolent of lemon grass and hinting of coriander), Santa Fe (fried clams coated in blue cornmeal) and French (tuna is paired with foie gras). Fruit is frequently used as an ingredient, occasionally overshadowing the fine flavors of the seafood but usually a refreshing surprise to the palate. The wine list is long and well chosen, the service excellent. Open Tues.–Sat. from 5:30–10:30 P.M. **One West Exchange St.; (401) 598-8011.**

Davio's—$$$

Northern Italian dishes with up-to-date flourishes predominate on Davio's menu, from which you can choose a straightforward pan-seared salmon entree or pasta and apple-wood smoked chicken dressed in a classy toasted walnut cream. The cafe serves lighter dishes, including pizza. Serving the needs of hotel guests, Davio's serves breakfast daily from 6:30 A.M., remaining open until 11 P.M. But don't mistake this popular spot for just another hotel dining room; the Biltmore's restaurant is as stylish as the hotel itself. It's also smoke-free and fully handicapped-accessible. The valet parking, available after 5 P.M. is free Sun.–Thur. **11 Dorrance St., at Kennedy Plaza; (401) 274-4810.**

New Japan—$ to $$

Small and casual in a traditional Japanese country decor, New Japan is best known for Sunday sushi. The price is right and the selection superior, with salmon, tuna, squid, octopus, eel and more. On other days hearty dumplings, soba and the usual tankatsu, teriyaki, sukiyaki and delicately light tempura are served. Open Tues.–Fri. from 11:30 A.M.–2:30 P.M. and 5:30–9:30 P.M., Sat. from 5:30–10 P.M., Sun from 5–9:30 P.M. **145 Washington St.; (401) 351-0300.**

Downcity Food and Cocktails—$$ to $$$

No longer the retro diner that Providence loved, Downcity has changed its image and its menu, but you can still depend on it for interesting combinations of new and traditional ingredients at reasonable prices. They still draw largely from American regional cuisines, with crabcakes and meatloaf, but with a definite melting pot twist: The meatloaf is served on Portuguese broa, and the next item on the menu might be a Thai specialty. It's right across the street from the new main gate of the downtown Johnson and Wales University campus. Open Mon.–Fri. from 11:30 A.M.–2 P.M., and 5:30–9 P.M., Sat. from 9 A.M.–2 P.M. and 5:30–10 P.M., Sun. from 9 A.M.–2 P.M. **151 Weybosset St.; (401) 331-9217.**

Pot Au Feu, The Salon— $$$$

One address, one name, two restaurants with entirely different style and menus: Pot au Feu has a split personality. Upstairs is the elegant Salon, with crisp proper service, linens, crystal and a sense that you are in a fine Paris dining room. The menu, which offers a la carte or prix fixe dining, matches the elegance of the room with sophisticated classic French cuisine—but always with the chef's modern signature. The menu, with a choice of 15 entrees, changes nightly, but a few of the favorites show up fairly regularly. You might find Pot au Feu au homard, a subtly seasoned melange of lobster, scallops, clams, mussels and shrimp in a broth of cider and cream, or a fresh grouper fillet baked in a crust of crushed pistachios. Rack of lamb, so difficult to find in American restaurants, is spread with pommery mustard and honey before being

roasted to a perfect turn. Open Tues.–Fri. from noon–1:30 P.M. and 6–9 P.M., Sat. from 6–9:30 P.M. Reservations are suggested, and proper dress is required (it's not stuffy here, but it's the kind of dining experience you'll want to dress up for.) **44 Custom House St.; (401) 273-8953.**

Pot Au Feu, The Bistro—$$ to $$$

Same address as the above Salon, but take the stairs down instead of up, and enter another side of Paris. It's pure bistro, the air filled with the fragrance of grilled meat and a wafting of herbs, the specials on a big chalkboard, the tables close and the steady electric hum of lively conversation. The menu features the less-formal dishes the French provinces are famed for: bouillabaisse, cassoulet (pheasant sausage lends a distinctive flavor to the white beans and duck), chicken livers sautéed with Madeira and our own favorite plate of assorted sausages and Alsatian sauerkraut. They also offer crepes, omelets and croques; the salad of chèvre and roasted red peppers is a fine light lunch. Open Mon.–Thur. from 11:30 A.M.–2 P.M. and 5:30–9 P.M., Fri.–Sat. from 11:30 A.M.–2 P.M. and 5:30–11 P.M., Sun. from 11:30 A.M.–2 P.M. and 4–9 P.M. No reservations are accepted for the bistro. **44 Custom House St.; (401) 273-8953.**

Federal Reserve—$ to $$$$

The menu looks like a giant thousand-dollar bank note, and the dishes inside are firmly based on native ingredients and New England styles but created with a panache that clearly separates them from old-fashioned Yankee cooking. You can order jonnycakes, a clambake or a full Thanksgiving dinner done with a whole Cornish game hen. Duck is roasted with a maple glaze and venison sausage is made with berries. They've made their point that New England cooking can rank with the best. The setting is spectacular, in one of Providence's most opulent banking halls. You can dine in the vault or enjoy a predinner drink at the marble bar, neatly converted from the long row of teller windows. Stained glass, marble and painted detail surround you here but can't outshine the food. Service is unhurried and highly intelligent. Prices really do cover the range indicated: Five items on the menu are over $20, and six are $10 or under; the remaining 16 entrees lie between. A nice addition for such an upscale restaurant is a children's menu with all entrees priced at $3. At **60 Dorrance St.; (401) 621-5700.**

RESTAURANTS: EAST SIDE—NORTH

3 Steeple Street—$$

Informal and usually busy, 3 Steeple is liked for its good-sized, well-prepared, but not overly complicated dishes. The setting is just over the river on the East Side in an old mercantile building; the interior walls are of stacked stone. The same menu is available all day, with hearty sandwiches and salads, pizzas and burgers available in the evening along with a specials menu offering full-sized dinner entrees and pasta dishes. Prices and servings are planned to suit all appetites: The German sausage plate comes at three price levels according to the amount of sausage ordered, or you can make a meal of a hearty salad and the quiche of the day or choose two appetizers instead of an entree. Sandwiches are interesting—tarragon-scented chicken salad served with broccoli and cheddar cheese on a toasted roll, or BLT with boursin. Open Mon.–Sat. from noon–1 A.M., Sunday from 5:30 P.M.–1 A.M. **3 Steeple St. (enter around the corner on Canal St.); (401) 272-3620.**

New Rivers—$$ to $$$

Very small, intimate and tastefully decorated with lamps and flowers on the table, this is the kind of place that you want to dress up for even if you don't have to. The menu is sophisticated, with entrees as varied as asparagus lasagna with portabella mushrooms wrapped in paper-thin pasta and sauced with a lamb ragout, or

pork tenderloin in a fresh peach and bourbon sauce. The southwestern chicken is coated with a jalapeño blue corn crust and is served with rattlesnake beans. The chef has a fine sense of presentation, and each plate is different and attractive. Desserts include extraordinary fruit and berry tarts prepared to order, as well as original sorbets. The menu changes seasonally, with daily specials. The wine list is extensive and truly international, with bottled wines starting at $14 for a good Chilean merlot. Open for dinner only, Tues.–Sat., from 5:30–10:30 P.M. Near the Steeple Street Bridge on the East Side. **7 Steeple St., Providence 02903; (401) 751-0350.**

Cafe Nuovo—$$$ to $$$$

This darling of the Downcity crowd isn't quite as nuovo as it was when it opened, but its attraction hasn't worn off. The view of the rivers and park are incorporated into the decor through oversized windows—or you can dine even closer in the summer, when tables are added outside. The food is California-inspired with heavy use of fruit, a little cute in its combinations and presentation, but always interesting. The salmon is smoked in-house, and the pasta-vegetable pairings are excellent. Handicapped-accessible. Open Mon.–Thur. from 11:30 A.M.–3 P.M. and 5–10:30 P.M., Fri. from 11:30 A.M.–3 P.M. and 5–11 P.M., Sat. from 5–11 P.M. In the Citizens Bank Building at **1 Citizens Plaza; (401) 421-2525.**

RESTAURANTS: EAST SIDE—SOUTH

Pakarang—$ to $$

A curving, cavelike ochre tunnel is not the entry you would expect to find at a Thai restaurant. The next surprise is that it leads to a large room decorated in black and white with a bar that once served as the sushi bar of a Japanese restaurant. Despite all of these incongruities, the menu is pure Thai and includes over 40 entrees as exotic as wild boar basil with green peppercorns, or shrimp,

31

scallop and squid in a hot pepper–garlic sauce. Menus for lunch and dinner are the same with a price differential of $3 to $8, reflecting the larger servings. Open Tues.–Fri. from 11:30 A.M.–3 P.M. and 5–10 P.M., Sat.–Sun. from 4–10 P.M. **303 S. Main St., Providence 02903; (401) 453-3660.**

Rue De L'Espoir—$$ to $$$

Not many city restaurants above the diner category serve three meals a day, but here you can begin your day with French toast made with Portuguese sweet bread or honey oat bread, or a Gorgonzola omelet. The dinner menu is varied—roasted salmon with pistachio, orange and basil crust, or a three-grain risotto with roasted vegetables—and changes five times a year. After 11:30 P.M. the bistro menu in the lounge offers lighter dishes such as chicken broccoli crepe with boursin, or grilled chicken, avocado and smoked Gouda sandwich on focaccia with ginger slaw. Dining hours are Tues.–Thur. from 7:30 A.M.–9 P.M., Fri. from 7:30 A.M.–10:30 P.M., Sat. from 8:30 A.M.–10:30 P.M., Sun. from 8:30 A.M.–9 P.M. **99 Hope St.; (401) 751-8890.**

Turchetta's Ristorante—$ to $$

The well-mannered rooms of a nice East Side house have been maintained to give Turchetta's a warm, intimate atmosphere. But the menu is Italian, and its fine aromas scent the air with a heady perfume of herbs. The menu doesn't *sound* all that different, but when the dishes arrive you know this is no ordinary Italian food. Chicken Franco is sautéed with artichoke hearts, roasted peppers, Vidalia onions and black olives, and daily specials might include eggplant stuffed with capicola and sharp cheese. Fillings for the ravioli first course change weekly. This is among the few better restaurants in the city that serve dinner on Sunday evenings. Open Wed.–Sat. from 5:30–10 P.M., Sun.–Mon. from 5–9 P.M. **312 Wickendon St.; (401) 861-1800.**

Al Forno—$$$ to $$$$

Undeniably the city's best-known restaurant in national food circles, Al Forno has been written about so exhaustively that there's not much more to say. Except that the reputation was not built on good press but on exceptionally good food. At the heart of Al Forno's food philosophy, as well as their menu, is the wood grill, where chefs cook everything, from pizza to pork chops. But neither will be like anything you've tasted elsewhere. The menu, a single-spaced typewritten plain Jane, doesn't describe the dishes in intimate detail, but it does tell you the basic ingredients; what the chefs do with them is the magic. Roasted veal tenderloins may be served with polenta and black beans, or a brook trout may be filled with herbs before grilling. Do share a pizza as a starter—the crust is so delicate you'll wonder how it holds together. The atmosphere is classy but crowded; a no-reservation policy assures a long (or longer) wait, which can be quite pleasant in good weather, when the patio bar is open. Order your made-to-order dessert with the main course to allow time to prepare it. The grand cookie finale is served on a pedestaled tray; sample a few and they'll wrap the rest for later. Open Tues.–Sat. from 5–10 P.M. **577 S. Main St.; (401) 273-9760** (but don't expect to make a reservation).

Raphael Bar/Risto—$$ to $$$

Why would we send you to a restaurant with no address? Because by the time you read this it will very likely be settled into its new quarters and will certainly be one of the best restaurants in the city. Recently moved to East Greenwich from his old digs on Water St., Raphael is looking for a place to reopen in Providence. You can count on a menu that will change constantly, but will include the likes of garlic-marinated lamb steak in barolo wine sauce, presented on a bed of creamy risotto abounding in porcini mushrooms. Ask around, check *Rhode Island Monthly* or call Raphael's in East Greenwich to find the new location; **(401) 884-4424.**

Rachel's Pastanova—$ to $$

With no pretense of being anything but a pasta shop with a restaurant attached, Rachel's draws pasta inspirations from all over the world—Jamaica, Thailand, India and other places not usually associated with this food. At the pasta bar you can create your own designer dishes, choosing your favorite pasta and combining it with toppings that include pesto, sun-dried tomatoes, olives, scallops and vegetables. The day's choices are written on a blackboard, along with the daily specials, which may include seafood lasagna (scallops, shrimp, clams and mushrooms) or a vegetable lasagna of zucchini, carrots, artichokes, broccoli and mushrooms. They serve half portions for children. The dining-in area is pleasant, with subdued lighting and a minimum of disturbance from the busy carry-out pasta business. Bring your own wine, easily found on nearby Wickenden St. Open Tues.–Wed. from 10:30 A.M.–9 P.M., Thur.–Sat. from 10:30 A.M.–10 P.M. **71 Hope St.; (401) 351-8585.**

Hemenway's—$$$

You don't just get oysters here, you can choose whether you're in the mood for Malpeque, Chincoteague, Caraquet or Wellfleet. The menu changes daily, so you know the pedigree of other seafood as well: The tuna is caught in waters off Point Judith, the catfish is from Mississippi, the scrod is fresh from the Grand Banks via New Bedford. Cooking style varies to suit the fish, from blackened Cajun to baked to grilled. The seafood chowder won the 1992 Chowder Cookoff for Rhode Island. You can get nonseafood dishes here, but who would want to? Free valet parking. Open Mon.–Thur. from 11:30 A.M.–3 P.M. and 5–10 P.M., Fri.–Sat. from 11:30 A.M.–3 P.M. and 4:30–11 P.M., Sun. from noon–9 P.M. On the river at **Old Stone Square, South Main St.; (401) 351-8570.**

Grille 262—$$$

Thirty on-tap microbrews and the city's only walk-in humidor are not the only claims 262 has to fame—the food is good, too. The cigar lounge is downstairs; the dining room is upstairs, serving innovative dishes such as duck-morel sausage in a kumquat basil glaze, Osso Bucco, a mixed sausage grill or wood-grilled chicken breast with portabella mushrooms. Start with clam-corn fritters or an herb-infused savory custard and finish with an open-faced ice cream sandwich—a brownie wedge with ice cream, caramel and hot fudge sauces. Open Mon.-Sat. from 5–10:30 P.M. It's on the Riverwalk at **262 South Water St.; (401) 751-3700.**

Tokyo Restaurant—$ to $$

Those who know Japanese food well will appreciate the wide range of the menu at this plain but good small restaurant. Along with the expected sushi, tempura, tankatsu and teriyaki you'll find an impressive list of sashimi, including sea urchin, plus warming bowls of chewy udon and pots of nabe. Share a Tokyo nabe with friends around a table in the tatami room. The restaurant serves beer and domestic wines. Open daily from noon–11 P.M. **231 Wickenden St.; (401) 331-5330.**

Kismet—$ to $$

A pleasant but not fancy Indian restaurant with tandoor oven and a chef who specializes in Kadahi dishes but also offers several of the hotter Madras curries. The Mughlai-style chicken is combined with cashews and almonds in a creamy sauce. The menu offers good descriptions of ingredients characterizing each dish. BYOB. Open Mon.–Sat. from 11:30 A.M.–2:30 P.M. and 5–10 P.M., Sun. from noon–9:30 P.M. **230 Wickenden St.; (401) 453-2288.**

Taste of India—$ to $$

Smaller than its counterpart, Kismet, across the street, this Indian restaurant offers spicy hot vindaloo dishes and a number of masalas. The house specialty is the thali, a sampling of three curries, with accompaniments. BYOB.

33

Open Mon.–Sat. from 11:30 A.M.–2:30 P.M. and 5–10 P.M., Sun. from noon–9:30 P.M. **221 Wickenden St.; (401) 421-4355.**

RESTAURANTS: EAST SIDE (RIVERSIDE NORTHERN HOPE STREET)

The Gatehouse—$$$ to $$$$

A riverside setting and attention to detail have earned this restaurant kudos from local foodies who come here for swordfish with mango salsa, angel-hair pasta paella or blackened tuna with sweet-and-sour roasted peppers. Especially popular is Sunday brunch, where a confit of duck hash is served with poached eggs and wild mushrooms. The brunch includes a buffet of breads and fruit along with the cooked-to-order entree. The chef will do several of the egg dishes with whites only for those who watch cholesterol. Live jazz is featured Tues.–Sat. from 8–12 P.M. on the river deck. Open Tues.–Fri. from 11:30 A.M.–2 P.M., dinner from 5–10 P.M., Sun. brunch from 10 A.M.–3 P.M. **4 Richmond Square** at the Providence end of the E. Providence bridge (the Red Bridge to locals); **(401) 521-9229.**

729 Hope—$

Breakfast and lunch are the big things here, but the cafe serves light entrees into the evening and offers a pasta bar on Friday and Saturday nights. Begin with the breads: fresh-baked focaccia, French baguettes or a seven-grain that's a meal in itself. Have them build a sandwich on it, with smoked turkey and grilled vegetables with Havarti, or fresh mozzarella, spinach, artichokes, roasted pepper and sun-dried tomato. They take special care to offer a full menu of low- or no-fat foods. The atmosphere is coffeehouse, with changing art exhibits. Friday and Saturday evenings feature performers, and Thursday nights members of the Rhode Island Songwriters Association meet and perform. Open Mon.–

Thur. from 8 A.M.–9 P.M., Fri.–Sat. from 8 A.M.–10 P.M., Sun. from 8 A.M.–5 P.M. **729 Hope St.; (401) 273-7290.**

Pizzico—$$$

An upbeat European air pervades this more-than-trattoria that has become a popular restaurant despite its location far from the center of Providence nightlife. Expect to find hearty provincial dishes such as grilled vegetables and sausages or pastas tossed with cheeses and tasty vegetables, as well as more gentrified offerings, such as the grilled veal with shitake mushrooms, pignoli nuts, roasted peppers and mustard seeds. The wine list is nothing short of astonishing, with literally hundreds to choose from. Open Mon.–Fri. from 11:30 A.M.–2 P.M. and 5–10 P.M., Saturday from 5–10 P.M. **762 Hope St.; (401) 421-4114.**

Garden Grille—$

It's tough to find a vegetarian restaurant in this land where food is the reason for living. The very thought of missing any nuance of flavor makes most capital-area residents shudder. We've found one good place (or, more accurately, our daughter did, just down the street from her house), barely over the line into Pawtucket, but so close we include it here. The chili is excellent, as are the grilled vegetables, although the plate is a little sparse for the price. Enchiladas and salads are good, too, but don't expect service with a smile. Everyone but the cook is positively dour. Open Mon.–Sat. from 9 A.M.–9 P.M. **727 East Ave., Pawtucket** (at the corner of Lafayette St., Providence); **(401) 726-2826.**

RESTAURANTS: FEDERAL HILL

Casarino's—$$

A chef-owned bastion of Italian food, Casarino's serves all the old favorites, with enough variety to keep it interesting: braciola, veal Marsala, shrimp in a creamy pink pesto sauce, clams over linguini, chicken with shrimp and artichoke hearts, tortellini carbonara. Open Mon.–Thur. from 3–9:30 P.M., Fri.–Sat. from noon–10 P.M., Sun. brunch from 11:30 A.M.–2:30 P.M., dinner from 2:30–8:30 P.M. **177 Atwells Ave.; (401) 751-3333.**

L'Epicurio—$$ to $$$$

Ask Providence foodies where they go for a special occasion, and L'Epicurio will very likely be mentioned. Its classic elegance is relaxed by the open kitchen; the service is impeccable. The chef concentrates on only six main entrees each evening and gives them his all. They might include veal medallions in Marsala cream with grilled oyster mushrooms, or a wood-grilled fillet of salmon over papardelle with radicchio and fennel. The pasta course, an entree for anyone who didn't grow up on Federal Hill, might be penne with pan-seared shrimp and scallops, fresh tomatoes and basil, or capellini with pan-roasted clams in white wine. If you are there with a group of four, order the appetizer platter for a sampling of incomparable starters, or begin with a garlic mascarpone polenta with sun-dried tomatoes and wild mushroom ragu. A number of good wine selections are available by the glass. No smoking; reservations are strongly suggested. Open Tues.–Sat. from 5:30–9 P.M. **238 Atwells Ave.; (401) 454-8430.**

La Campagnola Cafe—$

As we write, this upbeat corner cafe is open only for breakfast and lunch, but we expect that to change as the word spreads. The handwritten menu changes daily, according, the chef told us, to what he wakes up feeling like cooking that day. Be prepared to like this cheerful impresario who chats with customers as he designs their morning omelet, or offers a free serving of rabe to a diner who's never tried it. His restaurant is a fine addition to Federal Hill, with gingham curtains, bentwood chairs and murals of Vesuvius. Italophiles can start their day right, with crusty panini and *hot*

espresso. Lunch dishes may include sliced veal with prosciutto, mozzarella, mushrooms and white wine, or succulent ravioli with cream, ham and mushrooms. No reservations; bring your own wine. Open Mon.–Sat. from 7 A.M.–3:30 P.M. **188 Atwells Ave.; (401) 861-3463.**

Christopher's on the Hill— $$ to $$$

There's nothing quite like a fine chef with free reign in his own kitchen, and Christopher Turner can now indulge his two culinary loves—Italian and classical French. He blends ingredients and methods of each with a deft hand, adding a few New World surprises, such as cranberries to the cognac sauce for an oven-roasted duck. Look for wood-grilled swordfish with shallot-chive butter, or chicken breast and oyster mushrooms in a red wine and peppercorn sauce. Our choice of appetizer is calamari tubes filled with olives, shrimp, feta cheese and roasted red peppers, then grilled. Who needs an entree? At lunch, try a brick-oven pizza with garlic sausage, caramelized onions, roasted red peppers and goat cheese. The restaurant has its own parking lot, a real plus on Federal Hill. Open Tues.–Fri. from 11:30 A.M.–2 P.M. and 5:30–9 P.M., Sat. from 5:30–9:30 P.M. **245 Atwells Ave.; (401) 274-4232.**

Cafe Verde—$

This neighborhood cafe/restaurant/bar serves down-home Italian favorites (penne with meatballs) and a few purely Rhode Island dishes— like snail salad (this is such a hallowed local dish that we know an anthropology student who wrote his thesis on it). Hearty dishes and small bites make Cafe Verde a good choice when hunger strikes at any time of day. Pizza combinations are delectable: Try tomato, basil and artichoke hearts. Stand at the beautiful marble bar to drink your espresso, and find out what's happening on Federal Hill. Open Mon.–Sat. from 10 A.M.–10 P.M., year-round. **441 Atwells Ave.; no phone.**

35

Angelo's—$ to $$

The ambiance at Angelo's is as far from the white linen and subdued lighting of other Federal Hill restaurants as Sicily is from Venice, but so are the prices. Well-prepared hearty dishes—baked eggplant, chicken marinara, grilled sausages with potatoes and peppers, veal with peppers and a variety of pastas—are listed on a sign. Fruity wine comes by the juice glass. When they are crowded you may have to share a long Formica table (although recent renovation has created more small tables). For a quarter you can watch the model railroad engine make its way along the track overhead, just under the tin ceiling. No espresso or rosemary-infused oil in this family-owned place, just good solid family-style food and good solid value. Open Mon–Thurs from 11 A.M.–8:30 P.M., Sun from noon–6:30 P.M. They have a parking area out back, a real blessing on the Hill. **141 Atwells Ave.; (401) 621-8171.**

RESTAURANTS: KNIGHTSVILLE (CRANSTON)

L'Osteria—$$

A dozen tables and an espresso bar fill a storefront overlooking the center of the unique Italian community of Knightsville. The menu is as bright and upbeat as the room and its music: marinated grilled chicken breast with mascarpone, pasta stuffed with fresh lobster in a vodka sauce, sole with sun-dried tomatoes and artichoke hearts, grilled veal tenderloins with shitake mushrooms over risotto. But we go for the specials, which may be grilled shrimp in a sauce of plum tomatoes, tangerine, red onion and lime, or an almost architectural serving of swordfish in a delicate savory sauce. Begin with the antipasto for two—although you might not have room for dinner afterward. Wines are all Italian and start at an amazing $12 a bottle. The lunch menu offers hot or cold panini (eggplant and fresh mozzarella, sopressata and provolone), grilled pizza and an even dozen pasta dishes, most in the

$4–$8 range. Open Tues.–Thur. from 11:30 A.M.–3:30 P.M. and 4:30–9:30 P.M., Fri.–Sat. from 11:30 A.M.–3 P.M. and 4:30–10:30 P.M. **1703 Cranston St.; (401) 943-3140.**

Cafe Itri—$$

Itri is the Italian town that most of Knightsville came from, and stunning photographs of it decorate the walls of this cafe. On Mondays, when many restaurants close, you're likely to meet some of Providence's best-known chefs here, sampling the butternut ravioli in Gorgonzola walnut sauce, or the antipasto of stewed tripe in a zesty Neapolitan sauce. Calamari is sauced with roasted garlic and anchovies, veal scaloppine is flavored with wild mushrooms, Tuscan sausage is grilled over oak. The menu changes seasonally. Surroundings are informal and a sidewalk cafe is enclosed in the winter. Lunch menu includes panini (try the grilled chicken with baked mozzarella, roasted peppers and pesto), pastas, polenta, gnocchi and a memorable Farmer's Special of prosciutto, red onions and cannellini beans over focaccia, nearly all in the $4 to $8 range. Open Mon.–Thur. 11:30 A.M.–3 P.M. and 4:30–9 P.M., Fri.–Sat. 11:30 A.M.–3 P.M. and 4:30–10 P.M. **1686 Cranston St.; (401) 942-1970.**

Marchetti's—$ to $$

If you can't find something to tempt you on Marchetti's long menu (14 veal dishes, 10 chicken, 15 seafood, plus specials) you just don't like Italian food. Then there are the specials: calamari with roasted peppers, hot cherry peppers and black olives, or the cioppino of littlenecks, crab, shrimp, scallops and clams, both priced under $10. In fact, most of the menu is priced under $10. Look for all the classic southern Italian favorites served in an attractive dining room. Families will feel welcome here, but it's classy enough for a night-out dinner, too. It's just off Cranston Ave. in the center of Knightsville, at **1463 Park Ave; (401) 943-7649.**

Services

Visitor Information

The main information center is at **The Greater Providence Convention and Visitor's Bureau, 30 Exchange Terrace,** in the Old Union Station at the end nearest The Westin Hotel; **(800) 233-1636** or **(401) 274-1636.**

A free flyer from **Historical Attractions of Rhode Island** includes $1 discount on admission for each of several properties, including the John Brown House and the Aldrich House (also Slater Mill and Blithewold). You can pick these up at any tourist information rack.

International visitors can find assistance at **International House of Rhode Island, 8 Stimson Ave.; (401) 421-7181.**

In an emergency, dial 911 from anywhere in Rhode Island.

Public restrooms in the **City Hall** and **U.S. District Court** on **Kennedy Plaza** and **Garrahy Judicial Complex** at **1 Dorrance Plaza** are open only Mon.–Fri from 8:30 A.M.–4:30 P.M. Restrooms are also available at the **Providence Public Library** at **225 Washington St.; The Arcade** at **65 Weybosset** (also access from Westminster); **the Amtrak Train Station** at **100 Gaspee St.** and the **Traveler's Aid Society, 177 Union St.** (the only one open 24 hours a day).

Money

Most banks are in the downtown area; ATMs in the downtown area are located on Empire St. near Perishable Theater, on Washington at Aborn St. and on Westminster St. at Weybosset. On the East Side they are on Main St. opposite the Old Stone Bank, at the Brown University Bookstore, across the street at the corner of Thayer and Angel and at Waterman and Brook Sts. There is also one near Cafe Nuovo, at the end of the Steeple St. Bridge, and another on Frances St. behind the State House and Veterans Auditorium. On Federal Hill there is one opposite DePasquale Plaza on Atwells Ave.

Parking

Many lots and garages offer early-bird specials on all-day parking for those who arrive before 9 A.M. The largest downtown parking garage is on Eddy St., behind the Biltmore Hotel. A large garage is at the train station close to Waterplace Park. Behind Old Union Station on Memorial Blvd. are two lots. There are three on Pine St., which runs parallel to Weybosset, behind the Johnson and Wales campus, and several more on Weybosset and Westminster Sts. On Frances St., close to the Veterans Memorial Auditorium, is a 600-car facility.

Taxis

Taxi fares in Providence are $1.25 for getting into the cab, plus $2 a mile. Taxi ranks are in Kennedy Plaza and in front of all the downtown hotels. Major cab companies are **Arrow (946-5333), Red & White (941-9888)** and **Economy (944-6700).**

Access for the Disabled

Because so much of Providence is in historic properties, access can be a problem. All the theaters and performance venues have full access. Restaurants in newer buildings do, as well. These include Cafe Nuovo, both Trinity and Union Station brewpubs, Davio's in the Biltmore Hotel and Agora in The Westin. Other accessible restaurants are Christopher's on the Hill, L'Epicurio, Rachel's, Turchetta's, Hemenway's and Al Forno. The Art Museum at Rhode Island School of Design has wheelchair access, as does the Winton Bell Gallery at Brown and the Visitor Center at the Roger Williams Memorial. All the major hotels have fully accessible rooms available.

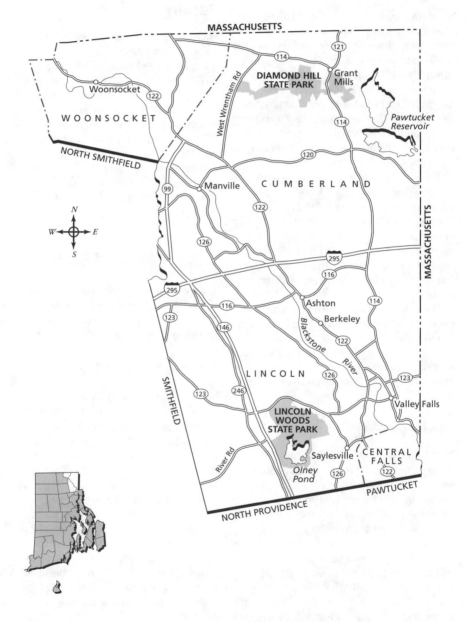

The Blackstone Valley

The Blackstone Valley

No one but a historian (or a Rhode Islander) would list the Blackstone among the world's great rivers. A mere 46 miles long, it rises in Worcester, Massachusetts, where it joins Mill Brook and the Middle River from an underground pipe. From Worcester it flows southeast, falling at the rate of ten feet per mile through towns and cities, swamps and countryside until it joins the tidal Seekonk River at the Slater Mill dam in Pawtucket, 438 feet lower than where it began.

From the first, this drop in elevation was an important asset to settlers, providing them with a reliable source of power for mills that produced lumber and ground their grains for market. During the height of its use, 400 of the 438-foot drop were used to produce power. The production system born here was the first shot fired in America's Industrial Revolution. The Blackstone, short as it is, changed the face of the United States.

This chapter contains the cities of Pawtucket, Central Falls, Woonsocket and the towns of Lincoln, Cumberland and North Smithfield. Inside these towns and cities along the river are many smaller settlements whose names read like a roll call of the beginnings of the American manufacturing industry. Also included in this section is the Massachusetts part of the river, since it is so inextricably linked to the story of Rhode Island.

Today the lands along the banks of the river are in transition. The massive textile industries that once crowded its shores, borrowed its waters for power and used its stream as a waste disposal system have largely disappeared. Environmental concern has led to substantial cleaning of the river and to its increased recreational use. On the downside of the equation, however, the closing of the mills has cre-

ated unemployment and left a blight in some areas, most notably cities like Woonsocket whose mills lie empty and derelict.

Cumberland, on the east side of the river, is mostly rural, except for Valley Falls (the seat of the town government) at its southern edge. Valley Falls, and Central Falls to its south, share the industrial history of Pawtucket. North of Valley Falls, Rte. 122 follows the river through Berkley, Ashton and Cumberland Hill, all small mill towns that shared in the growth, and decline, of the fabric industry. Ashton, backed up to the steep riverbanks, has a classic series of brick duplex mill houses.

For the traveler, the Blackstone Valley offers wildlife preserves, canoe adventures, a winery, ethnic festivals and historic sites of the American Industrial Revolution. Some of the finest examples of American industrial architecture lie along the banks of the river and its tributaries, from the first rudimentary wooden structure to the brick and concrete giants of the late nineteenth and twentieth centuries. One of the country's earliest canals runs alongside it. Innovative museums educate and entertain, and all around is the color and gusto that is the legacy of Rhode Island's ethnic communities. Woonsocket is even one of the Northeast's principal venues for the live performance of jazz and blues. Long an industrial center, the valley is relatively unknown to tourists.

History

In 1623, a twenty-eight-year-old English clergyman named William Blackstone came to New England with a small group of settlers. All but Blackstone soon returned to England. Unhappy with the Church of England, he settled alone on the side of Beacon Hill: He was the first resident of Boston. When, in 1630, Governor Winthrop brought his company of settlers to establish a colony, Blackstone invited them to join him. After only four years, however, he found that he could not live with these doctrinaire and contentious Puritan neighbors, and he sold off most of his farm and made his way south into the wilderness to the southwest.

He settled on a plateau above a ford on a river the Indians called Pawtucket, where he lived until his death in 1675 at the age of 80. This first European settler of what would become Rhode Island was at the beginning of a long line of independent-minded philosopher-clerics who pioneered the state. When Roger Williams founded his Providence Plantation in 1636, they became close friends, and Blackstone preached to Williams's congregation even though they differed on theological matters. Blackstone had a library astonishing for his time—184 books—and came to be known as the "Sage of the Wilderness." The Pawtucket River was known by the settlers as Blackstone's River.

Although first to arrive, Blackstone is not known as a founder of the state, because he brought no other colonists with him. Roger Williams gets that honor for the founding of Providence, the first permanent settlement in Rhode Island. Both shared beliefs in the right of freedom of conscience and the separation of civil government from religion, common threads among all of the early colonial settlers here.

After Providence was settled, the population grew rapidly, with shipbuilding, fishing and coastal shipping and farming expanding as settlement moved inland. Dams were built on the Blackstone to power grist and lumber mills and to run forges that used bog iron found in area wetlands. By 1761 the Blackstone was so heavily dammed that the General Assembly authorized the digging of a passage around the Pawtucket falls so fish could pass. In 1671 the falls at Pawtucket were harnessed for a smithing forge, and the manufacture of iron tools and farm implements began. During the Revolution these ironworks were converted to firearms production.

In the late 1780s, Moses Brown of Providence decided to manufacture cotton thread. Samuel Slater, a young immigrant who had extensive knowledge of the power-operated spinning machines used in British industry, heard of Brown's venture and, combining Brown's capital and Slater's knowledge, they established mills at the falls of the Blackstone in north Providence, now Pawtucket. When President Madison wore a suit made of Pawtucket cloth to his inauguration in 1809, the future of U.S. fabric manufacture was secured.

While the first mill made cotton thread, power weaving machines were soon invented, and woven cloth became a major industry. No sooner was machinery invented than forges and machine shops were built to make it. Small wooden mills rose along the banks of the river, spreading north, and around them grew villages and mill towns. The dangers of fire led to the building of stone mills, such as those at Slatersville, and then to the massive brick-building complexes of the 1890s and early twentieth century.

The industry that was spreading up the Blackstone soon needed a better way to transport finished products to the port of Providence. Farther upriver the growing town of Worcester faced the same transportation problems. Goods from Worcester and the rest of western Massachusetts had to travel by wagon over the slow muddy roads to the port of Boston. In 1823 the General Assembly issued a charter to build a canal along the Blackstone, and five years later the canal's first horse-drawn barges began operating. While flooding often made passage difficult or impossible, the new canal expanded the market for the valley's goods from Pawtucket all the way to Worcester. The new canal so damaged Boston's shipping interests that some tried to get the Massachusetts legislature to withdraw the charter for the Massachusetts part of the canal.

Unfortunately for the backers of the canal, its life was short. In 1844 the Providence and Worcester Railroad was built, and it was not only a lot faster than the canal's 4 mph, but more reliable. Unable to compete, the canal owners stopped collecting fees, and within a few years the locks and tow paths fell into disrepair.

Transportation, first via the canal, then by railroad and an improved highway network, allowed the mills and machine shops of the valley to expand even more. Until the 1920s, huge new manufacturing plants continued to spring up, employing increasing numbers of workers. At first the mills were staffed by men, then women and eventually even young children joined them in the factories. They came from the towns and then from the farms to provide additional cash income for struggling farm families. Children were particularly useful to the mill owners because their small hands could easily reach in among the spinning bobbins to repair broken threads. There was opportunity for some in the mills: In 1815 an eight-year-old boy began work at the Pawtucket Thread Company, and by the time he was nineteen, he was the plant superintendent.

By the mid–nineteenth century, French immigrants from impoverished areas of Quebec

Where to Find the Aulde Sod in Rhode Island

The potato famine and the rise of manufacturing industry along the Blackstone combined to bring a wave of Irish immigration to Rhode Island in the 1840s and 1850s. At the famine's end, one-tenth of the state's residents were immigrant Irish. They're still here, and their culture is alive and well. Newport's Fifth Ward, centering on lower Thames St., was once almost entirely Irish, and the influence is still strong. On St. Patrick's Day it engulfs the city, as residents celebrate in a giant parade and festival. In September Newport hosts an Irish music festival.

Elsewhere in the state, Irish music and camaraderie is best found in lively pubs: **Aiden's Pub** on **St. John St. in Bristol, (401) 254-1940; Tinker's Nest** on **Metacom Ave. in Warren, (401) 245-8875; Pancho O'Malley's** on **Rte. 108 in Narragansett, (401) 782-2299.** All offer Irish music at least one night a week, usually Sunday, although Tinker's Nest has performers on other nights as well.

had begun taking jobs on the low end of the pay scale. Irish, British and Scottish workers followed to fill the jobs created by the explosive growth of valley industry. These cultures brought new color and vitality to northeastern Rhode Island.

By the late 1930s the first signs of an increasing industrial crisis in the valley appeared. A few years earlier one of the largest mill complexes in Central Falls had closed and was torn down so that its owner could avoid real estate taxes. While World War II brought a respite, the rapid shift of fabric manufacture to the South and then overseas was going at full speed. Smaller industry occupied parts of some older buildings, but many were obsolete, too inefficient for modern manufacturing. Foreign competition had kept wages low, leaving the remaining jobs open for a new wave of immigrant workers from Portugal and Colombia.

Tourism is a new phenomenon here. Active groups on both ends of the river are working not only to help build tourist facilities but to preserve the area's heritage. In Massachusetts, the Blackstone River and Canal Heritage Park is a series of parks along the river canal system developed to preserve and interpret the remaining sections of the canal. In Rhode Island, this work is in the hands of the Blackstone Valley Tourism Council and the Blackstone River Valley National Heritage Corridor Commission. They work together to help communities identify and preserve buildings and canal segments and to develop walking and bicycling paths, canoeing routes and park land.

Getting There

The Blackstone Valley begins (physically and historically) in the middle of downtown Pawtucket, at Slater's Mill, just off of I-95. The primary routes from Pawtucket through Woonsocket are Rte. 122 east of the river and Rte. 126 on the west. These highways do not follow the river, but the map of northern Rhode Island produced by the **Northern Rhode Island Chamber of Commerce (640 Washington Hwy., Lincoln 02865-4243),** is in larger scale than the state highway map and shows roads that are closer to the river. In Massachusetts the primary route through the valley is Rte. 146.

Festivals and Events

The Blackstone Valley Tourism Council and the Blackstone River Valley National Heritage Commission keep a full schedule of events going on in the valley, many of which center around Slater's Mill in Pawtucket. New events are always being added, and you can get a current schedule from the **Blackstone Valley Tourism Council, P.O. Box 7663, Cumberland 02864-7663; (401) 334-7773,** fax **(401) 334-0566.**

The Blackstone River Festival
May

The towns of Central Falls and Valley Falls celebrate the Blackstone River and its modern use as a focus of recreation with riverboat rides, canoeing and kayaking on the river with an emphasis on the history and ecological value of the river. There are paddling lessons by qualified instructors all day long, music performances at the Blackstone River Theater and guided walking tours. The festival is also a chance to sample a unique Rhode Island dish: Chicken Family Style. Originally designed as a way to make a little chicken feed a big family, Chicken Family Style is now an area tradition; **(401) 334-7773.**

Jubile Franco-Americain
August

On the last weekend of August the Union Saint-Jean Baptiste Americain and other groups combine to celebrate the French Canadian contribution to Rhode Island. The Jubile is held in Woonsocket and it features French music, fiddling, arts and crafts and Franco-American culture. The celebrations are held in the high school and churches of various denominations throughout the city; **(800) 225-USJB** or **(401) 334-7773.**

International Steamboat Muster
August

Pawtucket celebrates its connection to steamboats in a festival that recalls David Wilkinson and Elijah Ormsbee, who built a steamboat from a longboat fitted out with a steam engine and a boiler made from an old still. They traveled to Providence and back with it in 1796. Daniel French heard about the boat and went to Pawtucket to examine it and talk with Ormsbee and Wilkinson and later told his friend Robert Fulton what he had found. During the nineteenth century and into the twentieth, small steamboats were popular pleasure boats in the bay, and they provided rapid transportation between the shoreside towns.

The Muster is a week-long series of events at the waterfront and at Slater Mill Historic Site: a showing of historic and operating steam launches, a steam engine exhibit, displays of steamboat-related art and artifacts, seafood and entertainment. Canoe, kayak and paddleboats can be rented, or bring your own for a trip on the Blackstone River. An old Wurlitzer band organ wagon provides turn of the century music. This is also a good chance to see the Pawtucket and Providence waterfronts aboard the *Explorer*. There are shore dinners, a Captain's Barbecue Dinner with live jazz, the Portuguese Social Club's annual feast and the Greek festival. Contact the **Blackstone Valley Tourism Council, P.O. Box 7663, Cumberland 02864-7663; (401) 334-7773, fax (401) 334-0566.**

Rhode Island Labor and Ethnic Heritage Festival
September

Labor Day is the appropriate date for this celebration of working men and women and the diversity of cultural and ethnic backgrounds from which they came. Sponsored by arts, history, tourism and labor groups, this is a day of fun on the banks of the Blackstone. Live performances for children, folksinging and storytelling, music from Ireland, Cambodia, Africa and American bluegrass provide entertainment. Exhibits by labor and community service organizations join art and craft exhibits of Native American culture, woodworking, jewelry making, folk arts and needlecrafts from around the world. The riverboat *Explorer* provides river excursions into the area's history. **Blackstone Valley Tourism Council, P.O. Box 7663, Cumberland, 02864; (401) 334-7773, fax (401) 334-0566.**

Pawtucket Jaycees Oktoberfest
September

The Jaycees Oktoberfest is a family event highlighting the Blackstone Valley and featuring children's entertainment, ethnic foods, crafts,

music and a parade. Although it's an Oktoberfest, it's held the last weekend of September; **(401) 726-1190.**

Fall Foliage Train Excursion
September

Sponsored by the Blackstone Valley Tourism Council, the train leaves Cumberland at 10 in the morning, traveling along the Providence and Worcester rail line to Worcester and returning at 2 P.M. It's a chance to travel a historic route, on which there are no longer passenger trains, for only $32 per person, and you can bring your own lunch or buy it in the dining car. Seating is very limited, so reserve early; **(401) 334-7773.**

Self-Drive Foliage Tour the Valley
September

As far west as Chepachet, Pascoag and Harrisville and all along the valley, fall brings a splendid display of colors. This route will take you through some of the prettiest of northern Rhode Island countryside, and it's all within an easy day's travel. For a map, contact **Blackstone Valley Tourism Council, P.O. Box 7663, Cumberland 02864; (401) 334-7773.**

Pawtucket Winter Festival
December

The Pawtucket Recreation Department holds a winter festival at Slater Memorial Park that centers around the carousel and the Daggett House. There are food and craft booths, hayrides through the woods of the park and roving minstrels and choral groups singing Christmas songs. The decorated carousel is operating and there are tours of the adjacent Daggett House; **(401) 728-0500, ext. 252.**

Outdoor Activities

Parks and Recreation Areas

Lincoln Woods State Park

This is a major state park surrounding **Olney Pond** and offering canoeing, kayaking and hik-

43

The Rhode Island Guide

ing trails. Its proximity to Providence makes it very popular and busy, but in the spring or the fall it's a different place, quiet and almost deserted. Much of the walking here is along paved roads, but there are also sections through the woods.

As you enter, ask for a trail map. The park is a fine place for family outings, with swimming, boating, walking and fishing. Primary access to the park is from Rte. 146 (Eddie Dowling Hwy.) on the west side, but there is also access from Rte. 123 (Breakneck Hill Rd.) on the east that will bring you around to the main lots. Open 6 A.M.–11 P.M. daily; there is no camping. **Rhode Island Department of Environmental Management, Division of Parks and Recreation, Lincoln Woods, Lincoln 02865; (401) 723-7892.**

Blackstone River State Park

This is one of the best places to see the remains of the Blackstone Canal and get a sense of how it operated. Park under the bridge at the park entrance and follow the path northward along the banks of the canal. In this deserted wood, one can almost see the white 70-foot passenger packet *Lady Carrington* being drawn by draft horses through here on her maiden voyage on July 1, 1828. The vessel was the first, and possibly the only, passenger ship on the canal and may have been the first passenger ship on any U.S. canal. A carpeted interior cabin that ran the length of the ship and seating on the upper deck allowed passengers to view the countryside; it was far more comfortable than a bouncing coach.

This section of the canal is so well preserved that it is hard to remember that it isn't still operating. It's a good place for a canoe since it is relatively long and clear of debris. The old tow path parallels it between the canal and the river. The hillside has collapsed at the north end, blocking immediate canoe access to the river, so canoeists will have to make a short portage. The entire canal route through this section is cool and wooded, and the sunlight comes through in dappled patterns. Across the river the two settlements of Ashton and Berkley are visible but seem to be in an-

other world, as does the giant bridge that crosses above.

The park runs both north and south from the bridge. Heading south along the tow path you immediately pass the Kelly House, former home of a mill owner. The walk to the end, at the falls in Lonsdale, is about two and a half miles one way. The park is open during daylight hours. It is a little hard to find. The main road along the west side of the river is Rte. 126, Old River Rd., between Lonsdale and the intersection with Rte. 116 (Washington Hwy.). From Rte. 116 take Rte. 126 south 0.7-mile to Cullen Hill Rd., turning left at the canal onto the Lower River Rd. Follow it to the parking lot at the end. **Blackstone River Valley Heritage Corridor, One Depot Square, Woonsocket 02895; (401) 762-0250.**

River Island Park, Woonsocket

Small and still in development, this green space is the first step in the long process of reclaiming the river and reusing some of the vast surrounding area once covered by mills. It's a metaphor for the city itself. There is a short walk along the river and a place for canoe access. Unfortunately, the concrete put-in is a little too high, so launching from it can be difficult; we'd use another spot along the bank. The park has benches and new trees; behind it is a collection of old stone mill buildings and a tall, abandoned and decrepit smokestack to remind you of these once powerful old mills. Follow Armory St. from the east side of Market Square to the bridge over the Blackstone River. Just before the bridge there is a small parking lot.

Slater Memorial Park, Pawtucket

It's easy to confuse the historic site downtown with this park, which is in the southeast corner of the city along the Ten Mile River, close to the Massachusetts border. Its 193 acres are filled with woods, picnic areas, walking trails, a carousel, art and history—and ducks to feed on a pond. There is plenty of free parking. From Slater Mill, cross the river on Main St., then follow Walcott St. to North Bent St. and then go right onto Armistice Blvd. (Rte. 15). Just before the river, the entrance will be on the right. There is also an entrance off the southern end of Narragansett Ave. (Rte. 1A). Inside the park are the Looff Carousel, the historic Daggett House and the Rhode Island Watercolor Society (see pages **43** and **47**).

Cumberland—The Monastery

In 1900 a group of Cistercian monks from the community of Petit Clairvaux in Nova Scotia established the monastery of Our Lady of the Valley. They built their new home in Gothic style, with a large chapel and an octagonal bell tower topped with a tall spire. The monks, who observed a vow of silence, cleared and farmed the land, praying and living on a vegetarian diet. The monastic life came to an end when fire destroyed the stone church and seriously damaged other parts of the building. The town acquired the property, and the remaining buildings are now used as town offices and a library. The massive stone steps march grandly up to the stump of the octagonal bell tower, Cumberland's own Gothic ruin.

Long before the monks arrived, many colonists had fled here following the 1676 King Philip's War battle at Central Falls. In Camp Swamp, only a short distance from the chapel, nine were killed at a place now called Nine Men's Misery. There's a trail to the spot where they fell and were buried.

In addition to the hiking, walking and bicycling trails, there is a large playground with swings and slides. Many details from the monastery remain, including several shrines along the entry drive. They have been joined by more modern memorials, and a howitzer and mortar that serve as the town war memorial. There is also a nicely restored garden, the **Ruth Carpenter Memorial Garden,** set within hedges next to the ruins of the church. It's on the **west side of Rte. 114 (High St.) north of Valley Falls.** It's open during daylight hours.

Diamond Hill State Park

North of Rte. 120 on Diamond Hill Rd. (Rte. 114), Diamond Hill State Park offers a chance to relax, picnic and sit by the pond. The name

of the hill derives from a vein of quartz visible in a 150-foot cliff. There is hiking on trails through the park and fishing in Silvy's Brook. There is no bicycling or skiing here, however (and they threaten a fine and jail time if you try). **Cumberland Recreation Department; (401) 728-2400.**

Canoeing

Blackstone River offers good canoeing from Pawtucket north along almost its entire length. Friends of the Blackstone has programs on the river and canoes for rent. Canoes are also available in Providence from **Baer's River Workshop, 222 S. Water St.; (401) 453-1633.** There is a put-in at the **Slater Mill Historic Site,** just off the parking area next to the mill.

Among the groups formed to protect and enhance the river and educate the public about it is Friends of the Blackstone. These volunteers intend to restore the river and its environs to its natural state. They offer guided canoe explorations on the river. Although you can use your own canoe, they have a fleet of 22 available. Their headquarters is in Cumberland, but they operate throughout the Blackstone River Valley. They give canoe lessons and special training sessions for kids at their pool. Although they were only formed in 1991, they have removed over *6,500,000* pounds of trash from the river's banks and adjacent lands (that's right, 6,500,000). They are also leading in the restoration of fishing in the river, stocking over 4,000 trout in the spring and fall and promoting the creation of fish ladders.

Both recreational and educational, their tours go into the **Valley Falls Marsh,** the second largest marsh in the state and an integral part of the Atlantic flyway, and along other river stretches, including the Uxbridge area of Massachusetts. You not only can enjoy the quiet of the river but may see otter, deer, raccoons and turtles as well. Friends' programs include lectures on the river, its Indian and European history and the wildlife that lives in and along it. Contact the group in advance for a schedule of trips, training sessions and lectures. You'll also find Friends at festivals along the river throughout the summer. The fee for most programs is about $15. Contact the **Friends of the Blackstone c/o John Marsland, 6 Valley Stream Dr., Cumberland 02864, or call Vin Mancini, (401) 272-8485.**

Anyone serious about canoeing on the Blackstone should get the *Canoe Guide for the Blackstone River*, published by the Blackstone River Valley National Heritage Corridor. The booklet divides the river into fifteen segments from Millbury St. in Worcester, Massachusetts, to the Slater Mill in Pawtucket, virtually the entire length of the river. It describes water classes, shows put-ins, take-outs and portages; describes the scenery and gives USGS map references. At the back there is also a brief description of five accessible tributaries of the Blackstone. **Corridor Commission, One Depot Square, Woonsocket 02895; (401) 762-0250** or **Blackstone River Watershed Association, Northbridge Town Hall, Memorial Square, Whitinsville, MA 01588; (508) 234-8797.**

Baer's River Workshop also gives canoeing and kayaking lessons and can tell you about the river. Rentals include paddles and flotation devices. Baer's people are usually at most of the river festivals with their rentals, particularly at the Steamboat Festival in Pawtucket. Baer's is located at **222 S. Water St., Providence; (401) 453-1633.**

Hiking and Walking

Lime Rock Preserve

The Nature Conservancy has a 157-acre preserve near Lime Rock with marble outcrops in a setting around an attractive pond. For a moderate two-mile walk, follow the bed of the old Providence/Woonsocket trolley line from the parking lot. The path will go through cuts in the ledge and after about a half mile will pass a pond on the right. Take the trail to the right just beyond the end of the pond. This curves around the end of the pond, eventually coming to a dam at its head, where the water

drains off into a small ravine. On the other side of the dam, the trail leaves the pond, then intersects another trail. Go right to the next intersection and again go right. The trail can be hard to follow at this point, but you can always go down the hill to the left and to the old rail track, which you can follow to the left back to the parking lot. This area is a good one for wildflower viewing and for amateur geologists, since the alkaline limestone and marble deposits make it a habitat for plants not usually found in this area. Some of the flowers you may see are northern green orchids, yellow lady's slippers, fringed gentians and bloodroot. There are also ferns, both on the rocks and on the forest floor. This land has the state's largest outcropping of marble, a fact consistent with the limestone that gives the town its name. Lime Rock Preserve is best reached from Rte. 246 or Rte. 123. From Rte. 246 take Wilbur Rd. west (the road is south of Lincoln Mall) about a half mile. From Rte. 123 take Wilbur Rd. east about a half mile. The entrance is on the north side of the road.

The Llama Farma

The unique way to see northern Rhode Island is in the company of a llama, who will be happy to carry your picnic lunch for you (you'll have to walk). The Llama Farma offers family hikes of three to four miles or adult hikes of up to nine miles. The trails will take you through fields, forests, farms and along marshlands in the rolling hillsides, and you'll have the pleasant company of these strange-looking South Americans. There are also sunset hikes with wine and cheese served along the way. The hikes cost $25 per person with two people per llama, and the sunset hike is $5 more per person. **Llama Farma, P.O. Box 7274, Cumberland 02864; (401) 334-1873.**

The Monastery

The grounds of a former monastery north of Valley Falls has trails through its 500 acres. From the parking lot a trail leads off to the right at the playground, going through woods to Nine Men's Misery. The area is covered with trails that lead through old fields and orchards the monks once tended (see page **45**).

Horseback Riding

Riders can take advantage of the trails at Lincoln Woods with horses from **Sunset Stables,** just off **Rte. 146 near the park.** They have trail riding for all levels from beginner to experienced. Open weekdays from 1:30 P.M. and on Sat. and Sun. from 9:30 A.M. The stables close an hour before sunset every day. The fee is about $12 per ride; **(401) 722-3033.**

Seeing and Doing

Pawtucket

Daggett House

This is the oldest house in Pawtucket, built in 1685 to replace one burned in the Indian raids of King Philip's War. It was built by Colonel John Daggett, a Revolutionary War veteran, and eight generations of the family lived here until 1894, when the house and farm were bought by the then new city of Pawtucket for a park. In 1902 the Daughters of the American Revolution leased and restored it. An impressive collection of historic memorabilia is on display here, and an ancient millstone serves as the front doorstep. Open June–Sept. from 2–5 P.M. Sat. and Sun.; **(401) 722-2631** or **333-1268.**

Rhode Island Watercolor Society

Opposite the Daggett House and the Looff Carousel, overlooking the pond, is the Rhode Island Watercolor Society's gallery and learning center, with changing exhibits of Rhode Island and New England watercolorists. The building itself is a work of art. Built in 1917 as the J. C. Potter Casino, its deep red brick and green-trim architecture is a fine example of public structures of the time. Inside are two floors of paintings, which are for sale. The noted watercolor artist Tom Nicholas serves on the society's panel of jurors. **Slater Memorial Park, Armistice Blvd., Pawtucket 02861; (401) 726-1876.**

Slater Mill Historic Site

In the center of downtown Pawtucket, Slater Mill sits adjacent to the falls where the Blackstone River meets the tidal Seekonk River. This is also known as the Pawtucket River, the last stretch of the river to bear its original name. The three buildings are the sole remainders of a complex of manufacturing buildings that once stood here and were the first of the mills to begin manufacturing fabric in the United States.

At the south an impressive stone double-arched bridge, built in 1858, crosses the Blackstone just south of the falls. From it you can look down on the dam that created power for the mills, and you can trace its canals and ditches. On the west side a marker notes the location of the Ezekiel Carpenter Clothier Shop, where Samuel Slater designed and built the first of the machines that broke England's monopoly on spinning thread for cloth and began the American Industrial Revolution. The building was destroyed in a flood in 1807 (along with the original 1730 bridge). To the north sits the second mill built by Slater for Moses Brown.

The pale yellow building is built in two sections with a tall bell tower that is slightly off center. Tours of the building are guided by docents well versed in its history and in the operation of the carding, spinning and weaving machinery on display. You might even see a demonstration by one of the mill workers who ran these machines at the end of their heyday.

The slightly newer stone Wilkinson Mill, built in 1810 by Oziel Wilkinson, father-in-law of Samuel Slater, is next door. It housed his cotton yarn factory and a machine shop that made spinning machinery for the burgeoning cotton-spinning industry. Operated by a massive waterwheel, which you can see outside the building, the mill is an impressive testament to the creative genius that sparked the Industrial Revolution and put the basic comforts of life within the reach of everyone. The world's first screw-cutting lathe was invented in this building by David Wilkinson and it was here that he built and improved upon the area's first successful commercial power loom.

47

The adjacent Sylvanus Brown House, built in 1758 as the home of the blacksmiths Nathaniel and Ebenezer Jenks, was later used by carpenter Sylvanus Brown, the pattern maker who helped Slater perfect his machinery. It was saved from demolition for the construction of I-95 in 1962 and moved here to house exhibits of early spinning and weaving techniques.

Surrounding these three historic buildings is a grassy landscaped park overlooking the river and falls that is often used as the location for festivals and exhibits. Open June–Labor Day, Tues.–Sat. from 10 A.M.–5 P.M., Sun. from 1–5 P.M.; Mar.–May 31 and Labor Day through the third Sun. in Dec., Sat. and Sun. from 1–5 P.M.; weekdays for group tours by reservation. Adults $5, seniors $4, children six to 12 $3. **Roosevelt Ave. at the intersection with Main St., Pawtucket; (401) 725-8638.**

The Slater Park Looff Carousel

In 1875 an immigrant furniture carver named Charles I. D. Looff carved 27 goats, camels, zebras, storks and horses and put them onto a platform at Coney Island New York. The platform was turned by horses, and it became a popular new ride. He soon built another at Bullock Point, and another at Roger Williams Park in Providence. By 1895 Looff had his own 50-acre Crescent Park at Riverside in East Providence and was manufacturing his rides in buildings at the park. In 1910 the Providence ride was moved to Pawtucket, where it ran until 1967. The city announced intentions to tear it down, but popular outcry led to a committee that refurbished and reopened it in 1979. The carousel has 44 horses, three dogs, one camel, one giraffe and two benches, and all of the figures, except for one horse, are original. Watch for the figure on the panels in the center, the one with the derby hat is Charles I. D. Looff himself. The ice cream truck inside was operated by Americo Pierini in Pawtucket about 1906. The carousel is open in June and from Labor Day–Columbus Day, Sat. from 11 A.M.–5 P.M. and Sun. noon–5 P.M.; July–Labor Day it's open Mon.–Sat. 11 A.M.–7 P.M. and noon–7 P.M. on Sun. Early in December

it is open for the Winter Festival (see page 43); **(401) 728–0500, ext. 257.**

Walking Tours of Pawtucket

All of the following tours start at Slater Mill, where there is ample parking. The first two are fairly short and don't involve long hills, and the third is more strenuous. Brochures for each of the walks are available from the **Preservation Society of Pawtucket, P.O. Box 735, Pawtucket 02862,** so we've just included the highlights here.

Churchill Industrial District

While the first mills rose along the river to take advantage of water power, the invention of powerful steam engines in the 1840s freed industry from the riverbanks. The next stage of industrial development took place in the fields, away from the dangers of flooding. In Pawtucket one of these areas was south of Main St. on land originally owned by the Jenks and Wilkinson families. The tour follows Main St. to Park Place, a triangular park that was a focal point for the mansions the industrialists built in the late 1800s. In its center is the statue *Liberty Arming the Patriot,* an 1897 bronze by Providence artist W. Granville Hastings. Several notable houses and churches surround the park. On Church St. are the Slater Cotton Company plant (1881) and the American File Company plant, built in 1863 and altered to art deco style in 1936. Across Pine St., on Main St. is the 1881 plant of the Rufus Bliss Manufacturing Company, and a short distance away is the James S. Brown Machine Shop, built in 1847, the first plant built in this section of town. The walk then turns up Commerce St. past the Steam Fire Engine Company #2 building (1861) and the Campbell Machine Shop (1888) before returning to Slater Mill.

Main Street: The Jenks Settlement

This tour goes up Main St. and Broad St., then down Summer St. to High St., returning to the mill. It traces the family of Joseph Jenks Jr., the first settler of Pawtucket, who established a forge at the falls. His descendants continued to live here and played prominent roles in the community. This and other early industry at the falls began the prosperity that led to the growth of the town after 1790. The sites of the Jenks homes show how the area changed from farms and residences to business and commerce. The brochure points out the home sites and describes the development of Main St. as a center of commerce. Pawtucket's decline from the 1930s to the 1960s caused several of the finest commercial buildings to fall into disrepair, and many of them were torn down during the urban renewal of the 1960s and 1970s, but a number remain, and brief histories of them accompany illustrations in the brochure.

Quality Hill

This walk is the most ambitious of the three, covering hills and a longer distance. As contrasted with the commercial and industrial focus of the other two, it shows the residential architecture of the rising community. Forty-two buildings and sites along the path are described in the Preservation Society's brochure. In 1800 Oliver Starkweather built a fine Federal-style house on the hill, the first to be built outside the area of the falls. Over the next century more mansions were built along Walcott St. and its side streets. These cover every major style of residential architecture from the end of the Revolution to the 1930s. Although the walk essentially follows Walcott St., it strays down side streets and over I–95 before returning to the Main Street bridge. You will pass both the 1840 Pitcher-Goff Mansion, at 58 Walcott St., and Oliver Starkweather's home, twice moved and now at 60 Summit St.

Woonsocket

To understand the apparent jumble of Woonsocket, you need to picture it as it once was: a thriving, lusty town filled with working mills. Three rivers meet here, and in 1810 their power was harnessed to spin cotton thread in a small plant near the Mill River,

Woonsocket is still recovering from the loss of its manufacturing industry, which left its downtown filled with empty mill buildings.

which was followed after the 1820s by the manufacture of cotton cloth. The Mill River now flows into a conduit in Social Park and ignominiously joins the Blackstone through a pipe. The Peters River, Woonsocket's third, also meets the Blackstone through a constricting conduit.

In 1840 Edward Harris started a small business making woolen goods, and by the time of the Civil War he had built the biggest and most modern woolens factory in the country. By the 1930s there were over 90 manufacturing plants in the city making more than 50 products. The canal and the railroad spurred even faster growth, drawing French Canadian workers from Quebec and Trois Rivieres.

Today much of that industry has either closed or moved away, and the enormous manufacturing plants lie abandoned. Woonsocket has been hit the hardest of any Rhode Island city by this decline, and with more lasting effect. Although a number of the most decrepit plants have been taken down, many remain along the banks of the river. The demolition has left the city with large random vacant spaces that leave the impression of an oversized Wild West ghost town. This is a city in a deep and fundamental transition of the most painful sort.

It is also a city, however, with a proud history and with a number of things to offer. The Blackstone River, the reason for its rise to prominence, wends and winds in every direction, providing the downtown area with plenty of riverfront. Here more than anywhere else in Rhode Island is a sense of the magnitude of the power that was harnessed for manufacturing. The mere remnants of the massive factories that once filled the city are staggering.

New hope is on the horizon as plans progress for a major National Park Service museum complex centering on the rise of American industry from the perspective of the mill workers. The museum will bring visitors into the everyday lives of these French–speaking immigrants, into their homes, schools, churches and meeting places. Along with the mills, it will focus on the French Canadian experience and influence throughout the Northeast. It is a major undertaking, and as plans progress, small exhibits are mounted in the old railway station in the center of town, where the tourist office is located.

Walking Tours of Woonsocket

Downtown Woonsocket

The Blackstone Valley Tourism Council has designed a walking tour of the downtown and Cato Hill area that gives a good overview of the city's development. For a copy of the tour, write to **Blackstone Valley Tourism Council, P.O. Box 7663, Cumberland, 02864; (401) 334–7773, fax (401) 334–0566.**

You can get a good taste of the town's heyday just by taking a walk up Main St., the commercial center of the city until the 1970s. Start from **Market Square**, which is in the process of redevelopment, and where there's a parking lot. On the west side of the square the tightly confined river thunders through its channel to **Woonsocket Falls**, feeding the Thundermist Hydroelectric Plant. On the south end of the square, there remain a number of former stone

mill buildings, several of which are planned for renovation and reuse. A good example of how these fine old stone buildings can be restored and used is at 1 Main St., where elderly housing has been created from the former Lippitt and Hanora plant. The earliest of these buildings was erected in the 1820s. The **Buel Building** at **75 Main St.** dates from a century later and is notable for the terra-cotta medallion of Samuel Fossa, founder of the town's early newspaper. At **93–119 Main St.** the **Commercial Building** (1902) has a water-powered elevator, and water from an old power trench still runs beneath it and the Buel Building. **Honan's Block**, up the street at **106–108,** is painted blue, and the upper floors still show the ornate cast-iron work popular when it was built in 1879.

In the nineteenth century, public philanthropy was an obligation of the wealthy, and wool manufacturer Edward Harris thus created Harris Hall. With an eye toward economy he put retail stores on the first floor to bring income for the support of the building. On the second floor was a free school to teach workers reading and writing, and on the third floor was a hall with seating for 1,100 people. The chandeliered room was the site of a speech by Abraham Lincoln on the campaign trail in 1860. The Harris Institute Library, the first free library in the state, was opened on the second floor in 1863. Since 1902 this building has been used as the city hall. The **Harris Block and City Hall** is at **169 Main St.** A full-sized wall mural on the wall of city hall records former buildings. The millstone in the park was found at the base of the falls.

Diagonally across the street, the old **Providence and Worcester Railroad Depot**, built in 1882, is a Victorian delight of decorative brickwork and terra-cotta tile with large overhangs supported by ornate wooden bracing. Be sure to note the copper locomotive on the weathervane. This is the office of the Blackstone Valley Heritage Corridor Commission (where you should stop to see displays about the river). Behind the depot, at **61 Railroad St.,** is the former **Harris warehouse.** It was built in 1855 and is made of stone rubble with a brick cornice and designed so that railcars of wool could be brought inside for unloading and loading. It is particularly unusual in that it curves to accommodate the track that ran into it. The old post office building at the corner of Main and Federal Sts. is built of granite and marble in the Beaux-Arts style popular in 1910.

Union Saint–Jean Baptiste D'Amerique

The Union was formed in 1900 of many French societies from throughout New England. It houses the **Mallet Library** (which opens to Worral St. on the east side of the building), a large collection of books, articles, photographs and other material relating to the French settlement of this area and in the United States. It is an important research center for anyone interested in Franco-American history. On the last weekend of August the Union presents the Jubile Franco-Americain, with concerts of French music, arts and crafts, special masses and a community brunch and fiddler's jam; **(800) 225–USJB** or **(401) 334–7773.**

Cato Hill Historic District

Named for Cato Willard, a free Black man whose wife inherited the property upon which the area was built, the restoration here is the work of the Woonsocket Redevelopment Agency. It bought and restored three houses, sold them, and used the profits to continue the restoration of the neighborhood. Private owners have also restored some of the houses on the hill. These are not grand buildings—this is not Benefit St. in Providence—but are representative of houses of the working classes of the city, many of them immigrant families. Some were single family houses, some group or family residences and others were transient housing, apartment houses and even ward rooms.

To explore this area, walk north on Main St. from the depot to Church St. The house at **28–30 Church St.** was built in 1840, an early duplex. At **61 Church St.** is the late Greek revival–Victorian **Second Vose House.** Its

neighbor, at **#62** is the largest of the Greek revivals in the district. The **Martha Kimball House, at #70 Church St.,** illustrates another aspect of life in the late Victorian period. This house was originally built in 1840 as a single-floor cottage. When the demands of the family grew, it was raised and another floor was built under it.

During the early and mid–nineteenth century, the community built ward houses, small single-room meeting places that were used for many neighborhood functions. They were used for voting, political meetings and social gatherings by newly arrived immigrants. These simple ward houses played a vital role in shifting political power from the old Yankee aristocracy to the new immigrants. The **Cato Hill Ward House** at **168 Church St.** is a good example. At the end of Church St. take Arnold St. south to Cato St. At **151 Cato St.** is a four-apartment house, an example of multifamily housing built during the influx of immigrants in the late 1800s. If you return to Arnold St. and walk down the hill to Railroad St. you will find a fascinating 1935 gas station made of hand-cut granite with a hexagonal tower, granite fireplace and oak paneling: It is at **339 Arnold St.**

Allen Street Historic District

Located opposite the entrance to River Island Park, this historic district contained some of the oldest mill properties in the city. Note the classic stone mill to the right, or east side, of the street. Allen St. is lined on both sides by two- and three-story brick and stone mills. This is a short easy walk, no more than a few hundred feet, but it emphasizes the difference in scale between the early mills along the river and the later ones as exemplified by the Hanora Lippitt complex inland.

The Countryside

Village of Arnold Mills

Although it's only five miles north of Valley Falls, Arnold Mills shows a different type of mill development typical to small communities

51

away from major rivers. In the early 1700s settlers built farms and started small mills along the banks of the local stream to grind their grain and saw lumber. They built forges to process the iron from nearby bogs and produce items needed elsewhere in the colony. Near the grist mill, sawmill and forge they built houses, forming a compact village. Today there is no large mill building, rather a place that gives a true picture of a small New England village at the very beginning of the American Industrial Revolution. Most of the parts of the revolution were here: the water-powered mills, the ironworks and forges all later converted to machine making, which changed the village from a farm-oriented economy to a wage economy. You can see everything from your car, but the distances are so short that this is a place you may want to explore on foot.

From Valley Falls take Rte. 114 north to Rte. 120 east. From I-295 take Rte. 114 north to Rte. 120, the Nate Whipple Hwy. The old town street is intersected by this newer road, so the old parts form two loops, one on either side of the new road. Less than a quarter mile from the Rte. 114 intersection, follow Sneech Pond Rd. left until it crosses a bridge. Park in the lot of the old granary, now an antique shop. This site and the area across the road from it were the center of industry in this small town. You can see the mill pond to the rear of the building. The stone foundations of the grist mill that operated here from 1745 until 1962 and that of the sawmill (operating from 1734 until 1862) are visible on the shore of the pond.

Across from the parking lot, the jumble of stone and brickwork was the Metcalf Machine Shop, built in 1825 to make textile machines for use in the Blackstone Valley and other area mills. Behind the granary you can trace the millrace that supplied the power and follow it to the machine shop ruins where the turbines, wheel pit and tailrace are visible. This small set of sites is about as close a view as you'll find of the opening stages of the Industrial Revolution in the United States.

Cross back over the river on the Victorian steel bridge with its period detail and go back up Sneech Pond Rd. This was the town's origi-

nal main street, with fine homes from the 1700s and 1800s. The **Amos Arnold house,** home of the builder of the area's first gristmill, still stands here. **Dr. Addison Knight's house** (1845) has a Greek revival porch with Doric columns. Follow Sneech Pond Rd. to Rte. 120 and, keeping to the right, take an immediate right on a curving road to the elegant white clapboard **Methodist Church** of 1827. To complete the picture of the heart of a typical mid–nineteenth century village, go to the other side of the highway and look for the school and Grange Hall. On the right is the schoolhouse (moved out of the way for the new road) and an original blacksmith shop. Farther down the road are the **Friends Meeting House** (1810) and the **Grange Hall** (1895), now a private home, the first in northern Rhode Island.

This is still an active community. If the big July Fourth parade in Bristol seems too much to handle, consider coming here to the **Arnold Mills Parade,** also on July 4. The village has been celebrating the Glorious Fourth since the Reverend Horatio Crawford started it all in 1927.

Diamond Hill Vineyards

On the east side of Rte. 114 just south of the Rte. 120 intersection, a pair of stone gates and a sign announce the vineyard. In 1976 the Berntson family planted their first vines and now have over five acres of pinot noir grapes and fifteen acres of fruit orchards on the rolling hillside. The farm is over 200 years old, and the old farmhouse (built about 1780) now houses a gift shop and tasting rooms. In addition to pinot noir, the Berntsons offer wines made from apples, peaches, plums and blueberries, all of which can be sampled and bought at the shop, along with jams, conserves and chutneys and gift basket selections. The vines are close to the shop, and you can see the next vintage growing there. Once a month, on a Sunday, they have special events that include guitars, bluegrass and other music, along with wine and cheese tastings. The shop is open Wed.–Mon. from noon–5 P.M., year-round. From April through November vineyard tours are given hourly on the half hour from 12:30 to 4:30 P.M. **3145 Diamond Hill Rd.,**

Cumberland 02864; (401) 333-2751 or (800) 752-2505.

The Great Road

In colonial times a road was built from Providence into the then unpopulated northern interior: It was known as the Great Road. Today Rte. 126 from Providence and Pawtucket covers part of the route, and Rte. 123 covers another portion of it. Traveling west, Great Road leaves Rte. 123 to the north just over a half mile from the Rte. 126 intersection. On this road you will pass Dexter Rock Rd. before Great Road branches off to the northeast, where it heads until it intersects with Rte. 116 just east of the Rtes. 116 and 146 cloverleafs. Throughout its length it may have other names, but it was a major thoroughfare of its day and many historic buildings line its routes. Most of the following sites are close together.

Historic District Tour

In early September the Society for the Preservation of New England Antiquities conducts a tour of many of the historic houses and buildings along the Great Road, including the Arnold House, Meeting House, Hannaway Blacksmith Shop and others described below. Call for dates; **(401) 364-8897.**

Eleazer Arnold House

This is one of the oldest "stone enders" in the state. These buildings are so called because one gable end, and sometimes two, is built of stone quarried or gathered around the new homestead. This one was built by Eleazer Arnold in about 1687, and it is a fine example of the primitive living conditions in the home of even a prosperous settler of the period. Clapboard covered the remaining three walls; the clapboards are narrow near the ground and become more widely spaced toward the top. The small windows with tiny leaded-glass diamond panes make the interior dark. Window shape and size is not a matter of style but a result of the period's scarcity of glass. The great room of the house has a massive summer beam, low ceilings and an enormous open-hearth fireplace.

Restoration did not include reconstructing the front gable that was typical of the time, but the original beams that carried it are still in the attic. The entrance to the drive is very narrow and difficult to spot. The house does not have regular hours and except for a tour or other scheduled events, you will need an appointment to visit it. **487 Great Rd. (Rte. 123)** just a few feet west of the intersection with 126, **Lincoln (Lonsdale) 02865; (617) 227-3956** (this is a Massachusetts number).

Just east of the intersection of Rtes. 123 and 126, on the north side of Rte. 123, you will find the very modern **St. Jude's Church**, which we mention because of its unique modern architecture, with a steeple that soars heavenward like a sheaf of wheat.

Quaker Meeting House

South on Rte. 126 (also called Cottage St., a part of Great Road), and on the west side of the street at #374 is a classic gray clapboard Quaker Meeting House that is still in use. The ell was built in 1703 and the main building in 1745, making this the oldest meeting house in New England in continuous use. Be sure to see it from the outside even if you can't arrange a tour. Behind is a small cemetery with very old headstones and in the yard is a stone used by women to mount horses. Meetings are held Sundays at 10:30 A.M., and all are welcome. The meeting house can also be seen by appointment. It's at **374 Great Rd., Lincoln 02865; (401) 723-2515.**

Hannaway Blacksmith Shop and Chase Farm

North along the Great Road at number 671, beyond the Eleazer Arnold House, is a restored and operating blacksmith shop. The building itself is a late-nineteenth-century single-story building where blacksmithing demonstrations are held. It is open the second Sunday of each month, Apr.–Nov. from 1–4 P.M. (in October it's open on the third Sunday rather than the second). Occasionally, special tours may be arranged. The shop is next to the Chase Farm at **671 Great Rd., Lincoln 02865.** For information call the Lincoln Town Offices; **(401) 333-1100, ext. 246.**

The adjacent Chase Farm is a reserve for walking and hiking. Parking for Chase Farm is at the Hannaway Blacksmith Shop, and the

53

trails leave from there. The old farmhouse on the property is not open to the public.

Hearthside and Butterfly Factory

Just before the Great Road joins with Break-neck Hill Rd., notice the elaborate stone house on the north side of the road. It was built in 1811 with the Louisiana lottery winnings of Stephen Smith, and he named it Hearthside. The house was reputedly a wedding gift for his bride-to-be. The story has it that the house cost so much to build that Stephen became nearly impoverished, so his ungrateful fiancée left him. The columned front is reminiscent of southern plantations, and it protects a door-way with an elliptical arch. The house is a unique example of early-nineteenth-century architecture. It is not open for visits, but it is the centerpiece of an active farm with a farm produce stand. Great Road turns to the north at the intersection just beyond this house. Across the street from the intersection is the so-called Butterfly Factory, named because of the pattern of colored stones on the front wall near the east end. Built about 1811, it has been a mill, distillery, printshop and riding school. It's not open for tours but is a good example of the multiple uses of former mills.

Lime Rock

The section of Lincoln known as Lime Rock takes its name from the large deposits of lime-stone, an important source of lime for the set-tlers, who used it to sweeten their acid soils and to make mortar to build their farms. Lime-stone is burned to convert it to lime and, once burned, it must be transported and used quickly. If it is not used, it attracts moisture and re-forms into lumps or, worse, bursts into flames if exposed to moisture. These deposits were particularly important to the mills, be-cause lime could quickly reach the sites of the hundreds of brick and stone buildings being constructed after 1790. Although demand for the lime has dropped and the lime-processing industry has nearly disappeared, one plant is still operating. At the intersection where Wilbur Rd. passes over Rte. 146 is the last lime-processing plant in town. Piles of lime-stone in the yard are mined locally, processed, then trucked off for use as a soil conditioner. Across the street in the bramble and jumble of undergrowth is a quarry and the remains of some of the old brick lime kilns. The center of Lime Rock is **at the intersection of Rte. 246** (also known here as Louisquisset Pike) **and Wilbur Rd.,** in north-central Lincoln.

Blackstone Valley Historical Society

A few feet south of the intersection of the Louisquisset Pike and Wilbur Rd. in Lime Rock is the **North Gate,** the original tollgate for the Louisquisset Pike, built in 1807 and now the headquarters of the society. A reproduction of a nineteenth-century keeping room is the set-ting for its collection of furniture, antiques and domestic implements. The exhibit room is open only during society meetings on the last Wednesday of the month from June–Sept. They start at 7:30 P.M., so go a little early. **Old Louisquisset Pike, Rte. 246, Lincoln 02865; (401) 725-2847.**

A short distance north of the same inter-section, on the west side of the road, what appears to be a pond is actually the remains of the **Harris Quarry,** first licensed as a quarry during colonial days and operated during the times of Roger Williams. The quarry was aban-doned near the turn of the century and it filled with water. Over 35 feet deep, at the far end the wall of the cut is clearly visible. Lovers of antique cars might stop to ponder here, for it is said that at one time this was a favorite spot for the disposal of "stolen" cars on which the owners wanted to collect insurance.

Valentine Whitman House

A stone-ender dating from 1694, this house was built by Valentine Whitman's father, who was a friend and associate of Roger Williams. The house shows the lifestyle of the second generation of settlers, who moved inland and became a bit more prosperous. The first town meeting of the town of Lincoln was held in the great room of this house. It has seen little al-teration since it was built. On the first floor are four rooms: a great room, a large kitchen and

54

two bedrooms. The great room and kitchen are on the end of the house that is composed of the massive stone chimney, and each has a huge fireplace. Unlike the Arnold House, the doorway of the Valentine house is not centered. The house is not open on schedule, but on the first weekend in December the Friends of the Valentine Whitman House decorate it for the holidays and open it to the public. You can also visit by appointment through the Lincoln town offices; **(401) 333-1100, ext. 289.** The house is **at the intersection of Whalen Rd. and Great Rd.** just north of Wilbur Rd.

Valley Falls and Central Falls

Cogswell Clock Tower

Jenks Park is adjacent to the Central Falls City Hall on Broad St. (Rte. 114) in the center of town. The highlight of the park is the Cogswell Tower, a tall free-standing square shaft climbing high into the sky. There is a clock face on each of its four sides. Built of rough-cut field stones, the tower is adorned with fine decorative wrought-iron balconies and decorative work.

The large rock outcropping here is known as Dexter Ledge, and it was used as an Indian lookout during King Philip's War. While it's not a tourist attraction, it is interesting to note that a short distance away to the northeast on the riverbank, one of the major battles of King Philip's War occurred in 1676. A stone monument commemorates the battle in Pierce Park on High St.

Valley Falls Park

This is a fine example of how a community with imagination can turn an eyesore into an asset. The park is on the east side of Broad St. (Rte. 114) at the north end of the bridge that separates Valley Falls from Central Falls. Between 1840 and 1900 a series of mill buildings was built on this site, growing until it covered several acres between Mill St. and the river. By 1934, however, the mill company was out of business, and in order to avoid having to pay the annual tax of $600 on the buildings, the roofs were removed, and over years the buildings eventually were torn down. The cellars, raceways and turbine emplacements were left to grow over with weeds and brush. This area has now been cleaned up, walkways have been installed and informative plaques have been put up to show the development of the site and explain the original uses of the areas visible from the walkways. Parts of the large hydraulic turbine system provide a look at the complicated water systems that once drove the factories above them. This is a rare opportunity to see a part of the process that is hidden beneath those huge complexes you see along the riverbanks. Be sure to go all the way to the far end of the park. This park is handicapped-accessible.

Be sure to stop to look at the imposing and stunning brick **Cumberland Town Hall**, **at the corner of Broad St. and Mill St.** It's an unrestrained expression of the civic pride of the town in its glory days at the end of the nineteenth century, and it hasn't been ruined with modern accretions. There is a public parking lot across Broad St. Next to the parking lot you may note a series of decorative arches crossing over the street. These are a part of the decorations for the several ethnic festivals that take place here every year.

Riverboat rides on the *Explorer* leave from a pier off Madeira Ave., just over the bridge from the park, where you leave Valley Falls and enter Central Falls. **Blackstone Valley Tourism Council; (401) 334-0837, fax (401) 334-0566.**

Airplane Rides

The Rhode Island North Central State Airport is along the west side of Rte. 123 as it loops into Smithfield and back into Lincoln. While the airport and North Central Airways are actually in Smithfield, they are included here because access is from Lincoln. North Central Airways has short scenic rides for only $15 per person. There is a sign announcing their rides on the right side of the airport road at the intersection of the road to the airport; **(401) 333-1212.**

Nightlife

Chan's

Don't ask us how a Chinese restaurant in the middle of a Franco-American mill town became one of the hottest jazz venues in the Northeast, but jazz, folk and blues lovers from all over New England know Chan's. At least one live performance is scheduled nearly every weekend, usually on Friday, but it's wise to call for the schedule. The cabaret-style shows may feature single performers such as Livingston Taylor, Rose Weaver or Tom Rush, or groups such as the New Black Eagles Jazz Band. Admission for the concerts varies but is usually $5 to $15. Seating is limited, so reserve for shows. See page 59 for information on the restaurant. 267 Main St., Woonsocket 02895; (401) 765-1900 or 762-1364.

Blackstone River Theatre in Central Falls

Musical entertainment, theater and children's programs are offered by this theater on the Central Falls side of the Blackstone River. Performances are on weekends in the winter and from Thur.–Sun. at other times of the year. The Blackstone River Theatre is the home venue for Pendragon, a well-known folk ensemble that celebrates the diversity of immigrant families that populated the valley. In addition to Pendragon, the theater showcases other New England folk, jazz, ethnic and acoustic blues groups. Other theater groups also occasionally offer productions here, and there are many special productions and plays for children. It's air-conditioned. On alternating Friday nights an intimate coffeehouse show with two performers runs from 7–11 P.M. in the lobby of the theater. The theater works closely with other groups in the valley and is an integral part of the Blackstone River Festival. Special programs are offered in conjunction with the Blackstone Valley Explorer during its operations from Central Falls. The theater is at 1420 Broad St. (Rte. 114) at the corner of Madeira Ave. in Central Falls 02863; (401) 729-1880.

The Community Players

In 1920 a group of area citizens got together and decided that Pawtucket needed a theater company, and 75 years later it is still presenting four productions each year. Most of these are on Friday, Saturday and Sunday evenings and may include musicals such as Man of La Mancha or Simply Sondheim or a comedy. Shows are presented at the Jenks Junior High School, Division St., usually in November, January, February, April, May and June. Contact The Community Players, c/o E. Babiec, 33 Calder St., Pawtucket 02861.

Shopping

OUTLET AND FACTORY STORES

The northeast part of Pawtucket has four outlet complexes that offer off-price shopping, and the area has become a major destination for bargain hunters.

The Yarn Outlet and Luggage Too

Knitters will find bargains and a large selection of knitting yarns and knitting accessories along with luggage, totes and sport bags. Discounts are in the 30% to 75% range. This outlet is handicapped-accessible. Open Mon.–Fri. 9 A.M.–4:30 P.M. and Sat. from 9 A.M.–1 P.M.; closed Saturday in the summer. From Slater Mill go north on Roosevelt St., then left onto Rte. 15 (Exchange St.). Follow Rte. 15 and take a right onto Conant. 225 Conant St., Pawtucket; (401) 722-5600.

Lorraine Mill Fabrics

One of the largest fabric stores in the country, with a wide variety of fabrics for sale, this is an off-price outlet, not a manufacturer's outlet. Open Mon–Sat. from 10 A.M.–9 P.M., Sun. noon–5 P.M. 593 Mineral Spring Ave. (Rte. 15), Pawtucket 02860; (401) 722-9500.

Slater Fabrics Store

On the east side of the river is a manufacturer's store with decorator fabrics for as little as $1.25 per yard, plus women and children's clothing. Cash only. From Slater Mill take Main St. over the bridge to School St. going south about one and a quarter miles to Beveridge Hill Ave. Slater Fabrics is open Mon.–Fri. from 10 A.M.–5 P.M. and Sat. 10 A.M.–2 P.M. **727 School St., Pawtucket 02860; (401) 725-1730.**

Textile Warehouse

Also on the river's east side, is a bed, bath and kitchen outlet with bed linens, pillows, comforters and towels (sold by the pound). Discounts range to 75%, cash only. Mon.–Fri. from 9:30 A.M.–4 P.M., Sat. from 9:30 A.M.–12:30 P.M., in Dec. until 4 P.M. Closed the week of July 4. From Slater Mill take Main St. over the bridge to School St., go right to Division St. about one mile. **Division St. at Industrial Hwy., Pawtucket; (401) 726-2080.**

Gorham/Lenox Factory Outlet Store

Just south of the airport access road in Lincoln, they carry a large selection of china, silver and stainless steel, with periodic clearance sales. **Rte. 123 (known locally as Jenkes Hill Rd.) Smithfield 02917; (800) 971-7709.**

Van Craft Knitting

This Central Falls factory outlet store carries hand-fashioned wool sweaters, caps and scarves. They also do custom-printed T-shirts. Open Sept.–May on Mon.–Sat. from 9 A.M.–5 P.M., but during the summer you will have to call for hours. From Rte. 114 take Sacred Heart Ave. to High St. north. From I-95 take Exit 30 to Roosevelt, then Charles St. and go north on High St. **678 High St., Central Falls 02863; (401) 725-5422.**

Woonsocket, with its still large number of manufacturing plants, has a number of factory outlets.

Tinsel Town and Patioland

An outlet for makers of holiday decorations and patio and summer furniture, Tinsel Town carries wreaths, garlands, summer porch and patio furniture. From Rte. 126, north of the Rte. 122 intersection, take a left onto East School St. Hazel St. is on the right. **93 Hazel St., Woonsocket 02895; (401) 766-5700.**

Turfer Jacket Factory

The outlet store sells a wide variety of jackets in nylon, corduroy and wool. Cash and checks only. A half mile north of Monument Square, where Main St. becomes North Main St. at **565 North Main St., Woonsocket; (401) 766-1088.**

Stitchers Inc.

This is the factory store of the firm that created Cape Cod–style curtains and is responsible for the recently renewed interest in Victorian swags. Bring your color scheme, samples and measurements. From Monument Square take Social St. to the junction with Rte. 126 (which becomes Social St. at this point) and follow it north to the intersection with Rte. 114. The parking is across the street from the outlet.

FARM STANDS

In Lincoln, Rte. 116 is known as the George Washington Hwy., and along it is **Spatola's Farm,** open daily from Aug.–Oct. from 2–5:30 P.M.; **(401) 333-0582.** Near the Rte. 146–Rte. 116 intersection, take Great Rd. south to **Butterfly Farm** at **679 Great Rd.,** near the intersection with Rte. 123. Open from 10 A.M.–5 P.M. daily; **(401) 723-5464.**

Spectator Sports

Baseball: Pawtucket Red Sox

With a season that runs from early April through August, the AAA Red Sox farm team offers a full schedule of lively baseball at **McCoy Stadium.** The schedule is arranged so that there are one or more games during most weeks of the season. The stadium opens two hours before game time and doesn't allow carry-in food or beverages. Handicap tickets are available in advance at the ticket office at the stadium. Admission prices are $4 for adults, $3 for children and seniors. Box seats are available by reservation for $1.50 more per ticket. The stadium is at the intersection of

57

Columbus Ave. and South Bend and Division Sts. Free parking is to the south of the stadium off Columbus Ave.

Tours

Riverboat Rides on
Blackstone Valley Explorer

The *Explorer* is a good example of the strong community spirit alive in the valley. It is a joint project of the Tourism Council, the Heritage Corridor Commission, local businesses and individuals. Built in the early 1990s, this all-weather 49-passenger boat offers the only riverboat cruise in the state, with 45-minute narrated tours throughout the valley and upper bay. The schedule changes from year to year but includes tours of Slater Mill Pond and Pawtucket Harbor as well as other tours in Cumberland, Lincoln, Central Falls, Woonsocket and Uxbridge, Northbridge and the Blackstone Gorge in Massachusetts. The *Explorer* operates from each location for periods of a few days to two weeks. It also offers special events, including a Haunted River Tour in October. Rates are $7 adults, $6 seniors and ages 12–18, $5 children. A brochure of dates and locations is available at tourist kiosks or the **Blackstone Valley Tourism Council, P.O. Box 7663, Cumberland, 02864; (401) 334-7773, fax (401) 334-0566.**

Where to Stay

Whipple-Cullen
Homestead—$$$

The Whipple-Cullen Homestead is a 1736 family farm that has become a B&B with five comfortable guest rooms. Some of the rooms have fireplaces and all share the use of the keeping room, which doubles as the dining room for Continental breakfast. Attractions in this part of the state are no more than 15 minutes away, including Providence. Reservations only, with a two-night minimum on weekends, prepaid in cash or by check. **99 Old River Rd; (401) 333-1899.**

Comfort Inn—$$

Right on I-95, the Comfort Inn has fairly large rooms, some with second sinks and a vanity in the room. The second-floor rooms have recently been renovated and are more attractive than those on the first floor. The rooms are surprisingly quiet, even those on the I-95 side. The lobby is small and serviceable, well maintained and manned by a friendly and helpful staff. There is one handicapped-accessible room, but the lobby is not yet accessible. An outdoor pool is available to guests. Cable TV and movies, game room. Children under 18 stay free. **2 George St., at I-95 Exit 27, Pawtucket 02860; (800) 228-5150 or (401) 723-6700.**

The Woonsocket Motor Inn—$$

Close to the center of the city, this motel inn offers pleasant clean rooms at prices that are hard to beat; it's also the only place in town. The rooms are large and comfortably furnished and are individually air-conditioned. Nonsmoking rooms are available. Some rooms have a queen bed, most have twin doubles. Rates do not change with the season. It's less than a quarter mile from the visitors center at the old railroad station. From Market Square take Main St., and at the Railroad Station go straight ahead and downhill. **333 Clinton St., Woonsocket 02895; (401) 762-1224.**

Hi View Motel—$$

Just south of the Woonsocket exit on Rte. 146 you will see the sign for the Hi View Motel. The 21 rooms are basic clean lodging. If you plan to be in the area on weekends, reserve ahead—the motel tends to fill up early. **797 Eddie Dowling Hwy. (Rte. 146) North Smithfield 02895; (401) 762-9631.**

Where to Eat

Spumoni's—$$ to $$$

With tables on three levels and wood-paneled booths, the atmosphere is that of a turn of the century bistro or pub. If you ask locals for Italian food, this is where they'll send you, and for good reason. Spumoni's also specializes in seafood (and serves fish and chips on Fridays). While this is a busy place at night, service is not only fast and friendly but accommodating. If you want to add shrimp to your fettucini Alfredo, just ask the waiter, he'll arrange it. In addition to the regular menu there are daily specials and Mon.–Thur. early-bird specials from 3:30 to 5:30 P.M. Open Sun.–Thur. from 11:30 A.M.–10 P.M., Fri.–Sat. from 11:30 A.M.–11 P.M. Wines are very reasonably priced. The restaurant has take-out service and is fully handicapped-accessible. Just north of the Providence line on Rte. 1A. **1537 Newport Ave., Pawtucket; (401) 726-4449.**

Lisboa a Noite—$ to $$$

The menu is filled with seafood specialties and features the best traditional Portuguese dishes. The lobster comes with a spicy green cilantro sauce, and the pork Alentejo is done in the classic style, but with ocean, not freshwater clams. Several offerings are prepared for two to four people. In addition to early-bird specials, they have a Wednesday special of $3 for typical plates. The decor is not ornate, but tables are set with linen, good china and flowers. This is a good place to experience the ethnic diversity of Pawtucket. On Friday and Saturday nights a singer performs Portuguese music. Lisboa is in the center of downtown and only two blocks from Slater's Mill. Open from 11 A.M.–1 A.M. daily. Handicapped-accessible. **17 Exchange St.; (401) 723-2035.**

Ground Round—$ to $$$

Family dining is the strong point of this eating place at the Comfort Inn just off of I-95. From 6:30 A.M. until midnight, seven days a week, this restaurant provides good solid dining at reasonable rates. The dining room is attractive and handicapped-accessible. **2 George St., Pawtucket; (401) 724-5522** or **(800) 4-CHOICE.**

Valley Park Cervezaria—$ to $$

From the outside this little neighborhood restaurant looks like a pizzeria, but on the inside it's a piece of Portugal transported. The Portuguese influence in Valley Falls goes back to the turn of the century. Upon entering you will find the bar in the far corner with tables around the room and in the more formal dining room of this family owned and operated restaurant. Try the cod or shrimp cakes as an appetizer. The staff can describe any of the dishes you're not familiar with. This is a relaxed friendly place where families with children come to watch TV from Portugal via satellite. Handicapped-accessible. The embarkation point for the *Blackstone Valley Explorer* is just across the river in Central Falls, a block away. Open Tues.–Fri. from 10 A.M.–11 P.M., Sat.–Sun. from 9 A.M.–11 P.M. **Broad St. at the corner of Mill St., Valley Falls.**

Serra d'Estrella—$ to $$

Serra offers Portuguese dining in a more up-scale setting, although it's still a comfortable place to bring the family. Included are all of the Portuguese specialties, such as caldo verde, shrimp *(gambas)*, pork with clams *(porco Alentejo)* and a variety of cod *(baccalau)* dishes as well. The tables are set with linen and nice china, and the service is friendly and helpful. Although the staff speaks English, don't be surprised to hear Portuguese being spoken around you. They have a good wine list, including many of the best Portuguese wines. Open daily from 11 A.M.–midnight. **168 Broad St., Valley Falls; (401) 725-9597.**

Chan's—$ to $$

Nearly a century old, Chan's is still run by the family that founded it. While the Chinese food they serve is well prepared, Chan's is best known as one of Rhode Island's premier jazz venues. A separate but equally attractive room in the former Fleet Bank building provides a small stage where top performers draw crowds from all over New England. The main dining room decor is elegant in red and mahogany, and the menu features more than 110 old favorites and lesser-known entrees. On most weekends there is at least one live performance, most often on Friday, so expect a crowd here, especially for big names or especially popular groups, such as the New Black Eagles Jazz Band. Admission is charged for the concerts, usually $5 to $15. Seating is limited, so reserve ahead for shows. Open daily from 11:30 A.M., closes at 9:30 P.M. on Mon. and Tues., and at 10:30 P.M. on Wed., Thur. and Sun. On Fri. and Sat. open 12:30 P.M.–midnight. **267 Main St., Woonsocket 02895; (401) 765-1900 or 762-1364.**

Bocce Club—$ to $$

Chicken Family Style is a northern Rhode Island tradition, and nowhere is it more traditional than at the Bocce Club, a real neighborhood club that has grown into a classy restaurant. A somewhat formal decor sets the tone, but the atmosphere is never stiff. The menu includes traditional Italian favorites along with roasts and northern Italian dishes. The antipasto is legendary. Go on Sunday (with a reservation) for the crown roast of pork and to see children in their starched Sunday best celebrating Nona's birthday or other special events. You may think you're lost if you are following a local's directions from downtown; the quiet residential neighborhood seems an unlikely location for a restaurant, but it's only a block off Rte. 114, west of town. The Chicken Family Style is $7.95. **226 St. Louis Ave., Woonsocket; (401) 762–0155.**

Gian Carlo's—$ to $$$

The menu here draws from cuisines all over Italy, with fish and meat dishes that include veal loin and their signature carne mista, a platter of mixed meats. Pasta dishes begin at $8.95. Open Tues.–Sat. from 5–10 P.M. and for lunch on Fri. from 11:30 A.M. to 2:30 P.M. **153 Hamlet Ave., Woonsocket; (401) 765-3711.**

Ye Olde English Fish & Chips—$

In Market Square, in front of the new parking area and next to the Blackstone Falls, this is the place to go for fish and chips. A family restaurant with red-plastic booths, it's plain and simple with a menu of fish and chips, fish alone, fish cakes and fish burgers, plus boneless chicken or shrimp—and chips. Order your meal and carry it into the dining room next door or take it to River Island Park. Open Tues., Wed. and Sat. from 10 A.M.–6:30 P.M., Thur. from 10 A.M.–7 P.M., and Fri. from 9 A.M.–7:30 P.M. **Market Square, Woonsocket 02895; (401) 762-3637.**

Chelo's—$ to $$

The modern brick-and-glass building contains three large dining areas on different levels and a separate bar area and sports bar. Chelo's offers a fine assortment of burgers, steak sandwiches, deli sandwiches, pastas and full dinner selections. Specials change daily, and most are under $8. It's lively and very popular, particularly on weekend nights, and a short walk from the Woonsocket Motor Inn. **490 Clinton St., Woonsocket 02895; (401) 769-6692.**

Services

Visitor Information

The Blackstone Valley Tourism Council office is an invaluable source of information on the valley and everything in it. The staff is friendly, knowledgeable and helpful. A calendar of events throughout the Blackstone River Valley is published seasonally. The phone is staffed

24 hours a day. **Blackstone Valley Tourism Council, P.O. Box 7663, Cumberland 02864-7663; (800) 454-2882, fax (401) 334-0566.**

Parking

In Pawtucket, **Slater's Mill** has a large parking area right downtown.

In Woonsocket there is parking in municipal lots at **Market Square,** with more spaces near the old train station off Main.

61

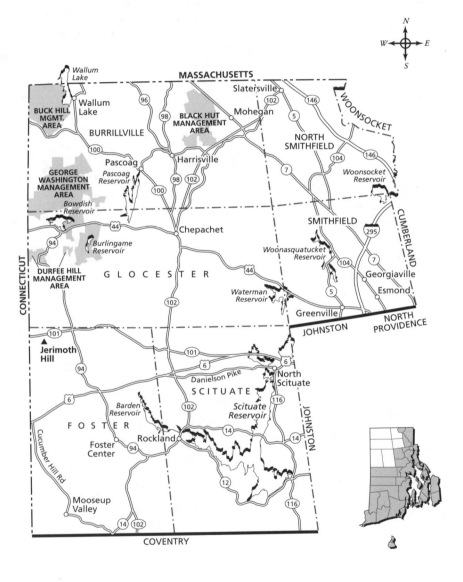

The map shows:

MASSACHUSETTS

Wallum Lake

Slatersville

WOONSOCKET

BUCK HILL MGMT. AREA

Wallum Lake

96

98

102

146

BLACK HUT MANAGEMENT AREA

Mohegan

5

BURRILLVILLE

100

NORTH SMITHFIELD

Pascoag

Harrisville

104

146

GEORGE WASHINGTON MANAGEMENT AREA

Pascoag Reservoir

98

102

7

Woonsocket Reservoir

Bowdish Reservoir

100

44

SMITHFIELD

295

CUMBERLAND

94

Chepachet

Burlingame Reservoir

Woonasquatucket Reservoir

104

7

DURFEE HILL MANAGEMENT AREA

G L O C E S T E R

44

Georgiaville

Esmond

5

CONNECTICUT

Waterman Reservoir

102

Greenville

NORTH PROVIDENCE

JOHNSTON

101

101

▲ Jerimoth Hill

6

6

94

Danielson Pike

North Scituate

S C I T U A T E

116

JOHNSTON

6

Barden Reservoir

102

Scituate Reservoir

F O S T E R

Rockland

14

14

Foster Center

94

12

Mooseup Valley

Cucumber Hill Rd

14

102

116

COVENTRY

The Northwest Territory

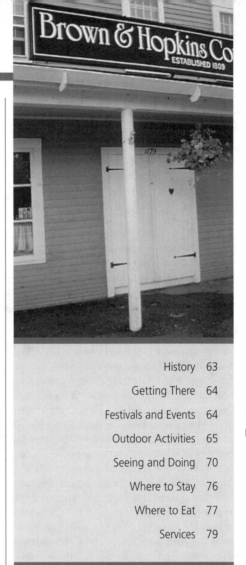

Roger Williams's Providence Plantation was a huge grant stretching north to the Massachusetts border and west to Connecticut. Most of it remained backcountry, some of the last land in the colony to be settled. Today, while hardly primitive, it is still one of the least developed parts of the state, and one of the most rural. The area includes the towns of Burrillville, North Smithfield, Smithfield, Glocester, Foster and Scituate, six towns covering much of the state's land, none of which is a large town or city. Here you'll find small villages, towns and outdoor activities all within a 45-minute drive of downtown Providence. While the area is included in the Blackstone Valley for tourism promotion, it is different in many ways. Like Blackstone, it has mill villages built along rivers and streams that have been dammed to provide power, but they are smaller and less urban. There is more space and forest here, and a different pace.

63

History

All the towns in Rhode Island's northwest are second and third generation: towns that were carved from older towns, in this case Providence. This land was so sparsely settled that it escaped the Revolution almost entirely. While it did serve as a refuge for colonists escaping occupied Newport, and the woods and fields provided some men, food and lumber for the war, life on the frontier went on as usual.

Although the American Revolution was a victory for democracy, the right to participate in it was limited to the "haves." In Rhode Island prior to 1842, only male landowners and their first-born sons, were allowed to vote. At least half of the adult male population could not. Although attempts were made to change this, the landholders controlled the government. In 1840 Thomas Wilson Dorr, son of a well-to-do manufacturer, a Harvard graduate and lawyer with a respectable position in his community, founded the Rhode Island Suffrage Association. Its purpose was to expand the vote to all men (it was still too early for the concept of women's suffrage). The association formed the People's Party and held a constitutional convention in 1841 that adopted a new constitution and held a plebiscite in which all men were allowed to vote. Of course, the legally elected government had authorized neither the convention nor the plebiscite. In May

1842, Dorr was inaugurated governor under the new constitution, and Samuel King Ward was inaugurated governor under the legitimate government.

Clearly, both men could not govern the state, and during the nights of May 17 and 18, Dorr's followers tried to capture the armory in Providence but failed. Their artillery, captured from Burgoyne in 1777, would not fire. Dorr left the state and Governor King rounded up Dorr's followers. By June Dorr was promised a force of 500 men to enforce the new constitution, so he returned to join his followers at the Stage Coach Tavern in Chepachet (still a tavern today). Only about 50 men showed up, and after Governor King's troops attacked them on Acote Hill (with no loss of life) Dorr was convicted of treason. He served a year in jail before being released. In a real sense, however, he won the war. In November 1842 Rhode Island held a new constitutional convention that gave suffrage to men who held real property of a value of $134 or paid taxes of at least $1 a year.

Six mill villages developed in the area as centers of wool and cotton manufacturing, with lumber and gristmills, a tannery, a brickyard and a nail factory. Ironware, silk, felt hats and liquor were also made here during the eighteenth century. Some of the mills still stand, but in Chepachet the mills that once lined the river have disappeared. While there were some significant factories in these towns, they did not reach the size and power of those of the Blackstone Valley. The area has always maintained its rural character with farms and small industry.

Getting There

From Massachusetts, Rte. 146 leads to North Smithfield from Worcester. Rte. 102 heads southwest to the village of Chepachet and on through Foster. From Connecticut, US 44 enters Glocester, meeting Rtes. 102 and 100 at Chepachet. From the east and south, I-295 provides rapid access to Smithfield and Rtes. 44 and 7, both of which lead into the heart of the region.

Festivals and Events

Dorr Days
June

A reenactment of Thomas Dorr's "Rebellion" celebrates the champion of universal suffrage. It's sponsored by the **Glocester Heritage Society; (401) 568-4077.**

Country Sampler of Historic Homes and Gardens
June

The Glocester Heritage Society holds lectures by eminent gardeners and tours of local gardens. For information, write to **Glocester Heritage Society Tours, P.O. Box 745, Chepachet 02814; (401) 568-4077.**

Ancients and Horribles Parade
July

If you've wondered what ever happened to community spirit, you should spend July 4 in Chepachet. The parade and other village activities are fun for the whole family.

Foster Old Home Days
July

Old Home Days are held on the last weekend of July on Rte. 94 in Foster. There is a bit of the old country fair to it with animals, demonstrations and exhibits as well as craft sales. Go on Friday night for chowder, clam cakes and Bingo, or for a ham and homemade baked bean supper on Saturday after the oxen pull and tractor pull. On Sunday a chicken barbecue is sponsored by the 4-H from 1–3 P.M., which will allow time to see the draft horse demonstration. There's also a Fiddlers Bee and other live entertainment; **(401) 392-5522.**

Heritage Day
August

Chepachet celebrates the many immigrant groups that came to work in its mills with ethnic foods and a special craft show. **Glocester Heritage Society; (401) 568-4077.**

Herbal Tea
August

Held at the **Job Armstrong Store** in the center of Chepachet, the tea includes lectures on herb growing and use; **(401) 568-4077.**

Scituate Art Festival
October

On Columbus Day weekend every year, over 60,000 visitors come to the festival held on the Village Green in North Scituate as they have been doing for more than 26 years. Although paintings are the primary focus, there are also exhibits of fine craft works. Over 200 artists and craftsmen from several states exhibit and demonstrate during this three-day show. Crafts include stained glass, leatherwork, wood crafts and pottery. All are juried for quality. There are also food booths. It's an outstanding show in a picture-perfect setting. At the **junction of Rtes. 6 and 116; (401) 647-0057.**

Hooked Rug Show and Antique Hunt
October

The rug show features both a show and sale of traditional hooked rugs and wall hangings; **(401) 568-8779.** The Antique Hunt features a unique treasure hunt, with clues to be dug out at the dozen or so antique shops in town. The hard part is remembering the game while doing serious browsing; **(401) 568-4077.** On the same weekend there is music at the **Free Will Baptist Church; (401) 568-4351.**

Peddlar's Faire
November

A celebration of the harvest offers a farmer's market, hayrides, craft sales and family entertainment. Routes for self-guided foliage tours are provided. The **Heritage Quilt Show and Sale** is usually held at the same time, sponsored by the **Glocester Heritage Society; (401) 568-8779.**

Candlelight Shopping in Chepachet
December

The shops and streets of town are decorated for the season, Christmas music plays, and horse-drawn wagons offer rides. In **Music at the Meetinghouse,** the Free Will Baptist Church celebrates the holidays with traditional music; **(401) 568-4351.**

Christmas in the Country Historic House Tours of Glocester
December

Sponsored by the **Glocester Heritage Society,** tours run from 11 A.M.–5 P.M. and feature historic homes decorated for the season. There are also wagon rides, refreshments and demonstrations of traditional crafts such as weaving, quilting and rug hooking; **(401) 568-8779.**

Outdoor Activities

Parks and Recreation Areas

Casimir Pulaski Memorial State Park

On the Connecticut border a short distance west of Chepachet, the park has day-use facilities that include picnic sites in a pine grove or a pavilion, plus horseshoe pits, an attractive beach, ball fields and a choice of walking trails. These are all easy enough to reach for a family outing with small children.

The shortest of the trails is **Peck's Pond Trail,** which starts on the shore at the white blazes and follows the shore around the pond. Look for waterfowl, particularly on the north end, where you will see wood-duck houses in the pond. For a longer walk, about three hours, follow the blue-green-blazed trail crossing the ball field along the left side and pick up the blazes on the other side. This trail leads through several different environments, including a wet marshy area and the shores of Peck's Pond.

Take Rte. 44 from Chepachet past the reservoir to the entrance road on the right. It's well marked. Day-use fees are $2 for children and $4 for adults. The trails of the park are available for cross-country skiing in the winter, and the internal roadways (barred to wheeled traffic) are available for snowmobiles in winter.

George Washington Management Area

Adjacent to the Pulaski facility is the George Washington Management Area, and a less crowded and much quieter beach than at Pulaski. The camping area has 55 sites and two shelters in a wooded area and does not take reservations.

The pond has a boat launch and is popular for motorboats, often with water skiers in tow, so we don't suggest planning a quiet canoe excursion there in the summer. During spring and fall, it is almost empty. The beach area is the trailhead for the **Walkabout Trail** (see page **68**). The park is **west of Chepachet on Rte. 44 near the Connecticut border; (401) 568-2013.**

Blackstone Gorge

The gorge is part of the Blackstone River Valley National Historic Corridor. In this park the river falls over the edge of Rolling Mill Dam, then tumbles through the rock-lined gorge that barred navigation before the canal. It's an impressive sight, especially when the water is high. From Rte. 146 in Forestdale take the exit to Rte. 146A. At the end of the ramp take Rte. 146A south to St. Paul Street, on which you go left into Blackstone, Massachusetts. Go left onto Rte. 122, which goes left at the next intersection. Just as the road passes over a bridge, take County Rd. to the left. Park at the end of the street. The trail to the gorge is to the left through the woods.

Birding

Large tracts of land devoted to wildlife management areas make northwestern Rhode Island ideal for birding. Wetlands have been created especially as bird habitat, and fields have been planted with grain crops to further attract them. **Black Hut, Buck Hill** and **Pulaski Marsh** are primary locations for ducks, swallows and a number of songbirds. **Powder Mill Ledges,** headquarters of the state Audubon Society, is in Smithfield, with a habitat planned to attract birds and a blind for observation (see below).

Hiking and Walking

Powder Mill Ledges Refuge

The **Audubon Society of Rhode Island** headquarters at the Powder Mill Ledges Refuge in Smithfield is more than a building. The society owns and oversees a wildlife refuge in the midst of what first appears to be commercial overdevelopment. Rte. 44 (Putnam Pike) at the Sanderson Rd. intersection is crowded with shopping centers, but at just a few feet away the refuge seems miles distant. The headquarters is right behind a large Brooks Drug Store.

The headquarters building is a buffer between the world and the refuge. Inside it has a gift shop, brochure racks with materials on flora, fauna and the environment and facilities for the society's wide range of programs. Outside is a butterfly garden and an observation blind at the end of the herb garden where you can watch the resident birds. Programs here have included sundial making, sunset walks and a fall migration bird walk. **The Rhode Island Wild Plant Society** is also headquartered here. It conducts programs on wild plants and their environments, including a coastal marsh and wetlands walk and other walks and programs. There is usually a small fee, and advance registration is requested; **(401) 949-0195.**

For a quick look at the nature of this area the **Orange Loop** is the best choice. This self-guided trail is described in brochures that are tailored to each season. The eleven stations explain the glacial kame terrace on which the building sits, the forested swamp, the role of fields and how they are maintained and even special trees, such as a muscle tree and cigar tree. A station-by-station narrative of the trail is available at the headquarters, and its descriptions and line drawings of the plants are a good guide. Along with an amazing variety of trees, you'll find cinnamon, lady and sensitive ferns, pasture rose, Virginia creeper, bluet, red clover, Canada mayflower, wild sarsaparilla, Solomon's seal, false Solomon's seal, oxeye daisy, jack-in-the-pulpit, pipsissewa, lady's slipper, Indian cucumber, goldenrod, reed canary grass, Turk's cap lilies and joe-pye weed—and that's only a few.

The **Blue and Yellow Trails** are longer: The Blue will take about 40 minutes, the Yellow about an hour and the trip around the outer perimeter of all of them about an hour and a half. The walking is easy to moderate, and the trails are used in the winter for cross-country skiing. Mountain bikes, motorized bikes and ATVs are not permitted. The trails are open daily from dawn to dusk, and the headquarters is open weekdays from 9 A.M.–5 P.M. year-round. The gift shop is open from noon–5 P.M. From I-95 take Exit 7-B and then Rte. 44 west toward the village of Greenville. **Audubon Society of Rhode Island, Powder Mill Ledges Refuge, 12 Sanderson Rd., Smithfield (Rte. 5) 02917; (401) 949-5454.**

Black Hut Management Area

This 1,500-acre management area, although close to the greater Providence area, is one of the least-used in the state and therefore one of the best places for a solitary walk in the woods. The trails are not blazed, and the variety of paths and old roads can be very confusing, so be careful. Rte. 7 bounds the area on the east, Joslin and Spring Lake Rds. on the south and west and West Ironstone Rd. on the north.

At the parking area are two barred paths: Take the path to the right through forest for about 0.3 mile where another path leads off to the right. Follow this to a small marsh created

long ago by the damming of a small brook. At the far end of the pond are remnants of the dam. Return to the main trail by the same path and turn right, following the trail about 500 feet to the second path that passes off to the left (if you miss this turn you will immediately come to a power line cut, in which case turn around and look for the path, which now will be on your right). Follow this trail through a mixed forest where it turns left, meeting the beginning of the trail you started on. The parking lot is to the right. This walk is just under three miles over mostly level terrain through a mixed forest of oak, maple, pine and chestnut. You will also find sassafras and laurel. In the marsh area and in the vicinity of the fields, you may come across ducks, pheasants and songbirds, as well as deer, woodchucks, foxes and squirrels. Some of the fields on the property have been planted to provide feed for the resident wildlife. There is nothing spectacular here, just quiet solitude. Cross-country skiing is permitted on the trails in winter.

From the Providence area take Rte. 7 to Rte. 102 south, following it to Joslin Rd. in the village of Glendale. Follow Spring Lake Rd. from the village to its end.

Buck Hill
Wildlife Management Area

In the far northwest corner of the state, this preserve has over 2,000 acres on which special habitats have been created to encourage wildlife. Park at the lot, which is about a third of a mile off Buck Hill Rd. just beyond the barway. The strange structure you see is a deer weighing station, a reminder not to go walking here during hunting season. Be sure to note the small sassafras tree to the left of the barway. Its mitten-shaped leaves are distinctive, and not all are the same shape. This is not a common tree in New England. During late August you'll also find wild blackberries growing in profusion near the bar-way.

Follow the path straight ahead. To your left is a small pond that has been created to support wildlife. About a quarter mile from your car you'll cross a brook; note the path with white blazes entering from the left—this is your return trail. Continue on, following the yellow blazes to a large marsh on your left. This area was made by damming the brook in order to create a habitat for ducks and the other wildlife in this area. The small boxes you may see are provided to encourage the elusive wood duck, whose nesting habits require a hole in a tree trunk. Stay well away from these boxes, especially during the spring nesting season. The many skeletons of trees that died with the flooding of the area provide perfect nesting and perching places for a multitude of birds.

In about a mile an old road crosses the path at right angles, leading to the west shore of **Wallum Lake.** Cross it and continue to another old road lined with stone walls. (About 500 feet straight ahead is the Massachusetts border.) Follow it to the right a few yards to a knoll on the right to see the cellar hole of one of the earliest farms in the area. Return along the old road, past the point where you entered, and continue on for about a half mile to a grass-covered path on the left. (The road goes to the Connecticut border, a stone marker, about a half mile away.)

Take the grass-covered path to the left past small ponds and fields that were created as habitat for birds and other wildlife. You can take the shorter paths to them for wildlife-watching. You will begin to notice white blazes, which you should follow until the trail becomes sandy, then look for a path to the left that will take you to the dam at the end of the large marsh you saw at the beginning of this walk. This path leads over the dam and back to the road where you began. If you miss it, the path you're on will take you back as well. This hike is just under five miles and should take about three hours. Watch carefully for birds, particularly water birds such as wood duck. These trails are available for cross-country skiing during the winter.

To get there, take Rte. 100 west from Pascoag through Bridgeton. Past Wilson Reservoir you will see Jackson Schoolhouse Rd. on the left. About three-quarters of a mile past it take Buck Hill Rd. to the left. The entrance is 2.3 miles from Rte. 100. Just before the entrance is a sign for the Gabeler Rifle Range; the Management Area entrance road is on the right.

Walkabout Trail

A few miles south of Buck Hill is **George Washington Memorial State Park and Wildlife Management Area,** 3,489 acres featuring hills, ponds, white cedar swamps, boulder fields and wetlands and abounding with wildlife. In 1965, while waiting for the completion of their new ship, the H.M.A.S. *Perth,* 300 Australian sailors volunteered to work with the state of Rhode Island, the U.S. Navy and National Guard to create trails in the George Washington Management Area. Working in teams of 100 for two-week stretches each, Operation Black Swan built over eight miles of hiking trails—walkabouts the Australians call them—and several picnic sites. In addition to the Walkabout, there are a number of other trails and roads here.

The Walkabout Trail begins at the triple-blazed **Angel Loop** opposite the end of the boat put-in. There are three options: The blue-blazed trail is two miles, the red about five miles and the orange about eight miles. From the beginning you will follow the triple blaze along the shore of **Bowdish Lake,** where short side tracks lead to the lake's edge. The trail turns away from the lake and passes by a camping area (on the left) and continues, following the triple blazes. The trail splits when it reaches a gravel path, at which point you can make a choice: The red and orange trails take you around **Wilbur Pond** and uphill into an open woodland before the red-dot trail turns off to the right. The red trail goes over undulating terrain and past some wet areas before it rejoins the orange trail. The orange route crosses a wet area on a bridge and continues to the shores of **Pulsaki Wildlife Marsh** and across the earthen dam that creates it. Over the dam the trail continues through thicker growth and wet areas before it rejoins the red-dot trail. With all these low-lying areas, this trail isn't a good choice in the spring.

Along the way look for the great variety of trees here, including several oaks and birches as well as hemlock and white cedar. You may also see rabbit, hare, red and gray squirrel, deer, fox, coyote, raccoon and at the marsh perhaps even a muskrat. Pulaski Marsh was especially created as a habitat for waterfowl, so look for wood ducks (those wooden boxes were installed for them), black and mallard ducks, kingfishers, herons and swallows. Trail maps are available at the park entrance, but a detailed map is available from **U.S. Orienting Federation, P.O. Box 1444, Forest Park, GA 30051** showing all of the roads, trails and features of the Management Area. The trails throughout the park are available for cross-country skiing during the winter.

To get to the trail, take Rte. 44 (Putnam Pike) west about 4.5 miles from Chepachet. The entrance is on the north side of the road. Just over a quarter mile up the entrance road you will come to the park office. There is a primitive campground on-site and a larger full-service RV and tenting campground nearby (see page **77**). Park along the nearby road. **2185 Putnam Pike (Rte. 44), Chepachet 02814; (401) 568-6700.**

Durfee Hill Wildlife Management Area

This whole area is filled with trails, but they are not blazed, and the entire web is often confusing. One fairly short (about two miles) circuit, however, takes you past some nice ledges, a small cave, a gristmill and two stone dams—quite a lot of extras for a short, pleasant woodland walk. As you walk you may see rabbits, waterfowl or even wild turkeys or pheasants. This is a hunting area, so you should not plan to walk here in the fall. No maps are available and trails are neither marked nor blazed, so follow us carefully here.

Park at the weigh station on Rte. 94, walk south along Rte. 94, watching, in a little under 200 yards, for a trail off to the right. (If you take a trail that goes to a field, it's the wrong one. Return to Rte. 94 and go a bit farther on. If you come to a barred woods road, you've gone just a little too far.) The trail you want leads almost immediately past a series of ledges on the right, then comes out onto a woods road, where you should turn right. Follow it to a swampy pond, where it will go left around the edge, then veer left again. This is a good place to look for birds. Don't take either fork you see to the right (the first just leads to the pond's edge), or the trail that leads uphill to the left. Stay on the woods road, which leads past a bar gate to a gravel road. Turn left here and watch the woods to your right for the well-preserved cellar hole of an old farm. You will soon come to an old gristmill, also on the right, with grindstones in the grass and among the stones of the dam and sluiceway, both of which are in pretty good condition. Shortly past the mill turn left onto another gravel road and follow it a few yards until it crosses a stream. You will see Rte. 94 just ahead, which you can follow to the left back to your car. But a more interesting route parallels Rte. 94, following a trail to the left just past the bridge. It leads past the ruins of another mill and stone dam and up a hill, where you will see another set of ledges, this one with a small shallow cave in it. The trail meets the same woods road you followed earlier and that you should take to the right. It becomes overgrown with brush for a short stretch but is still clearly defined. When you get to Rte. 94, you are quite close to the point where you entered; your car is about 200 yards to the left.

The gristmill and dam, as well as the cellar hole, are on roads that can also be reached by car: Continue along Rte. 94 about three-fourths of a mile from the Durfee Hill sign and turn right onto a gravel road, then right again. The mill is on your left, but since you are almost in someone's front yard, you will need to drive a little farther to park at the barred woods road and walk back.

To reach Durfee Hill, follow Rte. 94 south from US 44 (the turn is opposite the Waterfront Cafe at the Bowdish Reservoir), and at about 1.2 miles you'll see the sign for the Durfee Hill Wildlife Management Area on the left. Just past it is a parking lot and a hunter checking station, where you should park your car while you explore the trails.

Skiing

All of the management areas and **Pulaski Memorial State Park** have hiking trails that are open to cross-country skiers in the winter. The heaviest snowfall is in this part of the state.

Swimming

Casimir Pulaski Memorial Recreation Area, near the Connecticut border west of Chepachet, has an excellent lakeshore swimming beach. Nearby, the **George Washington Management Area** has a smaller beach, which is less crowded and used mostly by the people staying in the adjacent campground. **Spring Lake Recreational Facility** has a very nice swimming area on the lake, with a changing room and a snack bar. The gradual incline of the beach makes this a good place for families, and there is usually a lifeguard on duty. Swimming is allowed from 10 A.M.–8 P.M., and the park closes at 9 P.M. There are also inexpensive boat rentals. Admission fees are $2.50 for adults, $1 for kids under 10. To get there follow the directions for Black Hut Management Area (see p. **XX**).

Seeing and Doing

The Smithfields

Slatersville

The power of the Branch River attracted John Slater to this small settlement with grist and sawmills and a forge in 1803. (John was the brother of Samuel Slater, who founded the Pawtucket Mills.) He built a cotton mill, and his new company rebuilt the town, opening a store and creating the first planned mill village in the United States. At the foot of the hill on Rte. 5, the big granite building with its tall central bell tower is, although not used today, still as sound as when it was built in the late 1820s. A two-arched stone bridge built in 1855 carries Rte. 5 over the Branch River.

Note the power canal that carries water from the dam upstream to the mill. On the north side of the canal a small stone building was the "picker house," where workers removed sticks and leaves from the cotton. Uphill from the factory Rte. 5 intersects Main St., and directly ahead are two three-story buildings that were the first commercial structures in town. The stone building on the right was built as a store in 1850 and later used as a bank. The other was erected in 1870 and is more ornate, made of stone and brick. Farther west along Main St. are the earlier homes, many of which predate the mill.

At the **corner of North Main St. and Green St.** is the **Bartlett House,** a Greek revival dating from 1843. Dr. Bartlett was married to a Slater. Next door is the home of the first mill superintendent and a series of three colonial-style mill workers' homes on Green St. While they now look like fine old colonials, they were put up as the company housing for Slater's new mill. The Greek revival **Congregational Church** was built in the 1840s, and if the steeple seems a bit shorter than it should be, it is. The original was blown off in the 1938 hurricane. After John Slater's house, next door on School St. is a colonial with an outstanding ornate—and unique—doorway made by a local craftsman.

In 1994 the fifth-grade class of Halliwell School wrote and illustrated a wonderful little brochure describing the main buildings of the town, which any visitor should try to find. The Blackstone Valley Tourism Council often has copies (see page **60,** under Services).

Forestdale

This small industrial village is just east of Slatersville on School St. In the eighteenth and early nineteenth centuries it was famed for the manufacture of scythes and scythe stones and later as the home of Forestdale Mills, makers of flannel blankets. On the east end of Main St., near the Rte. 146 intersection, the **North Smithfield Heritage Society** has its headquarters in an old schoolhouse. Attractive older buildings here include a striped-stone house, duplex and quadruplex company housing and some interesting storefronts, one of which houses the post office.

Union Village–North Smithfield

Union Village is close to the southwest edge of Woonsocket (and was originally a part of that settlement) on Rte. 146A, also known as Smithfield Rd. Along this road are scattered many of the town's finest antique buildings, almost all of them dating from the late 1700s and early 1800s. Rte. 146A was Great Road, the main route between Providence and Worcester, with several taverns for stagecoach passengers and the homes of well-to-do settlers. The home at the corner of Pound Hill Rd. and Rte. 146 was the Seth Allen Tavern (1804). **Pound Hill Rd.** was the route of the followers of Thomas Wilson Dorr on their June 1842 rendezvous with history at Chepachet. At the **Peleg Arnold Tavern,** on the corner of Woonsocket Hill Rd., a stack of 100 firearms was cached during the Revolution in case of a British invasion. Just opposite the South Main St. junction is the **Union Cemetery,** where Peleg Arnold, Revolutionary War soldier, member of the Continental Congress and chief justice of the Rhode Island Supreme Court is buried. Diagonally across the street is the **Friends Meeting House,** built in 1881 to replace an earlier building put up by a congregation that gathered in 1715. During the years when the British occupied Newport, this was the primary meeting house of the Rhode Island Quakers. Just north of it is the old Quaker cemetery, its headstones now becoming lost among the trees. Several of them did not have inscriptions even when they were new.

Wright's Dairy Farm and Bakery

The Wright family has been operating this farm since 1900, and their dairy, gift and pastry shop is within the farm buildings, in fact as you drive in you might be concerned that you're about to drive into the barnyard. During the summer an ice cream stand serves the dairy's own ice cream. In addition to a full line of fresh dairy products, the shop has wine and pepper biscuits, a whole list of egg-free products, pocket pies, real pies (the kind with real fillings, flaky crusts and no fancy edges), pastries and breads, jams and jellies and a variety of honeys including thyme, cranberry and blueberry. You can see the cows milked between 3:30 and 6:30 P.M. any day. Open Mon.–Sat. from 8 A.M.–7 P.M. and Sun. from 8 A.M.–4 P.M. From Rte. 146A in Union Village (North Smithfield) take Woonsocket Hill Rd; **(401) 767-3014** or **(800) 222-9734.**

Smith Appleby House

In the 262 years between 1696 and 1958 only two families lived in the historic Smith Appleby House, now the headquarters of the Historical Society of Smithfield. Originally a one room stone ender it was built by the grandson of one of Roger Williams's original band of settlers. In the early 1700s another house was moved from Johnston and annexed to it. The twelve rooms of the house are furnished in items from several periods, from the early colonial kitchen and keeping room to the Victorian parlor. There are examples of marbleizing on the living room floor, stenciling from 1830 in one of the bedrooms and some fine built-in cabinetwork. It is, unfortunately, open only by appointment, except for special events. In late June is a Strawberry Social, followed by an Ice Cream Social in mid-July, a Blueberry Social in mid-August and an Apple Social in mid-September. The exact dates vary each year. From I-295, take Exit 8B to Rte. 7 north, and follow it about three-quarters of a mile, then head west on Rte. 116 a short distance to Stillwater Rd. south. The house is opposite pole 67. Write to **Historical Society of Smithfield, c/o 185 Old County Rd., Esmond 02917; (401) 949-4441** or **231-7363** (Esmond is part of Smithfield).

Burrillville and Glocester

Harrisville and Pascoag

These two villages are only a few miles apart on Rte. 107 in Burrillville, and both grew around the nineteenth-century mill buildings that dominate them. During their height, everything in these towns revolved around the

71

Betty the Elephant

On the opposite side of the bridge from the museum look for the plaque on the bridge's railing commemorating Betty the Elephant, who met an untimely end in Chepachet. She was traveling through with a carnival when some pranksters took a well-aimed shot at her from the upper floor of a Main St. building. That much is pretty well agreed upon, but a whole mythology of local legends have taken the story from there.

mills, and the towns are good examples of small villages that owed their existence to water power. Along with the architecture of the mills themselves, look for the mill-worker housing, rows of identical houses built by the factory owners. Harrisville, the more attractive village of the two, was owned by the Stillwater Worsted Company, and its mill has a very nice white-brick bell tower. While most of these villages sit in valleys, the river in Pascoag (pronounced *Pasko*) winds so much that the main street following it doesn't have a straight block in town. There is an enormous ledge on the western side of town. The big mill building is the Uxbridge Worsted Mill, started in 1814. This mill building was put up in 1865.

Shrine of Saint Theresa the Little Flower

The first shrine to Saint Theresa in America has been a pilgrimage site since a miracle cure occurred in this parish in 1923 on the day after its founding. On August 20 the Feast of Saint Theresa is celebrated here with an outdoor solemn High Mass, procession of the saint, a concert and blessing with the relic. In addition to a shrine, there is an outdoor rosary and a stone Scala Sancta, a replica of the 28 stairs Christ ascended and descended during the Passion. The chapel upstairs has nice modern stained glass windows. A brochure with a history of the parish, its miracle and the shrine is available. **35 Dion Dr., (close to the junction of Rte. 102) Harrisville; (401) 568-8280.**

Chepachet Town Pound

South of town on Rte. 102, at the corner of Pound Rd. on the left, is an especially good **Town Pound**. These enclosures of stone walls were used to pen livestock that were found wandering loose in the community until their owners were able to reclaim them (and pay for their upkeep). This one has high walls and is in very good condition.

Job Armstrong Living Museum and Country Store

In 1827 Job Armstrong built and opened a flour and grain store near the river in downtown Chepachet, which he expanded by adding other goods until it became one of the most prosperous dry-goods stores in town. Today the store houses a museum of Chepachet history. While today's town may not look large enough to have supported several dry-goods stores, it was once a major mill center. When you leave the store, walk to the bridge and try to picture it a century ago, with enormous mills lining both sides of the bridge along that quiet river that now tumbles through the woods. You'll find pictures of the mills upstairs in the museum.

Other photographs in the museum show the taverns, shops, inns and schoolhouses and bring to life the mills that once lined the banks of the river. There is also material on Dorr's rebellion, the medical bag and artifacts of the town's Civil War–era physician, period clothing from the nineteenth and early twentieth centuries and displays of early textile looms. The museum frequently has artisans demonstrating spinning, weaving, quilting and rug hooking, and there is an herb garden adjacent to the building with herbs that would have been used by early residents.

The country store, part of the museum, carries handmade sweaters, shawls, quilts, hooked rugs, wrought-iron implements and objects, jewelry, bandboxes (lined with real nineteenth-century newspaper), baskets, pottery, furniture, herbal wreaths, potpourri and other items, many made by local craftsmen. There is also a visitor center with maps, brochures and information on eating and dining in the area. Tours run periodically in the summer and can be arranged through the **Blackstone Valley Tourism Council, (401) 334-7773,** or through the **Glocester Heritage Society. Job Armstrong Store, The Glocester Heritage Society, 1181 Main St., P.O. Box 745, Chepachet 02814; (401) 568-4077.**

Theatre Company of Rhode Island

Chepachet has its own resident theater company that has been putting on theatrical productions for over 11 years. From September through June there are six productions, each presented twice. The company tries for a mix of mysteries, comedies, drama and musicals. Productions are in the **Playhouse Theatre,** the classical brick building behind the library; **(401) 568-2929.**

Aaron Smith Farm

The gourmet dining workshops taught in this 1730s farmhouse may include using the open hearth or learning the mysteries of cooking on an old-fashioned cast-iron woodstove. The menus and ingredients are seasonal, all food used is organically produced. During the holiday season, the restored house is decorated in greenery. Dinners include appetizers, entree and dessert served with coffee or herbal tea, and after your hands-on cooking experience it will be served to you by waitpersons in black tie. Class size is limited to six to 10 people. Call for a schedule of current workshop dates. From Chepachet, take Rte. 102 north (it's also Rte. 100 for a short section). Just after Rte. 102 diverges from Rte. 100, Victory Rd. is on the right. The farmhouse is along this country road on the left. **Aaron Smith Farm, 264 Victory Hwy., Pascoag 02859; (401) 568-6702.**

Chepachet Farms

Up in the hills east of Chepachet, Neil and Jody Esposito have a new and nicely kept farm that offers hayrides during the summer and fall and sleigh rides in winter as snow conditions permit. Rides take about an hour, winding through two and a half miles of backwoods trails or, if you prefer, along the back roads of Chepachet.

They also have an animal petting corral with a miniature donkey, a horse, sheep, goats, cows and Barbados sheep. On Sundays in October they have several special events: You can pick your own pumpkin, sit around a campfire or enjoy a foliage ride through the backwoods. No reservations are required during the fall specials, but the rest of the year they are. Rates are $5 per person with a party minimum of 10 persons. Call them to see if there is a group that you can join. East of Chepachet off Rte. 44 on Tourtellot Hill Rd. **Chepachet Farms, 226 Tourtellot Hill Rd., Chepachet 02814; (401) 568-9996.**

Scituate and Foster

Cherry Valley Herb Farm

A "full-service" herb farm, with dried herbs, plants and gardening accouterments, Cherry Valley has a series of theme herb gardens that shows herbs as integral to the whole human experience: gastronomical, medicinal, social and mystical. In April–June extensive courses and lessons on crafts and herbs, from wreath making and painting Ukrainian Easter eggs to growing everlastings, culinary uses of herbs and even aromatherapy, are taught. Course prices are $10–$30. During the summer afternoon teas are served; tea accessories are for sale as well. From Chepachet, take Rte. 44 east to West Greenville Rd. and take it south to Snake Hill Rd., close to the Rte. 116 intersection. **969 Snake Hill Rd., North Scituate 02857; (401) 568-8585** or **568-3901.**

Swamp Meadow Covered Bridge

This is the only covered bridge on a public roadway in the state, and although it represents a fine old New England tradition, it's not old. In 1994 a group of volunteers got together and built this 40-foot replica of a covered bridge from the last century. The timbers were cut from trees donated by owners of local woodlots. They did a superb job, and the bridge is well worth a visit. Take Rte. 94 south from the Rte. 6 intersection to Central Pike, a dirt road. Take Central Pike west a very short distance and you'll be at the bridge.

Foster Town Meeting House

Foster has the oldest town meeting house in the United States that is still used for town meetings. Built in 1796, it is a classic, with wooden benches and a three-sided gallery. When it was built by the Second Baptist Church, the town house was a civic, religious and social meeting place (unusual for Rhode Island). The first town meeting was held here in 1801, and the building has sheltered everyone since. In 1822 the church deeded it to the town. The 12-over-12 paned windows on the first floor are topped on the second floor with 12-over-8 windows. This is a fine example of early civic architecture, when function dictated form but frugality didn't sacrifice beauty. It still sits in a rural setting. Tours can be arranged by appointment, but if you're passing by you can peek in through the windows; **(401) 392-9200.**

Windsor Blacksmith Shop

Built in about 1870 and several miles away from the town meeting house, this building and its tools were sold to the Foster Preservation Society, and the shop was reassembled on the town house lot. Although the shop is not open frequently, it is easy to see it by looking in through the windows. The shop has a rare oxen sling used to shoe oxen, and an equally rare wheel stone that was used for the repair of wagon wheels. It's open from 1–4 P.M. one day a month, and three days during the last weekend of July from noon–8 P.M. for Old Home Days or by appointment; **(401) 392-9200.** Heading south on Rte. 94, take Howard Hill Rd. The town complex is on the east side of the road just past the Killingly Rd. intersection. **Foster Preservation Society, P.O. Box 51, Foster 02825.**

North Scituate

The whole village is in the National Register of Historic Places. The settlement is filled with white colonial houses and a village green with a tall spired Congregational church. The church and the buildings of the former Smithville Seminary are also on the National Register. **Near the intersection of Rtes. 116 and 6.**

Seagrave Observatory

In the nineteenth century an amateur astronomer in Providence named Frank Seagrave acquired an eight-inch refractor telescope, but as the city grew he found its lights interfered with his view of the night sky. In 1915 he moved the telescope to Scituate and continued to share its use with other interested amateurs. When he died without heirs in the 1930s, his astronomer friends formed Skyscrapers to preserve the instrument and their opportunity to probe the nighttime skies. More than 60 years later, this group of dedicated amateur astronomers still use the instrument and meet on the first Friday of each month. The public is welcome at their meetings. They also have public viewings on the third Saturday of each month (weather permitting), when visitors can look through the telescope with a trained observer nearby to explain its use. There is no fee for the public viewing. Private observatory sessions can be arranged for groups of 12 or more. Membership fees are $15 for the first year and $25 for subsequent years. From Rte. 44 in Glocester, take Rte. 116 west and south. At about the Glocester town line the road swings sharply south and becomes West Greenville Rd. Just before this road reaches Rte. 101, and opposite the west end of Moswansicut Pond, Peep Toad Rd. leaves to the right (west). The observatory is a short distance on this road to the right. **Skyscrapers' Seagrave Observatory, 47 Peep Toad Rd., Scituate 02857; (401) 828-0702.**

Shopping

Welcome Rood Studio

Welcome Rood was a keeper of a general store which he opened in Foster in the 1820s. His old store now is the home of a professional potter who throws functional pieces of stoneware in his shop adjacent to the store. The store also carries quality woven goods, blown glass, forged iron and other handcrafted items at moderate prices. It's at the intersection of Rte. 94 and South Killingly Rd. **Welcome Rood**

Studio, South Killingly Rd., Foster 02825; (401) 397-3045.

ANTIQUE AND CRAFT SHOPS

Chepachet is a center for antique shops, craft stores and general stores.

Country Cupboards

On Rte. 44 just west of the intersection with Rte. 102, the shop shows antiques and collectibles in a 1746 home. Open Wed.–Sun. from 11 A.M.–4:30 P.M. at **1503 Putnam Pike, Chepachet 02814; (401) 568-0606.**

Chestnut Hill Antiques

On Rte. 102 north of the intersection with Rte. 44, this shop handles furniture, glass, china, sterling, jewelry, watches and postcards. It's in the home of Dr. Potter, whose medical equipment is in the Job Armstrong Museum. This is a chance to see a historic home as well as do some shopping. Open April–Nov., on Wed.–Sun. from 10 A.M.–5 P.M. **1 Victory Hwy., Chepachet 02814; (401) 568-4365.**

Harold's Antique Shop

Rte. 102 south of the intersection with Route 44 is Main St., and shops line both its sides. The shop carries kerosene lamps and chimneys, furniture, prints and frames, and they also offer caning, splint and rush repairs. Open Thur.–Sun. from noon–5 P.M.; **1191 Main St., (401) 568-6030 or 568-2590.**

Cool Papa's Collectibles

Cool Papa's has sports cards, autographs and memorabilia. Mon.–Fri. from 10 A.M.–7 P.M., Sat.–Sun. from 9 A.M.–5 P.M. **1184 Main St.**

Noni's Things

In the old Franklin Bank Building, they deal not only in antiques but painted furniture, grapevine wreaths, sprays and handcrafted items. Open Sat. from 11 A.M.–5 P.M. and Sun. from noon–5 P.M.; **1187 Main St.; (401) 647-7562.**

The Lion and the Swan

In the same building as Noni's and owned by Barbara Kissack, who is very active with the Glocester Heritage Society, the shop carries furniture, linens, china, vintage clothing, books and Victorian items. Open Thur.–Sun. from 11 A.M.–5 P.M.; **(401) 568-1800** or **568-4077.**

The Old Post Office

At **1178 Main St.** this shop sells furniture, primitives, early lighting and other antiques. Thur.–Sat. from 11 A.M.–5 P.M. and Sun. from noon–5 P.M.

The Shed

Also at **1178 Main St.,** The Shed is a group of dealers specializing in collectibles and nostalgia items, including things as recent as the 1980s as well as country antiques; **(401) 943-4336.**

Stone Mill Antique and Craft Center

A change of pace, they feature European antique furnishings, carriages and sleighs. All are housed in an 1814 mill building that is worth visiting in itself. Open Sat.–Sun. from 11 A.M.–5 P.M. **1169 Main St.; (401) 568-6662** or **885-2182.**

The Old Curiosity Shop

On the same side of the street as Stone Mill and a few doors down, it has collectibles, antiques and used furniture that has not yet achieved the patina to warrant being called "antique." It's open Thur.–Sat. from 10 A.M.–5 P.M. and Sun. from noon–5 P.M.; **(508) 883-3420.**

Brown and Hopkins Country Store

They claim the title as the oldest continuously operating country store in the United States (as does Gray's in Adamsville). The building was put up in 1799 and renovated for use as a store in 1809. Although it has passed through many hands since then, it has always operated as a general store. Many of the early features remain, including its pot-bellied stove. It carries a wide range of items, from gourmet foods to country furnishings, handcrafts, antiques, collectibles and penny candy. **1179 Main St.,** open Thur.–Sun. from 11 A.M.–5 P.M.; **(401) 568-4830.**

Old Armstrong General Store

At **1182 Main St.,** it's practically across the street from Brown and Hopkins. It, too, handles general merchandise, which means you will find just about anything there—antiques and collectibles as well as consignment craft items. Open Tues.–Sun. from noon–5 P.M.; **(401) 568-8886.**

Farm Stands

In North Smithfield at the junction of Rtes. 104 and 5 (at this point also called the Providence Pike) is **Goodwin Brothers Farm,** open daily in June–Oct., from 8 A.M.–6 P.M.; **(401) 765-0368.** In Smithfield are three farm stands within a short distance of the Rte. 44 and Rte. 116 intersection, west of I-295. **Appleland Orchard** is at **135 Smith Ave.,** with apples from the early August varieties to the better keepers, which are sold all winter, along with cider, pies and apple wine. Open daily from 9 A.M.–5 P.M.; **(401) 949-3690.** North of the intersection on Rte. 116, **Pleasant View Orchards** is open daily in April–Dec. from 8 A.M.–6 P.M. The farm is at **143 Pleasant View Ave; (401) 231-4620.** Farther north on Rte. 116 (Pleasant View Ave.) take Swan Rd. to **Jaswell's Farm.** It is open daily in June–Dec. from 9 A.M.–5 P.M. It handles a wide variety of produce.

    Smiths Farm is in Pascoag on Rte. 100 west of the Rte. 107 intersection. Open daily in May–Oct. from 9 A.M.–6 P.M. In Chepachet, **Petersen Farm** is at **451 Putnam Pike** (Rte. 44 west of the village). Open from 10 A.M.–5 P.M. on weekends only from July–Dec.; **(401) 949-0824. Snowhurst Farms** is south of the village center on Rte. 102, known as Chopmist Hill Rd. (and also as Victory Highway, an example of the delightfully schizophrenic aspects of Rhode Island nomenclature). Snowhurst is open daily, year-round, from 8:30 A.M.–6 P.M.; **(401) 568-8900.**

Where to Stay

ACCOMMODATIONS

Susse Chalet Inn—$$

Basic low-cost motel accommodations, well kept and well located. **George Washington Hwy., Rte. 116, Smithfield; (401) 232-2400.**

Willingham Manor—$$$

Guests at this small B&B have their own house. The two tastefully appointed bedrooms share a spotlessly clean modern bath, a living room furnished in fine (but very comfortable) antiques, a dining room and a fully equipped kitchen, where guests can cool a bottle of wine or have a glass of juice at any time. The Elephant Room, the more elegant of the two bedrooms, has a queen bed, air-conditioning and overlooks the front lawn. The Shell Room has twin beds and is light, bright and airy, with a view over the backyard and to the forest beyond. The bath is between the rooms and has thick, fluffy monogrammed towels and bars of 4711 soap. The hosts, whose home is attached to the guest house, are a fascinating couple who have lived in outposts of Africa, South America and the South Seas. You'll know it when you walk in, since their furnishings show their eclectic good taste and the places in which they have lived. All of the furniture, except one bed, are family heirlooms. A choice of Continental or full breakfast starts with fresh fruit, coffee or brewed tea (with a fine selection of loose teas), and you will have homemade jams with your muffins or English-style toast. All of the muffins and breads are homemade. The thoughtful gestures of the hosts (such as the loan of an insulated picnic bag, plates and napkins for a picnic lunch) make you realize that here you really are a house guest. (We consider this our home in northern Rhode Island, so you may meet us here on our wedding anniversary.) No credit cards are accepted, but they will take personal checks.

570 Central Ave., Mapleville. Mailing address 570 Central Avenue, Pascoag 02859; (401) 568-2468.

Stone House Motor Inn—$$

The Inn takes its name from a small stone building that serves as the office for this 11-room motel. It's clean and has TV but is also pretty basic. Around Foster there aren't many places to stay, and this one is quite adequate. It's open year-round. **Danielson Pike (Rte. 6), Foster 02825; (401) 647-5850.**

CAMPGROUNDS

Bowdish Lake Camping Area

Close to the George Washington and Pulaski Memorial State Parks, this private area has frontage on Bowdish Lake and Wilber Pond. It's a large area, with over 200 sites for RV and tenting campers. Although most of the sites are set in forested areas, they are rather open and less than optimal for privacy. In addition to good supervised swimming beaches, there is boat access to both the pond and the lake, where there is good fishing. Hayrides, a playground, horseshoes and volleyball are all available, as well as a craft and activity program that includes supplies and instruction. In addition to electrical hookups, there are dumping stations, a camp store, recreation halls, a snack bar and campfire sites with picnic tables and firewood. Weekend prices for wooded sites with water and electricity are $20 a day; sites near the water will cost up to $30. Weekday rates are $14 to $21. On holidays there is a three-day minimum stay. Rates are for two adults and children under 16. For additional people, rates are $3 (under 16) and $5 (adults). Call for reservations. Open April 30–Columbus Day. Rte. 44 west of Chepachet (Glocester), less than a mile from the Connecticut border. **Rte. 44, Putnam Pike, P.O. Box 25, Chepachet 02814; (401) 568-8890.**

George Washington Camping Area

This camping area, run by the state Department of Environmental Management, offers 45 primitive sites near Bowdish Lake. There are no water nor electricity hookups, and only two shelters are available. The sites are wooded, with toilets and water nearby. A nice beach area is available to campers, and a boat launch provides access to Bowdish Lake. This is a special area for tent camping, the site of the camp of the Australian sailors who, as part of Operation Black Swan, built the Walkabout Trail (see Outdoor Activities, page 68). The sites are in a pleasant older forest, but although they are well spaced, they are open. In addition to the beach and water access, miles of hiking trails are available in the Management Area; this is the beginning point of the Walkabout Trail. The campground is open from April–mid-Oct. Rates are $25 for shelters and $8 per site for state residents, $12 for nonresidents. There are extra charges for visitors and second vehicles. **George Washington Campground, 2185 Putnam Pike (Rte. 44), Chepachet 02814; (401) 568-6700.**

Where to Eat

SMITHFIELD

Bushberry, Ltd.—$

Afternoon tea and the proper accompanying small dishes are served daily. Also for sale are gift baskets, jams, chutneys, teas and coffees. Open Tues.–Sat. from 10 A.M.–5 P.M. **466 Putnam Pike, Greenville (Smithfield) 02828; (401) 949-5230.**

BURRILLVILLE

Creative Pies and Cakes—$

Here you'll find not only good pastry but a full breakfast and lunch counter as well. It's

77

clearly a grill, but you can get breakfast for under $3, and there are burgers, sandwiches and other fried foods. **Rte. 107, Harrisville; (401) 568-7117.**

The Doughboy—$

Not gourmet, but a good place for breakfast, sandwiches or for an ice cream break on a hot afternoon. This roadside eatery is on **Rte. 102 just south of Rte. 7 in Burrillville.**

Wright's Farm Restaurant—$ to $$$

One of the joys of Rhode Island is its food traditions, and Chicken Family Style is one of the most treasured. Wright's, run by the Galleshaw family since 1972, is one of the most popular places for this specialty. The meal includes tossed salad, macaroni salad, french fries, rolls and chicken. There is also a 14 oz. steak for those who don't like chicken, but that's the full extent of the menu. The children's portion for kids under 10 is $4.20, adults $7.25 and the steak $14.50. They also have a full bar and wine by the carafe at reasonable prices. This place is so popular that there is seating for over 1,500 in five dining rooms of varying sizes. The Carriage Room Lounge is open May–Aug. On Rte. 102 south of the Rte. 7 intersection. Open Thur.–Fri. from 4–9 P.M., Sat. from noon–9:30 P.M. and Sun. from noon–8 P.M. **84 Inman Rd., Harrisville; (401) 769-2856.**

Stagecoach Tavern Restaurant—$ to $$$

Tradition has it that this inn was the meeting place of the supporters of Thomas Wilson Dorr when he returned to the state to defend his reform constitution. While the dining room is a bit more comfortable now, it still has the feel of a rustic inn of the colonial period: There's lots of old wood and antique implements around, as well as a cast-iron cookstove. You can dine in high-back wooden booths or at tables. The menu is American and Italian, with

a lot of seafood, all well prepared and served in prodigious quantities. A heart-smart menu has five selections for under $10. You may be lucky enough to go when the restaurant offers a lobster dinner for two: a pair of one-pounders, each stuffed with scallops and the meat of another lobster and served with clams and mussels on the side, for only $28—dinner for two at the price of one elsewhere. A full-service bar in the separate tavern, open daily. The dining room is open Wed.–Thur. from 4–9 P.M., Fri.–Sat. from 4–10 P.M., and Sun. from 4–9 P.M. **Rte. 44, Main St., Chepachet; (401) 568-2275.**

The Purple Cat—$$ to $$$

Rose La Voie started this restaurant in 1929 as a diner, and three generations later it is still run by her family, now as a full-service restaurant. Antiques add to a pleasant and casual atmosphere. The flowers on the table are grown by the owners. While the menu tends toward French, there are other options. Steaks include steak au poivre, veal is served Marsala or Saltimbocca style. In addition to daily specials they also have a Saturday prime rib special, under $15, but go early—it's popular. Open Tues.–Fri. from 11:30 A.M.–2 P.M. and 4:30–9 P.M., Sat. from noon–9 P.M. and Sun. from noon–8 P.M. Reservations are helpful on weekends. **Junction of Rtes. 44, 100 and 102 in Chepachet village; (401) 568-7161.**

Stateline Restaurant—$ to $$$

A good family choice, this restaurant is close to the Bowdish Lake and George Washington camping areas. The menu is American, with baked scrod, chicken parmigiana, steak and prime rib, with a few adventurous choices like chicken Atlantis, sautéed with shrimp, scallops, broccoli and scallions in a tomato lemon butter. On Friday and Saturday nights they have a Rhode Island clam chowder and clam cakes special—all you can eat for only $5.95—and an all-you-can-eat fish fry for only a dollar more. There are also early-bird specials Monday through Thursday, with several dinners starting at $5.95. Nightly specials, Family Day specials (Wednesday and Thursday) and Saturday and Sunday specials (you get two entrees for $11.95 from a list of ten offerings) make this restaurant a bargain. Open for three meals daily. Six miles west of Chepachet on Rte. 44. **2461 Putnam Pike, Chepachet; (401) 568-1967.**

Services

Visitor Information

Blackstone Valley Tourism Council; (401) 334-7773.
Glocester Heritage Society. Job Armstrong Store, 1181 Main St., P.O. Box 745, Chepachet 02814; (401) 568-4077.
Foster Preservation Society, P.O. Box 51, Foster 02825.
Glocester Historic District Commission, c/o 1241 Putnam Pike, Chepachet, 02814; (401) 568-5457.

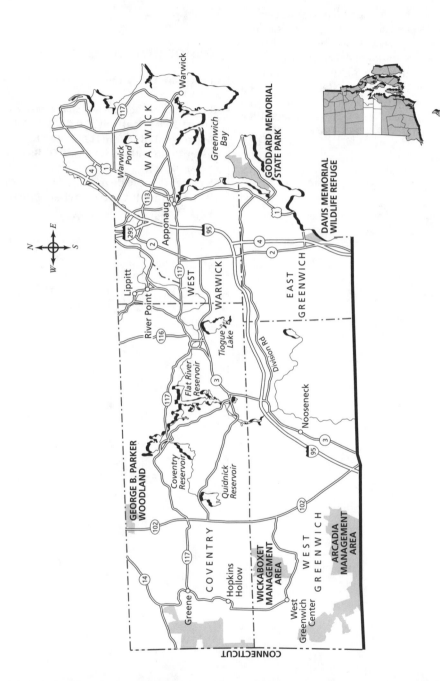

The Midlands

Kent County forms a narrow stripe across the exact center of Rhode Island's mainland reaching from the Connecticut border to the waters of Greenwich Bay. From the rural villages and wild parklands of its west to the historic coastal ports and urban sprawl of the Narragansett Bay coast, these midlands offer a sampling of many of the attractions found in the rest of the state: colonial history, period architecture, rural farmlands, beaches, little harbors, wild areas to hike, wildlife reserves and mill towns. It is particularly rich in associations with the American Revolution.

Since the eastern towns in this region are small and compact and the western ones long and thin, we have divided the attractions not by town names, as we have done elsewhere, but by east and west. Warwick, West Warwick and East Greenwich, plus the villages of Anthony and Washington, are grouped as the east, and West Greenwich and Coventry as the west.

History

A young woman who couldn't help smiling in church may have changed the history of Warwick. Samuel Gorton, one of the four original settlers of Rhode Island, took such affront when Massachusetts Bay Colony magistrates censured his maid for smiling in church that he was exiled. He moved to join Hutchinson's and Coddington's settlement at Portsmouth, Rhode Island, but his temper made him unwelcome there, too. He tried Roger Williams's tolerant Providence but became involved in a street riot, moved on to Pawtuxet, and was sent packing by a citizenry who asked the Bay Colony for protection from this highly excitable man.

In 1643 he and a few followers bought land from the Indians south of Providence and later settled it, but by 1645 they were expelled at the request of their neighbors. Gorton went back to England for a guarantee of safety from the Earl of Warwick, after which he returned to his land (which he named for the earl) and lived happily until King Philip's War, when they were all forced to leave again.

After that war, settlers returned and commerce began with gristmills and sawmills. Manufacturing grew, and shortly after Samuel Slater's innovations, Job Greene started a cotton-thread mill in Warwick. As technology improved, several fabric-manufacturing plants opened. Warwick was heavily involved in the Triangle Trade of molasses, rum and slaves, with over thirty ships participating, and was in the vanguard of the American Revolution: Here in June 1772 the British revenue vessel *Gaspee* was lured to the shallows and burned. Today Warwick is still a major manufacturing and commercial center and the home of the T. F. Green Airport, the state's major airport.

Encompassing approximately 62 square miles, Coventry, which was originally part of Warwick, is the largest town in the state. While villages in northeastern Coventry such as Washington and Anthony were involved in manufacturing, the western area remained agricultural. Local boy Nathaniel Greene rose to the rank of major general in the Continental Army while in his early twenties and was one of George Washington's most trusted and respected associates.

Most of the territory that is now Rhode Island was claimed by the colonies of Providence and Warwick (in the north) and Westerly (in the south), but there remained a small unclaimed segment between them. In 1677 the General Assembly created the town of Greenwich to protect the colony's rights from claims being made by Connecticut and by a group of speculators known as the Atherton Company.

The Atherton group, which included Governor John Winthrop of Connecticut and citizens of Massachusetts, New Hampshire and Rhode Island, tried to acquire Indian land, contrary to the law, and annex it to Connecticut. There were no settlers to secure the new town for Rhode Island, so land was given to 50 veterans of King Philip's War as a reward for their service, 13 of whom settled on it. The long strip that eventually became West Greenwich was bought in 1709 by a group of 13 investors for 100 pounds. East Greenwich grew into a cotton and fiber town with a small port. West Greenwich remained a farming town, and eventually the two were split, as we find them today.

East Greenwich's only contact with the sea is at Greenwich Cove in the far northeast corner of the town, but it is a beautiful meeting. The harbor, which once was filled with packets and was known as the Shellfish Capital of Rhode Island, is now less commercial and serves as the home base for hundreds of plea-

sure craft. The East Greenwich Historic District lies to the west of this stretch of water. Fry's Hamlet Historic District is almost in the center of the town, and the Tillinghast Historic District is in the south-central part of town. Today East Greenwich is an attractive and prosperous community where the median price for a home is $250,000. It shares with Barrington the title for the community with the state's highest median income.

Getting There

From Providence, I-95 goes through Cranston into Warwick and then on to East and West Greenwich. Warwick proper and the airport can be reached via Rte. 1, as can the East Greenwich Historic District. To get to the heart of Coventry, take Rte. 117 west at the Apponaug exit in Warwick. West Greenwich can be reached via Rte. 3 or by the interstate and Rte. 102 north. The Escoheag area is reached from Rte. 165 west from the interstate in Exeter.

Festivals and Events

Gaspee Days
May

Warwick's early entry into the Revolution is celebrated annually during May and half of June. Its highlight is the **Gaspee Days Arts and Crafts Festival** on Memorial Day weekend with a wide variety of crafts and food booths with everything from baked goods to barbecued chicken. At the end of the festival is a symbolic burning of the *Gaspee* and a great parade with militias in full uniform and lots of bands. The best place to see the burning of the *Gaspee* is from **Salter Memorial Grove** on Narragansett Parkway, off of Post Roast just south of the Cranston line or from Warwick Ave. (Rte. 117). There is also a colonial encampment, mock colonial battle and children's colonial costume contest; **(401) 781-1772.**

American Indian Federation Pow Wow
August

Held in West Greenwich, this meeting is open to the public and features Native American crafts, food, drumming, storytelling, dancing, sack races and a tug-o-war. 10 A.M.–8 P.M. on Sat., 10 A.M.–6 P.M. on Sun. Usually the first weekend of August at **Stepping Stone Ranch, Escoheag Hill Rd., West Greenwich; (401) 231-9280.**

Fest & Feast
August

The East Greenwich Chamber of Commerce sponsors this weekend festival, with live entertainment, art, crafts, ice carving, clowns, pony rides and food by local restaurants. 10 A.M.–9 P.M. on Sat. and 11 A.M.–5 P.M. on Sun. at **Academy Field, Rector and Church Sts., two blocks west of Main St. in East Greenwich; (401) 885-0020.**

Cajun and Bluegrass Festival
August

Louisiana comes to West Greenwich when Stepping Stone Ranch in Escoheag hosts a celebration of Cajun culture and music. Major Cajun and bluegrass musicians perform and conduct music workshops. Free dance lessons are given during the day, and two dancing areas open at night. Cajun and Creole foods such as gumbos, alligator, blackened catfish, etouffee and jambalaya are served, also barbecued chicken. Advanced sale tickets (one week prior to the event) are $12 to $20. Camping and RVs are $40–$65. **Cajun Music, 151 Althea St., Providence 02907-2801; (401) 351-3612.**

Annual Luminaria Candlelight Tour
December

East Greenwich features tours of historic buildings and private homes, the only time some are open to the public. This is an excellent chance to peek inside some of the state's finest old homes to see the restorations; **(401) 885-0020.**

Outdoor Activities

Parks and Recreation Areas: The East

Goddard Memorial State Park

The seventeenth-century mapmakers did a strange thing to Warwick. Between the Potowomut River and Greenwich Cove a long peninsula of land is part of the city of Warwick, even though there is no land route to it except through East Greenwich. Goddard Memorial State Park lies on this peninsula. In 1874 this area was nothing more than a sand barren when Henry Russell started an intensive tree-

83

A huge Victorian barn is almost overgrown by the trees at Goddard Memorial State Park.

planting program that he carried on until the property was sold to the Goddard family just after the turn of the century. They continued planting for another twenty years until the land was given to the state. Its forests have been called "the finest example of private forestry in America." Trails through the groves also wind along the coast of Greenwich Cove overlooking East Greenwich. (For detailed descriptions of these, see *More Walks and Rambles in Rhode Island,* described on page **xvii.** In addition to trails, the park has sandy swimming beaches, shoreline fishing, picnicking, bridle paths, riding rings and boat-ramp access to the cove and to Narragansett Bay. Naturalist programs are conducted during the summer, and a carousel building has been restored as a performing arts center. There is also a golf course on the eastern end of the park. In the winter the park is open for cross-country skiing and ice skating. During a low or dropping tide the shoreline is a good place for beachcombing, and from the northeastern corner the Mount Hope Bridge and parts of Prudence Island are visible. To get there take Main St. south from East Greenwich. At the Warwick–East Greenwich town line take Forge Rd. east (opposite the Rte. 401 intersection) to Ives Rd. on the left. The park is run by the Rhode Island Division of Parks and Recreation; **(401) 884-2010.**

Warwick City Park

Protected by two long coves, this 200-acre park offers swimming, a nature trail, golf, tennis, ball fields, a picnic area with handicapped access and other recreational facilities. The shore of Greenwich Bay here is claimed to be the scene of the first New England clam bake—others say this is simply where they became so well known. A scenic coastal trail through the forest is paved and open to foot or bicycle traffic (for access, park near the entrance, before you come to the gate). Unpaved trails also traverse the pine barrens and light coastal oak woods. Look for the sadly broken stones of Assylum Cemetery for residents of the poor farm that was once located here, and the potter's field for others. Open daily from Apr.–Oct, dawn to dusk. Take Buttonwoods

south from Rte. 117 to Assylum Rd. There is an entrance charge for cars; **(401) 728-2000, ext. 354.**

Conimicut Lighthouse and Park

A small narrow point jutting sharply into Narragansett Bay, Conimicut is completely covered in parkland, with a beach and snack bar. There is a fee for use of the park. Follow Shawomet Ave. to its end. The shoreline here is a favorite fishing spot. The lighthouse off the point was the last in the United States to be electrified, in 1960.

Parks and Recreation Areas: The West

Alton Jones Environmental Education Center

The Environmental Education Center is part of the W. Alton Jones Campus of the University of Rhode Island. You can't just drop in for a hike here, but it is open to the public through regularly scheduled programs. They are a half day to five days in length and deal with topics as wide-ranging as expedition camps and wildflowers. Weekend retreats are guided and taught by trained staff members. These change frequently, so contact the center in advance for details. They also have hayride tours on wagons drawn by draft horses by reservation; **(401) 397-3304.** Wildflower walks are held at the **Nettie Jones Nature Preserve.** Reservations are required and there is a $25 fee, which includes a lunch at the **Whispering Pines Lodge,** an elegant hunting and fishing lodge that has been visited by everyone from President Dwight Eisenhower to the king of Nepal. **Rte. 102, West Greenwich 02817; (401) 397-3361.5**

See also Hiking and Walking (page **85**) for the Parker Woodland, an Audubon Society property.

Birding

The **Parker Woodland** (see Hiking, page **85**) is an excellent bird habitat where you may see swallows, bluebirds, woodcock and sparrows in the fields near the house; scarlet tanagers, chickadees, woodpeckers, brown creepers, hermit thrushes, kinglets and warblers in the hardwood forest; and in the wet areas nuthatches, yellow throated vireos, veeries, American redstarts, Canada warblers, common yellowthroats, yellow warblers, ovenbirds and blue-gray gnatcatchers.

Fry Woods, at the Tillinghast Mill site, has good bird sightings, and there are waterfowl nests at the millpond (see page **90**).

Golf

Warwick has two nine-hole courses open to the public. **Seaview Country Club, 150 Gray St.,** is a USGA course on Warwick Neck, with a PGA pro, putting greens, driving range and practice fairway. From Warwick Neck Rd. take Leroy Ave. west to Carlton Ave., then south to Gray St. west; **(401) 739-6311.** Another nine-hole course is at **Goddard State Park, Ives Rd.** open April 15 through the last Sat. in November from 8 A.M.–dusk weekdays and from 7:30 A.M.–dusk on weekends; **(401) 884-9834.**

Hiking and Walking

The George Parker Woodland (Coventry)

Owned by the Audubon Society of Rhode Island, this area offers walking trails through the woods, archaeological sites and a place to see how nature recovers from the changes made by humans. The society maintains a headquarters and meeting room at the **Isaac Bowen Farm,** a collection of farm buildings dated to the eighteenth century. The land is part of a tract bought from the Narragansetts in 1642, and on it you can see remnants of a charcoal industry, sawmill ruins, the ruins of several prosperous eighteenth-century farms and mysterious stone cairns. Archaeological excavations have been, and continue to be carried out by the University of Rhode Island. The area is crisscrossed with trails for which maps are sometimes available at the **nature center.** We have chosen a route that shows most of the

area's many highlights and provides interesting but not difficult walking. There are only a couple of rough rocky spots. For a list of the birds you may see here, see Birding, page **84.**

Take Maple Valley Rd. (also called Waterman Hill Rd.) east from Rte. 102. On the left you will immediately pass the manager's house and the society facilities, but continue on not quite a half mile to a parking lot off the north (left) side of the road. Note that this is an area with deer ticks (see page **xiv**). The trail leaves from the parking lot. After about 500 feet it crosses a low mound, the site of the charcoal operation. Interpretive panels explain the process that made charcoal for the iron-smelting furnaces at Hope.

When the trail crosses a brook on a bridge, take the blue trail to the right along the brook. The path is stony, climbing into a laurel grove before coming to an old road, Biscuit Hill Rd. Local legend relates that a load of hardtack biscuit being brought to the French general Rochambeau during the Revolution overturned on the rocky highway, spilling the biscuits down the hill. The stone-foundation walls of a sawmill, a dam and other structures are beside the trail at this point. The dam and raceway are on one side of the road and the sawmill is on the other. This is an excellent example of how natural topography and watercourses became sources of power to tame the wild forests in the eighteenth century. It is one of our favorite places for a picnic.

Just uphill from the mill site the trail continues through the woods and a glacial boulder field. A 15-foot boulder marks the intersection of the blue and yellow trails. Take the yellow trail along a brook, through another boulder field and along the base of a cliff. The trail then comes to a small natural dam with a tiny waterfall and wooden bridge. Look for the pothole in the bedrock. When the trail intersects the **Milton Gowdey Trail,** keep to the right until you come to Pig Hill Rd. Go left. (If you follow the blue trail across the road it will take you to a swamp and a pair of old quarries before bringing you back out to Pig Hill Rd. It's a good extension if you want a longer walk. Take Pig Hill Rd. about 1,700 feet to the point where the blue trail enters from the right (a blue pipe

85

marks the point). On the right you will find the stone foundations of an old farmhouse.

Take the blue trail on the left side of the road through the woods, where you will pass stone walls and the foundations of a small farmhouse with the base of a huge center chimney, and the barn and outbuilding foundations. This is a good example of the layout of a small frontier farm, but be careful of the well. Continue downhill, through a woods that was once pasture, to a brook. On the left is a pile of rock against a boulder that may have been a rude shelter, and beyond is the ruin of another fireplace on the right. This one is more clearly defined, one end raised six inches above the surrounding ground. Could these be the original temporary quarters of the first settlers, or was one of them the home of a hermit wood-cutter who is said to have hanged himself from a tree close to his cabin?

At this point the trail goes back down the incline and along the brook to the bridge at the small waterfall, where you retrace your steps to the large boulder with trail blazes. Take the blue trail over the ledges, cross another ledge and then cross the dirt road. Along the next ledge look for the cantilevered rock, a seven-foot piece of fractured cliff that turned until it points straight out over the path. Through stone walls the trail reaches the homestead site of the farmer who owned the sawmill at the beginning of this walk. Excavated in the 1980s, the site contains the foundation of a large house with a big center chimney, dairy room and stone stairs to the cellar. The site is on the old Biscuit Hill Rd., which is lined with handsome dressed-stone walls, indicating the prosperity of this family. Across the street are the barn foundations.

Follow the blue trail to a large rock out-cropping. From this point there are dozens of stone cairns scattered through the woods, the trail passing among them. No one knows their purpose or origin; excavation has revealed no clues. It's fun to speculate about them. Were they Celtic, Narragansett or the result of a wry Yankee's sense of humor? The trail descends to a brook and a bridge at the intersection of the blue and yellow trails. Cross the bridge and take the trail uphill to parking lot #2.

To get to the Parker Woodland, take Rte. 6 west to Rte. 102, then go south to Maple Valley Rd. The woodland headquarters are at the first parking lot on your left. The trail begins at a second small lot a bit farther on. Trail maps are sometimes available at the trailhead or at the Society Nature Center. No dogs or horses may be brought onto the property. **George Parker Woodland, Audubon Society of Rhode Island, 1760 Maple Valley Rd., Coventry 02827; (401) 397-4474,** or call the **Society headquarters in Smithfield; (401) 231-6444.**

Horseback Riding

Stepping Stone Ranch on the Escoheag Hill Rd. in West Greenwich offers horseback riding and wagon rides. Public horseback riding is $15 per hour. From Rte. 3 in Exeter, take Rte. 165 west. Escoheag Hill Rd. will be on the right, past the Arcadia Management Area. **201 Escoheag Hill Rd., West Greenwich 02817; (401) 397-3725.**

Ice Skating

Mickey Stevens Sports Complex is a giant city-owned rink, home to a world-champion figure-skating team; **(401) 728-2000, ext. 6806.** Outdoor skating is available at **Goddard State Park** (see page 83).

Skiing

Goddard Park's many level trails are popular with skiers (see page 83), and the **Tillinghast Mill Site** in East Greenwich has trails as well (see page 90).

Swimming

Warwick City Park (see page 84) has a beach with bathhouse and picnic facilities; **(401) 728-2000, ext. 354.** The once-smart summer-cottage neighborhood of **Oakland Beach** is pretty tattered now, but the beach is still thriving in the summer. It is **south of Rte. 117 on Oakland Beach Ave.** It has a good beach, but not nearly enough parking and no public rest rooms or changing facilities. **Conimicut Point,** east from Rte. 117, has a beach with facilities. All charge a parking fee. **Goddard Park** has a bayfront beach on Greenwich Cove with lifeguards, changing rooms and picnic area; **(401) 884-2010.**

Seeing and Doing

The East

Apponaug Village

This part of Warwick is the historic heart of the town, with more than 30 historic buildings still standing. These are described in a free walking-tour brochure that you can get at the **Department of Economic Development** at the **City Hall, 3275 Post Rd., Apponaug 02886.** The City Hall itself is an interesting structure built a century ago, and the staff will give tours that include the old jail cells in the basement. The village lies along **Post Rd., between Greenwich Ave. and West Shore Rd. (at the junctions of Rtes. 1, 5 and 17).**

Pawtuxet Village

From the burning of the village in King Philip's War and the burning of the British ship *Gaspee* even before the Revolution to the Triangle Trade and the Underground Railroad, the harbor village of Pawtuxet seems always to have been where history was happening. But history comes easy here—this is New England's oldest village. Its National Historic District has more than 25 buildings of note. Pawtuxet is on the northeast corner of Warwick, where it meets Cranston at the mouth of the Seekonk River.

Drum Rock

A huge boulder, weighing, we hear, about two and a half tons, sits on another rock in such a way that it can be moved back and forth on its base to make a reverberating noise. Most accounts say these rocks (this is not the only example in the state) were used to send messages, although a bronze plaque on this one

In summer, the beach at Goddard Memorial State Park is filled with people; off season, it's a good place for beachcombing.

says it was a trysting place for the Cowesets and Narragansetts. Our thought is that no one especially wants to announce to the world that they are trysting. Along with the rest of the state's unusual and unexplained balancing stones, we'll probably never know for sure what these were used for. You can no longer follow Drum Rock Rd. to get here. Instead, take Gilbane St. south off Rte. 117 just west of the Rte. 1 junction in Apponaug Village, in Warwick. When Gilbane ends in a housing development, go right, and follow the loop along the edge of the woods. You'll see the drum rock on your right, before the drive turns left.

John Waterman Arnold House

Built in stages (as most early houses were) between 1770 and 1810, this center-chimney colonial has beehive ovens, a winding front staircase, wide-board floors and a paneled dining room. Period furniture and household goods include some from the original Arnold family, as well as Samuel Gorton's soup tureen. A colonial garden is in the front yard. Open Sun. from 1–4 P.M. and by appointment. **25 Roger Williams Cir., Pawtuxet; (401) 467-7647.**

General Nathaniel Greene House

The amazing young Major General Nathaniel Greene was a Quaker by birth but was dropped

87

from membership in the Society of Friends due to his fascination with military science. In 1773, at age 23, he was appointed Commander of the Rhode Island Company sent to the Continental Army surrounding Boston; a year later he was made a major general in command of the troops on Long Island. Having passed the winter of 1777 in Valley Forge, he became the quartermaster general of the Continental Army. In 1780 he was given command of the southern army and was so popular there that Georgia and South Carolina both gave him land grants. His house in the village of Anthony on Rte. 117 was built in 1770, when he was sixteen. The large gray clapboard house has four rooms downstairs and four rooms upstairs, typical of the period. On the 13-acre lot are a historical cemetery and a trail through the forest to the Pawtuxet River. From Rtes. 117 and 33 in Anthony, take Laurel St. to just west of the large mill building. Take Taft St. left: It will turn to the right and the Greene House will be on the left. It's open Mar. 1–Oct. 31 on Wed.–Sat. from 10 A.M.–5 P.M., Sun. from 1–5 P.M. **Nathaniel Greene Homestead, 50 Taft St., Coventry (in the village of Anthony); (401) 821-8630.**

Paine House

The original parts of this colonial farmhouse were built in 1669, but unlike many of the period, this is not a stone ender. The big brown shingled house has a series of additions that give it an odd shape in the rear. Once a home, then an inn, it is partially restored with period rooms and houses the Western Rhode Island Civic Historical Society. It's just off of Rte. 117 a short distance west of Anthony, behind the Coventry Fire Alarm Headquarters building at a traffic light. Parking on Station St. is limited. It is open May–Oct. on Sat. from 1–4 P.M. by appointment. **7 Station St., Coventry (in the village of Washington); (401) 521-0784.**

Lakeview Amusements

Specializing in outdoor activities, Lakeview is a good place for a family outing. You'll find a three-flume waterslide, a 19-hole miniature golf course, USA miniature basketball court,

fast- and slow-pitch softball and hardball batting cages (slow pitch). It's in Anthony, on the north side of Rte. 3 opposite Tiogue Reservoir, at **475 Tiogue Ave., Coventry 02816; (401) 823-8250.**

East Greenwich Harbour District Walking Tour

Start this tour at the old **Kent County Courthouse on the corner of Main and King Sts.,** the two most historic streets in town. Main St. developed from an original trail of the Pequot Indians, and King St., which runs downhill to the cove, was planned as the grand ceremonial street of the new town. It changed the town in an unexpected way, however. Unpaved, steep and a straight shot to the harbor, it served as a runoff flume. During storms, huge quantities of soil and debris washed down its length, silting the harbor until it could no longer take deep-draft ships.

Cross to the south side of King St., traveling downhill to **#19,** the **Jonathan Salisbury House.** Built in 1765, this was the home of a prosperous whaling captain of the early nineteenth century and shows the social status this street once enjoyed. Diagonally across **King St.** at **#32,** the **Benrett House,** erected in 1870 in the Second Empire style, shows that this was still a prestigious address more than a century later. Be sure to see the carriage house to the rear of the Benrett House.

Back on the south side of the street, the **Pink House** at **39 King St.,** at the corner of Duke St., was built in the Greek revival style in about 1830 and has a late Victorian addition. Across the street are two houses showing the architectural style of the end of the eighteenth century. The **Varnum Bailey House** at **#42** was built in 1800, but the rear portions may be part of an even earlier building erected in 1766 by Nathaniel Greene. Next door at **#50,** the **Nathaniel Cole House** is also from 1800.

Continue down King St. to the **King Street Railway Bridge.** This twin-arched granite bridge dates from 1837, when the Stonington Railroad opened. Its arches seem to cut the town off from the harbor. One of its two designers was Major George Washington Whistler, uncle of American painter James McNeill Whistler. Continue through the arches to the end of the street and the **Second Kent County Jail**, a large yellow two-story colonial, like many homes of the period. In a different take on equality, it once displayed a carving of two handcuffed men of different races, to symbolize the town's belief in equal justice. Back up King St. on the south side of the street, is the Greek revival **Bay Mill,** an early example of a mill from the period when steam power replaced water power. Cross back under the arches and follow Crop St. to its end. The 1800 **Barnet Marvel House** is at **#3** and is one of the least-altered architectural examples of this period. Cross Wine St. and take it east to the **East Greenwich Baptist Burying Ground,** which has many gravestones dating from the mid-eighteenth century. Return up Wine St. past Crop St. and take Bicknell St. to Division St., which is also the boundary with Warwick. Walk Division St. west to Main St. If you still feel like walking, continue up Division St. to **#144, The Windmill Cottage** which was built in 1800 and given to the grandson of General Nathaniel Greene in 1866 by Henry Wadsworth Longfellow. In 1870 Greene bought an old windmill and had it moved and made a part of the house. This National Register property is well worth a drive by if you don't walk to it.

At the corner of Main St. and Division St. you'll see the **Varnum Memorial Armory and Military Museum**, a twin-towered castlelike structure built in 1913 (see **opposite column**). Take Main St. south to the **W. P. Salisbury House** at **#69–75**. In the Second Empire style, it shows the effects of prosperity and influences from abroad during the mid-Victorian period. Farther south along **Main St.,** at **#99–101,** is the **Thomas Spencer House**, a private residence built in 1800, just before the courthouse was erected. The courthouse, where you began, is just ahead.

Kent County Courthouse

The somewhat severe Georgian revival–style Kent County Courthouse was built in 1803, replacing an earlier one that was once the

home of the Rhode Island General Assembly and site of a 1775 vote chartering the arming of two sloops to protect shipping from the British. This act of the General Assembly made this spot the birthplace of the United States Navy. The present building was remodeled in 1909. The courtroom has a semivaulted ceiling, a crenelated molding around the judge's bench and wainscoting ornamented with rope molding. Be sure to note the outstanding bronze war memorial on the front lawn, in a style seldom seen. The courthouse is open all year by appointment; **(401) 886-8645.**

Varnum Memorial Armory

This huge medieval revival–style building was erected in 1913 as a memorial to General James Varnum. On its lower level it has a museum with items, particularly uniforms and armaments, from all of the wars the United States has been involved in, from the Revolution through Vietnam. The Varnum Continentals, formed in 1907 as a patriotic, military and social organization, meet and train at the armory on the second Monday of each month. The Continentals seek to perpetuate the uniforms, traditions and values of the American citizen soldier during the Revolution, and they march in local parades, including the annual Memorial Day Parade. The museum is open for tours by appointment. Call or write for information on both the museum and the continentals; **6 Main St., East Greenwich 02818; (401) 884-4110.**

Armory of the Kentish Guards

In 1774 Nathanael Greene and James Mitchell Varnum gathered 56 men from Kent County to form a militia company. Trained by Greene and Varnum, the company served with valor in the Revolution and in all American wars up to World War I. The company still exists as a volunteer militia unit answerable only to the Governor of Rhode Island and is the fifth oldest militia company in the country. It is dedicated to the preservation of "the military traditions of our forefathers." The company's fife and drum corps provides field music for parades and musters. The corps will take volunteers

89

Several walking trails begin at the old millpond at Frenchtown.

from ages 14 to 70. The headquarters of the company is an outstanding Greek revival frame structure at 111 Pierce St. built in 1842 with four Doric columns and a classic pediment. While the practice sessions are not open to the public, people in East Greenwich sometimes gather close to the headquarters on hot Wednesday nights to listen. **Kentish Guards– Rhode Island Militia, 111 Pierce St., East Greenwich 02818** and **Kentish Guard Fife and Drum Corps, 1774 Armory St., East Greenwich 02818; (401) 821-1628.**

General James Mitchell Varnum House Museum

When James Varnum built this house in 1773 he was a prosperous young lawyer. It's a fine example of American Georgian residential architecture. Varnum served as commander of the Kentish Guards throughout the Revolution and became a close friend of Washington, Lafayette, Rochambeau and Sullivan, each of whom visited here. Every room has a fireplace; a particularly attractive one in the dining room was copied by Stanford White. General Lafayette slept in one of the upstairs bedrooms, and the portrait of Napoleon hanging on the wall in that room was given to General Varnum by Lafayette. There is also a collection of colonial and Victorian children's toys. An

eighteenth-century garden displays annuals and perennials popular in the period. The museum and gardens are open June 1–Sept. 1 from 1–4 P.M. on Thur.–Sat. by appointment. There is a small admission fee. To see the gardens when the museum is not open, you can enter from the Church St. side. A small parking lot for the museum is on Church St., opposite the telephone building. The museum is at **57 Pierce St., East Greenwich 02818; (401) 884-1776.**

Colonel Micah Whitmarsh House (The Brick House)

Erected in 1767, this historic home was almost razed in 1967 for a parking lot. The threat, however, served as a rallying point for preservationists in the community and it was not only saved but restored, and the group has gone on to save other structures. This classic brick Georgian building has a chimney at each end and 12-over-12 windows and a classic colonial doorway. The house is at **294 Main St., East Greenwich.**

Fry's Hamlet Historic District

This early farming area still retains three typical eighteenth- and nineteenth-century farms with outbuildings: They are the Spencer-Bailey House, 1735, the Joseph Fry House, 1794, and the Spencer Fry House, 1815, and they function today as a single operating farm. Two of them are distinguished by white picket fences with granite posts. Unfortunately they lie along the very busy Rte. 2 and are hard to see. Fry's Hamlet lies along Rte. 1 from the Middle Rd. intersection to Frenchtown Rd. From the latter intersection continue on to the next two attractions.

Tillinghast Mill Site and Frenchtown Park

This National Register site is on Frenchtown Rd. east of Rte. 2. The "Frenchtown" reference in the street name, and the name for this section of town, is to Huguenot settlers who came here to take up the land they had bought from the Atherton Company in 1686. Unaware of controversy over the title to the land, they began farming and building their homes. In the fall of 1687, opponents of the Atherton claims harassed the settlers and drove most from the land. In 1813 Thomas Tillinghast and General Christopher Rhodes saw the success of Samuel Slater in Pawtucket and built a cotton-thread factory at the confluence of Frenchtown Brook and Mawney Brook. Long abandoned, the site contains the foundations of the mill, the raceway, the millpond and dam, the steam boiler building, the foundations of four houses, a well, privy and outbuildings. The town has been acquiring the land and has developed an attractive park on it that includes hiking trails. The trail to the mill ruins leaves from the rear of the parking lot behind the yellow parks department building and leads past the mill ruins and the millpond. Another trail leads through **Laurel Woods,** to **Fry Woods,** the best part of the park for bird-watching and wildflower identification. This well-developed park is a nice place for a family outing and has both historical and natural attractions. There is a good trail map posted at the entrance to the park trails. The park is open during daylight hours daily. From Rte. 2, take Frenchtown Rd. west to the yellow parks department building.

Tillinghast Historic District

At the nearby intersection of Frenchtown and Tillinghast Rds., turn south onto Tillinghast Rd. The historic district runs along both sides of the road to the point where it intersects South Rd. Conservation easements on the bordering lands have ensured no further development of this area. The road is narrow and has been paved to appear as gravel. Along the roadside are a few farmsteads from the late eighteenth and early nineteenth centuries, particularly the **Briggs homestead** at #864, the original part of which dates to 1702. The area looks much as it did when these farms were first built, and the purpose of the historic district is to keep this rural climate.

New England Wireless and Steam Museum

As a young man, Robert Merriam fell in love with radio, and in order to operate his transmitter in the wilds of Alaska he had to use a steam-powered generator. Later, settled in Rhode Island, he and his wife, Nancy, created a museum of radios and steam engines that now fills five buildings and is home to an association of over 2,500 radio and steam-engine enthusiasts. Throughout the summer the National Association of Power Engineers conducts classes here, and in another building is the oldest radio station in the state. It was built in 1908 at Point Judith and moved to its present site in six pieces. A classic white New England meeting hall built in 1822 has also been moved here. The exhibits include fully operational steam engines of all sizes and an original George H. Corliss engine, as well as an engine made by the Herreshoff family of Bristol and an 1899 Sears-Roebuck engine. Radio equipment includes receivers and transmitters, both commercial and private, and follows the development of radio from early crystal sets through the vacuum-tube sets of the 1950s. There is even a forerunner of TV, a 1934 scanning-wheel set. There are two major events during the summer when the museum is open to the public all day. These are the Yankee Tune-Up, devoted to the exhibit and demonstration of radio related equipment, and the Yankee Steam-Up, on the second Saturday after Labor Day. On these days the public can see the collections and additional equipment and engines brought and demonstrated by museum members. In 1995 over 1,500 people attended the Steam-Up. The public can see the museum at occasional other times as well. Admission is $5. From Rte. 2 take Frenchtown Rd. about a mile to the museum entrance on the left, just beyond Tillinghast Rd. Call the museum for dates or information. **Frenchtown Rd., East Greenwich 02818; (401) 884-1710, fax 884-0683.**

The West

Stepstone Falls

Falls Brook drops over layers of stone so evenly broken that they appear to be cut stairs, an illusion heightened by the piles of stone left from nearby quarries. It isn't spectacular, but the series of short falls is a safe

Stepstone Falls near the Connecticut border in West Greenwich, is a cool shady spot for a picnic.

place for children (or adults) to cool off on a hot summer afternoon or to picnic around at almost any season. However, it's not easy to find. From Rte. 3 west in Exeter, take Rte. 165 (Ten Rod Rd.) west. Just short of the Connecticut border, take Escoheag Hill Rd. to the right to an unmarked dirt road (Falls River Rd.) on the right, about 0.6-mile beyond Stepstone Ranch. The falls are at the bottom of a long steep hill.

Rattlesnake Ledge

Although rattlesnakes haven't been seen in Rhode Island for 20 years or more, this was one of their favorite spots because of the rock outcropping where they could sun themselves. It is in the 678-acre **Wickaboxet Wildlife Management Area** in the western part of West Greenwich. The main reason for a visit to Rattlesnake Ledge is the view from the ledges. The surrounding terrain is relatively level and the ledges tower above it, creating a view that is pretty close to what the original settlers found. Miles of forests below you make it hard to believe that Rhode Island is one of the two most densely populated states in the United States. From the parking lot go past the bar gate to a fork and take the right branch. If you look in the brush to the left of the trail at the

fork you'll find an old foundation. After about a quarter-mile walk you'll see the ledge rise above you on the left. Climb it from the far end, but be careful, because the rocks can be slippery. There is also a pleasant, relatively level, five-mile walk in the Wickaboxet Wildlife Area. Wildlife include deer and lesser mammals as well as flycatchers, thrashers, grosbeaks, woodpeckers and towhees. From Rte. 102 take Plain Meeting House Rd. about three miles to the Wickaboxet Management Area parking lot, on the right.

Carbuncle Pond

Although there are some good, challenging walking trails here, we include this area for a story about a time when this was home to the Narragansett. It is told that there lived a great snake that had in the center of its head a huge brilliant red gem, the glow of which announced its presence. Just before the white man came, the Indians managed to surprise it and kill it. The gem was prized as a talisman, and for several years its glow increased as a warning when danger approached. When the white men heard about the stone they organized an expedition to seize it and, attacking the village, killed most of the men. But the chief threw the stone as far as he could, into this pond, whence it has never been recovered. To get to the scenic pond, take Rte. 14 or Rte. 117 west from Rte. 102, to the **Carbuncle Pond Fishing Area** on the left. Take this dirt road to the pond. See *More Walks and Rambles in Rhode Island* for details on the hikes here and the nearby Place Farm, Perry Farm and Nicholas Farm (see page **xvii**).

Nightlife

Warwick Music Theater

From June through September, top-name professional acts and entertainers are featured at the theater. The list varies but includes mostly popular music. The theater is on Rte. 2, about halfway between the East Greenwich line and Rte. 117. For schedule and ticket information, call **(401) 823-8910.**

Greenwich Odeum

This classic theater is in the process of being restored by a dedicated group of theater lovers. A feature of the effort is the return of live dramatic theater and performance featuring well-known celebrities. The group also hosts a busy schedule of touring opera, dance, jazz, symphonic music and drama, such as the National Shakespeare Company. A child- and family-oriented series called Bookity-Book presents plays and storytellers. The theater also plans to have its own professional equity company by the turn of the century. Much of the work is being done by volunteers, and they are always looking for interested people. Tickets are $5 for the family programs and $12.50 to $20 for other productions. Call for the schedule. **Greenwich Odeum, 11 Main St., East Greenwich 02818; (401) 885-9119.**

Shopping

Pontiac Mills

Abraham Lincoln dedicated the tower of this brick mill complex in 1863. It's better known, however, as the home of Fruit of the Loom underwear. The old mill buildings now house a lively collection of small shops and artist studios. You can shop here for everything from antique teacups to a custom-made and painted canvas floorcloth. The **Pontiac Antiques and Art Emporium** is as eclectic a blend as you're likely to find, combining a group antiques center with studios for unique crafts; **(401) 739-8993. Handled w/Care** is a crafts cooperative with well-chosen work of a number of local artisans; **(401) 739-8787. Pontiac Treasures** is a wholesale bead outlet; **(401) 723-7693.** The signage in this complex leaves a lot to the imagination, but you can pick up a brochure and map in any of the stores that will lead you to others. It is on Rte. 5, opposite Warwick Mall, at **334 Knight St.; (401) 737-2700.**

Indigo Moon

A different kind of a shop, with things seldom found elsewhere: vintage linens, antique buttons and more modern collectibles, handmade dolls and French wired ribbons. At **192 Pilgrim Ave.,** Rte. 3 in Anthony, at the eastern edge of Coventry. Open Tues.–Sat. from 10 A.M.–5 P.M. From Rte. 117, take Laurel St. just west of the big mill and watch for Pilgrim Ave. on the right; **(401) 823-7471.**

Encore

Buying clothing from a consignment shop in such an upscale town as East Greenwich leads to real bargains. This one has fine clothing at good rates. Open Tues.–Sat. from 10 A.M.–4 P.M. **5853 Post Rd., Plaza 1, East Greenwich; (401) 884-1113.**

Where to Stay

ACCOMMODATIONS: THE EAST

93

Radisson Airport Hotel— $$$$

While high season rack rates put this in the expensive category, frequent special offerings coupled with a convenient location only a few minutes from Providence and adjacent to T. F. Green Airport make it a good value. A Stay and Fly package for only $82 includes a night's lodging, coffee and muffins in the morning, free transport to the airport terminal and two weeks of free parking. Add to that the free use of a complete health club (also with free transportation), and it's hard to beat. Romance packages include champagne, dinner and breakfast for two and upgrade to a suite. All suites have whirlpool tubs, separate sitting rooms and bars. Rooms are nicely furnished, with extras like hair dryers, daily newspapers and turn-down service. The staff is made up of students from the Johnson and Wales University hotel and restaurant management program, but don't expect untrained or sloppy service. On the contrary, we have rarely encountered friendlier staff or stayed in a better-managed hotel. On Sunday a mammoth brunch is served buffet-style in the ballroom, with tables of fruit and pastries, chef stations for creating omelets and other dishes to order and an entire table of chocolate delicacies. The cost is $14.95, and the brunch is served from 9 A.M.– 2 P.M. every Sunday. The hotel's restaurant is a bistro in the lobby (see **below**). **2081 Post Rd., Warwick 02886; (401) 739-3000 or (800) 333-3333, fax (401) 732-9309.**

Susse Chalet—$$

Nicely maintained rooms with some extras— irons and ironing boards, Continental breakfast, free local phone calls—as well as laundry facilities and free airport shuttle service make this a real value. A tip for Susse Chalets anywhere: A last-minute check directly to the hotel may get you a room when the 800-number-reservation desk says the hotel is filled, because the chain always has to hold a few rooms for its VIP Club members. Next to Bugaboo Steak House on **36 Jefferson Blvd., Warwick; (800) 5-CHALET or (401) 941-6600.**

The 1873 House B&B—$$$

Only one suite, with a private entrance, this B&B is right in the middle of the historic district, not far from the museum houses and Main St. It has a living room, fully equipped kitchen and a twin bed bedroom. **162 Pierce St., East Greenwich 02818; (401) 884-9955.**

Vincent House B&B—$$$

Bright and pleasant air-conditioned rooms are furnished with twin beds that can be converted to king if you prefer. After a day of touring you can relax by the fireplace in the living room. On Cedar Ave., which runs from Division to Main St. **170 Cedar Ave., East Greenwich 02818; (401) 885-2864.**

CAMPGROUNDS: THE WEST

Hickory Ridge Family Campground

Exclusively for RVs with the usual hookups, the sites here are close together, but with a choice of open sites or wooded areas. A few are on a pond. Many of the sites are taken on a permanent basis. The campground has a recreation hall and a swimming pool, and activities include Friday-night Bingo, Saturday-night potluck supper and Sunday-morning coffee and doughnuts. It's close to the Parker Woodland. **Hickory Ridge is at 584 Victory Hwy., Green (Coventry) 02827; (401) 397-7474.**

Oak Embers Family Campground

This family area has a lot of RV sites, tent sites and some shelter camping with rates at about $15 without hookups and slightly higher with water, electricity and shelters. Showers, a game room, laundromat, grocery store and dumping station are available. There is a pool, horseshoes, play area, badminton and hiking trails. It's across the street from Stepping Stone Ranch, which has horseback riding, and close to Beach Pond, where there is swimming, boating and fishing. Labor Day weekend prices are higher, and there may be a three-day minimum stay on some weekends. Advance reservations are required and may be paid by check, but the management won't take checks on-site. There is also winter camping. There is usually an activity or entertainment events on summer weekends at the campground or across the street. From Rte. 3 take Rte. 165 west, then right on Escoheag Hill Rd. **Oak Embers Campground, 219 Escoheag Hill Rd., West Greenwich 02817; (401) 397-4042.**

Where to Eat

THE EAST

The Bistro at Hillsgrove—$ to $$

Deluxe hotels are usually the last place we'd look for a good deal in dining, but The Bistro offers gigantic portions of well-prepared dishes from a menu that ranges from old New England favorites to innovative offerings such as a ragout of grilled shellfish and grilled shrimp in a lobster sauce served with penne. The ambiance is bright and open, and service is on colorful fiestaware, which includes mega–coffee cups. Two-thirds of the entrees are under $10. The knowledgeable and friendly service, as well as the management, is by students in the Johnson and Wales restaurant management program. Your tips are contributions to their scholarship fund. Open until 11 P.M. every day of the year. The **Radisson Airport Hotel, 2081 Post Rd., Warwick 02886; (401) 739-3000.**

Cherrystones—$ to $$

In a beach cottage that was once the home of Rhode Island's carousel king, Joseph Carrolo (who owned seven), Cherrystones is located right on Oakland Beach, where one of his carousels stood. A pleasant atmosphere and reasonably priced seafood makes it essential to call here for a reservation. Pasta is topped with shrimp, clams or mixed seafood, veal is served in all the traditional Italian styles, the Bay Platter includes fish, clams, scallops and shrimp. Open Sun.–Thur. from 11:30 A.M.–10 P.M., Fri. and Sat. from 11:30 A.M.–11 P.M. (with slightly earlier closing in the winter). **898 Oakland Beach Ave., Warwick; (401) 732-2532.**

Nonna Cherubina—$$ to $$$

This little cottage creates a corner of Italy and is incongruous amid the roadside businesses that surround it. Linens, candlelight and a restrained decor highlight the food, which is excellent. Chicken breast or a pale veal scaloppine is sautéed with porcini and wild mushrooms, shell pasta is served in a sauce of rosemary, lentils and goat cheese, farfalle is tossed in a creamy blend of peas and smoked bacon. Seasoning is deft, as we would expect in this relative of two of Newport's favorite Italian restaurants. Open for dinner Tues.–Sat. from 5–10 P.M., Sun. from 3:30–9 P.M., lunch on Fri. from 11:30 A.M.–2 P.M. **2317 West Shore Rd. (Rte. 117), Warwick; (401) 738-5221.**

Tomato Vine—$

Mostly pasta and pizzas are available here, also chicken or veal cutlets and wood-roasted chicken. The atmosphere is informal and bright, the service is a little slow but friendly. Penne with artichoke hearts and Asiago cheese is a good choice, as is the linguini with shrimp. Located in the Apex Mall, **545 Greenwich Ave., Warwick; (401) 732-2569.**

Iggy's Doughboys—$

An institution at Oakland Beach, Iggy's dispenses burgers, clam cakes and the doughboys the sign promises, daily in the summer. **887 Oakland Beach; (401) 737-9459.**

Portofino—$$ to $$$

Busy isn't the word for it, but it's easy to see what keeps people coming back to this upbeat taverna atmosphere. Southern Italian favorites get a lighter touch here without losing their gusto. The menu is pretty straightforward. Ingredients are impeccably fresh. Scaloppine with red wine, mushrooms and roasted red peppers or with broccoli and sherry; tenderloin in garlic with hot cherry peppers; chicken with artichoke hearts and roasted red peppers join the classic saltimbocca, sole Florentine and linguini alla vongole. Open Mon.–Thur. from 5–9 P.M., Fri.–Sat. from 5–10 P.M. Look sharp, because Portofino is hard to spot in a tiny storefront row on the west side of the road. **897 Post Rd. (Alt. Rte. 1), Warwick; (401) 461-8920.**

Bugaboo Creek Steak House—$$

The Canadian theme could be called *Rose Marie* rustic, with snowshoes, a talking moose head, lumberjack tools, fishing equipment and

Adirondack log furniture on the terrace. We hope it's comfortable, because the no-reservations policy may mean a two-hour wait here on summer weekends. Offering steaks, chops, meat loaf with wild mushrooms, chicken, baby back ribs and catfish, or create your own combo plate. Root beer by the pitcher served in frosty mugs, and more than 20 beers are available. Handicapped-accessible. Open Mon.–Thur. from 11 A.M.–10 P.M., Fri.–Sat. from 11:30 A.M.–10:30 P.M., Sun from noon–9 P.M. **30 Jefferson Blvd., next to Susse Chalet; (401) 781-1400.**

Twenty Water Street and Warehouse Tavern—$ to $$$

The Warehouse Tavern offers outside dining overlooking the harbor and inside dining with a more extended menu. Outdoors, the offerings are sandwiches and lighter fare. Indoors, appetizers, from Littleneck steamers to tavern fries and jalapeño shrimp poppers, are served. Chowder, soups and salads are also available. Entrees include baked scrod and chicken pesto. Twenty Water Street is the more elegant restaurant on the second floor, and it has a more sophisticated menu. The upstairs specialties are rack of lamb, veal and swordfish specials and, of course, seafood. Water Street runs along Greenwich Cove. The prices rise as you move inside and up. Both restaurants are at **20 Water St., East Greenwich 02818; (401) 885-3703.**

The Blue Parrot—$ to $$$

Right next door to Twenty Water Street, The Blue Parrot has an equally good menu and view of the harbor, with a more casual atmosphere. There is a dining room and bar on the first floor and another dining room on the second floor. The ambiance is romantic without being dark. During the summer there are three choices of dining: The Deck, with soups, salads, pizza and sandwiches from $5 to $10 and served outdoors; The Cafe, with a broader range of the same items plus pasta, chicken,

veal and fish entrees in moderate serving sizes all generally under $10; and the second-floor dining room, with a more complete menu, a better view of the harbor and bigger servings at slightly higher prices. The Deck is closed in winter, of course, but the rest of the restaurant is open every day year-round for dinner and in the summer for lunch from 11 A.M. In the summer there is live entertainment in the evenings. Wine by the glass starts at $4. **Water St., East Greenwich; (401) 884-2002.**

Harbourside Lobstermania—$ to $$$

This could well be the most popular seafood restaurant in town—it is busy even in the off-season. The first-floor dining room serves light and fast meals, and the one on the second floor serves larger meals from a broader menu. The view from both is of the marina filled with boats, some of which are bigger than our house. Just across the water is the green shoreline of Goddard State Park. The downstairs menu has a large selection of appetizers and the usual burgers and sandwiches plus 15 seafood entrees, three steaks and chicken teriyaki. Upstairs also offers a large selection of seafood dishes, seven sea-and-land combinations and a large choice of steak and beef. Lobstermania is a lobster stuffed with shrimps and scallops mixed with cracker crumbs and Chablis. Lobstermania serves different early-bird specials each night from 5–7 P.M. all year. At the foot of King St. to the right on **Water St., East Greenwich; (401) 884-6363.**

Post Office Cafe—$$ to $$$

Instead of licking stamps in this recycled U.S. Post Office, you may want to lick your plate. If you've brought a big appetite, begin with a bruschetta of shrimp and roasted peppers or veal sausage and cannellini. Or order your shrimp as an entree, served with angel-hair pasta in a lemony champagne and sherry sauce. Open Tues.–Thur., from 4:30–9:30 P.M.,

96

Fri.–Sat. from 4:30–10:30 P.M., Sun. from 4–9 P.M. **11 Main St., East Greenwich; (401) 885-4444.**

Raphael's Bar/Ristro—$$ to $$$

Raphael's is on the shortest of our short lists of places we'd like to have dinner tonight. Although we never know what we'll find on the constantly changing menu—it might be a pasta dish with braised duck, pancetta and sundried tomatoes in a Madeira cream sauce. The service is genial and intelligent, and you will not be hurried, so settle in to enjoy several courses, especially dessert, where even the now-cliché tiramisu is vibrant. Open for dinner Tues.–Sun. from 5 P.M.–. **5600 Post Rd., East Greenwich; (401) 884-4424.**

Jigger's Diner—$

In a diner that's been here since it was rolled into town in 1950, but recently refurbished and spotless, Jigger's serves up generous portions of old diner favorites that are several cuts above the ordinary. The meat loaf is fine-textured and well seasoned, the corned beef hash is legendary, the turkey croquettes are made right here with the dark meat of a roasted turkey. Vegetables are fresh, and the jonnycakes are some of the best. Open at 6 A.M. **145 Main St., East Greenwich; (401) 884-5388.**

THE WEST

Pete's Pizza Plus Family Restaurant—$ to $$

Coventry is not bursting at the seams with places to eat, but this family-run restaurant is a good and inexpensive place to have lunch.

From pizzas (under $5 for a small) to grinders (under $5), spinach pies and broccoli pies to pasta and gyros. A four-piece chicken dinner is under $5. At the intersection of Farm Hill Rd. and Rte. 117, and the closest place we've found for lunch after a morning hike in Parker Woodland. **21 Farm Hill Rd., Coventry 02816; (401) 397-3323.**

Services

Visitor Information

Be sure to pick up a free copy of the pocket-sized fold-out map of Warwick, with dining, lodging, shopping and other attractions indicated on it, as well as a copy of the very well done *The Insider's Guide to Warwick,* also free. This guidebook format booklet is one of the handiest and most complete community guides we've seen, useful to residents and tourists both. Available from the **City of Warwick Department of Economic Development, 3275 Post Rd., Warwick, 02886; (800) 4-WARWICK, TTD (401) 739-9150.**

Coventry Chamber of Commerce, 64 Phillips Hill Rd., Coventry 02816; (401) 397-8555.

East Greenwich Chamber of Commerce, 127 Main St., East Greenwich 02818; (401) 885-0020.

Taxis

For airport (or other) transportation, call **Apponaug Cab** at **(401) 737-6400** or **Airport Taxi** at **(401) 737-2868.** Remember that many of the hotels in Warwick have stay-and-fly specials that allow you to leave your car and take a free airport shuttle.

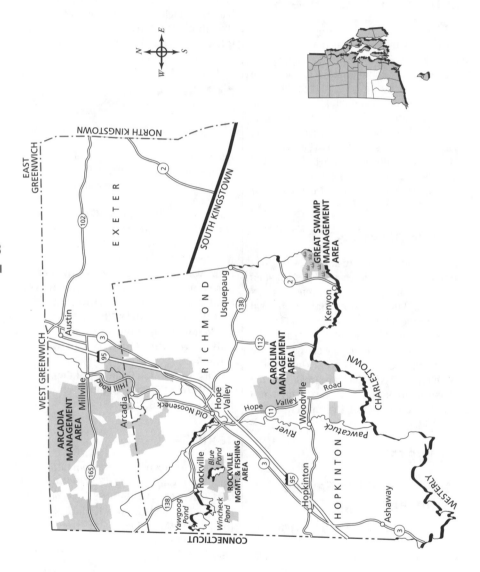

Arcadia

A vast (at least in Rhode Island distances) section of the state stretching from the Greenwiches south to the coastal towns and from the Kingstons to the Connecticut border, Arcadia is a rural place, sparsely settled and characterized by woods, streams and quiet. The panhandle of Exeter and the northern part of Hopkinton and Richmond are dominated by the enormous Arcadia Management Area, which contains more than 13,800 acres and extends well into West Greenwich. This section includes the towns of Exeter, Hopkinton and Richmond.

History

Exeter began life as a part of Kingstown, while Hopkinton and Richmond were carved out of the sprawling Westerly, all in the mid–eighteenth century. Richmond and Hopkinton were at first agricultural communities but were quickly transformed by the Industrial Revolution in the early 1800s. The decaying remains of textile plants can still be found in town centers and along the edges of streams.

Despite the mills that sprang up along the rivers, these communities have remained essentially rural. Today many of the farms of the last two centuries have disappeared, and the farmlands have returned to forest. Here are some of the most heavily forested areas of Rhode Island, with large tracts dedicated to conservation and outdoor recreation.

Getting There

I-95 and Rte. 3 parallel each other through western Exeter and Hopkinton. The interstate brings you quickly from Providence to the heart of the Arcadia Management Area, which can be reached from Rte. 165 in Exeter. Rte. 102, which intersects with I-95 in Exeter, connects Exeter to West Greenwich and northern areas. Rte. 138 runs through Richmond from the interstate exit at Wyoming.

Festivals and Events

Washington County Fair
Mid-August

The beginning of the harvest season brings the county fair with its traditional rides, shows and exhibits. The **Washington County Fairgrounds** are on Rte. 112 in Richmond. The fair runs for four days during the third weekend of August.

Outdoor Activities

Canoeing

The Arcadia area offers several canoeing opportunities on the Usquepaug, Charles, Wood and Pawcatuck Rivers, which offer some of the best nontidal canoeing in the state. As with any area, a good canoeing guide is essential for safety. (The *AMC River Guide,* vol. 2 covers this area and is updated regularly. Available in bookstores or from the Appalachian Mountain Club, 5 Joy St., Boston, MA 02108.)

Usquepaug River

The river's run is about five and a half miles; water levels are high enough for passage from March through June. Predominantly flat water with some quick water, it passes through the historic **Great Swamp,** where bushes and brush make passage more difficult. Park and put-in on the southwest side of the bridge on Rte. 138, at the Richmond–South Kingstown town line. Finding the right channel through the swamp can be tricky. On the far end of Great Swamp, the **Chipuxet River** (at this point named the Charles) enters from the left. Follow it to an access on Biscuit City Rd. The nine-mile run from here to the Wood River confluence is a combination of flat water and Class II, with four portages around dams along the way. For overnight trips there is camping at the state's **Carolina Management Area.** Conditions vary according to the water levels (high water is from January to early April, with medium water as late as mid-June.), but there is a Class II chute just below the bridge at Carolina that must be scouted.

Wood River

The Wood River rises in West Greenwich (part of it is called the Fall River) and runs to the village of Alton, where it meets the Charles to form the **Pawcatuck River.** The total distance of this run is 16.5 miles, with five portages and water classifications of flat, quick and Class I waters. The best water conditions exist from January through May, but it is runnable most of the year below Rte. 165. You can start in the **Escoheag Management Area,** but that section is narrow and shallow. You can access from the bridge over Rte. 165 and after three and a half miles take-out on the left *before* the bridge at the Barberville Dam. There are then some Class I rapids and flat water to the dam at Wyoming. Take-out to the left and portage down Rte. 3. After a mile of quick and flat water there is a portage around an old mill. The river passes under I-95, and there is a state put-in on the west bank. There is a nice flat water run from here to **Woodsville Dam,** where the easiest portage is on the right. South of the dam when the river forks, keep to the left. The river deepens, then passes through a marshy area into the pond at **Alton Dam.** The take-out is on the right, close to the dam. A parking area is close to the intersection of Rte. 91 and the Alton-Woodsville Rd.

Pawcatuck River

The best access to the Pawcatuck is from the Wood River, south of the Alton Dam, for the 11.5-mile run to **Potter Hill Bridge.** There are three portages and two camping areas along the way. We don't suggest canoeing past Potter Hill because the conditions at White Rock can be extremely dangerous. Park at the Rte. 91 parking lot and carry along the right bank about 100 yards. After about three-quarters of a mile the **Charles River** joins from the left and the river is now officially the Pawcatuck (these name changes must keep mapmakers on their toes). About a mile downstream a broken dam at Burdickville has a short portage to the left. At this point the river runs almost due south into the **Burlingame Management Area,** where there is camping on the left. More camping is available shortly at **Indian Acres Camping Area.** Downstream, at **Bradford,** there is a fishing access near the Rte. 91 bridge. Approximately 150 feet past the bridge, portage to the right for a short distance around a dam. From this point there is a pleasant six-and-a-half mile flat-water paddle through an unsettled area to the take-out at Potter Hill. This section alone makes a nice short trip.

Golf

Richmond Country Club

The club is set in rural Richmond along the banks of the Wood River. The grounds of this new 18-hole par 71 club are meticulously maintained. Full facilities include pro shop, carts and a clubhouse with a lounge and restaurant (see page **107**). From Rte. 3 in Hope Valley, take Nichols Ln. east to North Switch Rd., following it to the club (when it passes under I-95 it becomes Old Switch Rd.). **Clubhouse (401) 364-9292, pro shop 364-9200.** Also in Richmond is the **Meadowbrook Golf Club**, at the **intersection of Rtes. 112 and 138.**

Hiking and Walking

Arcadia Wildlife Management Area

Thousands of acres of deciduous and coniferous forests broken by ponds and miles of streams make this a mecca for walkers and hikers. Access to the **Ben Utter Trail** is from the Escoheag Hill Rd., north from Rte. 16. A bit farther west, **Beach Pond** access is off Rte. 165. Dirt roads crisscross the interior of the area, with parking pull-outs near attractions such as **Breakheart Pond.**

In Richmond, the **John B. Hudson Trail** leads to **Breakheart Pond** through pine forest and mountain laurel thickets that are spectacular in late spring. Also on the trail are a tower with views of the area, an early-nineteenth-century cemetery (about three-quarters of a mile from the trailhead) and a fish ladder at the pond. Access this trail from Rte. 165 (Ten Rod Rd.) about two and a half miles west of the Rte. 3 intersection. Drive into the angled dirt lane on the north side of Rte. 165, and you will see a parking area that is out of sight of the main road. A trail map at the beginning of the trail shows the Hudson Trail and others in the area. This is about a three-mile walk, most of it on easy-to-traverse terrain.

Carolina Game Management Area (Richmond)

This is not a place to hike in the fall, when hunters play their part in game management,

but just about any other time of year you can enjoy this area's history, wildlife and fine examples of human provision for the preservation of other species. Intensive management techniques are used in this 1,875-acre tract of evergreen and deciduous forests and wetlands. Special plantings of berries and grains support birds and small mammals. **Carolina Trout Pond** offers good fishing.

Hikers should follow Rte. 138, then Rte. 112 south to Pine Hill Rd., which runs between Rte. 112 and Hope Valley Rd. A barred gate and parking area marks the beginning of the **Andrews Trail.** Stop for a moment to see century-old headstones in the small cemetery set amid fruit trees just west of the parking area and trailhead. **Andrews Trail** leads out past a field planted with bird-feeding grains, where **Nicoll Trail** enters on the left (east). The trail straight ahead leads past several more management fields, where birders are likely to find a good variety. If you take the left, Nicoll Trail, to another trail on the left, **White Brook Trail,** it will take you back to Pine Hill Rd. and to your car, a short walk to the left. If you go straight ahead at the intersection of the Nicoll and White Brook Trails you will come to the Pawcatuck River and two camping sites for canoeists. Just south of this trail intersection is a cellar hole on the left, and a bit beyond is another cemetery, with stones dating from the time when this was an active farm.

If you follow Pine Hill Rd. west from the parking area, you will cross over Meadow Brook and find **Meadowbrook Trail**—a dirt road—leading north. Follow this to the first left, which is **Shippee Trail.** Take Shippee to its intersection with **Essex Trail** at a gate. Follow Essex left to **Laurel Trail,** again on the left (south), where there is another gate. Take Laurel Trail south to Pine Hill Rd. From there it is a short walk to the left (east) back to the parking area. In the spring the laurels, which give the trail its name, bloom in profusion, a glorious sight you will share with mosquitoes. Think of these as bird food.

Fisherville Brook Wildlife Refuge

The Audubon Society of Rhode Island owns this 722-acre tract on both sides of the Pardon

101

The Rhode Island Guide

Joslin Rd. in Exeter. The five-plus miles of walking trails are level and easy, passing through woodlands of oak, beech and pine, along a pond and across wetlands on raised walkways (made of recycled postconsumer plastic). The parking lot is on the south side of Pardon Joslin Rd. Be sure to look at the garden that is specially designed to attract butterflies and hummingbirds.

From I-95 take Exit 5A in West Greenwich and follow Rte. 102 south (it actually runs east). At the town hall and library take Widow Sweets Rd. left to Pardon Joslin Rd. and go right. The parking lot is just past the bridge. From Rtes. 1 or 2 take Rte. 102 north, which actually leads west. (Are you still with us, or have you been distracted by wondering what stories these roads could tell of the people for whom they were named?)

Take the **Blue Trail** from the end of the parking lot near the kiosk. (The **Split Rock Trail,** with orange blazes, leads off to the left; the Blue Trail is in the center, and the return of the Blue Trail is to the right.) The wide grassy path passes through a white pine nursery, after which you should follow Blue Trail right to the dam at the end of **Upper Pond,** an old human-made pond that once powered a sawmill. The trail crosses the dam and follows the south shore of the pond before entering a wetland. At a stone wall, a side trail on the left leads to the eighteenth-century cemetery of the Gardners, early settlers of this area. Continuing on the main trail, you will cross a bridge over **Fisherville Brook** and pass the **Cedar Swamp Trail** (yellow blazes) on your left. This is a short side loop through an attractive wetland; it returns to Blue Trail at a T intersection. Regardless of which trail you take, it will bring you back to the parking lot. The Blue Trail is about a mile and a quarter without the yellow trail loop. By taking the Split Rock Trail east from the end of the parking lot, you can lengthen the walk by about three-quarters of a mile. Follow the orange blazes to the intersection with Blue Trail, which you follow from that point.

The refuge offers pleasant walking and a good chance of seeing a variety of birds, in-

cluding great blue herons and hooded mergansers. Painted turtles can also be found in the spring and summer. Across the street from the parking lot is a private residence that dates from the 1720s, once the home of this area's original settlers. Two trails lead from the driveway: the **Outer Loop Trail** (red blazes) and the **Inner Loop Trail** (white blazes). The Outer Loop is the most difficult trail in the refuge, leading through wetlands, then uphill through pines to a hardwood forest. The Inner Loop illustrates the reversion of farmland to forest.

Long Pond and Ell Ponds Natural Areas

In the northwest corner of Hopkinton, known as Rockville, the lands around Long and Ell Ponds are managed jointly by the Audubon Society, The Nature Conservancy and the state. Its 1974 citation as a National Landmark cites its exceptional value as an illustration of the nation's natural heritage. It's not an idle boast.

Not for the out-of-shape, the trail leads up and down some fairly steep hills and through a boulder-strewn ravine, so good hiking shoes are suggested. The round-trip along the ponds, returning on the same trail, is about two and a half miles through hillside forests of oak, birch, hickory and hemlock, with second-level growth of rhododendron and mountain laurel. Birds found in the area include hawks, scarlet tanagers, rose-breasted grosbeaks, woodpeckers and vireos.

Park off North Rd. and take the trail south to an intersection of trails. In the early summer this section is filled with rhododendron and mountain laurel blossoms, one of the finest and tallest groups in the state. At the top of the rocky climb (where you will go over and among giant boulders and outcrops) you can take either a short side trail to overlook Long Pond to the left or Ell Pond to the right. One of the rare true bogs in the state, this area has white cedar and other plant life unique to bog environments. Back at the intersection, the trail immediately drops through a huge break in the granite hillside into a very steep descent with tricky footing. Stones have been arranged to form very rough stairs, but be careful. At the bottom the trail passes through a low, wet and fragile area where wetland plants and trees predominate, another example of the diversity of environments here. The trail then rises again to an overlook at the west end of Long Pond and up, over and down steep hillsides and rocky cliffs along its south shore. We love this never-never land of magnificent hemlock forests, craggy cliffs and groves of rhododendron—one rock outcropping looks like a dragon. At the east end of the pond the yellow-blazed trail bears right to **Ashville Pond,** but we suggest you retrace your route back to the parking lot.

Fishing

Carolina Trout Pond

Located in the northern end of the **Carolina Game Management Area,** the pond is well stocked and scenic, with forest-lined banks. From Hope Valley (Rte. 3) south of the Rte. 138 intersection, take Nichols Lane to Hope Valley Rd. (also called Old Switch Rd. on some maps). South of this intersection, on the left, you will come to the Shippee Trail which you take to the first left. A sign points along a gravel road to the fishing area.

Wood River

The Wood River runs to the southern border of Exeter, where it forms the boundary between Richmond and Hopkinton. While we haven't fished this section personally, we are told that it is well stocked for good fishing, including salmon (15-inch minimum). You'll find a canoe put-in where the river crosses Arcadia Rd. Keep in mind that some maps refer to the river here as the Pawcatuc. You can canoe downstream or carry above the dam to **Frying Pan Pond.** In August the riverbanks here are covered with cardinal flower, and it's not unusual to find the nests of cedar waxwings. Just north of the bridge over the river, opposite Cherry Lane, is **Bob's Bass Fishing,** providing fishing and guide service in Rhode Island and southeastern Connecticut. Call **(401) 539-7340.**

You can get to Arcadia Rd. by going north from the intersection of Rtes. 138 and 3 (just west of Exit 3 on I-95).

Skiing

Yes, there *is* skiing in Rhode Island, at the **Yawgoo Valley Ski and Recreation Area** in Exeter. While the drop is measured in hundreds of feet, not thousands, there is a ski school for all ages, equipment rentals and access by two double-chair lifts and a small tow. During the summer Yawgoo offers other activities, including volleyball and a water slide. From Rte. 2 (South County Trail) on the south end of Exeter, take Yawgoo Valley Rd. east to the ski area. Call **(401) 295-5366** for conditions.

Seeing and Doing

Exeter Town Pound

For the early settlers a fence was made of whatever tree part or rock pile came to hand, so it was common for animals to break loose and wander about town, raiding gardens along the way. When found, these strays were taken to a special area surrounded by strong stone fences, where they were impounded until their owners claimed them and paid for the damage they had caused. A fine example of such a "pound" is on the north side of Rte. 102 in Exeter about a mile west of the Exeter town offices.

Queen's Fort

On the North Kingston–Exeter town line, Queen's Fort is one of the few remaining Indian structures on the East Coast. Its stone walls are the remains of fortifications built during the late 1600s by Stonewall John, an English-trained stonemason, to provide protection from the increasingly aggressive European settlers. Taking advantage of a steep rocky hillside thick with tumbled boulders and interspersed with tall trees, the fort was built so its walls enclose a large area with good views of anyone approaching. The circular stone walls of one small redoubt, four feet high and about six feet in diameter, remain near the high point of the hill. Walk the walls of the fort in order to appreciate how well it is sited. Below, on the hill on the road side of the fort is a jumble of huge glacial boulders called Queen's Chamber where Queen Quaiapen was believed to have taken refuge during King Philip's War. Also known as Matuntuck (a name you'll run into in this area), she left the fort only to be killed by the militia from Connecticut. While the site has had a few abusive visitors, it is in good condition, without any special protection or maintenance. Approach it from Rte. 2 just south of the Greenwich–North Kingston town line. Turn west onto Stoney Ln. at the traffic light (it's the first left if you came north from Rte. 102 and the second right if you came south from the town line). In about 1.2 miles you'll see a dirt lane on the south (left) side of the road, not far past a road entering from the right. Park and take the dirt lane, then the path left and uphill to a flat hilltop. There you will see a path downhill to the left toward a rock-strewn knoll. Keep to the left as the trail descends and rises again. The fort will be on the hillside ahead of you.

Kenyon Gristmill

Kenyon Gristmill began grinding grains for farmers in the same year that the American Revolution began. It was once one of many such mills, only a few remain, but Kenyon still actively uses the huge stone wheels to prepare flour. The people at the mill are glad to explain the process and tell the story of the mill and its owners. They also sell Rhode Island's famed jonnycake flour and stone-ground whole wheat and cornmeal. The mill is just off Rte. 138 in Usquepaugh on the Richmond–South Kingstown line. Call **(401) 783-4054** to make sure it's open if you're making a special trip.

Hope Valley Dam and Mill Site

Even in this remote area, eighteenth-century settlers dammed rivers and put them to work long before their descendants expanded the uses of the rivers to support factories. At Hope Valley the Wood River is impounded by an outstanding example of an early horseshoe dam. Erected about 1765, the dam is still impressive and strong. On either side of the stream are the ruined foundations of the mills that once used its stored power. Remnants of the sluiceway are still visible along the banks, and just over the edge of the wall at the end of the parking area you can see the remains of an old stone-arch bridge. Cross the river on Nichols Ln. (and into Richmond) and take the first right at North Switch Rd. At that corner from the woods rises a big square brick chimney, the ghost of yet another abandoned mill. The mill is on Mechanic St., which is just south of the intersection of Rtes. 138 and 3; the dam is on the left.

Farm Markets and Pick Your Own

During summer and fall, Rte. 102 is lined with farm stands offering fresh vegetables and fruits. Fresh corn is ready from August into the fall. Also available during August are pick-your-own peaches; apples are ready for picking from late August into the fall.

Schartner Farms

Farming has always been an integral part of life in Arcadia and an enduring example is the Schartner Farm in **Exeter**. Farming its own 120 acres along with some rented land off-site, this family operation comes as close to a year-round farm as is possible in the Northeast. Periodic programs teach kids about farming, and it's a good place for anyone to breathe country air and rediscover farm life, if only vicariously. Throughout most of the year, the farm sells seasonal fruit and vegetables, and in the autumn adds winter squashes and pumpkins plus decorative gourds and Indian corn. Also available are the farm's own bakery products and the jams and jellies to spread on them. You can pick your own bouquet in the flower fields for $4.50 or your own raspberries from the farm patch. On weekends they feature curly French fries made from their own potatoes. The farm is open Mar.– Dec., opening at 7:30 A.M. during the harvest season. It's on Rte. 2 in Exeter; **(401) 294-2044.**

Shopping

The Christmas House

On Rte. 165 in western Exeter is one of the largest Christmas stores in all of New England. Three floors of ornaments and decorations are displayed on dozens of theme trees. Ornaments are made of everything from plastic to thin iridescent glass. Santas abound, and collectibles include Annalee dolls, Byers' Choice Carolers, Department 56 lighted villages and an entire regiment of German nutcrackers. On the grounds is a village of playhouse-sized buildings, and during the holidays this is the scene of all sorts of seasonal displays and activities. Open Mon.–Sat. from 10 A.M.–5 P.M. and on Sun. from noon–5 P.M. After Labor Day, open on Sun. at 10 A.M. and closed on Thursday at 9 P.M. **1557 Ten Rod Rd. (Rte. 165), Exeter 02822; (401) 397-4255.**

Richmond Antique and Craft Marketplace

The shop has a large selection of antiques to chose from, spanning everything from fine early pieces to things our kids still have in the bottom of their toy box. It is also a center for local craftspersons. It's open every day, year-round, from 10 A.M.–6 P.M. From Exit 3A on I-95 take Rte. 138 east about 3 miles. **318 Kingston Rd.; (401) 539-0350.**

Hope Valley Antiques

This two-floor shop in a large and attractive nineteenth-century brick building has a collection of fine antique furniture and in quantities seldom seen elsewhere. The shop is nicely kept—it appears to be dusted daily. Secretaries, tables, beds, chairs, clocks and just about every variety of furniture can be found here. As you leave, be sure to notice the fine Victorian fretwork on the house across the street. Open Wed.–Sun. from 10 A.M.–4 P.M. **1081 Main St., Hope Valley; (401) 539-0250.**

Wood River Antique Center

This antique center is close to the center of the village of Hope Valley and carries a wide variety of antiques, from furniture to glass, toys to advertising, jewelry, military items, lighting and more. **1017 Main St., Hope Valley; (401) 539-0070.**

Hack And Livery General Store

From the outside the Hack and Livery looks like a general store, and the merchandise inside carries through on the theme. There are *lots* of jars of penny candy (now more than a penny, unfortunately), rock candy, preserves and jellies, country-store foods and other delectables. They also carry fine soaps, candles and a large variety of old-fashioned cooking gear, including wire pie stands. Upstairs is a Christmas shop with Annalee dolls, Department 56 villages and the Fontanini nativity collection. The shop is open daily from 10 A.M.–7 P.M., but from Jan.–July it is closed Mon. and Tues. **1006 Main St., Hope Valley; (401) 539-7033.**

Meadowbrook Herb Garden

Meadowbrook is one of the best-known herb gardens in the state. While it doesn't have large formal display gardens, visitors are welcome to stroll in the beds of herb plants meant for propagation and sale. The attractive shop sells teas, herbal toiletries and crafts, books, seeds, garden accessories of all kinds and tools, in addition to their organically grown live herb plants. Open Mon.–Sat. from 9:30 A.M.–5 P.M., Sun. from noon–4 P.M. **Rte. 138, Wyoming; (401) 539-7603.**

Morgan's Woodwork Shop

We stumbled across this small workshop well off the traveled path in Richmond while wandering aimlessly one afternoon and were impressed by the handmade rush-seat porch chairs. Along with the porch chairs are children's rockers, stools, lazy Susans and turned candlesticks, and a seat weaving and caning service. From the intersection of Rtes. 138 and 3 (just a short distance west of Exit 3 on I-95) go north on Rte. 3 to the second left, K G Ranch Rd. Morgan's Woodwork Shop is at **30 K G Ranch Rd., Hope Valley; (401) 539-7121.**

Where to Stay

ACCOMMODATIONS

Country Acres B&B—$$

You couldn't ask for nicer hosts than Weltha Hopkins and Michael Fayerweather, who share their modern home and backyard swimming pool with travelers. One of the rooms has a double bed and half bath, another a double and a single bed. These rooms share a full bath. Two more rooms downstairs share a bath. A hearty country breakfast is served in the kitchen, and on chilly evenings there's a fireplace to curl up by. In order to maintain the quiet of this intimate place, the policy is no children under 12 and no pets. Cash, travelers checks and personal checks are accepted. Michael is second councilman for the Narragansett tribe and an excellent source of information about the tribe. On Rte. 112 just south of Rte. 138. **P.O. Box 551, 176 Town House Rd. (Rte. 112), Carolina 02812; (401) 364-9134.**

Richmond-Inn The Woods—$$

This two-room B&B is deep in the country and surrounded by woods and quiet. In a two-level home, the inn section is on the first floor with access to the herb gardens and a meadow. The rooms share a sitting room with a woodstove, and there is a kitchenette as well as a gas grill on the patio for guest use. The rooms share a bath. Up to three children (minimum age 6) can be accommodated, but no pets are allowed. Rates are $68 per room, $12 per extra person, with discounts for longer stays. From Rte. 138 (east of I-95) take Rte. 112 south to the first left, Wilber Hill Rd., then the first left onto Deer Run Rd. When the road turns sharply to the east, take the dirt road on the left (Boulder Dr.) to the inn. **17 Boulder Dr., Carolina 02812; (401) 539-6021.**

The Cookie Jar—$$$

The core of this three-room B&B is an old blacksmith shop built in 1732. Originally part of a plantation, it now offers accommodations that are quiet, set amidst an orchard with over 50 fruit trees, berry bushes and gardens. The first-floor rooms have sinks and share a bath; the room on the second floor has a king bed, a full bed, sink and shower. They also have special rates for children, and all rates include a full breakfast. Pets are not accepted. On Rte. 138 about three-quarters of a mile east of I-95 Exit 3. **64 Kingstown Rd., Wyoming 02898; (401) 539-2680** or **(800) 767-4262.**

CAMPGROUNDS

Whispering Pines Campground

Whispering Pines is one of the nicest camping areas we've seen in the state. The 55-acre property is covered (not surprisingly) with tall pines that shade most of the sites. Campsite "floors" are covered with a layer of soft pine needles. Camper trailers, RVs and tents are all welcomed. Some areas are shared by RVs and tents, while other sections are reserved for tents only. Most of the 180 sites have electric, water and sewer hookups, and hot showers are available. There is a laundromat, ice, firewood and a well-stocked store, too. In addition to swimming, the facilities include miniature golf, a game room, a stocked fishing brook, horseshoes, basketball, baseball, canoeing and entertainment on many weekend nights. Distances are so short in Rhode Island that you can camp here even if you plan to spend most days at the beaches and wildlife areas on Block Island Sound. It's popular, so reservations are almost mandatory. No personal checks, but credit cards and cash are accepted. From the center of Hope Valley, take Rte. 138 west to Saw Mill Rd. Whispering Pines is at **P.O. Box 425, Saw Mill Rd., Hope Valley 02832; (401) 539-7011.**

Where to Eat

Richmond Country Club—$ to $$

Surrounded by the lush green of the Richmond Country Club, the clubhouse is open to the public for lunch and dinner. The dining room and the porch overlooking the greens and fairways offer sandwiches ranging from turkey (white meat only) to Reubens and clam rolls, all for under $5, and full lunch entrees under $10. The dinner menu has a wide range of seafood, with a baked scallop casserole, baked stuffed scrod, sole or shrimp. Meat dishes include Delmonico steak, surf and turf, veal (Marsala and Parmesan) and chicken offered in three styles: Parmesan, zingarella (with red peppers in cream sauce) and piccata (with mushrooms, scallions and a lemon white sauce). The dining room is handicapped-accessible. From Hope Valley, take Nichols Ln. east to North Switch Rd., following it to the sign; **(401) 364-9292.**

West's Bakery—$

At the center of Hope Valley, West's serves breakfast and lunch in a clean, friendly setting. Locals eat breakfast here: An egg sandwich is $1.05, or two eggs, sausage and toast is $2.50. Sandwiches are made on the bakery's own rolls. Ice cream specialties include the Turtle—a soft-serve vanilla sundae with pecans, hot caramel and hot fudge topped with chopped pecans—or the Black Forest—chocolate cherry ice cream with cherries, hot fudge and chocolate shavings. Breakfast is served from 5:00 A.M. (you won't find *us* there at that hour) to 11 A.M. and lunch until 5 P.M., Mon.–Sat., Sun. from 5:30 A.M.–2 P.M. This is a cash-only place. At the **corner of Main and Spring Sts. 995 Main St., Hope Valley; (401) 539-2451.**

Services

Several B&Bs in this area have joined in a referral group, so you can call one number to learn which have vacancies. Member lodgings are also located elsewhere in the South County region; **(800) 853-7479.**

107

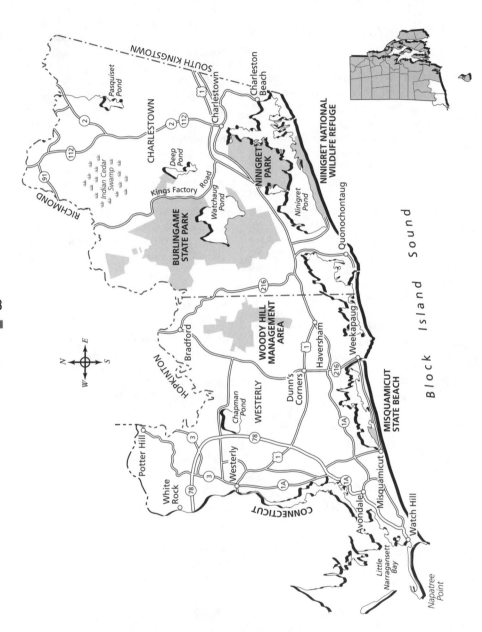

South Coast: Westerly and Charlestown

Westerly was built on a firm foundation: a bed of fine quality granite up to 80 feet thick, jutting to the surface on one end and sloping at an angle of about 10 degrees until the quarriable stone is over 50 feet below the surface. That layer of granite, while not the original reason for its settlement, became the foundation of the city's economy by the late nineteenth century. Westerly's appreciation for stone still shows in its buildings—which are by no means all constructed of native granite. Indiana limestone, Vermont marble and granite from Deer Island, Maine, join Westerly red and blue in the impressive structures lining the city's streets.

Small, lively and above all friendly, Westerly is the commercial center for an area that caters to summer tourists with sandy beaches, water sports and sailing harbors. Spring and fall, it attracts walkers and birders with its miles of seaswept beaches, salt ponds, and abundant migrating birdlife. Throughout the year an active arts community supports concerts, theater and other cultural events. From late April, front yards and gardens burst into bloom with bright forsythia, masses of flowering bulbs and magnolia, heralding a succession of bloom that lasts well into October and is visible in both public and private gardens throughout the area.

Although the boundaries of Westerly extend south to the shore of Block Island Sound and west in a long point that nearly encloses Little Narragansett Bay, the settlements in those

109

areas are known as Misquamicut and Watch Hill, respectively. Each of these has its own distinct character and geography, and although the traveler will move among them easily, they do seem like separate towns.

The Pawcatuck River, which appears to run through the center of Westerly, actually defines its western border. The downtown blocks across the bridge are in the Connecticut village of Pawcatuck, part of Stonington.

Charlestown sits to the immediate east of Westerly and was originally a part of it. Much of Charlestown is set aside as wildlife management areas, refuges or parks, the largest of which are Burlingame State Park and Ninigret

National Wildlife Refuge. Charlestown has a double shoreline, for a sand barrier lies along the entire length of its shore, behind which lie large saltwater ponds.

History

Westerly had a romantic beginning. In 1648, John Babcock, who worked for Thomas Lawton of Newport, fell in love with his employer's daughter, Mary. They eloped by open boat, traveling quite a distance along the shore and up the mouth of the Pawcatuck River before settling and building a home at the point where Mastuxet Brook flows into the Pawcatuck. For the first few years the Babcocks lived on the south side of the creek and the Indians on the north. Other settlers soon joined them, and by the end of the century, shipbuilding, fishing and agriculture were well established. Docks were built along the riverfront, and packet ships ran regularly from Westerly to New York. Fishing and whaling ships were built in Westerly until the middle of the nineteenth century. With the Industrial Revolution came mills, which used the river to power machinery. The Pawcatuck River would have given Westerly its fair measure of prosperity, but when Orlando Smith discovered the outcrop of granite in 1846 on the hilltop overlooking town, the granite industry quickly became the city's economic mainstay. More than 800 workers manned the quarries and stonecutting shops at their height.

The last Westerly granite quarried was used for the foundation and window and door frames of the addition to the Westerly Memorial Library in 1991. The drawings for the stonework were done by Ike Smith, grandson of the quarry's founder. Thus this building is probably the last large-scale use of Westerly red granite, because the source has been exhausted; much of what was used was salvaged from material quarried over 50 years ago.

Charlestown shares its early history with Westerly because Richmond and Hopkinton were all part of Westerly. The town's unwieldy size and the resulting difficulty in getting to

town meetings led to a series of divisions. It is interesting to note that the town was, by 1755, 37% nonwhite, with a large number of Narragansett Indians living in town. Many of their descendants still live there. Originally a town of farmers, at the end of the 1800s, its beaches and coastal ponds began to attract summer people. During World War II the area that is now Ninigret National Wildlife Refuge was the Charlestown Naval Auxiliary Air Facility, where Avenger torpedo bomber pilots trained for carrier and night landings.

Getting There

Westerly is three miles south of I-95, at the extreme southwest corner of Rhode Island. US 1 passes through it. **Amtrak** provides regular train service from New York (128 miles away) and Providence (40 miles away). The railway station is **at Canal and Railroad Sts.,** two blocks from the main square. A municipal airport just south of the center provides hourly flights to Block Island, just 12 minutes away by air. The part of town called Watch Hill is reached from Westerly via Rte. 1A to Avondale and from there via Watch Hill Rd. The villages of Misquamicut, Weekapaug and Shelter Harbor are on or just off Rte. 1.

Festivals and Events

Summer Pops, Chorus of Westerly
June

Everyone sits on the lawn-covered slopes surrounding the temporary stage built for this occasion. By 10 A.M., the park is filled with blankets and chairs—although not with people. Locals and well-prepared visitors bring blankets to leave spread on the grass, then go on about their business until about 4 P.M., when the chorus rehearses. Those who retire early come to hear the full rehearsal and stay for the concert at 6 P.M. given by the high school band. But all day people have drifted in and out, enjoying picnics, meeting friends. When the concert begins, not a blade of grass is showing between the blankets. The climax of the day is the Boston Festival Orchestra playing the 1812 Overture, accompanied by professional fireworks and the bells of the church across the street; **(401) 596-7761.**

Shakespeare in the Park
July

The Colonial Theater presents a free production of a Shakespeare play each summer. The Theater is a charter member of the Shakespeare Theatre Association of America and the productions draw audiences from across the country. Performances are held in beautiful **Wilcox Park** right in downtown Westerly during the month of July and are packed every night. For more about the Colonial Theater, see page **119.**

Narragansett Indian Pow Wow
August

On the second Sunday in August the Narragansett Indians hold the annual meeting of the tribe. Festivities, including dancing and rituals in full costume, take place at the Narragansett Indian Church and meeting grounds on age-old Indian lands near **Cedar Swamp** and **School House Pond.** The church, a small granite structure, was built in 1858 by a missionary to the tribe. Of three built, it is the only one remaining. It has not been open to the public since a fire damaged the interior. Take Rtes. 2 and 112 (South County Trail) a short distance north of Rte. 1 to Lewis Trail on the west side of the road and turn left.

Outdoor Activities

Parks and Recreation Areas

Westerly Town Forest

On the northwest corner of Westerly, the Pawcatuck River makes a long arc before turning south and heading to the ocean. In that section, known as **Potter Hill,** is a new 204-acre park where hiking, bicycling, canoeing and horseback facilities are in development. It preserves an attractive area abutting the river. The park is open daily from dawn to dusk. From Granite St. take Grove Ave. (Rte. 3) north. It turns into High St.; take Upper High St. north. After crossing Rte. 78, turn right on Potter Hill Rd., then left onto Laurel Ave. to the park entrance.

Napatree Point Conservation Area

At **Watch Hill, Napatree Point Beach** extends westward from the end of Bay St. While the beach and bathing facilities are privately owned, the point has a fine wildlife conservation area that extends a half mile out to the point. Wiry sea grass and wild rosebushes hold the sand from the wind and sea. Ospreys nest here. It's a fine example of a sandy dune–covered sand spit that protects the harbor. The

111

Napatree Point is the site of ruins of a fort from the Spanish-American War.

ruin of a Spanish-American War fort sits at the end. At the carousel end of Bay St., walk out toward the point, ignoring the ugly gray plywood wall and chain-link fences of the private beach club. Stay on the path to protect the dunes. The best time to come is on a fall, spring or even a sunny winter day. Parking is limited in town, so get there early.

Ninigret National Wildlife Refuge-Ninigret Park

Getting to any part of Ninigret can be somewhat of a problem if you are coming from the east and traveling west on Rte. 1. The highway is divided in this section, so you have to overshoot and drive back east on Rte. 1 to the entrances. When crossing into Charlestown, keep a careful watch for signs. Traveling east on Rte. 1, the wildlife refuge will be first, then the park. If this place seems a bit strange, with roads leading through fields for no apparent reason and an enormously long parking lot, the reason is that this was once the **Charlestown Auxiliary Naval Air Station.** The roads were once company streets between barracks and the parking lots tarmac or landing fields. During the height of World War II, navy pilots trained here for night flying and carrier landings, flying Avenger fighter bombers, Hellcats and Helldivers before heading off to the Pacific and war. A simple stone monument by the entrance memorializes the names of the 61 men who died here during training. Former President George Bush trained here before setting off to the Pacific. (An Avenger similar to the one he flew is at the **Quonset Air Museum;** see page **136.**) The base closed in 1972 and grass grows in the expansion joints of the runways. The spirit of Ninigret's war years seems to linger here; this is a fitting monument.

Ninigret National Wildlife Refuge is a strange combination of high-volume human activity and peace and quiet. It sits between a busy highway and the largest saltwater pond in the state. The western part of the land is the wildlife refuge, and the eastern part is accessed through the town-operated Ninigret Park. Across the pond, reached by a third road, Ninigret Beach constitutes a third part.

As you enter the eastern portion, signs direct you to fitness trails, nature trails, picnic areas, baseball fields, basketball courts and bicycle trails.

The town's Ninigret Park is heavily used, and it has an active senior center and a nature center with interpretive programs throughout most of the year. There are picnic areas, a pavilion, charcoal barbecue pits, a small swimming beach on the pond and a playground for the kids. The **Frosty Drew Observatory,** a celestial observatory open year-round on clear Friday nights, is billed as the "best buy in town." They ask only a small donation. The Nature Center, directly opposite the observatory, is a good place to start and pick up trail maps, information on migration dates and informative interpretive programs.

The eastern part of Ninigret National Wildlife Refuge, on Ninigret Pond behind Ninigret Park, is 407 acres of mixed environments. Grasslands, wooded swamps, emergent forests, and fresh- and saltwater ponds are protected across Ninigret Pond by a barrier beach that makes the pond into a nursery for fish and waterfowl. Swans, ducks, cormorants and a full panoply of resident birds from woodcock to the endangered yellow-breasted chat nests or passes through here (see page **114**).

On the western end, trails wander out over the grasslands to the shore and a point overlooking **Foster Cove** on the pond. In this part of the refuge the trails are for walkers; bicycles are not allowed. On the eastern end is access to a saltwater marsh area and to **Grassy Point,** where you can watch the wildlife and landscape from an observation tower. The vegetation along the paths is thick, filled with small trees, brambles, wild roses and vines that provide cover and food for small birds and mammals.

There is a different view of the area's wildlife from **Ninigret Beach.** A long sandbar stretches along the shore, creating miles of barrier beach good for beachcombing and walking. It runs all the way from **East Beach** to the **Charlestown Breach,** the opening of Ninigret Pond to the sea, almost at the South Kingstown line. At times thousands of starfish wash up on the shores, and since this is an important breeding ground for fish and shellfish, shells can be found along the shore as well. It is a fine example of a sandy, marshy, intertidal zone. For access information, see page **115**. Horses, dogs and other pets are prohibited. Ninigret National Wildlife Refuge, **U.S. Fish and Wildlife Service, Shoreline Plaza, P.O. Box 307, Charlestown 02813; (401) 364-9124.** Office hours are from 8 A.M.–4:30 P.M. weekdays.

Burlingame State Park and Wildlife Management Area

More than 3,100 acres have been set aside for recreational and wildlife management just north of Ninigret. The area is divided into two sections: the state park, with more intensive use, and the management area, where the uses are less intensive.

Burlingame State Park has a public swimming area on **Watchaug Pond,** an area that is also a good one for canoeing, boating and fishing. There are also picnic facilities for day visitors and a large campground. The park surrounds Watchaug Pond, and trails travel around it. A fee is charged for use of the state park, and the area and facilities of the campground are not available to noncampers. Access this part of the park from the westbound lane of Rte. 1 onto an unmarked piece of Old Post Rd. at the west end of Ninigret Pond. If you miss the first turn, there is another a short way on, just past East Beach Rd. on your left. From it take Klondike Rd., and then the entrance road for the park on your right.

The management-area section is more remote. You are more likely to find such mammals as coyote, fox, white-tailed deer, rabbit and muskrat here, as well as wild turkey and other forest birds. Two human-made marshes are designed to provide increased habitat for the wildlife. A word of caution: Management areas are intended for hunting, so don't plan to visit here in the autumn. If in doubt, check with the Department of Environmental Management. This area is past the state park entrance, up Klondike Rd. to Rte. 216 (Ross Hill Rd.). Take that route a short distance to Buckeye Brook Rd., and follow Buckeye about two miles to the entrance, which is on the left.

A third area of the park is accessible on the east side of Watchaug Pond, but it abuts another area. For information on that area, see the following section on Kimball Wildlife Refuge. **Rhode Island Department of Environmental Management, Division of Parks & Recreation, Burlingame State Campground, 75 Burlingame Park Rd., Rte. 1, Charlestown 02813; (401) 322-7994** or **322-7337 (summers), 277-2632 (off-season).**

Kimball Wildlife Refuge

Abutting Burlingame State Park, the Kimball Refuge covers 29 acres close to the south shore of Watchaug Pond. The refuge is wooded and has kettleholes. These are depressions in the ground, left when huge pieces of the last glacier were buried in the accumulating gravels as the glacier retreated. When the huge ice chunks melted, they left voids that collapsed. One of these kettleholes is filled with water: **Toupoyesett Pond,** in the southeast corner on the orange-blazed trail.

The trails of the refuge wander through fields, woods and along the sides of ponds. There is also an attractive memorial garden along the blue-blazed trail that begins opposite the Nature Center. It attracts hummingbirds and butterflies in season. Trail maps are available at the nature center, as are scheduled programs for adults and children on weekends throughout the spring, summer and fall. If you're here in the spring, be sure to look for the many varieties of wildflowers growing, including lady's slippers.

Kimball Refuge is also the best access for the **Vin Gormley Trail,** an eight-and-a-half-mile trail through Kimball Refuge and around Watchaug Pond through Burlingame Park with marshland, woodland and shore walking. The Vin Gormley Trail has yellow markers; pick it up on the right side of the road as soon as you enter the gates.

To get to the Kimball Refuge, take Prosser Trail to the right from the westbound lane of Rte. 1. Follow it 0.6-mile to Montauk Rd. on the left, then turn left at the end of that road. The refuge is operated by the **Audubon Society of Rhode Island, 12 Sanderson Rd.,**

113

Smithfield 02917. Kimball Wildlife Refuge, 180 Sanctuary Rd., Charlestown 02813. For program information, call **(401) 783-4369, 792-6664, 783-5254** or the society offices at **949-5454.**

Birding

In Westerly, the **Napatree Point Conservation Area** is a good place to view ospreys and during the migration seasons it also has large flocks of migratory fowl. It is particularly well known for the number and variety of migrating hawks in the autumn. On the harbor side of the point are tall poles with osprey nests, and in the cove itself are often several varieties of ducks. There are, of course, gulls everywhere.

In Charlestown, **Weekapaug Beach** runs between the Atlantic Ocean and **Quonochontaug Pond,** a wonderful habitat for shorebirds such as cormorants. During the migration seasons most of the migrating species of ducks, geese and loons, as well as several species of sandpipers, are found here. During the winter grebes, scoters and even eiders can be found.

The entire **Ninigret National Wildlife Refuge** offers outstanding bird-watching. During migration in the spring and fall canvasbacks, goldeneyes, buffleheads and red-breasted and common mergansers are among the varieties of duck spotted. You'll also find Canada geese and an occasional swan or loon. In addition to the many songbirds that inhabit the thickets of undergrowth are the yellow-breasted chat, warblers, flickers, robins, woodcock, cormorants, several species of gull, sandpipers, plovers, ospreys, marsh hawks and the seldom-seen bald eagle (see page 112 for refuge access information, and page 115 for Ninigret Beach access through East Beach). Migration dates for this part of the state are: Waterfowl from March, April and August–September; shorebirds from April–June and August–September; raptors from April–May and September–October. Parking is limited to three hours and in summer is restricted to town residents. There is no sign in the winter months.

Fishing

In Westerly the best surf casting is off of **Westerly State Beach** on the barrier beach that protects Winnapaug Pond. From Rte. 1A (Shore Rd.) take Winnapaug Rd. south to the beach, then turn left on Atlantic Ave. along Westerly State Beach. Fishing is off the eastern part of the beach. There is also good fishing farther along the shore at the **Quonochontaug Pond** breach. If you are on Atlantic Ave., continue on over the outlet of Winnapaug Pond, and at the next intersection turn right onto Wawaloam Ave., which turns into Ninigret Ave. in a short distance. If coming from Rte. 1A, take Weekapaug Rd. (in some places this is referred to as Noyes Neck Rd.) west of Shelter Harbor. It turns into Wawaloam and then Ninigret Ave. The road peters out at the barrier beach of Quonochontaug Pond; walk up the breach to the beach. All of this beach is privately owned, but the public is allowed to use it. There is no parking here in summer, so it's best to come in spring or fall. There is also boat fishing in the pond.

A bit farther east, the miles of barrier beach of **Ninigret Beach** offer more surf-fishing opportunities, and **Ninigret Pond,** the largest saltwater pond in the state, offers a different kind of fishing. Ninigret Pond is a nursery for quahog clams, oysters, scallops, eel, flounder and many other species. Note, however, that clamming and shellfish-gathering require special licenses, and that there are size limitations for some species of fish. For access to the beach area, see page 115 for information about **East Beach.**

There is also some good freshwater fishing at **Watchaug Pond** in **Burlingame State Park.** The state campground there has a special area for fishermen near the ramp (see page 113).

Swimming

Westerly's largest beach is **Misquamicut State Beach,** on the south shore. Access the beach from Rte. 1A (Shore Rd.) by taking

Winnapaug Rd. south to Atlantic Ave. The beach has a 3,000-car parking lot, but on weekends and holidays it fills fast. There are state fees for use of the facilities. The beach has areas for body- and board surfing.

Charlestown's shorefront is a continuation of Westerly's and offers a number of good beaches. On the west end, closest to Westerly, take East Beach Rd. from Rte. 1 to reach **Sam Ferretti Blue Shutters Town Beach** (straight ahead when the road meets the sea) and the state-run **East Beach** (just down Beach Rd. to the left). Both beaches are accessible all year, and in the summer they have lifeguards. Sam Ferretti Blue Shutters has a bathhouse and concessions. Both are beautiful sandy beaches with surf that tends to be heavy, especially East Beach, which is covered at high tide. East Beach is a barrier beach that protects saline Ninigret Pond behind it, which is used for windsurfing and canoeing. On the other side of the breach, which opens Ninigret Pond to the sea, is **Charlestown Beach,** reached from Rte. 1A (Old Post Rd.). At the fire station take Matunuck Schoolhouse Rd. a short distance, and then take Charlestown Beach Rd. to its end. The beach has lifeguards and a fee in the summer but is accessible all year. The beach extends to the east into South Kingstown and abuts **Green Hill Beach,** but the road doesn't go through. If you follow Charlestown Beach Rd. to the west at the shoreline, it will take you to **Charlestown Breachway,** also open all year, with a boat launch and a small open beach with lifeguards and rest rooms, and a use fee.

There is a freshwater beach in **Burlingame State Park.**

Seeing and Doing

Historical Sites

Babcock-Smith House

This outstanding eighteenth-century colonial home has double historic value for the town of Westerly. Built about 1732, its owner, Dr. Joshua Babcock, was a longtime physician in

town, its first postmaster (he was a friend of Benjamin Franklin), a member of the state legislature and chief justice of the state supreme court for 16 years. His home has a wealth of outstanding architectural features, particularly the handsome carved spiral newel post and the raised paneling in the stairway and in the parlor. The building is furnished with fine quality antiques, many from the Babcock and Smith families. Dr. Babcock's property was bought by Orlando Smith in 1848, who discovered here the high-quality granite that made Westerly one of the most important granite quarrying and processing centers of its time. Open Sun. from 2–5 P.M. in May–June and Sept.–Oct.; in July–Aug. on Wed. and Sun. from 2–5 P.M. It can also be seen by appointment. A nominal donation is requested. **P.O. Box 91, 124 Granite St. (Rte. 1), Westerly 02891; (401) 596-4424.**

Westerly Public Library and Civil War Memorial

The late nineteenth century saw most New England towns erecting Civil War memorials and at the same time building their first public libraries. Steven Wilcox, a wealthy inventor and industrialist, combined the two ideas and added a multipurpose building with a bowling alley in the cellar, a mineral collection and meeting rooms. The building is in the Richardson Romanesque style popular at the turn of the century and is built of brick and red Westerly granite. The library serves as the attic of the town, the archive for manuscripts, diaries, ledgers and daybooks from several centuries, as well as documents, business records, photographs, tools and oral histories from the quarry days. These records list all the monuments ordered, their designer and cutter and the dates of shipment. Towns that have lost track of the sources of their own Civil War monuments often conduct research here. The library also has a public art gallery. The library is open Mon.–Wed. from 8 A.M.–9 P.M., from 8 A.M.–5 P.M. on Sat. and from 8 A.M.–3 P.M. on Sun. On Granite St., next to the handsome granite post office.

115

Wilcox Park

Wilcox Park, a Victorian strolling park, is behind the library in downtown Westerly. In late April, when the magnolia blossoms fall like snow and the little blue squills and violets spring up amid the thick grass of the lawns, you can almost see the starched nannies pushing wicker prams along the walkways. A wide variety of exotic and native trees, including a regal pawlonia and a dawn redwood, earn the park its classification as an arboretum as well as a public garden. Benches face the pond, where you will usually find children feeding the ducks, and throughout the park picnics (alas, sans wine) are allowed. Bicycles are welcome, although pedestrians always have the right of way. Skates or skateboards are not welcome. Next to the caretaker's house, which faces into the park, is a raised-bed garden for the blind with braille labels and plants rich in texture and scent.

In summer Wilcox Park is a center for cultural activities, including Summer Pops Concerts and Shakespeare in the Park (see page 111). Although you'll hear the sounds of children laughing, you shouldn't have your reverie interrupted by boom boxes, since park rules forbid "electronic sound systems." This is a thoroughly lovely place right in the center of the city, made possible by the generosity of the Wilcox family and still privately maintained. Harriet Wilcox donated the land for the park in memory of her husband, the benefactor of the Westerly Memorial Library. The fountain in the park is lovingly called "Harriet" in her honor. Open daily from dawn to 11 P.M.

Westerly Railroad Station and Westerly Armory

The station was built during the heyday of the railroads in 1912. It's a single-story rambling building of granite and stucco-covered brick, and, unusual for New England, it has a red tile roof. Take High St., in front of the post office, to Canal St., then a left onto Canal to Railroad St. on the right. Across the street on the corner of Dixon St. is the red-brick and white-granite Westerly Armory, built in 1902, in Norman revival style, at each corner of the main building there is an octagonal tower topped with battlements.

Old Westerly Town Hall

A handsome building when it was new in 1872, it is abandoned and sad today but still bears the mark of good architecture. Plans exist to restore it and turn it into a town museum, a fine idea that we applaud. It's on Union St. just off Granite St., across from the new town hall and courthouse, which date from 1912.

Florence Nightingale's Cap

The **Westerly Hospital** has a display in the lobby that includes a nurse's cap worn by Florence Nightingale, as well as a book of her writing; **(401) 596-6000.**

Westerly Granite

Out Granite St., behind Ray Hoxsie Buick, is a large quarry hole that was first opened in 1846. There are quarry holes in several places around town. This quarry operated for over 90 years. The granite building on the corner of Tower St. served as the company store. While most of the industry closed by the late 1940s, one cutter still operates: Richard Commoli's sheds are north of town on Rte. 3, on the right just over the Meetinghouse Bridge. His father, Ferrucio Commoli, cut the granite bear that is the symbol of Bowdoin College in Maine. Many of the houses on John St., off Granite St., belonged to stonecutters. You can tell which they are: They have the best granite steps and walkways. The Smith granite works produced the main monument at the Antietam Battleground (which was exhibited at the Philadelphia Centennial Exposition in 1876) and more than 250 other monuments at the same battleground. At Gettysburg there are 62 Westerly monuments. Other examples are closer, at **Riverbend Cemetery.**

Riverbend Cemetery

The late nineteenth and early twentieth centuries were the high point for the carving of memorial cemetery monuments, and Riverbend has some fine ones. Look for the Langworthy plot, with an outstanding granite angel on a cross done by one of the finest area stonecutters, Angelo Zeberini. It was his last work. The cemetery, which rises gently from the river, has trees and shrubs along with its granite art, a fine Victorian cemetery park. It is on Beach St. (Rte. 1A) south of the center of Westerly, opposite Riverview Ave.

Watch Hill

This village occupies a narrow spit of rock and sand that juts out into Block Island Sound to form the boundary with Connecticut. Beautiful old "cottages" fill the town, built by wealthy New York, Connecticut and Rhode Island families who summered here in a style only slightly less opulent than that of Newport. The small business district on Bay St. overlooks Watch Hill Cove and its yacht club moorings. The sidewalk in front of the turn-of-the-century stores is covered with a colonnaded porch. In summer the village is crowded and busy, and it is almost impossible to find a parking space. The best time for wandering around is in spring or early fall, when the warm weather is still there but the crowds are not. On Bluff Ave. be sure to look at **Ocean House,** one of the last operating, or even existing, "grand" beach hotels from the last century. A little bit tired-looking now, it still has the majesty of a grand dame. Just past the hotel, a little street leads to the beach, where you can get a wonderful view of the hotel, the lighthouse and a fine sandy beach. Note the little round birdhouse in the marsh to the left. Walk or drive out Niantic Ave., Ocean View Highway and Manatuck Ave. for the best views.

Bronze Statue of Chief Ninigret

In front of the harbor at Watch Hill, a bronze statue of Chief Ninigret is posed kneeling on one knee, holding a fish in each hand. The statue was given to the community by Mrs. Clement Grisom and was modeled in Paris by Enid Yandell. Buffalo Bill's Wild West Show was playing in Paris at the time, and one of the show's Indian performers was used as a model for the statue.

Lighthouse

Watch Hill's handsome granite lighthouse sits on a point that extends out into Block Island

Sound. The original lighthouse was built in 1808, the present one in 1856, and the lamp was changed from oil to electricity only in 1933. During the War of 1812 the young Oliver Hazard Perry almost ended his career when his coastal patrol boat wrecked on the rocks here. In 1872 the steamer *Metis* collided with the schooner *Nettie Cushing*, sinking quickly. Thirty-three of its 100 passengers were saved by local men who manned a lifeboat that had been unused for 23 years. The lighthouse is approached from Larkin Rd. by the carousel. The best views are from Niantic Ave. and the beach.

Fort Mansfield

At the end of **Napatree Point** are the remains of Fort Mansfield, built during the Spanish-American War but abandoned after World War I. When it was new there were over 50 buildings in the fort. Now only low walls and circular gun emplacements mark the site (see pages **111–112**).

Flying Horse Carousel

During the nineteenth century, Rhode Islander Charles Looff invented the carousel, and over 3,000 were built around the world. Only 150 remain in the United States, and one of the earliest is at Watch Hill. It is thought to date from 1876. It was originally drawn from place

117

Even birds have custom-built mansions in Watch Hill.

to place by a horse, which also provided the power to turn it. Now permanently settled and motorized, its hand-carved and brightly painted wooden horses are different from most—suspended on chains to swing out as speed increases. This gave the carousel the name "flying horse." The saddles are real leather, and the tails are made of real horse-tail hair. It is said that the original horse that took the carousel from place to place was memorialized at his death by having his tail hairs implanted in one of these carousel horses. Rides on the carousel are limited to children under 12 years. You can see it any-time, but it's open for rides in mid-June–Labor Day, Mon.–Fri. from 1–9 P.M., Sun. and holidays from 11 A.M.–9 P.M. At the **end of Bay St., Watch Hill (Westerly) 02891; no phone.**

Fort Ninigret

This park was the site of an early Dutch fort dating from the seventeenth century. Abandoned by then Dutch, it was used by the Niantic and Narragansett Indians and may be the place where they met Captain John Mason to create an alliance to destroy the Pequot tribe. It sits overlooking **Fort Neck Pond,** a large cove of the tidal **Ninigret Pond.** You can see the worn remains of the rubble earthworks and the shallow moat that protected the fort. A stone monument at the corner of Rte. 1A and Fort Ninigret Rd. memorializes the Niantic and Narragansett Indians as "unwavering friends and allies of our fathers." Get to the fort from Rte. 1 in Charlestown by taking Rte. 1A (Old Post Rd.), almost parallel to Rte. 1. Turn onto Fort Ninigret Rd. at the monument.

Royal Indian Burying Ground

This is believed to be the burying place of the great colonial-era sachem Ninigret and his family. An iron railing surrounds the simple unmarked stones. It sits on a high spot in an undeveloped state park, and although it was once open ground, there are now many small sapling trees growing among the stones. A quiet place, it seems almost lost in the woods. From Rte. 1 just west of the Charlestown-South Kingston line, take Narrow Ln. north.

The roadway may not be marked. It's just opposite the Sunset Motel. Go 0.7-mile on Narrow Ln. and look for a small dirt lane on the left just past a sand pit and 0.2-mile from Old Coach Rd. (on the right). There is no sign. Follow the path as it winds up a small hillside to the site.

Charlestown Naval Auxiliary Air Station

During World War II the U.S. Navy needed increasing numbers of trained pilots. When the facilities at **Quonset** (see page **136**) were inadequate, the navy took farmland along the southern shore to create Charlestown Naval Auxiliary Air Station. Today **Ninigret Park** and **Ninigret National Wildlife Refuge** cover its grounds. While most of the buildings are gone, there are lots of reminders, including the runways where fighters and bombers trained for the war in the Pacific (see page **112**).

The Arts

Artists Cooperative Gallery Of Westerly

The gallery, (next to Kelly's Deli) in the Arcade, gathers together works by several local artists in a gallery setting. The media and style of the artists vary widely. Special shows are run periodically. Open Tues.–Fri. from 10 A.M.–5 P.M., Sat. from 10 A.M.–4:30 P.M. and Sun. from 11 A.M.–2 P.M. **High St., Westerly; (401) 596-2020.**

Chorus of Westerly

When the Immaculate Conception parish decided to build a new church down the street, they left behind a wooden structure with the finest acoustics of any building in town. The Westerly Chorale, active since 1959, raised the money to buy the building as a permanent home and concert hall. In addition to their two regular classical concerts—Christmas Pops Concert and Twelfth Night Celebration—they are the star attraction at the annual Summer Pops Concert in Wilcox Park (see page **116**); **(401) 596-8663.**

Colonial Theater

For more than a dozen years the Colonial Theater has presented a varied program of live professional drama, comedy and musicals. Its home, a handsome converted nineteenth-century Greek revival church, sits overlooking Wilcox Park. The season runs from the last week of April to just after Labor Day. Special productions run between Thanksgiving and Christmas, such as *A Christmas Carol*. The programs vary from Gilbert and Sullivan to musicals such as Cole Porter's *Anything Goes* or *The Fantasticks*. The theater also runs a very popular Shakespeare festival during July (see page **111**). Performances are Thur.–Sat. at 8 P.M. and Sun. at either 2 or 5 P.M. A dinner and theater special is offered at times during the summer. There are also special children's programs and a children's play at the end of August. The theater is on Granite St. (Rte. 1) in the center of town. Park at Christ Church, Central Baptist Church, Washington Trust Parking Garage or the town lot next to the post office. Tickets run from $15 to $20. **3 Granite St., Westerly 02891; (401) 596-0810.**

Shopping

Watch Hill

In addition to its beaches, Watch Hill is noted for the number and quality of its many small shops and boutiques, nearly all of which are on Bay St. **Puffins** is an interior design shop with accessories and gifts for the home; **(401) 596-1140. Honore M. Sullivan** is a specialty import store with pottery and accessories. **Shell Boutique** has, of course, shell jewelry and crafts, and **Comina** specializes in international furniture, accessories and artwork; **(401) 596-3218. Pumpkin Seed** has jewelry, plus one of the largest selections of children's tea sets we have ever seen. **Watch Hill Gourmet** has a big selection of kitchen accessories and exotic packaged foods. **Small Axe Productions,** next to the carousel, has both domestic and foreign goods from pottery and mugs to clothing; **(401) 348-1050. Book and Tackle Shop,** also close to

Watch Hill retains its exclusive air, with mansions overlooking its beaches.

the carousel, has thousands of old and rare volumes; **(401) 596-1770.** Nearby, **Farruska's** has a mixture of Moroccan and French-design clothing, china, brass and jewelry; **(401) 348-0047.** Almost all of the businesses are seasonal and close during the winter. They begin opening in April, and most are open by mid-May. Some shops close after Labor Day, but many remain open through December. While wandering around shopping, you can get quick snacks at **Biagio's Pizza,** hidden in a corner opposite the carousel and specializing in stromboli, calzoni and—pizza. For a sandwich, try **Bay Street Deli,** which also has hot pretzels. **The Village Bakeshop** has doughnuts, scones, muffins, turnovers and other pastries as well as coffee, or try **141 Bay St.,** where they have pastries and also ice cream. The oldest ice cream place is **St. Clair Annex,** which has been making its own ice cream since 1880.

The Fantastic Umbrella Factory

This collection of shops is one of the most unusual shopping centers you'll find anywhere. The three main buildings were erected between 1790 and 1870 together with several more recent accretions that look equally rustic. The shops carry a diverse collection: vintage clothing and accessories, jewelry, local and imported crafts, candles, Andean handknit sweaters, Guatemalan crocheted bags, art supplies, African carvings, drums, flutes, pottery (from flower vases to full dinner services) and collections of other things you never knew about or imagined. Bob Marley music sets the mood. Exotic birds walk the grounds or can be seen in their cages, or you can wander in the gardens of hardy perennials, also for sale. If you get hungry, try the **Spice of Life Cafe**, where the food is good and prices are reasonable. The whole place is a trip back to the sixties, and you'll see "stuff" you haven't seen elsewhere. The factory is open all year from 10 A.M.–6 P.M. daily from June–Labor Day and Thanksgiving–Christmas, and on Wed.–Sun. from Sept.–Thanksgiving and Jan.–June. Take Old Post Rd. on the south side of Rte. 1 just east of the Rte. 216 intersection. There are *two* old Post Rd. sections here, and you want the western one. **Old Post Rd., Charlestown; (401) 364-6616.**

Charlestown Village Shops

This small shopping center fills a log-cabin village—each shop is settled into its own small log cabin in a tree-covered setting. Rhode Island's own chocolate company, **Sweenor's,** is here, making its own chocolates and other candies. One of its specialties is a "Choco-hog," its own version of the quahog clam, made of chocolate and bedded in "seaweed." The other shops sell country furniture, wool products and Christmas decorations. **Rte. 1, Charlestown; (401) 364-3339.**

Where to Stay

For bed and breakfast accommodations throughout the southern part of the state, you can call one number to reserve a room or check availability. This saves making a number of calls to locate a room; **(800) 853-7479.**

ACCOMMODATIONS

Ocean House—$$$$

Bates bedspreads remind us of 1950s dorm rooms, but for all its fading grandeur, Ocean House is a rare piece of seaside Americana, one of very few grand hotels remaining. Rattan easy chairs fill its rather bare public rooms, but the view from its wraparound porch is splendid—across the lawns to the sea and the lighthouse. The restaurant is on the lower terrace. A fine beach is reserved for guests, who can check out as late as 5 P.M. on Sundays and holidays. Ocean House is open only from late June to Labor Day. Rates include breakfast and dinner; the European plan (no meals) is $20 per room per day less. Amenities are few, but rooms are bright and sun-filled, and the location is only a block from the harbor and shops of Watch Hill. **2 Bluff Ave., Watch Hill 02891; (401) 348-8161.**

The Inn at Watch Hill—$$$ to $$$$

Nicely appointed rooms arranged in a single row overlooking the harbor and main street appear more like a motel than an inn but make up for the lack of a lobby or public rooms by offering amenities such as Murphy beds for extra guests, microwaves, cafe tables and balconies. The roof of the Arcade over the historic harbor shops forms the balconies, each of which overlooks the pleasure boat harbor. An ocean beach, restaurants, boutiques and the historic carousel are within easy walking distance, as are the beach paths of a nature reserve. While the location may sound noisy, the shops close early and the town is quite sedate in the evening because it attracts an older crowd. Kitchenettes in each room have microwaves, sinks and refrigerators, but no dishes.

You'll need to reserve early, since many of the guests have been coming back for years. The managing family is particularly responsive to the individual needs of guests. A shower and changing room is available for guests who wish to stay at the beach on check-out day.

Weekday rates are less than those on weekends, and off-season rates during the spring and fall (both very mild here) are almost half the high-season rates. Weekly rates for seven consecutive nights are also lower. Open from May–October. **118 Bay St., Watch Hill (Westerly) 02891; (401) 596-0665.**

The Villa—$$ to $$$$

Clearly, The Villa is no ordinary B&B, as you can see the minute you start up the driveway. The grounds are alive with flowers, and a fountain springs from the center of the swimming pool. Rooms, some of which are suites, are just as impressive—each is individually decorated with stylish flair and a real eye for color. Each has some unique feature—skylight, working fireplace, Jacuzzi, kitchenette, ocean view, private garden. Homebaked breakfasts are served on the poolside terrace in the summer, and arriving guests are welcomed with such treats as strawberry shortcake. The Verona Suite is for incurable romantics, but any room here is designed for a getaway à *deux.* **Shore Rd. (Rte. 1A), Misquamicut (Westerly); (401) 596-1054.**

Pleasant View Inn—$$$$

Balconies overlook the beach from most of the rooms in this three-story shingled hotel that sits right on the beach. A lifeguard watches over hotel guests, who have exclusive use of one of the finest stretches of sand and surf in the state. For those who don't like the sand, there's a pool, too. This family-owned and operated hotel has been in business close to 50 years but was completely redone after a recent hurricane washed the sea through its lobby. Not exactly how we'd choose to do *our* fall house cleaning. The beachfront location and family clientele mean that rooms get heavy wear during the season, but they are well-kept, clean and bright. For beach-lovers, the location couldn't be better. The restaurant overlooks the sea. From Rte. 1A just west of Watch Hill take Winnapaug Rd. to the beach, then turn left to **65 Atlantic Ave., Misquamicut (Westerly), 02891; (401) 348-8200** or **(800) 782-3224.**

Breezeway Motel—$$$ to $$$$

While this neat and trim motel looks small from the road, what you see is only the front of a spacious quadrangle surrounding a courtyard with pool, poolhouse, a sundeck and immaculately kept lawns. Watchful parents have a good view of play areas from balconies and terraces surrounding the courtyard. Fountains, gardens and ornamental trees turn the grounds into a parklike setting. Rooms are just as perfectly manicured, although not fancy in decor. Several rooms have cooking facilities, two have whirlpools. Cabins and suites are also available. Continental breakfast is served in the poolhouse, and you can get special packages that include other meals at the Bellone family's nearby restaurant, **Maria's** (see page **125**). Free parking at the beach, umbrellas and chairs are available at the restaurant as well. Family-owned for more than 25 years, this place gets a lot of personal attention, and it shows. Open Apr.–Oct. The best rates are in April, May, September and October, about half the high-season rate. Weekly rates offer savings as well. **Winnapaug Rd., Misquamicut (Westerly) 02891; (401) 348-8953.**

Winnapaug Inn—$$ to $$$$

The attractive modern building takes full advantage of the views over the neighboring 18-hole golf course and a farm, where guests can watch sheep gambol. Most rooms have balconies, and all have TV, radios and refrigerators. A family-owned inn. The outstanding upkeep of the well-designed, recently decorated rooms makes them equal in quality to far more expensive lodgings. The entrance lobby is small and very plain; the decorating energy seems to have been spent on the rooms and pool area. The property is a favorite of golfers, who can't get much closer to the course than this.

Guests get complimentary passes to the ocean beach, only a mile away. The heated pool has an attendant, changing rooms and showers, and shuffleboard, swings and a game room are available. The inn has handicapped-accessible rooms, designated smoking rooms and is glad to have children, but no pets. Open Mar.–Thanksgiving. **169 Shore Rd. (Rte. 1A), Misquamicut (Westerly) 02891; (401) 348-8350, (800) 288-9906, fax (401) 596-1297.**

Grand View—$$ to $$$

If you prefer the homey comforts of a B&B and the quiet of the country, this is a perfect place to settle in for a while. The host, Pat Grande, is as gregarious as she is helpful—and guests are immediately drawn into the homelike atmosphere. The breakfast tables on the sunporch are covered with vintage embroidered linens, and rooms are furnished with mixed antiques and color-coordinated linens, carpets and towels. Touches like fresh flowers make guest rooms especially welcoming. Breakfasts are beautiful, with fresh-baked breads. There is a fax machine available to guests. Returning guests and families that require more than one room get discounts. There is an ocean view, and in the living room guests enjoy the stone fireplace on cool evenings. Pat also has another B&B, **Seven Granite Street,** in central Westerly. On Rte. 1 between Watch Hill and Shelter Harbor. **212 Shore Rd., Westerly 20891; (401) 596-6384** or **(800) 441-6384.**

Shelter Harbor Inn—$$$ to $$$$

It's hard to believe the stately farmhouse that is the main building of Shelter Harbor Inn was in such bad condition less than two decades ago that the town was considering tearing it down. Fortunately, Jim Dey was tired of his Wall Street career and had the vision to picture the house as it is today—an elegant and inviting inn, with large airy guest rooms (some with fireplaces), a rooftop hot tub and a dining room that attracts a full house almost year-round. The farmhouse was once home to a colony of musicians who traveled by boat from New York to Watch Hill to play the season at Newport. It overlooks Quonochontaug Pond and Philharmonic Brook, which empties into Harmonic Cove. The success of the inn is due largely to its owner's ability to attract and keep a long-term staff. Their personal interest—from long-term chef Joe Collins to the equally talented gardeners—show in every detail. Rooms are nicely appointed, beautifully kept and comfortable. On the grounds are a professional croquet court, bocci and putting greens. Tennis and golf are available nearby. A fax machine is available for guest use. A private beach, although not on the property, is close, stretching along two miles of the finest of Rhode Island's beaches; a shuttle bus carries guests there daily from 10 A.M.–5 P.M. In the winter, rates are about $20 per night lower than high-season rates, and second and subsequent nights are at a 50% discount. **10 Wagner Rd., Shelter Harbor (Westerly) 02891; (401) 322-8883.**

Woody Hill B&B—$$ to $$$

A four-guest-room B&B in a colonial reproduction that's hard to tell from an original, Woody Hill sits on 20 acres in the countryside with beautiful gardens and a 40-foot in-ground pool. Dr. Ellen Madison runs the B&B that sits on land that has been in her family for generations. She tells of an airplane that crash-landed on the side lawn during Prohibition; when people ran to rescue the pilot he begged them not to call for help. It seems the cargo would have caused more harm to him than the help would have done good. You can see a picture of the plane in the hallway. Rooms have antique furnishings, and most have a private bath. Privacy is predominant here. Shared common areas include a living room furnished with antiques, a fireplace and an overflowing library. It's easy to tell that the owner is a teacher. One room is handicapped-accessible. A full breakfast is served. No credit cards, but checks are accepted. As Woody Hill Rd. widens and turns to the left, keep to the right. **149 South Woody Hill Rd., Shelter Harbor; (401) 322-0452.**

Hathaways B&B Cabins— $$ to $$$

In the early days of the automobile, travelers stayed in cabins called "motor courts," and Hathaways is a modern and better take on that old idea. The main house was built as a farmhouse in 1863, and the first of the seven cottages was put up at the turn of the century for the summer people who were just beginning to come to the shore. The vintage cottages are well cared for and comfortable, with the ultimate advantage of cottages: privacy and quiet. All have a shower or tub, TV and air-conditioning. An efficiency cottage has cooking facilities. A Continental breakfast is served every morning in the dining room of the main house. Guests get passes to the Charlestown Town Beach or to Blue Shutters Beach. Open mid-May–mid-October. From Rte. 1 just west of the South Kingstown line, take Cross Mills Rd. and turn west onto Old Post Rd. (Rte. 1A). **4470 Old Post Rd., Charlestown 02813; (401) 364-6665.**

Willows Resort—$ to $$$$

The Willows is a modern, immaculately maintained family resort right on the water with motel-style motel units, efficiencies and apartments that are bright and comfortable. All rooms have TVs and firm king or queen beds, writing desks and tables and chairs. Many have balconies or patios, and there are deluxe apartments with screened porches. All of the apartments and efficiencies come with microwaves. The resort sits on 20 acres and has a very large outdoor pool, tennis courts, shuffleboard, practice golf holes and a game room. It's a short drive to the beach, or you can sail or paddle your own boat there. You can bring your own boat or canoe or, if you stay for more than two days, the management will let you use a canoe, rowboat or Sunfish without

charge. Weekly rates are good buys: A family efficiency for two adults and two children is $625, even less before the last weekend of June or after Labor Day. They also have a full seafood and steak restaurant on premises and offer a New England clambake. Rates including breakfast and dinner are usually available, as are several special packages. The Willows has been run by the same family for more than 50 years. It's on Rte. 1. **P.O. Box 1260, Charlestown 02813; (401) 364-7727, (800) 842-2181.**

One Willow B&B—$$ to $$$

A small B&B, One Willow offers attractive accommodations near the coast at attractive rates. Two rooms and a two-room suite share a bath, and guests have the use of a refrigerator and a barbecue grill. No pets are allowed during the summer. A full breakfast starts each day. No credit cards, but cash, personal and travelers checks are accepted. The B&B is open year-round.

Be sure to get directions when you reserve since the divided Rte. 1 access is complicated. **1 Willow Rd., Charlestown 02813; (401) 364-0802.**

CAMPGROUNDS

Burlingame State Park

The largest campground in the state, Burlingame has 750 sites for campers, vans and tents. The park sits on the shores of Watchaug Pond and has swimming facilities and access to the hiking and walking trails of Burlingame State Park and Wildlife Management Area.

There are a recreation hall, playground, ball field, boat launching area and a camp store with the essentials, including camping supplies and propane fill-up. The park does not accept reservations, has no hookups, and allows no alcoholic beverages and no pets. The rather dour gate attendants won't let you look

123

the area over before deciding whether you want to stay (as all other state parks do), so you may have to take potluck on the sites.

Fees for state residents are $8, nonresidents $12 per night. Open from Apr. 15–Oct. 31. Rhode Island Department of Environmental Management, Division of Parks and Recreation, Burlingame State Campground, **75 Burlingame Park Rd., Rte. 1, Charlestown 02813; (401) 322-7994** or **322-7337 (summers), 277-2632 (off-season).**

Ninigret Conservation Area

The 20 primitive camping spaces are for four-wheel-drive self-contained campers only. Run by the Rhode Island Department of Environmental Management, Division of Parks and Recreation; **(401) 322-0450 summers** or **277-2632 year-round.**

Where to Eat

Dylan's Steaks and Seafood—$$

At the corner of Canal and High Sts., Dylan's offers a pretty standard lunch and dinner menu as well as bar snacks and a kids' menu. Steak, seafood and pasta dominate, with additional daily blackboard luncheon and dinner specials, and a pub menu until midnight every day. Lunch is served Mon.–Fri., dinner seven days a week. **2 Canal St., Westerly 02891; (401) 596-4075.**

Olympia Tea Room—$$

When you walk into the Olympia in Watch Hill and glance around at its tall wooden booths, dark walls, shop windows overlooking the busy marina and vinyl tablecloths, you're sure nothing has changed in this venerable tea room since it opened early in the century. You'd be wrong. The menu is an up-to-date and unpredictable blend of old-time Yankee favorites

(clam chowder, pork chops, lobster and oysters on the half shell) and spicy newcomers from Latin kitchens. Jamaican jerk wings, guacamole, and at breakfast the owner's Taos tortilla and occasional specials are inspired by a variety of South American and Caribbean flavors. Stop at midafternoon for a giant old-fashioned apple dumpling, or, if they've run out, a wedge of pie. Ten beers are offered; the wine list is almost All-American—only the everyday house wine is French. **Bay St., Watch Hill (Westerly); (401) 348-8211.**

Watch Hill Inn—$$ to $$$

Stake out a place on the deck for lunch, with its good view over the harbor and street, and watch the tourists go by. Good salads and sandwiches make this a popular midday stop or an attractive spot for a drink and appetizer before you move on to dinner elsewhere. On the harbor at **50 Bay St., Watch Hill (Westerly); (401) 348-8912.**

Shelter Harbor Inn—$$ to $$$

The same careful attention to detail that distinguishes the Inn (see page **122**) characterizes the dining room and its outstanding menu. The chef for over 10 years, Joe Collins combines variety, surprise and a basic reverence for good ingredients to create a rare dining experience. While combinations may be unexpected—pecan-encrusted salmon served over a bed of spinach and garlic lentils—they are chosen for their flavors and textures, not just for the sake of cleverness. There are Rhode Island jonnycakes. The menu (with the help of a well-trained staff) describes the dishes clearly, a treat to those who enjoy contemplating their food before it arrives. The wine list is particularly surprising, not because it offers 92 different selections, but because they are almost all from American vineyards. Although it is difficult, try to save room for dessert— mango ice, a chocolate turtle pie, Indian pudding or a cloudlike lemon mousse. **10 Wagner Rd., Westerly; (401) 322-8883.**

Maria's Seaside Cafe—$$

Maria's offers Mediterranean cuisine in an informal setting, prepared in a spotless kitchen. Try the popular rigatoni vodka or the ravioli alla Maria, topped with sun-dried tomatoes, roasted peppers, garlic and basil and laced with cognac—just two of the many choices on the long pasta list. Four tempting selections highlight a special "healthy" menu section, although the usual dishes are not heavy in fats. This is not fancy nouveau northern Italian, but you'll find really good Italian cooking with a creative flair. Save room for tiramisu and espresso. Open daily from noon–10 P.M. in the high season (when dinner reservations are a good idea); during the spring and fall low seasons, hours are Thur.–Sun. from 4–10 P.M. Closed from Jan.–April. From Rte. 1A west of Watch Hill take Winnapaug Rd. to the beach and turn left. **132 Atlantic Ave., Misquamicut (Westerly) 02891; (401) 596-6886.**

Mary's Italian Restaurant—$$$

A varied menu of classic southern Italian dishes includes Florentine tripe and pork chops Calabrese style, simmered with roasted garlic, both rarely found in restaurants. Hot breads are baked on the premises, and servings are plentiful. Pastas are priced from $6.95. On Saturday nights after 9 P.M. a pizza and sandwich menu is offered; all dishes are available in smaller portions. Open Tues.–Sat. from 5–11 P.M., Sun. from 2–10 P.M. Located at the junction of Rte. 1 and scenic 1A on **Old Post Rd., Shelter Harbor (Westerly) 02891; (401) 322-0444.**

Cousins—$ to $$

Fish and chips, chicken pot pie, stuffed flounder, a daily pasta, lobster rolls and sandwiches fill the strictly what-you'd-expect menu in this lunchroom setting of tall wooden booths. Servings are generous. Beer and wine only. Open Sun.–Thur. from 7 A.M.–8 P.M., Fri.–Sat. from 7 A.M.–9 P.M. **241 Post Rd. at Dunn's Corner, (Rte. 1), Westerly (Misquamicut); (401) 322-7904.**

Wilcox Tavern—$$ to $$$

New American cuisine adds sparkle to this classic early American tavern, offering such dishes as salmon fillet served over a tomato-basil salad, or boneless chicken breast flavored with balsamic vinegar and hazelnuts. The pork loin is roasted with a maple mustard sauce. Even some of the more traditional seafood dishes take on a new life, for example the snowcrab pot pie. There is a nice extended wine list of domestic and imported wines. On Old Post Rd. near the General Stanton Monument. Major credit cards accepted. Open Mon.–Thur. from 4:30–9 P.M., Fri.–Sat. from 4:30–10 P.M., Sun. from noon–9 P.M. **Old Post Rd., Charlestown; (401) 322-1829.**

125

Nordic Lodge—$$$$

All the lobster you can eat, plus unlimited shrimp, clams, frog legs, smoked fish, scallops, filet mignon and prime rib. The atmosphere is pleasant, with a choice of long banquet-style tables or more intimate tables for four in several dining rooms. Each type of food—shellfish, appetizers, roasts, salads, desserts—has its own buffet, and you can return as often as you wish. Go for the big stuff here and skip the chicken and hot-table appetizers, although you may be tempted by the impressive array of desserts and fresh fruits. Meats are grilled to order. The lakeside grounds are beautifully kept, with gardens and peacocks—a pleasant place to stroll after dinner. Open weekends only in spring and fall from 5–10 P.M.; July 4–Aug. on Mon.–Fri. from 5–10 P.M., Sat. from 3–10 P.M. and Sun. from 1–7 P.M. Closed mid-December to late April. It's tricky to find, but you'll see signs. Take Shannock Rd. north from Rte. 1 in South Kingstown, just east of the Charlestown line. After several miles, turn left onto Old Coach Rd. and almost immediately right onto East Pasquiset Trail. You can also reach the lodge from Rte. 2/112 by taking Narrow Rd. east just north of the Rte. 1 intersection and then Old Coach Rd. north to East Pasquiset Trail. **178 E. Pasquiset Trail, Charlestown 02813; (401) 783-4515.**

Services

Visitor Information

Westerly-Pawcatuck Chamber of Commerce, 55 Beach St., Westerly 02891; (401) 596-7761.

South County Tourism Council, Stedman Center, 4808 Tower Hill Rd., Wakefield 02879; (401) 789-4422.

State Parks: Rhode Island Department of Environmental Management, Div. of Parks and Recreation, 22 Hayes St., Providence 02908; (401) 277-2632.

Parking

Parking is free in downtown Westerly for two hours, both curbside and in a small lot next to the post office on Granite St. A parking garage faces the square. Check to see which local businesses will validate your charge ticket. Three long-term lots in Watch Hill charge fees. Street parking, while available, is *very* limited both in the number of spots and the amount of time you can stay, especially in the summer.

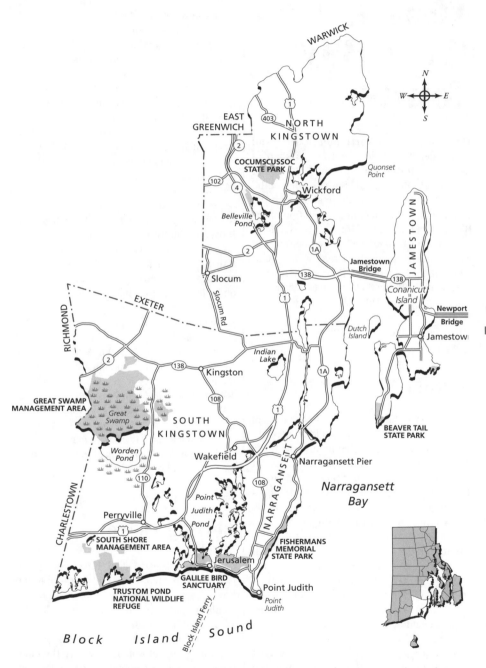

WARWICK

EAST
GREENWICH

NORTH
KINGSTOWN

COCUMSCUSSOC
STATE PARK

Quonset
Point

Wickford

Belleville
Pond

JAMESTOWN

Slocum

Jamestown
Bridge

Conanicut
Island

Newport
Bridge

Jamestown

EXETER

RICHMOND

Slocum Rd

Indian
Lake

Dutch
Island

Kingston

GREAT SWAMP
MANAGEMENT AREA

Great
Swamp

SOUTH
KINGSTOWN

BEAVER TAIL
STATE PARK

Worden
Pond

Wakefield

Narragansett Pier

Narragansett
Bay

CHARLESTOWN

NARRAGANSETT

Point
Judith
Pond

Perryville

SOUTH SHORE
MANAGEMENT AREA

FISHERMANS
MEMORIAL
STATE PARK

Jerusalem

TRUSTOM POND
NATIONAL WILDLIFE
REFUGE

GALILEE BIRD
SANCTUARY

Point Judith

Point
Judith

Block

Island

Sound

Block Island Ferry

N
W   E
S

The West Bay Towns

The West Bay Towns

The Kingstowns—North and South—and Narragansett form the western lower shore of Narragansett Bay, curling around the end of the Bay into Block Island Sound. Some of the state's best beaches are here, along with the fishing port of Galilee, jumping-off point for Block Island. Inland are attractive small villages, hiking, fishing, the largest body of fresh water in the state and the Great Swamp Management Area, a managed habitat where wildlife abounds. Within these three towns are the historic villages of Wakefield and Kingston, the fishing port of Galilee, the resort of Narragansett Pier and the old seaport village of Wickford.

History

The earliest settlement of Kingstown began in 1637, when Roger Williams and Richard Smith set up trading posts for commerce with the Indians and Dutch. Smith bought a large but ill-defined tract of land from the Indians in 1641 and later bought out Roger Williams's trading-post building, known as Smith's Castle. His trading post, in which Roger Williams stayed and preached on many occasions, exists to this day. While the Royal Charter of 1663 gave title of the area to Rhode Island, a land dispute with the colony of Connecticut created so much trouble that the king designated the area as the King's Province until the dispute could be settled. Rhode Island incorporated the town as Kings Towne in 1674 in hopes of enhancing its claim, but it wasn't until 1694 that Queen Mary declared the area part of Rhode Island. In 1723 the colonial legislature divided north and south Kingstown. (Note that the spelling of the village of Kingston differs from the spelling of the town of Kingstown, in which it lies.) By the outbreak of the Revolution, North and South Kingstown had a combined population of about 4,500, most of whom were engaged in maritime trade at the harbor of Wickford village.

The Revolution hit the 4,500 settlers along the bay hard. A British blockade of the bay and periodic British raids on the towns effectively ended shipping and fishing and made Narragansett Bay a liability instead of the asset it had once been. Population declined dramatically as settlers left for the interior, where they would be safer from British raids.

Narragansett was settled by Roland Robinson in 1675 as part of South Kingstown. It was originally a shipping and fishing community, but by the late nineteenth century it had become a fashionable resort area. Narragansett Pier had a dozen grand hotels and a huge casino, whose towered stone entrance spanned the roadway. The towers, designed by McKim, Mead and White, are all that remains of the casino, which was destroyed when fire spread from the nearby grand, but wooden, Rockingham Hotel in 1900. Although the town was incorporated in its own right in 1901 it was on a downhill course, and by the 1920s most of the other grand hotels were gone, also victims of fire. Today Narragansett Pier is once again a lively summer resort with modern hotels mixed among the fine old mansions. Several of these mansions are now elegant inns.

Getting There

US Rte. 1 winds like a giant thread through the center of this area. From Exit 9 of I-95 at the East Greenwich–Warwick line, take Rte. 4 south to Rte. 1. To follow the shore, take Rte. 1A south from Wickford.

RIPTA buses connect the Wakefield Mall and the village of Kingston, where the main University of Rhode Island campus is located, with Providence and Newport, each about a 50-minute ride. The fare is $2.50. RIPTA also connects from Providence to the port at Galilee, where ferries leave for Block Island. For RIPTA schedules and information, call **(401) 781-9400** or **(800) 244-0444.** The best and often only way to get to many parts of this area is by automobile.

Festivals and Events

South County Events Calendar

The South County Tourism Council publishes a pair of excellent, almost day-by-day, calendars of events, one covering spring and summer, the other fall and winter. In addition to established events, they also list those one-time events which travelers rarely learn of. They cover the entire area of the west side of the bay from West Greenwich and North Kingstown south to the sea and Block Island. Write or call **South County Tourism Council, 4808 Tower Hill Rd., Wakefield 02879; (401) 789-4422, (800) 548-4662, fax (401) 789-4437.**

South County Museum
May–October

Special events take place almost every weekend from the beginning of May through October. The schedule changes from year to year, so it is important to check in advance. In recent years the offerings have included programs such as Snake Oil to Sulfa—Medical Practices from the past and 100 Years of Bridal Fashions, featuring gowns from the museum's extensive collection. There are also annual events such as the Children's Festival (early June), Herb Garden Day (mid-June), Beekeeping Day (early July), Rug Hooking Day (mid-July), Gourmet Dinner (last weekend of July), Annual Blacksmithing Day (first weekend of August), Annual Quilt Show (third weekend of August), Jonnycake Festival (late August), Model Train Show (mid-September), South County History Day (mid-September) and the Harvest Festival and Apple Pie Con-

test, in the beginning of October. For a full schedule, call or write the museum at **Rte. 1A, Canonchet Farm, Narragansett 02882; (401) 783-5400.**

Wickford Art Festival
July

The Wickford Art Association sponsors this event on the second weekend of July, highlighting artists from all over New England and the United States. The works of over 250 association members are in oil, watercolor, pastel, pen and charcoal, along with sculpture, photography, print and other media. In addition to the art and the fresh air, there are exhibits at

The stone town hall in Wakefield stands beside an old burying ground.

the association gallery and food vendors. Main and Brown St., Wickford. For specific dates, programs and details, contact **Wickford Art Association, 36 Beach St., Wickford 02852; (401) 294-6840.**

South County Hot-Air Balloon Festival
July

Sponsored by the Wakefield Rotary, this three-day festival on the last weekend of July has been an annual event for over 15 years. It features hot-air balloons, antique cars, crafts, a bluegrass festival and other activities. It's at the **Athletic Field of the University of Rhode Island, Rte. 138, Kingston; (401) 783-1770.**

Blessing of the Fleet
July

The fishing and pleasure craft of Galilee get all dolled up for the annual Blessing of the Fleet on the last Sunday in July. This colorful event fills the tiny harbor of Galilee at the end of Point Judith; **(401) 789-9491 or 783-7121.**

The Lafayette Band— Wickford
July–August

The town band of Wickford offers band concerts from the bandshell during the summer. This is a well-known band that you may also hear at parades throughout the state. Call **(401) 295-1129** for dates and times, or ask at your local lodging.

International Quahog Festival
August

For years the village of Wickford (in the town of North Kingstown) has been celebrating and consuming this hard-shelled clam that is native to Narragansett Bay. On the last Sunday of August everyone converges on the town to eat them fried, steamed, stuffed and baked. There are quahog crafts, shucking contests and a cook-off, and a tent provides music throughout the day. **Middle School grounds, Tower Hill Rd., Wickford, at the intersection of Rtes. 1 and 102; (401) 884-6160.**

Festival of Lights
December

The annual Christmas festival in Wickford begins on the Thursday of the first weekend of December with a band concert, carol singing and the lighting of the town tree, and carries through the weekend with hayrides, caroling, house tours, special tours of Smith's Castle, a Christmas concert by the Community Chorus and an art show and sale. There is a full schedule of events each day. **North Kingstown Chamber of Commerce, 55 Brown St., North Kingstown 02852; (401) 295-5566.**

Outdoor Activities

Parks and Recreation Areas
Wilson Park

The history of this 55-acre parcel in Quonset (North Kingstown) over the past 60 years is dizzying. Starting as a dairy farm, it became part of the booming Quonset Naval Air Facility and ultimately a recreation and natural area. It has baseball, basketball, soccer and tennis facilities as well as bike and hiking paths. It is a good place for a family outing and a picnic or a hike on the footpath to the tidal areas of the cove. There is a boat ramp at **Long Cove.** Travel north on Rte. 1 from the Rte. 102 intersection, then turn right onto Intrepid Dr. (just after the police and fire stations); **(401) 294-3381, ext. 54.**

Birding

Narrow River

The Narrow River between Narragansett and South Kingstown offers some of the best waterfowl viewing in the state, with black, canvasback, goldeneye, bufflehead, Atlantic brant and mallard ducks, plus mergansers, Canada geese, mute swans, herons (great blue, black-crowned and little blue) glossy ibis, great and snowy egrets, terns, plovers, rails and a variety of gulls. Since roadside access is limited, the best way to sight birds is from a canoe or kayak, although there are bridges on Bridgetown Rd. and Middlebridge Rd. (see pages **140–141**).

Galilee Bird Sanctuary

This area is in a large area of forests and ponds covering much of the Galilee area of **Point Judith.** There is no interior access, but the fringes are Galilee Escape Rd., Galilee Connector Rd. and Sand Hill Cove Rd. at the south end of Point Judith.

Great Swamp

In the southern part of South Kingstown, west of Point Judith Pond. Take Succotash Rd. south from Rte. 1 toward Jerusalem. The road passes through a salt marsh that is filled with birds. You are likely to see egret, various ducks, ibis and herons right along the roadside. In South Kingstown over 100 bird species have been reported in the **Great Swamp Management Area** on the north end of **Worden Pond.** For access information see page **133**.

Trustom Pond National Wildlife Refuge

From Rte. 1 take Moonstone Beach Rd. south. At its end is a trail to the beach and the narrow strip of sand that separates the pond from the waters of Block Island Sound. The pond is an important part of the Atlantic flyway—the great thoroughfare of migratory wildfowl—and a nesting site for the piping plover.

Canoeing

Worden Pond

Located at the south end of the **Great Swamp Wildlife Management Area,** Worden Pond offers some fine flat-water canoeing with an opportunity to do some bird-watching as well. Worden Pond is the largest freshwater body in the state, however, and during windy weather it can become very rough and choppy, so be sure of the weather when you set out. The in-

Swans and other waterfowl are a common sight in the ponds at Manatuck.

131

lets and shores of the north and east sides offer some of the best birding, especially during the spring and fall migrations. Access to the lake is along Rte. 110 and off Worden's Pond Rd. on the south end of the lake. The pond outlet in the northwest corner goes through **Great Swamp** and leads to the **Usquepaugh and Pawcatuck Rivers** (see page **133**).

Narrow River

For most of its length the Narrow River forms the boundary between Narragansett and South Kingstown, extending farther north into North Kingstown. It's a long tidal river that extends both north and south of its outlet to the bay in Narragansett Pier. Much of the shoreline is undeveloped, and it offers attractive scenery and bird-watching. Access at Middlebridge Rd. north of Narragansett Pier by taking Boston Neck Rd. off of Rte. 1A.

Card's Camp Canoe & Boat Rentals

Located right along the shore of Worden Pond in South Kingstown. Canoes are $3 per hour or $10 per day. **1065 Worden's Pond Rd.** No reservations, just appear at the door.

Narrow River Kayaks

The best way to see Narrow River is from a canoe. Narrow River Kayaks rents fully equipped canoes and kayaks. Rentals are by the hour ($10 to $15), half day ($25, $45 for a double kayak) or full day ($40, $66 for a double). They also have guided canoe and kayak tours. There is a two- to three-hour bird-watching tour on Sats. and Suns. at 8 A.M. for $30, a two- to three-hour history tour any day of the week for a minimum of two people for about $30 and an all-day tour (from six to eight hours, depending on the skill level of participants) to Beavertail, including lunch, for $45. Lessons are available. It's best to call and find out what programs are available. Take Torrey Rd. from Rte. 1, then right on Middlebridge Rd., or take Old Boston Neck Rd. to Middlebridge Rd. from Rte. 1A (Boston Neck Rd.) north off Narragansett Pier. **Narrow River Kayaks, 95 Middlebridge Rd., Narragansett 02882; (401) 789-0334.**

Fishing
Surf Casting

Surf Casting is a popular sport along much of the coast of South Kingstown and Narragansett. In South Kingstown there is fishing off the shore of **Trustom Pond National Wildlife Refuge.** Take Moonstone Beach Rd. south from Rte. 1. There is also fishing at **Deep Hole Public Fishing Area** in Matunuck. From Rte. 1, take Matunuck Beach Rd. through Matunuck. **Worden Pond** and the **Great Swamp Wildlife Management Area** are popular spots for freshwater fishing. Bring your own canoe or rent one locally, or fish from the boardwalk under the power lines in the management area. See page **133** for access information.

In Narragansett, fish off **Roger W. Wheeler Memorial Beach** and off **Point Judith** at the **East Breakwater.** Take Rte. 108 south from Rte. 1, then take Sand Hill Cove Rd. for Roger Wheeler Beach, or stay on Rte. 108 to the lighthouse-access road for Point Judith and access to the East Breakwater. You might also want to try your luck off **State Pier #5** south of Narragansett Pier on Ocean Rd. (Rte. 1A), or farther north on that road from the **Governor Sprague Bridge** over the **Narrow River** or along **The Narrows** at the river's outlet to the sea north of Narragansett Pier. Incidentally, every year the Richmond-Hopkinton Economic Development Commission sponsors a sunrise-to-sunset **Great Rhode Island Trout-Out** on the **Pawcatuck/Wood River** watershed with a prize of up to $1,000. For details call **(401) 539-0230.**

Deep-Sea Fishing

Frances Fleet

Gail Frances, Inc., operates a fleet of deep-sea fishing boats from **Galilee,** south of Narragansett Pier, that are modern, Coast Guard–inspected and equipped with the latest safety and fish-finding gear. Half, three-quarter or full-day trips will probably send you home with a good supply of fresh fish. The shorter trips are about 90 minutes out from the harbor, well within sight of land, where you can bottom-fish for porgies, scup, blackfish and sea bass. The full-day trips concentrate on deeper waters and search for the fish that made New England, the cod. The fleet also offers overnight trips to Georges Bank, tuna fishing off the continental shelf and "wreck trips" to fish for the hake, pollack and cod that congregate around such sunken ships as the *Andrea Doria.*

The ships offer tackle rental, and the bait is supplied free, or you can bring your own. There is a galley to serve breakfast, lunch and dinner (when appropriate) as well as snacks and beverages. Don't forget to wear rubber-soled shoes, to dress warmly (the wind on the ocean even on a hot day can be cold), and bring your sunscreen, sunglasses and camera. Reserve as early as possible to make sure that a trip is available for the date you want. A deposit of half the total amount is due at least seven days prior to the trip, and checks aren't accepted at sailing time. Full-boat charters are also available. Rates for adults are about $20 for the half day and $30 for the three-quarter-day trips from July through September. Cod trips, which run from Nov.–mid-April on Wed. and Fri.–Sun. and daily from mid-April–Sept. are about $40. The boats leave from Galilee. From Rte. 1, take Rte. 108 (Old Point Judith Rd.) south, then turn right onto Galilee Escape Rd. to its end. The boats will be in front of the Captain's Table Restaurant. **Gail Frances, Inc., P.O. Box 3724, Peace Dale 02883; (408) 783-4988 or (800) 66 CATCH.**

Hiking and Walking

Davis Memorial Wildlife Refuge

In the northwest tip of North Kingstown, the Audubon Society of Rhode Island owns and manages a small, 102-acre reserve along the Hunt River between Davisville Rd. and Rte. 4. The site has a trail that winds through a forest, wetlands and along a bog, offering a chance to see greatly varied environments within a small area. There is also canoe access. Take Rte. 403 west from Rte. 1. Park on Davisville Rd. (Rte. 403), on the south side of the river. The canoe put-in is on the north side. Contact **Audubon Society of Rhode Island, Powder**

Mill Ledges Refuge, 12 Sanderson Rd., Smithfield (Rte. 5) 02917; (401) 949-5454.

Great Swamp Management Area

Great Swamp is 3,349 acres of wild area at the north end of **Worden Pond** in South Kingstown. The area is managed for hunting, so it's best to avoid it in the autumn, or at least wear appropriate (blaze orange) clothing. The interior can be reached via the access road to the **Great Swamp Fight Monument** and also from Great Neck Rd. (not a through road) off of Liberty Ln. in the village of West Kingston.

Park at the barred gateway and follow the road. It will take you through forests and marshy areas to the shores of Worden Pond. It includes substantial areas of red maple, white oak, alder and holly as well as dogwood and a profusion of berry varieties. The state maintains small plots of land totaling 88 acres, which provide grain crops for the animals. White-tailed deer, coyote, fox, raccoon and mink are commonly found here, and there is abundant bird life, with over 100 species reported. Look for game birds such as pheasant, wild turkey, ruffed grouse, woodcock and bobwhite and a great variety of waterfowl, especially during the spring and fall migrations. If you are going into this area you should probably pick up USGS topographic quad maps for Kingstown at a book or sporting goods store. Access the area from Rte. 138 in the northern end of South Kingstown. Just west of the village of West Kingston take Liberty Ln. south. At the railroad tracks take the dirt road to the left about one mile. The parking lot is one-half mile past the headquarters building. To reach the Great Swamp Fight Monument, take Great Swamp Monument Rd. off of Rte. 2 just east of where that road crosses the Usquepaugh River. It is marked with a sign.

Trustom Pond National Wildlife Refuge

Trustom Pond faces onto Block Island Sound, and its trails provide access to the rare ecology of a pond barely separated from the ocean by a narrow barrier of sand. Part of the Atlantic flyway, it is a good place for seeing waterfowl as well as the fragile ecosystems of the intertidal zone. The setting is an old farm with a combination of forests, open lands and fields. In the spring, rare azure butterflies the size of a penny are fresh out of the chrysalis. Alders, red maples (the state tree), water lilies and sedges grow in the pond fringes, along with hazelnut shrubs, pitch pine, wood anemone, shadbush, marsh marigold and the more rare Jack-in-the-pulpit. This is the state's only undeveloped salt pond (160 acres), and it is vented to the sea periodically to preserve its salinity. Over three miles of footpaths have boardwalks in the low areas. From Rte. 1 take Moonstone Beach Rd. south to the parking area. For information contact **Ninigret National Wildlife Refuge Complex, P.O. Box 307, Charlestown 02813; (401) 364-9124.**

Pettaquamscutt Wildlife Refuge

A little-known wildlife area skirting the southern end of the Narrow River, Pettaquamscutt's trails offer fairly easy walking, although it is a bit overgrown in places and muddy during wet spells. The path passes through vine-draped light woods with a forest floor of unusual plants that look like miniature trout lilies. The reserve attracts a wide variety of bird life, especially waterfowl, and also has some of the lesser mammals. The plant life along the shore is typical of such tidal areas, where the waters are brackish to saline and provide rich nutrients to the fish and other aquatic life of the river. From Narragansett, take Old Boston Neck Rd. to Middlebridge Rd. The path is just over the bridge on the left. There is a small parking space along the road. From Rte. 1 take Torrey Rd. east and then Middlebridge Rd. right, stopping just before the bridge.

Swimming

The beaches of South Kingstown and Narragansett are excellent; North Kingstown's beaches are open to residents only.

In South Kingstown, **Green Hill Beach** is near the west side of Trustom Pond Refuge. Take Shannock Rd. south from Rte. 1 to Green Hill Rd. and follow it to the end; **(401) 789-**

9301. Roy Carpenter's Beach is small, and the beach just to the east of it is private. From Rte. 1, take Matunuck Beach Rd., then a right onto Card's Pond Rd. The second right, just east of Theater by the Sea, takes you to the beach; **(401) 783-3076. Matunuck Beach State Park** has facilities and is abutted on the west by **A. B. Carpenter Beach.** At Rte. 1 take Matunuck Beach Rd. south to the coast; **(401) 783-4412.** To reach **East Matunuck State Beach,** take Succotash Rd. south from Rte. 1 toward Jerusalem, and the beach will be on your right just after the road turns east. It has lots of parking and bathhouses. Enjoy the beach grass, but stay on the path—the grass is fragile and holds the beach in place; **(401) 789-9301.**

Roger W. Wheeler State Beach is in Narragansett. Take Rte. 108 from Rte. 1 south and turn left onto Sand Hill Cove Rd. The beach is on the right; **(401) 789-1044. Scarborough State Beach** is on the east shore of Narragansett on Rhode Island Sound. Take Rte. 1A south along the east shore of Narragansett or north from Point Judith; **(401) 789-1044.** On Rte. 1A at Narragansett Pier, **Narragansett Town Beach** is one of the biggest and nicest. It has changing facilities in the pavilion and is a short walk from lots of lodging in Narragansett Pier; **(401) 789-1044.**

Whale-Watching

The waters of Block Island Sound and Rhode Island Sound abound with fish and plankton, good feeding grounds for whales. Boats operated by Frances Fleet have naturalists on board and side-scanning radar to help find whales. Humpback, finback, right and Minke whales are among the species seen on these trips. The three Coast Guard–inspected boats range from 65 feet to 105 feet. Trips are from 1–6 P.M. Thur.–Tues. in July–mid-Sept. and cost about $30 for adults, $20 for children. Call for reservations or, if you happen to be in the area, check at Capt's Tackle at the dock. From Rte. 1 take Rte. 108 (Old Point Judith Rd.) south, then turn right onto Galilee Escape Rd.

to the end. The boats will be in front of the Captain's Table Restaurant. Make reservations with **Gail Frances, Inc., P.O. Box 3724, Peace Dale 02883; (408) 783-4988** or **(800) 66 CATCH.**

Seeing and Doing

North Kingstown

Smith's Castle at Cocumscussoc

One of the oldest buildings in the state and the oldest original plantation in North America, this was called "castle" because it was originally a blockhouse. Built as a trading post about 1638 by Richard Smith and Roger Williams, it sits high on a hillside overlooking Narragansett Bay. It lay just off the Narragansett Trail, a path through the woods so well used that it is said to have been worn two feet deep in places by the footfalls of pedestrians. Rte. 1 overlies the original Narragansett Trail. Smith's Castle rapidly became a popular trading post frequented by Indians, and by the Dutch as well. Anne Hutchinson negotiated the purchase of **Aquidneck Island** (Newport) here. The plantation was used as a staging area for the **Great Swamp Fight** in 1675, and more than 40 casualties of that battle are buried on the grounds. After the original building was destroyed as part of the revenge of the Narragansetts in 1676, it was rebuilt in 1678 using many of the original timbers. Smith was interested in acquiring the Indians' lands and Williams their language and culture. One was a philosopher, the other was interested only in commerce. Commerce won out. Roger Williams sold his trading post to Smith and returned to Providence. Smith stayed here until his death in 1698. During the eighteenth century this was part of the **Updike Plantation,** where Benjamin Franklin, General Lafayette and General Nathaniel Greene all visited.

The castle is a fascinating place to visit and has been carefully restored after years of study. In particular, note the original paneling near the small fireplace in the old, small

The 1875 railway station in the village of West Kingston is a familiar sight to Amtrack passengers traveling south to Providence.

kitchen. The house is restored to its seventeenth-century appearance with appropriate furnishings and gardens with calendula, delphinium, Scotch thistle, lilies, trumpet vine and other period plants. **Queen's Island,** visible offshore, was given to Roger Williams by the wife of the great sachem Canonicus as a place for him to pasture his goats. The house is open in May and Sept. from Fri.–Sun., and July–Aug. from Thur. –Mon. Tours are conducted at 12:15, 1:30, 2:15 and 3:00 P.M., and there is a good video on the origins of the site. It's on Rte. 1 approximately 0.7-mile north of Wickford Village. **55 Richard Smith Dr., Wickford 02852; (401) 294-3521.**

135

Wickford Village

There is a magic to old seaport villages. Wickford is one of these, laid out in 1707 by Ludowick Updike, nephew of Richard Smith. Originally a small fishing and shipping port, it prospered until the Revolution, when it was damaged by the British blockade. It later enjoyed a renaissance as the place at which the railway from New York connected to steamships bound for Newport across the bay. Its harbor is still active, though not as commercial as before. This is a place to wander around and enjoy the colonial and early federal architecture; it seems that every building dates from the eighteenth or early nineteenth centuries and that each is in first-rate condition.

Be sure to see the **Old Narragansett Church.** It's an unspoiled gem built in 1707, and the oldest Episcopal church north of Virginia. It's open from 11 A.M.–4 P.M. in July and August. Services are held at 8 A.M. on Sundays during those months. For other arrangements call **(401) 295-5870.** On Church Ln. off Main St. Continue on to the town wharf at the end of Main St., where you'll find a special type of small fishing boat used here. A *Concise Walking Tour* of the village is available for $1 from **Historic Wickford, Inc., P.O. Box 261, Wickford 02852.**

Brandaris

In 1938 the owner of a Dutch shipyard built himself a private yacht following the lines of traditional Dutch sailing barge:, broad of beam and sturdy, but of steel, with a heavy wood keel that folds up along the starboard side. The *Brandaris* escaped the Nazis by sailing to Britain, and then helped in the evacuation at Dunkirk. Built for work and for luxury, with fully carpeted staterooms, a large saloon with fireplace and a head with a tub and heated towel racks, *Brandaris* is unique on the bay, and on the East Coast, and is available for sailing, naturewatch and special-occasion charters. Even if you don't sail on this beautiful historic craft, see her moored alongside the Brown Street Landing. There is parking close by. *Brandaris*, **c/o Somers/Burdick, 7 Main St., Wickford 02852; (401) 294-1481.**

The 1938 sailing yacht Brandaris, *a veteran of Dunkirk, is moored at Wickford.*

Gilbert Stuart Birthplace and Museum

Gilbert Stuart is one of the best-known American portraitists. If you don't know his work, look at a dollar bill: That's his portrait of George Washington. Born in this house in 1755, he went on to study in Europe and to paint the portraits of most major figures of his day, including Washington, Madison, Jefferson, Monroe and Adams. His birthplace is a fine example of an eighteenth-century working man's home. Stuart's father set up the first snuff mill in America here in 1751, in the basement. A partially reconstructed gristmill is nearby, as is a fish ladder, which swarms with herring in the spring as they return up the Mettatuxet River to spawn above the dam. Open Apr.–mid-Nov. from 11 A.M.–4:30 P.M. on Sat.–Thur. Look for the signs on either Rte. 1 or Rte. 1A south of Rte. 138 as it travels west from the Jamestown Bridge. **Gilbert Stuart Rd., Saunderstown 02874; (401) 294-3001.**

Silas Casey Farm

The farm was built in the mid-1700s and was occupied by the same family for over 200 years. Along with farming, they were also involved in the shipping trade in Newport. Three rooms are open to the public and display items belonging to the family over their two centuries on the farm. Its 300 acres are still farmed as part of a community program to preserve the farm and provide fresh organic produce. Notice the bullet hole in the parlor door, a reminder of a British raid during the Revolution. On Rte. 1A, in North Kingstown, about a mile south of the Rte. 138 intersection. The farm is owned by the **Society for the Preservation of New England Antiquities.** The hours are limited and vary, but you can also see the farm by appointment: **Casey Farm, Boston Neck Rd. (Rte. 1A), North Kingstown 02852; (401) 294-9182.**

Quonset Air Museum

A labor of love for about 25 dedicated volunteers, the museum is located in a brick hangar (the only remaining brick Quonset hut in the

East) that was once part of the Quonset Naval Air Station. The museum has a growing collection of about 20 aircraft, mostly from World War II and later. Among them is a TBM 3E Avenger, used as a crop duster after the war and pulled out of a crash site in Maine; a Russian MIG-17; a Grumman A-6 Intruder; a carrier-based attack bomber and a Hellcat fighter that crashed off Martha's Vineyard in 1945. It is undergoing restoration, as are several others. One, a 1948 French configuration of a World War II German Messerschmitt jet fighter, was discovered in a backyard on Cape Cod. The **Rhode Island Aviation Heritage Association** is the museum's parent organization, and its members perform the restoration work and, when necessary, even make the replacement parts themselves. They are always looking for new members. In addition to the aircraft, there is a small museum room with model planes and memorabilia including a Norden bombsight. The museum is open year-round on Fri.–Sun. from 10 A.M.–3 P.M. and by appointment. There is a nominal admission fee for adults. **488 Eccleston Ave., North Kingstown 02852; (401) 294-9540.**

Devil's Rock

Early settlers told the tale that this is the place where the devil first put his feet when coming across the bay from Conanicut Island. The rock bears an imprint like a huge human-shaped foot. (The Roger Williams and Richard Smith trading posts were located in an area called "Cocumcussoc" supposedly named for a stream, but other sources say that the word refers to "place of the marked rock," a reference to Devil's Foot Rock, or Devil's Footprint, other old names for Devil's Rock.) The granite here was quarried in the 1890s, and a wharf was built in Mill Cove off Smith's Castle to handle the granite blocks used to build the new Newport City Hall at the turn of the century. The mark is still there on the granite ledge. On Rte. 1 north of Wickford, look for a sandy pull-off on the west side of the road, opposite a car sales lot just south. It is not marked. Take the path through the brush at the right rear of the pull-out onto the rock outcrop.

An historic church sits atop a hill on South Ferry Rd. north of Narragansett.

Narragansett

South County Museum-Canonchet Farm

The museum, housed in a collection of old farm buildings, includes more than 10,000 artifacts that chronicle the lives and everyday technology of South County settlers from its earliest days. There is a general store with the merchandise they needed, a cobbler's shop and an exhibit on how crops were grown that includes a cross section of a live beehive. Exhibits concerning home life include an early country kitchen, a gentleman's study, a display on the development of lighting and a children's exhibit with antique dolls, dollhouses, trains and toys. Spinning and textile-weaving exhibits, vehicles and a print shop add another dimension. The property backs up to the south arm of the Narrow River, where there is a hiking trail and places to picnic. On Rte. 1A just north of Narragansett Pier. From Rte. 1 take Kingstown Rd. (near the Rte. 108 intersection) to Rte. 1A at Narragansett Pier. The museum is north, opposite the Beach Pavilion. Admission is $2.50 for individuals, $8 for families. **Canonchet Farm, Rte. 1A, Narragansett Pier; (401) 783-5400.**

Point Judith Light

Point Judith is one of the most dangerous spots on the New England coast, and the wa-

The wharves at Galilee are nearly always busy.

ters off its shores claim hundreds of ships. It was estimated that by 1889 as many as 30,000 ships a year passed through these waters; in rough seas and fog many missed their mark. While a beacon was kept on the point during the Revolution, the first lighthouse wasn't built until 1806. It lasted only until 1815, when it was blown away in a gale. The current light was built in 1816, an octagonal stone building whose original oil-fired light has been converted to electricity. While it's not open to the public, you can get a good view of the lighthouse and a sense of just how fearsome this point of land can be in a big storm from the small park just before its gate. The last German U-boat sunk in World War II was taken two miles off this shore. Take Rte. 108 south from Rte. 1, then Ocean Rd. south to the end. From the point looking west you can see the breakwater walls of the **Harbor of Refuge,** built at the turn of the century by the U.S. Army Corps of Engineers to provide a safe anchorage for vessels caught in rough seas. The harbor protects the area from Point Judith to Jerusalem–Port of Galilee.

Port of Galilee

One of the very few active fishing ports in the state, Galilee sits at the mouth of **Point Judith Pond** opposite its sister village of **Jerusalem.**

Sturdy piers lined with fishing vessels jut out into the protected harbor, providing a rare and colorful view of an industry common on the coast only a few decades ago. Fishermen unload their boats here, filleting and icing down their catch dockside. If you are on your way to or from Block Island, plan to spend a little time wandering around the docks, and be sure to look across the harbor to Jerusalem. Opposite the ferry landing is **May's Original Salt Water Taffy,** a local landmark with a history. Even if you don't eat candy, stop in and ask the owner for the latest tips on local restaurants. Her taste is impeccable, and she's never steered us wrong. The large area between Sand Hill Cove Rd. (along the south shore) and Galilee Escape Rd. (on the north and along Point Judith Pond) is the **Galilee Bird Sanctuary.**

South Kingstown

Kingston Village

It was here, in the northwest corner of South Kingstown, that warring colonists from Massachusetts and Connecticut gathered to plan their attack on the Narragansett Indians in Great Swamp a few miles away. Then known as Little Rest, the village later became the county seat and for a time the home of the state legislature. Its name was changed in 1885. There are a number of notable eighteenth- and nineteenth-century buildings in town along (or just off) Rte. 138. The **Fayerweather Craft Guild** occupies the small 1820 cape home built by George Fayerweather, a blacksmith and son of a former slave. It is open mid-May–Labor Day from 10 A.M.–4 P.M. on Tues., Thur. and Sat; **(401) 789-9072.** Also a gallery, the yellow clapboard **Helme House** was built in 1802 as a bank and is now used by the **South County Art Association.** It's at **2587 Kingstown Rd.; (401) 783-2195.** The gray-stone county jail, built in 1858 and used until 1956, is now the museum of the **Pettaquamscutt Historical Society.** Displays of toys and furnishings are in the former keeper's quarters. At **2636 Kingstown Rd.; (401) 783-1328.**

The Federal-style **Kingston Congregational Church** next door was built in 1820.

The West Bay Towns

The tan and gray library building with the cupola dates from 1775 and replaced an earlier one, which was one of the five homes of the Rhode Island legislature between 1776 and 1853; **(401) 783-8254.** West of the village on Rte. 138 at the railroad overpass, take the road down to the railroad station. It was built in 1875 and is being moved in order to preserve it. It still has its potbellied stove, ticket booth and dark wooden benches. For information, or to help, write to **Friends of Kingston Station, P.O. Box 191, West Kingston 02892.** Farther west on Rte. 138 take Dugway Bridge Rd. north to the Glenrock Mill. This stone building was a small water-powered woolen mill built in 1830. Today it is home to **Peter Pots Pottery,** itself well worth a visit.

University of Rhode Island Gardens and Arboretum

At its campus in the village of Kingston, the University of Rhode Island has collected more than 112 different species of trees and shrubs that landscape the grounds. Pick up a walking map and parking permit at the visitor's center, just inside the gateway to the campus. In the northeast part of the grounds a formal garden has perennial and annual beds and a water garden. The greenhouses nearby contain tropical research collections. On Campus Ave., the College of Pharmacy keeps a garden of medicinal plants. From Rte. 138 in Kingston village take Upper College Rd. **URI Cooperative Extension Education Center, University of Rhode Island, Kingston 02881; (401) 792-2900.**

Peace Dale

Rhode Island's villages are among its most interesting features. Peace Dale has heavy mill influences but is a rural town at heart, typifying the solid core of rural Rhode Island culture. Peace Dale centers around the intersection of Rte. 108 and High St., where the huge former **Peace Dale Mills** dominate with a tall tower. The mills were built between 1847 and 1883 and were the reason for the village. An attractive set of commercial buildings surrounds the square near the mills. The bronze sculpture on the grounds of the Romanesque library is *The Weaver* by Daniel Chester French. Opposite the library at Colombia St., the **Peace Dale Office Building** began life as the company post office, store and office building. Today it is the home of the **Museum of Art and Primitive Culture.** At the west end of the village is another mill complex with a surviving pump house, which is now the **Pump House Restaurant.** The owner occasionally schedules tours of this historic building at **1464 Kingstown Rd. (Rte. 108); (401) 783-4944.**

Museum of Art and Primitive Culture

The museum, founded in 1892, displays exhibits, collections of archaeology and ethnology and includes tools, weapons, household items, beadwork, utensils and hunting and fishing tools. While the exhibits focus on the New England Indians, they also include other cultures from places as diverse as Australia and Alaska. The museum emphasizes hands-on activities and programs for children. The collection is housed in the former office, boardinghouse and company-store building of the Hazard–Peace Dale mills. It's open on Wed. from 11 A.M.–2 P.M. but sometimes has extended hours, so contact the museum to find out or make an appointment. **1058 Kingstown Rd., P.O. Drawer A, Peace Dale (South Kingstown) 02883; (401) 783-5711.**

Great Swamp Fight Monument and Site

A tall obelisk marks the site of a battle between colonial troops and Indians that took place on December 19, 1675. Enraged by the depredations of King Philip's War, the settlers of the Connecticut, Massachusetts Bay and Plymouth Bay colonies, together with a scattered few from Rhode Island, gathered at North Kingstown to plan their attack on the Narragansetts whom they wrongly believed to be associated with the Wampanoag tribe of King Philip. Most Rhode Islanders, having maintained good relations with the Narragansetts, were not interested in joining the expedition. The Narragansetts had estab-

139

lished a winter camp and fort on high ground in the Great Swamp. Although this was normally protected by the swamp, extreme cold had frozen the swamp solid, and the colonists were able to approach during a blizzard. They set fire to the fort and the encampment, and while the Indians were able to kill 70 and wound 150 of the attackers, colonists killed about 600 Indians, including women and children. Most of the remainder, about 300 people, were taken as slaves. The monolith, erected to celebrate the victory, is today a sad monument to the Indians who were slaughtered that day. The massacre at Great Swamp brought the remaining 4,000 Narragansetts into the war and led to the burning of several colonial settlements, including Providence. From Rte. 2, south of the Rte. 138 intersection, take Great Swamp Monument Rd. to the left. Park at the circle. Reaching the monument requires a ten-minute walk on a dirt road.

Narrow River Cruise

At least three dates each year are set aside for the 48-passenger, pontoon-style riverboat *Blackstone River Explorer* to move south and cruise the Narrow River. These cruises offer a unique opportunity to see the wildlife and out-

The Great Swamp Fight Monument in South Kingston is a lonely sentinel to the struggle known as King Philip's War.

standing scenery of the Narrow River in the company of naturalists and from the comfort of a stable boat. The boat is handicapped-accessible. Trips run hourly from 10 A.M.–8 P.M., usually in August, and leave from the Middlebridge Marina on Middlebridge Rd. in Narragansett. Take Torrey Rd. from Rte. 1, then go right on Middlebridge Rd. From Rte. 1A in Narragansett, take Old Boston Neck Rd. to Middlebridge Rd. north of Narragansett Pier. For exact times and dates call **South County Tourism Council; (401) 789-4422** or write to them at the **Stedman Building, 4808 Tower Hill Rd., Wakefield 02879.**

Pettaquamscutt Rock (Treaty Rock)

To the side of Middlebridge Rd., on the west side of Narrow River, a historical marker records that at this spot (already a noted Indian landmark before the coming of the Europeans) the Narragansett sachems Quassaquanch, Kachanaquart and Quequaquenuet sold the surrounding land to Samuel Wilbor on January 20, 1657. It also records that here at Treaty Rock, Roger Williams, Anne Hutchinson and William Coddington probably completed the purchase of Providence and Aquidneck Island in 1638. It further suggests that it was probably here that the Atherton Company foreclosed its mortgage on the Narragansett lands in 1662, making this the real birthplace of Rhode Island. At the ball field, take the path up the hill that leads to a basketball court. A trail leads uphill through the woods to the right (north) to the base of the granite outcrop where the trail turns to the left and goes steeply up onto the rocks. The top is relatively flat with a striking view out over the Narrow River to the West Passage of Narragansett Bay, Jamestown, the Sound and with a nice view of the Jamestown Bridge to the north. The dramatic granite outcrop and the splendid view leave no doubt as to why this was an important Indian site. From Rte. 1 at the town line of the Kingstowns, take Bridgetown Rd. and, when it turns to cross the river, stay right onto Middlebridge Rd. You can also take Torrey Rd. east from Rte. 1 a bit south of that point, turning left onto Middlebridge Rd. From Narragansett (Rte. 1A) take Old Boston

Neck Rd. to Middlebridge Rd. over the Narrow River and then keep to the right.

Jerusalem

Opposite Galilee, across the narrow inlet to Point Judith Pond, the village of Jerusalem shares a narrow contorted sand spit with the other settlement of Matunuck. Here you see another view of Rhode Island's summer retreats—not grand estates of Newport or Narragansett Pier, but small cottages and vacation niches. On the short drive through this area into Jerusalem, look across the breach to the colorful harbor of Galilee. The road into Jerusalem passes through a salt marsh with abundant bird life right along the road. Jerusalem is an interesting combination of summer places, homes of working fishermen, docks and marinas.

Theatre by the Sea

One of the longest-running professional summer theaters in the state, this popular theater offers five plays, musicals and reviews throughout the summer, as well as a children's festival from early July through most of August, with shows at 10 A.M. and noon. Performers have included stars such as Helen Reddy and shows ranging from *My Fair Lady* to *Falsettos*. Behind the theater is the **Sea Horse Grill and Cabaret** for pre- and post-show drinks or dinner, and it's where the cast usually relaxes after performances (see page **147**). The season runs from May–Oct., and the box office is open from 10 A.M.–4 P.M. in May, from 10 A.M.–7:30 P.M. in June–Oct. Tickets are $20 to $25. From Rte. 1 in South Kingstown, take the Matunuck Beach Rd. south to Card's Pond Rd. and turn right. If you get to the Matunuck Town Beach you have just passed the road. For a current schedule and prices, contact **364 Card's Pond Rd., Matunuck 02879; (401) 782-8587. Sea Horse reservations; (401) 782-8587** or **789-3030 (after 3 P.M.).**

Shopping

Mom & Pop's Book Shop

Thousands of new and used books—4,000 cookbooks alone—cover every subject. Mom &

The harbor at Galilee is shared by whale-watch boats, fishing craft and the Block Island Ferry.

Pop's offers a search service for out-of-print books, and the shop carries vinyl recordings. We could spend a rainy day here quite happily. It stays open until 8 P.M. **239 Robinson St., Wakefield; (401) 782-2553.**

141

Historic Wickford Village

The two commercial streets in Wickford, **Brown St. and Main St.,** are lined with shops that even nonshoppers enjoy. Some of the best are at **Updike Square,** where Main St. and Rte. 1A intersect. Poke around in these shops, all within easy walking distance, where you'll find everything from Native American and western art to handcrafted furniture and eighteenth-century accessories to Nantucket baskets, art galleries, toys and antiques.

Wickford Place

This gallery has a collection of the works of over 170 craftspeople from around the state, and its showrooms contain woodwork, leather, stained glass, quilts, candles, baskets, jewelry, dollhouses and miniatures, pottery, whirligigs and many more. In a converted barn at the intersection of Rtes. 1 and 4, just north of the exits for the Jamestown Bridge. Open Mon.–Sat. from 9:30 A.M.–5:30 P.M. and Sun. from noon–5 P.M.

Wickford Art Association

The association, which runs the **Wickford Art Festival** in the summer, has a gallery exhibiting the work of contemporary artists that is open from the last weekend of January to December 23. Over 250 members of the association also hold 22 two-week special exhibits each year. The work includes oils, watercolor, pastel, multimedia, photography, sculpture, pottery, pen and ink, etching and other media techniques. Off of Rte. 1A on Beach St., south of the Rte. 102 intersection in Wickford center. **36 Beach St., Wickford 02852; (401) 294-6840.** Nearby, also look in on **The Artist's Gallery of Wickford at 5 Main St.**, specializing in the works of Rhode Island artists. Open Tues. –Sat. from 10 A.M.–5 P.M. and Sun. from noon–5 P.M.

Tours

M/V Southland sight-seeing boats leave from State Pier in the Port of Galilee for 11-mile narrated harbor cruises. From Memorial Day–June and all of September they leave at 11 A.M. and 1 P.M.; from July 1–Labor Day at 11 A.M., and 1, 3, and 5 P.M.. You will need reservations; **(401) 783-2954.**

Seven B's V sight-seeing cruises and fishing excursions for tuna and offshore species leave daily from the Port of Galilee from May–Oct.; **(401) 789-9250.**

Where to Stay

For bed and breakfast accommodations throughout the southern part of the state, you can call one number to reserve a room or check availability. This saves making a number of calls to locate a room; **(800) 853-7479.**

ACCOMMODATIONS

The John Updike House—$$ to $$$

A small two-room B&B, this house was built in about 1745 in the historic heart of Wickford. Rooms are furnished with a nice mix of antiques and modern pieces. Guests share a bath

but have access to a full kitchen and a guest parlor. There are baskets of menus and information about things to see. Look in the stairway for the picture of The General, which took nineteenth-century millionaires from their private railroad cars in Wickford to their "cottages" in Newport. Breakfast is served on a sunporch overlooking the fishing harbor, with dishes such as beach plum syrup with a breakfast bread pudding. **19 Pleasant St. (off Main St.), Wickford 02852; (401) 294-4905.**

Farmer Brown House—$$ to $$$

The two Victorian houses of this B&B are nicely decorated in Laura Ashley papers and linens. Furnishings range from wicker to mixed antiques and reproductions. During the process of renovation, care was taken to preserve the fine woodwork and floors of both buildings—the rooms have the charm and individuality that new buildings lack. The front yard is shaded by a copper beech tree considered to be one of the largest in New England. Amenities include air-conditioning, cable TV and robes; guests can enjoy the grounds from either of two porches or have afternoon tea in either of the two common rooms. No credit cards. Reservations are essential, especially on busy weekends, as the University of Rhode Island is close by. **2492 Kingstown Rd., Kingston 02881; (401) 783-5477, (800) 529-7300.**

Larchwood Inn—$$ to $$$

The Larchwood is a beautifully kept 165-year-old mansion in the heart of Wakefield, converted to an inn in 1926. Set back from the road in its own garden, it offers a quiet respite of comfortable lodging, dining and entertainment. The rooms are furnished with antiques and reproductions and are individually decorated. Some of the rooms have four-poster beds and fireplaces, and others, such as #3, have a double and a single bed. Three of the rooms in the main house and four of the rooms in Holly House share baths. Children of all ages are welcome, and the staff and owners are among the most accommodating we've found. The inn has its own lounge, **The Tam O'Shanter Room,** which is separate from the dining areas and offers entertainment on Fri. and Sat. nights. **521 Main St., Wakefield (South Kingstown) 02879; (401) 783-5454.**

The Village Inn—$$$$ (Narragansett)

This gray-shingled modern and comfortable hotel faces the beach on one side and the shops and restaurants of Pier Marketplace on the other. Some rooms have balconies and all are bright and attractively furnished in well-coordinated colors. Guests are provided with discounted passes to the long sandy beach across the street. The better the ocean view, the higher the room rate. The indoor swimming pool is heated. Rates are significantly lower in the autumn and even more drastically reduced in the winter and spring, to as low as $60 for a double. Special packages include dinner credits at the **Spanish Tavern** and **The Village Cafe,** both in the hotel. **1 Beach St., Narragansett Pier 02882; (401) 783-6767** or **(800) THE PIER.**

The Atlantic—$$$$

Facing the ocean, The Atlantic sits in a neighborhood of Victorian "cottages" and boasts new facilities where the emphasis is on the rooms instead of the lobby and public areas. Each room has a small sitting area with table and desk as well as a balcony. Quality reproduction Queen Anne furniture, first-class carpets, color-coordinated decor and well-thought-out lighting make the rooms enjoyable resting spots. **Ocean Ave., Narragansett Pier 02882; (401) 783-6400.**

Pier House Inn—$$$$

This inn started life as the large Victorian "cottage" of a wealthy family. Its past, however, was not always sedate and included smuggling

The shore between Narragansett Pier and Point Judith alternates between sandy beaches and rocky tidal pools.

through a tunnel from the sea and a stint as a speakeasy. The rooms in the original building vary greatly and retain many of their old features; front rooms overlook the sea. The rooms in the motel unit are well furnished and pleasant but, as might be expected, are more similar to one another. The motel units have either two king- or queen-sized beds, and they all have terraces. Coffee is available to guests throughout the day. Inn guests get complimentary wine and discounts with dinner in the restaurant. Seasonal rates do not fluctuate as much as they do for other lodging in the area. **113 Ocean Rd., Narragansett Pier 02882; (401) 783-4704, fax (401) 783-6096.**

Admiral Dewey Inn—$$$ to $$$$

In May of 1898 Admiral George Dewey entered Manila Bay in the Philippines in the *Olympia* and destroyed the Spanish fleet, so the Champlins named their then new boardinghouse at Matunuck Beach for the new national hero. It is open again, fully restored and under its original name. The rooms all have private baths and are furnished in period Victorian furnishings from Eastlake to marble top. Room

#1, with a four poster bed, has windows on three sides and a Victorian rocker, while room #5 has an ornate Victorian bed with oval marble-top side tables and a plush Victorian settee. There is a large and comfortable common sitting room furnished with overstuffed furniture. A Victorian tile fireplace is the focal point of the dining room, where Continental breakfast is served. Winter rates are about half of the summer rates and make this a good off-season buy. There is a minimum three-day stay on holiday weekends, two days on all other weekends. The owners recommend reservations a month in advance and require a 30% deposit. **668 Matunuck Beach Rd., South Kingstown (Matunuck) 02879; (401) 783-2090, 783-8298.**

Green Hill Beach Motel—$$$

Located right on the beach, this motel has average-sized rooms with tub and shower units in the bathrooms. Nothing fancy, the rooms are comfortably furnished and very livable. The motel's major advantage is its location just a few steps from the beach. Open from June–Oct., the motel is at the end of Green Hill Rd. south of Rte. 1 in South Kingstown west of Trustom Pond Refuge. **P.O. Box 24, Charlestown 02813; (401) 789-9153.**

Marantha—$$ to $$$

The most unusual place to stay in this area is on the *Marantha*, a 52-foot motor yacht moored on Great Salt Pond, which is the upper end of Point Judith Pond. The guest quarters hold a maximum of four in two bedrooms (one with a queen-sized bed and one with bunks). The bath has a tub. A private entrance is off the rear deck and there are shady and sunny decks overlooking the harbor. While this isn't suitable for little kids, older ones will love their ship's cabin. A breakfast of fresh fruit, juice, bagels, muffins and cereal is served. From Rte. 1 south of the Rte. 108 intersection, take Woodruff Rd. west, then Salt Pond Rd. south. It becomes William Schmidt Dr. and

brings you to West Dock. Stop at the Ram Point Marina and go out onto the wharf by taking the path between the service building and the fuel tank. Summers only. Reservations are required. **29 Whitman Rd., Worcester MA 01609,** or call **(508) 799-2136.**

Dutch Inn by the Sea—$$$

If for no other reason than convenient access to an early start on the ferry to Block Island, this is the place to stay in Galilee. It is in the heart of the port, within walking distance of the beaches and the bird sanctuary. Many of the rooms in the inn have been recently refurbished, and all are large and furnished like motel rooms, but comfortably so. They have access to the exercise room, whirlpool, saunas, game room and large indoor pool area. The Dutch Inn is a local institution, the best-known hostelry in the Point Judith area. After the high season (end of June to Labor Day), rates drop significantly. A minimum stay may be required on some weekends and major holidays. While there is a $15 charge for an extra person in a room, there is no charge for children under 12 or for port-a-cribs. Ask about special package rates on- and off-season. The inn is opposite the Block Island Ferry landing. **307 Great Island Rd., Galilee (Narragansett) 02882; (401) 789-9341, fax 789-1590, (800) 336-6662 from out of state.**

Cottrell Homestead—$$

The Cottrell Homestead is a small B&B on one of the few remaining dairy farms in the state. Only a short distance from the University of Rhode Island, it is open year-round and serves a full country breakfast. Baths are shared and there is no smoking in the house or barn. As this is also the owners' home, they don't allow pets and prefer no children under 10 years old. No credit cards, but they will take personal checks. From Rte. 2 north of the Rte. 138 intersection, turn right onto Waites Corner Rd. It's the second farm on the right, south, side of the road. **500 Waites Croner Rd., West Kingston 02892; (401) 783-8665.**

Hedgerow—$$ to $$$

Only a half mile from the URI campus, this three-room B&B is well situated. In addition to a pleasant verandah, guests also have access to attractive gardens, a private tennis court, a den, game room and sitting room. Children are welcome, and crib-sized babies stay free. From Rte. 138 go a half mile east of the light at the URI campus and look for the Hedgerow sign at the drive on the north side of the road. No credit cards, but personal checks are accepted. **Ann and Jim Ross, P.O. Box 1586, Kingston 02881; (401) 783-2671, (800) 486-4587.**

CAMPGROUNDS

Fishermen's Memorial State Park

The state of Rhode Island has built an attractive camping area in the southern end of Narragansett right on Rte. 108 (Old Point Judith Rd.) that offers 182 sites. Area 1 is intended mainly for RVs and offers electric, water and sewer hookups. Areas 2 and 4 have smaller sites with electric and water hookups, and Area 3 has no hookups and is limited to tents only. Sites are open and nicely kept and are accessed over paved roads, which cuts down on dust. The grounds are landscaped and have low trees, along with baseball fields, basketball courts, tennis courts, horseshoe pits and recreation fields. The big advantage, however, is that this is right at the end of **Point Judith,** a short walk from the beaches and from the **Port of Galilee.** As you would expect, it fills up fast, so reservations are a real necessity. From the third Monday in May through Labor Day there is a five-day minimum stay with a liberal maximum of 14 days. Reservations *must* be made on the campground's form. Send for it, enclosing a stamped self-addressed legal-size envelope. The reservation form must be received no less than two weeks before the date you desire. The park is open from mid-April–Oct. Pets are not allowed, nor is alcohol use or possession. Area 1 rates are $12 per day, Areas 2 and 4 are $10 and area 3 is $8, but check in advance for changes. **Fishermen's Memorial State Park, 1011 Point Judith Rd., Narragansett 02882; (401) 789-8374.**

Worden's Pond Family Campground

Right along Rte. 110 and opposite the east shore of Worden Pond, this campground couldn't be better situated for the enjoyment of the pond, the natural southern extension of **Great Swamp.** This is a lightly wooded camping area catering to families. Very nicely maintained, the **Cedar Lot** has low trees with close but pleasant sites, **Indian Orchard** has open woods and grassy field sites on the edge of the woods and **Bluebird Hollow** is a shady grassy area in an open grove of trees. The campground has its own private access to the pond via a sandy beach. Canoe and boat rentals can be made a short distance away at **Card's Camp** (see page 132). **Worden's Pond Rd., South Kingstown 02879; (401) 789-9113.**

145

From Galilee, you can look across the channel to Jerusalem.

Where to Eat

Duffy's Tavern—$ to $$$

Duffy's calls itself a "seafood in the rough place" and it is. It's sometimes noisy and boisterous, especially in the separate lounge/pub area. Duffy's has been a favorite in the area for many years not only for its food but for its longtime support of local charities and the Jimmy Fund. With the help of baseball great Ted Williams, Duffy's has raised thousands of dollars. Try the clam cakes or the seafood platter, a bargain at under $10. The seafood is available fried, grilled, baked or broiled. On Rte. 1 (Tower Hill Rd. in this section) just west of Wickford. From the village take West Main St. and turn left at Rte. 1. **235 Tower Hill Rd., Wickford 02852; (401) 294-3733 (takeout), 295-0073 (Tavern).**

The Pump House—$$ to $$$

This 1888 stone building was the pump house that provided water for the mills across the street. No longer needed for that purpose, it is now an attractive restaurant with many antique features and graceful touches. The big fireplace in the dining room, high open-beamed ceilings and etched-glass panels all add to the nineteenth-century atmosphere. Specialties include baked salmon, chicken with rosemary and chicken or sole with white wine and tarragon. The dining rooms are separated from the lounge by a stone wall. Reservations are accepted. Open Tues.–Sat. from 11:30 A.M.–10 P.M. On Rte. 108 just north of High St. **1464 Kingstown Rd. (Rte. 108), Peace Dale (South Kingstown); (401) 783-4944.**

Larchwood Inn—$$–$$$

This beautiful old inn has four attractive dining rooms, some of which allow smoking. The dining rooms (one has a mural), are nicely decorated and accented with antiques. Breakfast, lunch and dinner are served from a traditional American menu that includes prime rib, lobster Newburg, duck glazed with orange sauce and broiled lamb chops. The wine list is good, with over 36 domestic, French, German, Australian, Chilean and Spanish wines. Early-bird specials are offered from 5:30–6:30 P.M. on weeknights, and Sunday dinner is from 11:30 A.M.–9 P.M. Breakfast is served from 7:30 A.M., lunch from 11:30 A.M. and dinner from 5:30–9 P.M. **521 Main St., Wakefield (South Kingstown); (401) 783-5454.**

Woody's—$$$

Moved to Narragansett Pier from Westerly, Woody's brought a corps of happy diners who are pleased to see the same stylish dinner menu here. It changes seasonally and may include gnocchi with grilled wild mushrooms, duck in pomegranate sauce or cod cakes with roasted pepper tartar. Tapas are still a specialty. Woody's serves dinner only, Wed.–Sun. **21 Pier Marketplace, Narragansett Pier; (401) 789-9500.**

Spanish Tavern Restaurant—$$ to $$$

Located in the same building as the Village Inn, the restaurant overlooks the water and the stone towers of Narragansett Pier, which are visible through large windows. Candlelit tables are well spaced and the service is friendly. The chef is from Spain, and serves a good selection of traditional Spanish and Continental dishes. Some of the entrees are veal chops sautéed with mushrooms and asparagus, broiled sirloin steak with a creamy pepper sauce, a paella of lobster and seafood with a saffron sauce or breast of chicken stuffed with spinach and cheese in a mushroom sauce. The wine list is extensive and includes American, French, Italian, German, Australian and Portuguese selections. Reservations are accepted and recommended on busy weekends. There is live flamenco guitar music on weekend evenings. Lunches are under $10 and dinner is under $20. There is a separate area for smokers. Open Mon.–Sat. from noon–10 P.M., Sun. from 1–9 P.M.

The Village Inn, 1 Beach St., Narragansett Pier 02882; (401) 783-3550.

Chez Pascal—$$ to $$$

The emphasis in this small French restaurant is on French provincial and bistro cooking. Chez Pascal has no license, but you are welcome to bring your own wine. It has an auberge atmosphere with tables close together but not crowded, and there's only enough lighting to easily read a menu by. Read every word, since it includes appetizers such as the house pâté—a blend of pork and duck. Entrees include steak poivre, confit of duck and ravioli filled with goat cheese in basil cream sauce. Entrees are evenly split between seafood and meats in the winter and more seafood in the summer. Personal checks are accepted, a rarity for restaurants. Reserve early in the week for summer weekends and for Saturday nights even in the winter. Open Memorial Day–Labor Day, Tues.–Sat. from 5–10 P.M., fewer hours off-season. **944 Boston Neck Rd., Narragansett Pier 02882; (401) 782-6020.**

The Coffee Bean—$

A good place for breakfast or lunch or for picnics to-go, The Bean is popular with local people. Although there is no table service, there are tables inside and out of doors. The fresh-baked croissants and scones are all made on the premises, and the deli counter is well stocked with a good variety of salads and sandwich makings. The cafe and deli are slightly separated, so you can enjoy your lunch without being crowded by deli customers. Of course, they have a good selection of premium coffees and teas. No smoking. Open daily from 6 A.M.–6 P.M. Near the intersection of US Rte. 1 and RI Rte. 108 at **Salt Pond Plaza, South Pier Rd.**

Port Side Restaurant—$ to $$

A good place in Galilee for a quick lunch, the Port Side is right opposite the ferry landing for Block Island. It also serves dinner. It has no pretensions and no ambiance, but very friendly staff and very good food, which is mostly seafood and largely fried. But you'll find some broiled entrees and excellent salads of lobster or other seafood. An Italian shrimp and scallop salad features roasted peppers and black olives. A dozen clam cakes (like hush puppies and delicately seasoned) are under $4, fish and chips are under $8, but the best deals are probably the combination plates. They also serve veal cutlets, fried chicken, burgers and steak sandwiches. They use a separate fryer for each kind of seafood, and the batter for the fish and chips is made fresh for each order. Open daily from 8 A.M.–9 P.M., May–Oct. Shorter hours in spring and fall. Closed Dec.–Jan. **Great Island Rd., Port of Galilee, Narragansett 02882; (401) 783-3821.**

Vanilla Bean Ice Cream—$

A "cool" place to stop if you are exploring the southern reaches of South Kingstown or enjoying the sands of Browning Beach or Daniel O'Brien Estate Beach. Right at the entrance to the Matunuck Town Beach off of Matunuck Beach Rd.

Sea Horse Grill and Cabaret—$$$

An intimate part of the Theatre by the Sea, the Sea Horse begins your visit with a sensory delight. Allow enough time to savor the lush, almost tropical, gardens that line the path to the restaurant, at their height of glory in July and August. Once inside you'll find interesting appetizers and sandwiches such as turkey, avocado, Bermuda onion and Dijon mustard, or a grilled marinated chicken breast with Caesar dressing, onion, romaine and parmesan. Innovative entrees may include apple orchard chicken—chicken breast sautéed with cashews, apples and flamed in Fra Angelico—or Nantucket Sound scallops baked in sweet vermouth and topped with Mozzarella cheese. There are plenty of offerings under $10, such as the grilled chicken

The Rhode Island Guide

salad. The setting along the salt marshes and the lively atmosphere of the theater, where cast members mingle after shows for cabaret singing and comedy, makes this an enjoyable place to spend the evening. Reservations are recommended, especially for the cabaret following theater performances. Major credit cards accepted; handicapped-accessible. Open June–mid-Sept. from Tues. –Sun., 4–11 P.M. **Theatre by the Sea, 364 Card's Pond Rd., Matunuck; (401) 789-3030.**

South Shore Grill—$$$$

This pleasant restaurant is located on the north end of Point Judith Pond, next to the Point Judith Yacht Club. The restaurant is on the second floor, and the lounge and informal deck dining is on the first overlooking the marina. Seafood is a specialty here, but there are other dishes. A good choice for lunch is the lobster bisque. From Rte. 1 take Woodruff

Ave. west to Salt Pond Rd. Open Sun.–Thur. from 11:30 A.M.–9:30 P.M., Fri. and Sat. from 11:30 A.M.–midnight. Shorter winter hours. **Salt Pond Rd., South Kingstown; (401) 782-4780.**

Services

Visitor Information

North Kingstown Chamber of Commerce at 55 Brown St., North Kingstown 02852; (401) 295-5566.

South County Tourism Council, Stedman Building, Wakefield 02880; (401) 789-4422, (800) 548-4662.

South Kingstown Chamber of Commerce, 328 Main St., P.O. Box 289, Wakefield 02880; (401) 783-2801.

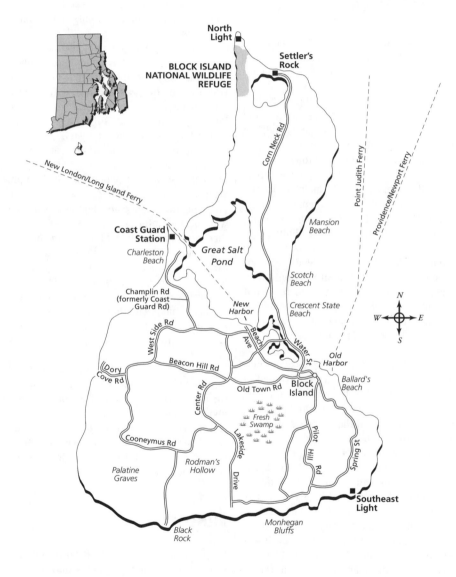

North
Light

Settler's
Rock

BLOCK ISLAND
NATIONAL WILDLIFE
REFUGE

Corn Neck Rd

Point Judith Ferry

Providence/Newport Ferry

New London/Long Island Ferry

Coast Guard
Station

Mansion
Beach

Charleston
Beach

Great Salt
Pond

Scotch
Beach

Champlin Rd
(formerly Coast
Guard Rd)

New
Harbor

Crescent State
Beach

West Side Rd

Beach Ave

N

W ⊕ E

S

Water St

Old
Harbor

Dory
Cove Rd

Beacon Hill Rd

Old Town Rd

Block
Island

Ballard's
Beach

Center Rd

Lakeside Drive

Fresh
Swamp

Cooneymus Rd

Pilot Hill Rd

Spring St

Palatine
Graves

Rodman's
Hollow

Southeast
Light

Black
Rock

Monhegan
Bluffs

Block Island

Although it's only 12 miles off the coast of Rhode Island, Block Island seems as far removed as Bermuda. Residents speak of being "on the mainland" as the British speak of "going to the Continent." Although the island is a separate town officially named New Shoreham, it's referred to as "the island," or Block Island, by visitor and native alike.

As with many New England towns, people here have settled in small groups in different parts of the island, but unlike mainland towns, these settlements don't have a separate village identity. The entire island is a single community, and that identity is strong. While some areas have names, such as Old Harbor, New Harbor and Southeast Light, these specify location only, as a street address would. The streets are named, but street numbers are not used. To provide the fire department with locations, all buildings are assigned fire numbers, but you can't use them to find a place.

The reason for this is a very funny, very Block Island story. While there, ask your innkeeper how the numbers were assigned in such a random order. If you have an emergency, however, give the fire number of the nearest building and the rescue squad will know just where you are.

Roughly the shape of a triangle with one long leg, the island is seven miles long and only three miles wide at the widest point. Great Salt Pond intrudes as a large circular bay that nearly cuts the island in half. Only a narrow section of land connects the north end of the island to the southern part, creating in essence two islands joined by a narrow isthmus.

This is not an island of theme parks or high designer-fashion shops, nor is it self-conscious Nantucket. It is a more contemplative place, one for sunbathing on some of the East's finest sand beaches, for long leisurely bike trips, for salt- and freshwater kayaking and canoeing, for short walks and long hikes on maintained trails and roadways and for some pleasant low-key sight-seeing. The sight of a full three-masted square-rigger sailing into Great Salt Pond harbor on a late summer afternoon is an unforgettable visual souvenir, one of Block Island's many happy surprises.

On the island all power is generated, and electric costs are astronomical. Remember, too, that every bite of food, gallon of gasoline (there's only one gas station), soft or hard drink, paper napkin and souvenir T-shirt has to be shipped in by boat, so you'll find prices higher here than on the mainland.

Roads are narrow and winding and, in the summer, are crowded with bicycles, mopeds and cars. Speed will seldom exceed 25 mph. While all parts of the island can be reached on paved highways, there are many dirt roads that wind off into interior and coastal areas. The dirt roads are fun to explore by car, bike or foot, but are off-limits to mopeds. While readily available for rent in Old Harbor, mopeds are not looked upon with approval by islanders, mainly because of safety concerns. Most users are not familiar with them and a rescue squad member told us that it's not unusual for there to be as many six serious moped-related injuries a day.

Bicycles are available at several places at reasonable rates, and walking is an alternative for many sights. From Old Harbor it's only about a mile-and-a-half walk to Payne's Pier at New Harbor. Crescent Beach and Ballard's Beach are within a mile, and even Southeast Light and Mohegan Bluffs are less than a three-mile hike.

History

Block Island, for all of its idyllic peacefulness, has a past with all the swashbuckling romance of its Caribbean cousins: confrontation, battles, pirates, shipwrecks, ghosts and tales of hidden treasure. Although it was seen by Verrazano as he sailed by on his explorations of the Atlantic Coast (he named the island "Claudia," after the mother of the king of

France, but the name didn't stick), it wasn't shown on maps until the Dutch explorer Adriaen Block found it in 1614. By noting it on his map and giving it his own name he achieved a measure of immortality.

The island is actually the end of a glacial moraine, a gravel-and-stone extension of the landmass of mainland Rhode Island, originally connected to it by a sizable causeway. As late as the eighteenth century, an island remnant of the causeway known as The Hummock remained off the end of Sandy Point. Colonists traveled over the connecting sandbar at low tide to collect berries on its low-lying hill. The Hummock is now just a shoal: Its hill is washed away and the sandbar is no longer exposed.

The entire coast, but especially the Sandy Cove end of Crescent Beach, has suffered severe erosion; it is estimated that when the first colonists landed in 1661 the shore along the beach was as much as a half-mile wide than it is today. The fierce storms that buffet this seaborne outpost, coupled with the conflicting currents of Long Island and Block Island Sounds, which meet and clash off the north end of the island, have caused the erosion. Even now, on a moderately calm day you can stand on the dune in front of North Light and watch waves coming from opposite directions crash into one another in a foaming mass off the north point.

At the time of Block's short stay, the island was inhabited by the Manisses, a relatively peaceful tribe related to the mainland Narragansett Nation. After the Narragansetts were defeated by the colonists of Massachusetts Bay in 1636, the colony was looking for a suitable reward for Governor John Endicott, so they gave him Block Island. He sold it to a small group of investors, who in turn convinced 16 men and their families to move to the island and establish a permanent settlement there. (A granite monument at the parking area for North Light honors these settlers.) In 1661 they appeared off Cow Cove, pushed their cattle off their boats and accompanied the swimming beasts to shore, causing some mirth among the remaining 300 or so Manisses.

While the Manisses were the primary inhabitants of pre-European Block Island, other tribes from the mainland and Long Island also were attracted by its abundant sea foods and made periodic attacks on the Manisses. The most famous of these attacks was recorded by a settler of 1760 and is based on the story told to him by the Manisses. While on their way to raid the Mohegans on the mainland, the Manisses discovered that a war party of Mohegans was on its way to attack the island. Returning, the Manisses waited in ambush and attacked, destroying the Mohegans canoes and pursuing the warriors. The hapless Mohegans dug trenches in front of the bluffs on the south shore but finally had no choice but to jump off into the sea. While their defensive trenches

The Rhode Island Guide

have long since fallen after them, the area is still called Mohegan Bluffs.

After the settlers arrived on the island, the Manisses became restive with their new neighbors, and somewhat aggressive. They had a refuge on an island in Trimms Pond, opposite what is now the marina near New Harbor. The settlers decided that they had to show their spirit, so 16 men and one boy marched against the fort where the Manisses were gathered, stopping at the opposite shore to make loud noises and beat on their drum. The show on both sides preserved face, and the "battle" of Fort Island led to improved relations between the groups.

Pirates, privateers and the French were a constant threat to all islanders. In 1689 a small fleet appeared offshore, and its leader claimed to be a friend of an English pirate who frequented the island. In reality it was William Trimmer, a French pirate. Gaining their trust,

A full-rigged sailing ship is not an uncommon sight in New Harbor.

Trimmer invited several islanders aboard. Taking them hostage, he captured the island, seized the islanders' goods and kept the people as captives. After a week Trimmer moved on to Fishers Island, where the now-alerted mainland militia attacked and killed him and his crew. The political instability caused by the French and British contest for the control of North America plagued the island until well after the turn of the seventeenth century; the colony of Rhode Island had to keep a company of troops stationed there to repel pirates and privateers.

During the Revolution the island suffered from British naval outfitting parties and from isolation from mainland markets. When, in 1812, the island was again cut off, residents achieved a sort of self-anointed neutrality and dealt freely with British naval officers seeking supplies for their ships. Again during World War I and even as late as World War II the island was cut off from mainland markets for its produce, and it is rumored that German submariners were known to barter here for fresh water and produce.

The island offered no safe harbor from the raging North Atlantic, and the early settlers decided to cut a channel to a large pond close to the island's center, making it a new harbor. But storms made it hard to keep this passage open, and it was abandoned. A new opening was cut to open ocean on the island's eastern side, and although it was also periodically closed by storms, it survived as a harbor. So important was the new harbor that every man and boy over 16 was required to provide several weeks' labor each year to maintain the pier and harbor. Try as they might, they couldn't keep up with nature, and by 1815 the harbor was closed again. It wasn't until 1899 that a permanent opening was created to the sea.

It is estimated that more than 500 ships have wrecked on or near the coasts of Block Island. Some of these gave names to parts of the island; others became the fabric of legend. In 1831 a ship, believed to be the *Warrior* (another source says it was the *Spartan*), a two-masted schooner with a cargo of calico fabric, wrecked on Sandy Point, and its cargo was tossed ashore. Salvaging the cloth, the islanders spread it on a hillside to dry, giving the hill the new name of Calico Hill. A monument to the people who died in this shipwreck is at the Island Cemetery.

A somewhat more mysterious legend tells of the *Palatine*, a ship filled with European immigrants from the lowlands that arrived here some time between 1720 and 1755. Legend suggests that the crew mutinied, imprisoning the hapless passengers and taking their possessions. Many died from starvation, and as the ship approached the island the crew abandoned it and rowed away with their booty. The few remaining survivors were taken ashore, the story continues, and the ship, while being towed, caught fire and drifted off to sea. A few years later islanders saw a strange glowing light at sea, the ghost of the burning *Palatine*. Called the Palatine Light, sitings of the strange glow were reported from time to time. Although the true name of the vessel is not known for certain, a monument to the dead of this shipwreck has been placed on the island's southwest bluffs, where shipwreck victims were buried.

Getting There

The most common port of access to Block Island is Point Judith, Rhode Island, but boats run seasonally from Providence and Newport and from Montauk on Long Island and New London in Connecticut. There is also air access from Westerly, taking less than 15 minutes flying time.

By Sea

Interstate Navigation Company operates year-round from **State Pier** in Galilee, with as many as 10 trips per day during the height of the season and one a day during the winter. From mid-June–Labor Day boats leave almost hourly, beginning at 8 A.M. The ferry carries cars and passengers and, during the season, has a snack bar. From the last weekend of June until Labor Day, passage is available on a limited basis from Providence (departing at 8:30 A.M., round-trip about $11) and from Newport (departing at 10:30 A.M., round-trip about $10) and arriving back in Newport at 5:30 P.M. and Providence at 7:30 P.M. Same-day round-trip rates are $10.50 per adult (children under twelve $5), and cars are $20.25 one way. One-way passenger rates are $6.50 and $3.15. It is crucial to reserve *well* in advance and be on the dock no less than an hour before sailing time. From I-95N in Connecticut, take Exit 92, skirting Westerly Rte. 78 and following Rte. 1 to the sign for Point Judith/Galilee. From Providence to Point Judith, follow I-95 south to Exit 9, and follow Rtes. 4 and 1 to Rte. 108 near Wakefield. The Providence ferry leaves from India Point Park off Gano St., on the east side. The Newport ferry terminal is at Fort Adams State Park. Follow the Fort Adams signs from Newport harbor. **Interstate Navigation Co., P.O. Box 482, New London CT 06302, Reservations; (401) 783-4613, (203) 442-7891 or 442-9553.**

NELSECO Navigation Company, an affiliate of Interstate Navigation Co., operates seasonal ferries from New London, Connecticut. The trip takes two hours and leaves at 9 A.M. daily from mid-June to mid-September (no cars after Labor Day). The ferry departs from Block Island at 4:30 P.M. Adult one-way fares are $13.50, $9 for children ($17.50 and $11 same-day round-trip); the one-way auto fare is $25. Reservations are required. Take I-95 north to Exit 83 (Huntington St.) or I-95 south to Exit 84S for downtown (Eugene O'Neill Dr.). Take either street to Governor Winthrop Blvd. and follow it to the ferry terminal. Park at the Water St. municipal parking lot. **Nelseco Navigation Co., 2 Ferry St., P.O. Box 482, New London, CT 06320; reservations in RI, (401) 783-4613, in CT, (203) 442-9553 or 442-7891.**

From Montauk on Long Island you can take *Jigger III*, a passengers-only ferry, from the first week of June until the third week of September. It leaves Montauk at 8:45 A.M. and Block Island at 4:30 P.M. Rates are $30 round-trip. Follow the Long Island Expressway (Rte. 495) to Rte. 46

The ferry brings cars and passengers from Point Judith to Block Island.

south, then at Rte. 27 go east. The ferry is at Pier 1 on the corner of West Lake Dr. and Flamingo Rd., and you should be there *no later than* 8:30 A.M. **Jigger III, P.O. Box. 461, Montauk NY 11954; (516) 668-2214.**

Viking Lines also runs a ferry from Montauk, Long Island to New Harbor. The one-hour forty-five-minute trip departs Montauk at 9 A.M. from Fri.–Sun. early May–mid-June and early Oct. and Mid-June–late Sept. daily at 9 A.M. From late July through Labor Day there are some limited weekend afternoon sailings. Fares are $30 round-trip. Viking sails from the ferry dock on West Lake Dr. **Viking Lines/ Montauk Ferry, West Lake Dr., Montauk, NY 11954; (516) 668-5700,** or from **Block Island (800)-MONTAUK.**

By Air

New England Airlines has regularly scheduled flights from **Westerly State Airport** every two hours from 7:30 A.M–7:30 P.M. daily. Return flights leave on the hour. During the summer flights run hourly and extend until 10:30 P.M. on Friday nights. Westerly State Airport is at Rtes. 78 and 1 (the Post Rd.). Charter services are available. Luggage space may

be limited. **New England Airlines, State Airport, Westerly 02891; (800) 243-2460, from Westerly (401) 596-2460, from Block Island (401) 466-5881.**

Resort Air has a twin-engine five-passenger charter service to the island operated by its owner/captain. **P.O. Box 577, Block Island 02807; (401) 466-2000, fax (401) 466-2707.**

Action Airlines has weekend service from **LaGuardia Airport** for about $150 from mid-May–Labor Day. It also will fly charter flights from Groton, Connecticut, or other airports. **Action Airlines, 155 Tower Ave., Groton, CT 06340; (800) 243-8623.**

By Train and Bus

You can't get all the way to the island by train, but **Amtrak** connects to New London, Kingston, Westerly and Providence. It's a short cab ride to the Westerly Airport from the train station, or from the Providence station to the ferry docks. Amtrak passengers arriving at Kingston station can connect to Point Judith via **RIPTA** buses. Those arriving at T. F. Greene Airport in Warwick can also take RIPTA buses directly to Point Judith or, if one is not running at a convenient time, can take the bus to the central RIPTA station in Providence to connect from there. **Amtrak (800) 872-7245; RIPTA (800) 244-0444** or **(401) 781-9400.**

Getting Around

By Bicycle and Moped

Beach Rose Bicycle Rental offers rentals of Raleigh 21-speed mountain bikes at $10 for a half day, $15 for a full day. Rentals include helmet. At the Rose Farm Inn, High St., at the end of the Atlantic Hotel access road; **(401) 466-2946. Seacrest Bicycle Shop** also has all kinds of bicycles available: Kids' bikes are $6 per day, 6-speeds $8 per day, and 12-speeds for $12 per day. They also do repairs. They are in the center of Old Harbor, not far from the ferry. Prices include helmet. At the corner of Weldon's Way. **207 High St., Block Island 02807; (401) 466-2882.**

Esta's Bikes also rents bicycles at competitive rates from its shop on Chapel St., just off Water St.; **(401) 466-2946.** The **Moped Man** is on Water St. just to the left of the ferry landing. They also have mountain bikes; **(401) 466-5011. Aldo's Bikes & Mopeds, (401) 466-5871,** and **Island Moped, (401) 466-2700,** are a short distance away on Weldon Way (on Water St. turn right, then take an immediate left). Check with your hotel or inn when you make your reservation, because many have bikes for guests to use free of charge.

By Taxi

Not the least expensive way to get around, but available. Taxi travel on the island is regulated by zones, so ask about the fare for your itinerary before you climb into the cab. **Wright's Oceanview Taxi, (401) 789-0400** or **(800) 698-2941; A. Ernst Taxi, (401) 782-5659; Riker Taxi, (401) 466-2062; Gann's Taxi, (401) 782-7097; OJ's Taxi, (401) 782-5826;** and **Wolfie's Taxi, (401) 466-5550.**

Outdoor Activities

Biking

Block Island is made for bicycles. Much of the terrain is low rolling hills with long relatively flat stretches, and bicycles can travel the dirt and gravel roads that cross over parts of the island most visitors never see. From Center Rd. take Beacon Hill Rd. over the highest point on the island (the top is 211 feet above the sea). Or follow Cooneymus Rd. west and north along the shore to Grace Cove Rd. and then back to West Side Rd. An *Official Visitors Map* is available from the chamber of commerce and most hotels, showing most of the dirt roads and all of the paved ones.

Birding

The entire island is a birder's dream, especially during the fall migration, when songbirds stop here on their way south. Take Corn Neck Rd. to its end at Settlers Rock on the north side of Chaqum Pond. This is the beginning of **Block Island National Wildlife Refuge,** a 46-acre reserve of sand dunes and beach growth that is a major rookery for gulls and an important part of the Atlantic flyway.

Canoeing

While there is great kayaking and canoeing in the waters around the edge of the island, with seaward views of the Mohegan Cliffs, Clayhead and the lighthouses, tides, winds, unexpected fog and storms make this the playground of only the most experienced kayaker and canoeist. For the beginner and novice, however, there are still a lot of places to paddle. **Great Salt Pond,** the large body of water at New Harbor, is one place to start. Much of the shoreline is not built up and is still in its wild state. On the north end you can either search out the 1889 cut that attempted to open the pond to the sea or circumnavigate Skipper's Island. At the southeast corner of the pond a narrow cut leads into **Trimm's Pond** and the **Hog Pen,** a marina favored by islanders. Heading southwest, you'll pass **Rat Island,** then travel by the site of the **Indian Fort.** On the east end of the pond another watercourse provides access to **Harbor Pond,** whose southern end is almost at Dodge St. in Old Harbor. These two smaller ponds provide a unique perspective of the island and pleasant flat-water canoeing. Elsewhere, there are in excess of 350 ponds, most of them spring-fed. Some of the small ponds are actually old peat beds that islanders dug up for fuel until the end of World War II. The largest of the freshwater ponds is Fresh Pond, about 90 feet deep. Canoes and kayaks can be rented from **Oceans & Ponds, The Orvis Store, Ocean Ave.; (401) 466-5131.**

155

The sand bluffs at Southeast Lighthouse continue to erode from the constant pounding of the sea.

156

Fishing

Sitting at the ocean edge of a major bay system, Block Island offers plenty of good fishing. Some of the species available are bluefish, striped bass, fluke, cod, marlin and dolphin (the fish, not the mammal). There are nine varieties of shark alone in these waters, including sand sharks, makos and great whites. Sport tuna fishing is available for the adventurous. For charter and rentals, call **G. Willie Makit at Dories Cove; (401) 466-5151.**

Many islanders with fishing boats will take guests out. Most innkeepers will be able to arrange this for you. The extensive shoreline of the island makes for miles of surf fishing. The major ponds of the island are also well provided with sizable freshwater species, including trout. The freshwater fishing here is one of the most underappreciated assets of the island. A license is required for freshwater inland fishing but not for surf and sea fishing. **Oceans & Ponds, The Orvis Store,** runs fly and spin inshore fishing trips and can also arrange for guides. It also sells and rents fresh- and saltwater fishing equipment and sells licenses. **Ocean Ave., (401) 466-5131.**

Hiking and Walking

Walking and hiking possibilities are limited only by your energy level. For a short two-mile walk over easy terrain, follow Water St. north from the ferry to Dodge St. Take Dodge St. to Corn Neck Rd. and follow it to Beach Ave. On this stretch you will be passing between dunes and Block Island Sound on the east and **Harbor Pond** on the west. Turn left onto Beach Ave. The big square white building sitting high above the road on the north side is the old Block Island weather station; it's about a mile from your start.

You can add about a mile and a lot of interesting scenery to the trip by taking West Side Rd. to New Harbor. It will pass over **Trimm's Pond,** past the **Indian Fort** and the **Hog Pen** to **Payne's Pier** in New Harbor. From the pier, rejoin West Side Rd. and follow it uphill to the right to the **Block Island Historical Cemetery.** Take a left at the cemetery to Beach Ave. and go to Ocean Ave. If you don't take the road to New Harbor, continue along Beach Ave. to Ocean Ave., which will be on your right. Follow Ocean Ave. back to Dodge St.

Another variant is to follow Beach Ave. past West Side Rd. to the Old Town Rd. and go left. This will take you through the old center of the town (from the 1700s–1900s). Continue on Old Town Rd. until it becomes Chapel St., following it to Weldon Way. Stop for ice cream or pastry along Weldon before returning to Water St. and your beginning point.

South of Old Harbor, the walk to Southeast Light is just under two miles each way. From the harbor, follow Spring St. up the hill past the **Manisses Hotel** and the **Spring House Hotel** (built in 1853). The Manisses gardens and exotic animal farm are on the right. The road passes through low growth to the lighthouse. For a good view back toward the light, continue past it to the entrance to the stairway down to the beach, where there is a platform. Retrace your route or, if you're up to more primitive terrain, take Pilot Hill Rd., a dirt road that goes inland. It will take you to High St., past the island school and back to Water St.

Rodman's Hollow is a large ravine left behind by the last glacier. While the beginning of the trail is high above the sea, the bottom is only a few feet above sea level. Saved from development, the 114-acre tract is now part of the island nature reserve system and has hiking trails running through it. The entrance is on the south side of Cooneymus Rd. (some maps show this as Cherry Hill Rd.). Just before the entrance is a sign and a good overview of the reserve.

The Greenway is a network of trails that runs from the central part of the island to the southern shore, a joint venture of the four major conservancy organizations on the island. It is for walkers only and runs through some of the most sensitive wildlife habitat on the island. Before taking this trail, get a map and further information from **The Nature Conservancy.** The office is **at the corner of Ocean Ave. and Legion Way at New Harbor; (401) 466-2554.**

For some island history, take Cooneymus Rd. west until the paved road makes a sharp turn northward and becomes West Side Rd. At the intersection notice the large painted stone. This is the island "message" stone, which may announce anything from a birthday greeting to a missing cat.

At the intersection with West Side Rd., continue straight ahead on Cooneymus Rd., which becomes dirt. As the road nears the shore it bears off to the right and past **Steven's Cove, Martin's Point** and **Dorie's Cove.** These coves were used as harbors by the Manisses and by the first settlers, who dried their fish on racks here. Beyond Dorie's Cove the road will bear inland. Take Grace's Cove Rd. left, and in about 0.4-mile there will be a small road to the left to Grace's Cove. The road continues to the right and meets West Side Rd. about a mile and a half north of the message stone.

Nature Walks

The walks described above all pass through areas of great natural interest but can be even more engrossing if done with a knowledgeable guide. **The Nature Conservancy** and **Block Island Conservancy** conduct an ongoing series of walks throughout the summer. Other walks are held during the fall. For specifics on which walks will be available during your stay, call **(401) 466-2129** or **(401) 466-2554.** The conservancies office is **at the corner of Ocean Ave. and Legion Way at New Harbor.**

Horseback Riding

On West Side Rd., **Rustic Rides Farm** gives you a chance to see the beaches from the saddle. In addition to guided rides on the beach, they offer pony rides for children. **P.O. Box 842, West Side Rd.; (401) 466-5060.** The farm is marked by a sign on the west side of the road.

Swimming

Block Island has some of the finest beaches along the entire Atlantic Coast. Except for the State Beach, there are no lifeguards. Tide and wind conditions can create dangerous undercurrents and riptides. Always keep an eye out for these conditions, particularly with children. Also, watch for the rising tide, which could cut you off from your path.

A beach at **Old Harbor** is within the area protected by the breakwater, but commercial boats make this a less savory place to bathe. A few hundred feet north of the harbor, starting at the Surf Hotel, **Crescent Beach**

If you don't mind the long climb back up, the beach below Southeast Lighthouse is quiet and uncrowded.

157

stretches northward along the east side of the island for more than two miles. This beautiful sandy beach is within easy walking distance of the ferry terminal. It is very popular and during the summer very crowded with day-trippers. Less than a mile farther along the beach is the **State Beach,** with restrooms and changing facilities. Farther out Corn Neck Rd. watch for Mansion Beach Rd., a dirt road on the east side, leading to the beautiful quiet town beach.

Also within easy walking distance of the terminal are **Ballard's Beach** and **Pebbly Beach,** just south of the harbor area. At Pebbly Beach look for rounded stones, known as cobbles. In the last century these were harvested here and sold to mainland cities as paving stones.

Farther out along Corn Neck Rd. the town has bought land and established a public beach at the end of Mansion Rd. This was the site of the 1886 dream-house mansion of mil-lionaire Edward F. Searles, an elaborate three-story house with a central hall open to the dome and the room on each side of the hall a duplicate of the other. With a boardwalk and a miniature replica of itself used as a beach pavilion, the mansion was the center of turn-of-the-century island society. Now long gone, bits of it remain to tease the imagination while the public plays on its beach.

If you're headed out to **Southeast Light** you might want to wear your bathing suit and bring a picnic lunch. Under the **Mohegan Bluffs** there is an attractive sandy beach with the 200-foot bluffs rising dramatically behind. The beach is at the front of a wooden stairway of 151 steps, although on the way back up it will seem about three times that number.

Follow Mohegan Trail, then Lakeside Dr., then Cherry Hill Rd. west past Rodman's Hollow to Black Rock Rd., where a narrow dirt road leads to **Black Rock Point Beach.** There's a big rock in the middle of the road, so you can't drive all the way and you can't turn around, so don't go by car. Take Cooneymus Rd. toward the former lifeguard station on the shore, or follow the main paved road (at this point it is the West Side Rd.) north less than a mile to Dorie's Cove Rd., and take it to the shore. These beaches are at the end of narrow dirt roads with little or no parking. Mopeds are not allowed, so it's best to get there on foot or by bicycle.

The beach at **Charleston Cove,** farther along the west side, is also a popular choice. It's near the Coast Guard station off of Champlin Rd., until recently called Coast Guard Rd. Follow the dirt lane to its end, past small farms, wild roses and views toward Great Salt Pond, to the parking area at the Coast Guard station. From the station there is a path to the beach that is known as **Charleston Beach** locally. There are actually two areas here: One is on the ocean side and the other is along the cut that opens Great Salt Pond to the sea. This is also a popular place for surf fishing and watching the boat traffic coming and going from the harbor. From Old Harbor take Ocean Ave. to New Harbor, and then take a left onto West Side Rd. to Champlin Rd.

Charleston Beach is close to the Coast Guard Station at the entrance to Great Salt Pond.

On the north end of the island there is a sandy beach on the west side that can be reached from the **North Lighthouse.** Take Corn Neck Rd. to the parking lot for the lighthouse, then follow the path along the beach to the light and take the stair over the dunes to the beach. It is important to avoid this beach during the spring and early summer nesting season because it is a breeding ground for herring and great black-backed gulls. Not only is it dangerous for the chicks to have you around, but their parents will dive-bomb anything that appears to be a threat to their young.

Seeing and Doing

North Lighthouse

The waters around the island are filled with hidden threats to ships, as the long history of shipwrecks in the area shows. To warn ships, lighthouses were built at either end of the island. The first light was put up in 1829 at a point now well out in the water off the north tip. When the sea encroached a few years later, the light was torn down, and its replacement went up in 1837 west of the northern end of Chaqum Pond. It, in turn, was destroyed by storm and its successor built in 1857, again toward the north tip but still at the wrong spot. Soon it was necessary to build another, and in 1867 a solid building of Connecticut granite was put among the dunes on the point. Although its light was replaced as a navigational aid by an electronic beacon, the lighthouse was restored in 1989.

The north tip of the island consists entirely of a dune system, and access to the lighthouse is on foot over a loose pebble and sand beach. (Handicapped persons can call for vehicular access, **(401) 466-3220,** with a 48-hour notice.) The building has an interpretive center with artifacts of the light and its predecessors, lifesaving equipment, shipwrecks and displays on the dunes and gull rookery. Compare the photos of the lighthouse in the museum with the actual land around it today to appreciate just how changeable the dunes are. The center

North Lighthouse was rebuilt several times after it was destroyed by storms.

is open June–mid-Sept. 10 from A.M.–5 P.M. daily, and weekends only mid-Sept.–mid-Oct. Admission is $2, children under 12 are admitted free.

Outside the light, a wooden stair leads up over the dunes and down to the beach on the other side. At the top of the stair you can see the skeletal remains of the second light. Walking among the dunes here is prohibited, but you can walk the long beach that runs along the west shore all the way to the harbor neck. Be sure to check the tide schedule and allow time for your return before high tide.

Southeast Lighthouse

While the weather has been kinder to southeast lighthouse, it, too, has had its travails. Construction began on the brick lighthouse in 1875 at a point 204 feet above the ocean at the southeast point of the island, and its oil-burning light was first used on February 1, 1875. To get to the light, follow Spring St. from Old Harbor. As you round a bend and crest a hill, it's suddenly there, a huge brick Victorian confection with a tall brick tower. There's a very small parking lot at the end of the drive, followed by an easy walk to the light. Threatened by the erosion of Mohegan Bluffs, by the 1990s the lighthouse had to be moved or it would have slid down into the sea. The huge structure, successfully freed from the foundation it had been built on 120 years earlier, was

Southeast Lighthouse on Block Island was moved when cliff erosion threatened to send it into the Atlantic.

moved back 208 feet from the cliff in 1994, the heaviest complete structure ever moved by humans. Its light, now electric, can be seen 35 miles out at sea, and the sound of its horn can be heard for 11 miles. The tower is open July–Oct. from 10 A.M.–4 P.M., and a tour is given for a fee of $5. An exhibit and the gift shop are open without charge; **(401) 466-5009.** Don't be surprised if it is closed during its "regular" hours—this is an island.

While the most impressive view of the lighthouse is from its own grounds, for the most photogenic view, travel west a short distance to a parking lot on the south side of the road. A short trail will take you to a platform that gives a full panoramic view of the light in its context on the edge of the cliff high above the sea.

Block Island Club

Anyone planning to be on the island for a week or more may want to consider a short-term membership in the Block Island Club. Although most of the members are islanders, visitors can buy one-, two- or four-week family memberships from $195 to $395. The clubhouse is a replica of a Block Island lifesaving station built by the Mystic Seaport Museum when the original was moved to the Connecticut museum. The club facilities are on Great Salt Pond but reached from Corn Neck Rd. and offer sailing, tennis and swimming lessons at all levels for children, teenagers and adults. Group lessons are $6 per session, and private lessons can be arranged. JY 15's, Lasers and Sunfish and a 20-foot Highlander as well as boards and rigs for windsurfing are available to members. The club also offers overnight camping for kids, teen dances and family cookouts. This is a bargain way to be a "native" and enhance your family's experience as well.

Block Island Historical Society Museum

Island history and a flavor of island life a century ago are preserved in a nineteenth-century farmhouse. Three furnished rooms are restored to the 1890s with interpretive displays explaining the island's Native and European settlements and the story of the rise and fall of its fishing industry. The museum shop has reproductions of old island photos for sale. Open from 10 A.M.–4 P.M. daily during June–Aug., from 11 A.M.–4 P.M. weekdays and 10 A.M.–5 P.M. weekends until Columbus Day and on weekends from 10 A.M.–4 P.M. in the spring and late fall. Admission is $2. At the **corner of Old Town Rd. and Ocean Ave.; (401) 466-2481.**

Indian Fort

By 1661 the Manisses Indians had erected a rude fort to protect themselves from the European settlers, and the settlers in turn found the presence of the fort threatening. The confrontation between them (300 Indians and 16 adult settlers and a boy, according to legend) led to a great deal of drum beating but little bloodshed. While nothing of the fort remains, a monument marks the spot today at a point opposite the **Hog Pen** on the road to New Harbor. While the origin of the name "Hog Pen" is lost, it is now the marina where most islanders keep their boats. Recent archaeological excavations on the shores of **Great Salt Pond** have revealed that this area was settled by Native peoples as long as 2,500 years ago.

Cemeteries

The **Block Island Historical Cemetery at the intersection of Center Rd. and West Side**

Indian Sites in Rhode Island

The Narragansetts, who made up about half the Rhode Island Indian population, occupied the land west of the bay, the Wampanoags occupied the Bristol County region and the Pequots nudged from the west in what is now Connecticut. A smattering of Nipmucks and Niantics made up the rest of the 8,000 to 10,000 Native people living here at the time of the first colonial incursions. All these groups were nations of the Algonquin.

They hunted, fished, gathered shellfish, farmed and were hospitable to the early settlers, who purchased their land and respected their way of life. This early relationship deteriorated until it erupted into King Philip's War and the near extinction of the local tribes. Indian place names and a wealth of archaeological evidence remain from their centuries of habitation. Brown University's **Haffenreffer Museum, The Museum of Primitive Art and Culture** in Peace Dale, the collections in the **Warren Library,** and the **Dovecrest Trading Post and Museum** in Exeter have major Native collections, but local historical societies throughout the state also have some finds. Of these, only the Haffenreffer is open more than a few hours a week, and it is in the process of moving from Bristol to Provi-

dence. The Dovecrest has, as we write, no regular hours but can be reached by telephone; **(401) 539-7795.**

The most interesting site, we think, is **Queen's Fort** in Exeter, near the North Kingstown line, a stone defensive position that is still clearly recognizable. In **Charlestown** is a burial ground, not far from the Indian church, which has unfortunately suffered a fire and is no longer in use. But the land around it is still the meeting place for tribal events. **Treaty Rock** in South Kingston and **King Philip's Seat** in Bristol are other landmarks.

The trails that once connected the settlements throughout the area were the first roads the settlers used, and along these they built their plantations. As a result, the roads we travel today follow the routes of the Pequot and Wampanoag Trails: US 1A and the various stretches marked Old Post Road, the old Route 1, follows the Pequot Trail through Wickford, Wakefield and Charlestown. Route 114 through Barrington is still called the Wampanoag Trail, and Weybosset St. in Providence winds along the route of the Pequot Trail as it forded the river and joined the Wampanoag and Nipmuck Trails on its east bank.

Rd. contains the graves of the island's earliest settlers, and just about everyone who has lived here since then. Many of the ancient headstones tell life stories or have somber angel faces. Although it doesn't have carved headstones, the **Indian Cemetery** has its own special feeling. From the Historical Cemetery follow Center Rd. to the cemetery about 0.2-mile beyond Cherry Hill Rd. (at Cherry Hill Rd., Center Rd. becomes Lakeshore Dr.). The cemetery is on the left side of the road, across from **Fresh Pond,** one of the largest freshwater ponds on the island. The Indians had a settlement here along the hillside above the pond,

and when the first Europeans came, they spent their first years here living in harmony with the Indians. The drought in 1995 forced the town to run a five-foot hose 3,700 feet from Fresh Pond so that water could be taken to refill the nearly empty town reservoir.

Littlefield Bee Farm

Chris Littlefield spends a lot of time on his duties with The Nature Conservancy and the Block Island Conservancy, and part of what is left over he spends on the family business. The Littlefields run an apiary from their farm on the Corn Neck Rd. opposite the entrance to the road to Clayhead Trail. In addition to native honey, they sell honey mustard, beeswax candles and gift baskets. They are open all year, and their products can also be found in several local stores and gift shops.

Where to Stay

All lodging on the island is in older hotels, inns and B&B accommodations. There are no motels and no chains. Nearly all of the older hotels have been completely renovated to add features of safety and comfort expected in fine hotels. Regardless of the price range, you'll find open hospitality and a clean place to stay.

The Island Home—$$$ to $$$$

This big old turn-of-the-century farmhouse has a new life as a bed and breakfast, and it's reminiscent of guest houses of the past. It's about three-quarters of a mile from **Old Harbor** and a half mile from **Crescent Beach.** While you wouldn't want to walk there with your luggage, it is an easy walk to major points once you're there. Twelve rooms are in the main house and in the converted carriage shed behind it. The rooms in the carriage shed all have porches that overlook **Trimm's Pond** and the hills beyond. While everything is clean and well maintained, this is a basic B&B, a good value during the off-season, but a bit overpriced during the high season. A full breakfast is served, restaurant-style, from a menu in the attractive breakfast room. The two rooms that share a bath are $60 to $82 in May and June, rooms with private bath are $75 to $100, rates for the shared bath rise to $100 to $125 in Aug. and early Sept. and for private bath $125 to $150. There is a $25 charge for an extra person and a charge for all children. Rates fall to the spring level mid-Sept.–Columbus Day. Closed from Columbus Day through May. The high end of the rates range is for weekends, when there is a minimum-stay requirement. Located at the **corner of Beach and Ocean Aves. P.O. Box 737, Block Island 02807; (401) 466-5944.**

The Atlantic—$$$$

High above the town and the harbor, The Atlantic catches the breezes that blow in from the sound. Front rooms and the porches and lawns have an expansive view of the town, harbor and water; on clear days the shores of the mainland are clearly visible. This is a fine old hotel (1879) that has been carefully renovated to retain the charm of its period while providing modern amenities. The pleasant and bright lobby and sitting room are furnished with a carved Victorian sofa and armchairs— a good place to read if you find the large porch too breezy. All of the rooms are on the second and third floors; the first is the dining room and bar. Room #5 is a corner room with nice cross-ventilation, and room #4 is papered in a pale green embossed wallpaper typical of the architectural detail of the late nineteenth century. Room #17, on the third floor, is perhaps one of the nicest—it's large, with a beautiful Victorian carpet. Its view of the town and harbor is remarkable. April–mid-June is called the "Nice Season," and the rates are $99 to $145, which jump to $110 to $195 during the "Inn Season," from mid-June–Labor Day. There is a two-night minimum stay on weekends in the spring, three-night minimum in summer. During the Nice Season, however, a third day is available for 50% of the regular rate. Rates return to the spring prices from Labor Day through Columbus Day. **P.O. Box 188, High St., Block Island 02807; (401) 466-5883.**

Seacrest Inn—$$$ to $$$$

When this building was erected, the first floor was a bowling alley with second-floor rooms for the staff of a nearby hotel. It has now been renovated into the 17-room Seacrest Inn. It's family-run and offers a less expensive option to the larger hotels. All rooms have private baths, with toilet and shower in the bathroom, sink in the sleeping room. While the rooms are fairly small, they are clean and nicely furnished, some with 1950s maple colonial reproductions and others with white painted wicker.

Room #19, a corner room on the second floor, is light and cheerful, with wicker furniture. Complimentary Continental breakfast is available from 8–9 A.M. There is parking, a fenced play area for kids and a gazebo and hammocks for their parents. It's right in the heart of the **Old Harbor** area, a five-minute walk from the ferry landing. High-season rates for two are $95 to $130, for three $100 to $145 and for four $105 to $150. In the off-season the rates run from $55 to $100 for the same categories. During the off-season a two-night stay will get you a third night free in midweek, but you have to reserve a week in advance. Ask about special weekly rates. Open May–mid-Oct. The Seacrest also has an on-premises bicycle rental shop. **207 High St., Block Island 02807; (401) 466-2882 during the season,** or **(407) 862-6746 in mid-Oct.–late April.**

Gables Inn, Gables Inn II— $$$ to $$$$

Another inexpensive lodging option on the island are these two Victorian homes close to the center of town. Although most of the rooms are small and share baths, they are pleasant, clean and nicely furnished. All of the rooms have ceiling fans and bureau fans. Guests have a nice outdoor sitting area, two ornate Victorian parlors and a small cozy reading and writing room, and the inn has barbecue grills and picnic tables, swings, horseshoes and croquet. There is limited parking on the grounds, and the inn is about an eight-minute walk from the ferry landing, even closer to the sandy **Crescent Beach.** During high season a room for two with shared bath is $75 to $90 (off-season it's $50 to $80), and a room with private bath is $95 to $125 (off-season $70 to $110). Efficiency apartments or cottages, for two to four guests, are $130 to $225, and they have weekly rates. (Meadowwood, for four, costs $765 a week). Other special rates are available. A two-night minimum is generally required, with a three-night stay during the high season, but you can check for availability of shorter stays. A Continental breakfast with homemade muffins or pastries is served in the

ornate parlor. You can't miss the wonderful Victorian reception desk window, and be sure to look at the metal ceilings. Open Memorial Day to Columbus Day. **Gables Inn, P.O. 516, Dodge St., Block Island 02807; (401) 466-2213, 466-7721 in season. Off-season write Gables Inn, c/o Nyzio, 1770 66th Ave. North, St. Petersburg FL 33702; (813) 526-4296.**

The National Hotel—$$ to $$$$

The white tower surmounted by a briskly flying flag draws everyone's attention as each ferry arrives from Point Judith. This five-story building, with an entire level of shops below its porch, has an unobstructed view of the sea. It has been here since the nineteenth century and is listed on the National Register of Historic Places. Unlike most old hotels, the National is also fully sprinkler-protected, and major renovation means that all of the rooms have the modern conveniences guests expect. The victim has been the hotel's nineteenth-century ambiance, but if you're looking for a quality harborfront hotel a five-minute walk from **Crescent Beach,** this is the place. Although the Water St. entrance is reached by stairs from the street, there is handicapped access from the rear of the building, where there is also limited off-street parking. The hotel has a fully handicapped-accessible room on the first floor. Rooms on the front have a bird's-eye view of the harbor but can be noisy in the summer, when Water St. is busy until the wee hours. The rooms are somewhat small but not cramped, and they are modern, furnished with mixed antiques and contemporary pieces. All rooms have a full modern bath and fan, color TV, phones and beach towels. The lobby is not a place to curl up with a book, but porch chairs on the opposite side of the porch from the lounge/dining room have nice views and the area is relatively quiet in midafternoon. Open May–Oct. Rates vary between weekends and weekdays and become higher toward August. A midweek double that costs $79 the first week of May will be $139 in August. The

163

Point Judith ferry landing is right across the street. **Water St., P.O. Box 189, Block Island 02807; (401) 466-2901, (800) 225-2449.**

The Surf Hotel—$$ to $$$$

In the 1870s this hotel was built for Victorian pleasure seekers, and it still retains the same ambiance 120 years later. It dominates the north end of the harbor area and is literally the boundary between the harbor and **Crescent Beach.** In fact, it is the only hotel on the island with direct access to the beach via its own private stair to the white sand below. While the grand old porch rockers on its Victorian porch look out over the harbor, the tables and chairs on the modern deck are right over the sandy beach. There should be no mistake about the modernity of this hotel. With a few exceptions, all rooms share bathrooms. This

The Surf Hotel stands above Block Island State Beach in Old Harbor.

gray-shingled building has been nicely maintained by the same family for more than 40 years, and they have taken pains to maintain the integrity of the hotel and its nineteenth-century ambiance. This is the real thing, tin ceilings and all, and although you give up some modern amenities, you get the rare chance to enjoy the lingering remnants of a golden age. The dining room serves breakfast only, and only to guests. An oceanside double midweek in the spring is $70, and the same room in high season will cost $90 (with shared bath). Weekend rates are slightly higher, but weekly rates offer good discounts. The hotel is clean as a whistle throughout, very nicely maintained and a good buy for the island, but if you have a thing about shared baths, look elsewhere. Reserve early; most guests reserve for next year as they check out. **Dodge St., P.O. Box C, Block Island 02807; (401) 466-2241.**

Rose Farm Inn—$$$ to $$$$

This inn has the most extensive grounds on the island, covering a former farm. The new Captain Rose House has views across 20 acres of rolling hillside, and the view in the opposite direction covers the town and the ocean beyond. The Farm House is the original farm residence from 1887, completely rebuilt as an inn in 1980. The second-floor rooms in the Captain Rose open onto both sides of the building, giving wonderful air flow and views of the fields from the private balconies and of the town from the entry deck on the other side. Tastefully decorated, and with such important amenities as good bedside reading lights, the rooms are furnished with fine antiques and reproductions, and several have double whirlpools. One could settle into room #12 for a long stay. Its Victorian-style rose-covered walls are a nice setting for the Sheraton four-poster bed with lace canopy. In fact, many of the rooms feature four-poster beds, and all have firm, comfortable mattresses. While the rooms in the Farm House don't have balconies, they do have nice views and are large and furnished in the same style as the Captain Rose.

The breakfast room at the Farm House has window-filled walls that let in the sun and the views. The complimentary buffet breakfast includes homemade breakfast breads. High-season rates are $115 to $160 in the Farm House and $135 to $175 in the Captain Rose; two shared-bath rooms are $90 each. Weekend rates in the spring and fall are the same, but weekday rates are lower. There is a substantial drop in winter-month rates. Minimum stays are required in the summer and at some other times. Open Mar.–Nov. Bicycle rentals are available on the inn grounds. **P.O. Box E (at the end of the Atlantic Hotel access road), Block Island 02807; (401) 466-2034.**

The 1661 Inn, Hotel Manisses—$$$$

In 1969 the Abrams family began the restoration of some of Block Island's historic inns, creating two of the island's most outstanding properties. While the two share reservation and other management functions, they are separate, with different atmospheres. Guests at each share the pleasures of the other, a nice marriage of function and style.

The 1661 Inn

This large rambling house, with 18 rooms in the main building and six additional rooms in the adjoining Sherman and Nicholas Ball Cottages, overlooks the sea. Even in breezy or rainy weather you can watch the surf and see the fog creep in. Breakfast on the sunporch of The 1661 serves both inns, and offers guests a large buffet with several varieties of fresh fruit, cereals, juices, pastries, muffins, breakfast meats, corned beef hash, bacon, home fries, pancakes and cooked-to-order eggs. The breakfast is complimentary for guests; nonguests can enjoy it for $11.50. The only flaw in the ambiance is the plastic chairs. Almost all the rooms have private baths, several have whirlpool tubs and many have decks, refrigerators and other extras. The Ball and Littlefield rooms are large, with private decks overlooking the wild freshwater pond and the sea. That privacy creates the impression of

having your own little cottage by the sea. The main building of the inn is just a minute's walk away along a beautiful flower-lined walk. The three bedrooms of Sherman Cottage are the only ones that share a bath, fine for a family or for friends traveling together. The nicely furnished rooms are separate from other guest rooms and share a full kitchen. In the main building the Deering room has silky pink walls with dark blue trim, a huge white Victorian four-poster bed and a view of the sea.

Hotel Manisses

When it was built in 1870, the Manisses was one of the island's grandest hotels, but by 1972 the once-famous hotel was so derelict that an appointment had literally been made with a bulldozer. Countless hours of labor later, it has regained its place as the island's unquestioned premier hotel. All the modern safety features (built-in sprinklers and fire and heat detectors) have been discreetly added, and comfort features such as large well-appointed bathrooms and telephones have been installed without sacrificing the aura of the golden age and the elegance reflected in small details and in the fine antique furnishings. Rooms in the hotel are all named for famous shipwrecks along the coast before 1870. Antoinette has its own entrance from the wide porch at the front of the hotel, as does the adjoining Almira. The rooms Palatine and Princess Augusta, on the second floor, are large rooms with king-sized beds, fine antique furnishings and fine old engravings on the walls. They also have whirlpools, large sink space and big showers. Even the smaller rooms, such as Palmetto, are spacious and comfortable. Two large public rooms off the lobby have the clear imprint of the old hotel, as does the wide front porch, where you can retire for people-watching.

Behind the hotel are the gardens and an eclectic farm. Don't be surprised to see an emu, llamas, a Sicilian donkey, a highland bull with long curving horns or other exotic creatures. Both guests and nonguests are invited to enjoy the farm and gardens. The hotel also offers other programs, most of which are unique.

165

Block Island is ringed by beaches where you can build sandcastles or just sit and watch the waves.

A daily complimentary guided sight-seeing tour is offered, and the hotel will make picnic lunches (including checkered tablecloths and wicker baskets), set up gourmet meals at your favorite secluded spot, arrange fishing trips and tell you where the best beaches are. It will even serve a romantic dinner for two in your room or overlooking the Mohegan Bluffs. There is usually a special program available, especially in the off-seasons, such as nature walks with an island naturalist, wine evenings, a pumpkinfest, pre-Christmas and New Year's weekend packages and special midwinter getaways. Rates in the high season (late July through Labor Day) are $146 to $325 weekdays and weekends. Rates are substantially lower in the spring, autumn and winter months. **Hotel Manisses/The 1661 Inn, 1 Spring St., Block Island 02807; (401) 466-2421 or 466-2063, fax 466-2858.**

Where to Eat

Eli's—$

One clue to a restaurant's quality is the look on people's faces when you mention its name. Eli's evokes a look of amusement and pleasure. Inside the small shingle-clad building are six small tables and a dining bar, the top of which is covered with handcrafted tiles with paintings of whales, sharks and other fish done by an island artist, Bill Kelley. The place may be small, but the food is big. Try the Gorgonzola tortellini—three kinds of tortellini prepared with broccoli florets, walnuts and Gorgonzola cream sauce—or the Thai chicken and shrimp, pan-seared with vegetables and sherry with a curry, peanut and ginger sauce over angel-hair pasta. The basis for most of the meals served here is pasta. Eli's has a beer and wine license. It's open 5–10 p.m. in the summer and closes earlier off-season, but it is open year-round. No reservations—in the summer there can be a formidable line, so eat early, or late. **Chapel St. at Weldon Way, Block Island 02807; (401) 466-5230.**

Winfield's—$$$

Winfield's has a good local reputation, and deservedly so. In business for over 10 years, it is consistent in quality. The adjoining Yellow Kittens Tavern opened in 1876 and is the oldest continuously operating tavern on the island. In season, the tavern serves lunch from 11:30 A.M–5 P.M., and the outdoor bar is open the same hours. At 6 P.M. the inside bar opens, and there are usually dance and rock bands nightly and reggae on Sundays. On the other side of the entry hall the restaurant is quieter, but casual, with touches of elegance. The menu has a broad range, including fresh swordfish, veal saltimbocca, chicken with thyme polenta, lamb and New York sirloin. Lobster pasta is lobster meat sautéed with snow peas, pignoli nuts and brandy over black pepper fettucini. The numerous nightly specials often feature game. The dining room itself has open beams with off-white walls and is sectioned to make it intimate but not crowded. Open from 6–10 P.M. daily Memorial Day to Columbus Day—and maybe a little longer if good weather holds. **Corn Neck Rd., Block Island 02807; (401) 466-5856.**

Highview Inn Eatery—$$$

Even if we didn't have a soft place in our

hearts for those visionary people who save old hotels from ruin, we would praise this restaurant for its really good food. The 1930s ambiance (a result of the hotel's age and its owner's good taste in decorating) creates the slightly languorous feel of a hotel favored by the expat characters in some classic movie set in a prewar island outpost. The menu is varied, but the chef really shines with a lengthy list of specials each evening: fresh Block Island swordfish prepared differently each day, or ravioli in a shitake and ginger demiglaze, rabbit or other game meat and the best of the day's catch. The chef clearly enjoys sharing his latest successful creations. The accent is on Caribbean and southwestern methods and ingredients, but it doesn't overwhelm the menu. The Caribbean clam chowder, for example, is made with a splash of dark rum. Salads are impeccably fresh and served in a giant bowl, the bread is hot and delicate in texture, the butter is seasoned with herbs. Desserts are presented on a tray, along with descriptions (the staff is extraordinarily well informed and can give intelligent advice): ganache served in a shell of solid chocolate with blackberries, a blackberry-peach tart filled with rum custard, whipped lemon cheesecake. The low markup on the wine list is particularly attractive, a good merlot is available for $11, barely more than the same wine in the island's only liquor store. **Connecticut Ave., Old Harbor; (401) 466-5912.**

Hotel Manisses—$$$ to $$$$

With all the panache and class of the hotel itself, the Manisses dining room overlooks the flower gardens from a wide porch. An inner room provides quieter corners for intimate dinners. The menu changes daily, reflecting the freshest ingredients. Appetizers range from a plate of smoked fish or escargot to chicken ginger Thai sausage or a choice from the raw bar. Entrees, which begin as low as $14, are about half seafood: bluefish baked with a two-mustard crust, scallops pan-seared with herbs and leeks or almond-crusted

striped bass. Mahimahi may be accented with a banana kiwi chutney, or the tuna with a salsa of pineapple. Even the old favorites like duck à l'orange take on new life, semiboned and sauced in Grand Marnier. Baked stuffed lobster is filled with oysters and walnuts, and the tournedos are topped with Brie and served with horseradish and a brandy cream. A prix fixe dinner includes both soup (try the renowned seafood chowder) and appetizer, main course, dessert and cappuccino or espresso. Those not dining at the hotel can still enjoy the coffees, which include several laced and flamed varieties, and dessert, in the elegant upstairs lounge. In the summer or on a weekend you should reserve ahead. **Hotel Manisses Dining Room, 1 Spring St., Old Harbor; (401) 466-2836.**

The Atlantic Inn—$$$$$

Built in 1879, the inn overlooks the town from a hilltop perch that provides a panoramic view from the dining room. There is nothing old-fashioned about the cuisine here: It blends the best of island seafood and meats with fresh herbs and vegetables grown in the inn's own gardens. The style includes influences from a number of cuisines, pairing couscous with grilled tuna steak, and dried poblano chiles and cilantro with scallops. The prix fixe menu, $37 plus taxes and tips, gives three choices of appetizer, two of soup, four of entrees and three of desserts. The latter includes local seasonal berries in dishes such as a blackberry flan, and a nightly chocolate creation such as a bittersweet truffle tart. Reservations are a must, especially in summer and on weekends. Open April–Nov. from 6–10 P.M. daily. In spring and fall, Thur.–Sat. from 6–9 P.M. **High St., Old Harbor; (401) 466-5883.**

Finn's—$$ to $$$

Finn's, in the heart of Old Harbor, is one of the islanders' favorites for casual dining. Located at the ferry landing, this fish-eater's paradise serves up steamers, chowder, lobster, fried clams and a fisherman's platter that's prepared either broiled or fried. There is also a selection of seafood-over-pasta dishes and a raw bar that is known for its marinated mussels and smoked bluefish plate. There is a children's menu. Reservations are not accepted here. Open mid-May–mid-Oct. daily from 11:30 A.M.–10:30 P.M. **Water St., Old Harbor; (401) 466-2473.**

The Ice Cream Place—$

Walk through the white arch and you'll see picnic tables covered with kids and adults slurping on the island's best ice cream and iced drinks. Inside you can also get lemonade and limeade made from fresh-squeezed fruit—squeezed right after you place your order. In cooler weather (if you're not a New Englander; if you are, you'll eat ice cream year-round) you can get hot chocolate, coffee or tea to go with a fat brownie or big cookie. Inside are photographs of old Block Island as well as postcards of the old hotels. Open Memorial Day–Columbus Day, daily from 9:30 A.M.–11 P.M. **Weldon's Way, Old Harbor; (401) 466-2145.**

Old Harbor Take-out—$

Right above the ferry landing, the take-out offers a few picnic tables for the patrons who line up here all day long for pita sandwiches, chowder, chili, burgers, burritos, bagels and soft ice cream. The quality is above average for take-out fare, and the prices ($6.25 for a brim-ming lobster roll and $6.95 for a huge chicken burrito) are reasonable. Stop here before taking the midday ferry back to the mainland and you can eat your lunch as you sail. Open mid-May–Columbus Day daily in the summer from 8 A.M.–8 P.M., off-season from 10 A.M.–5 P.M. **Water St., Old Harbor; (401) 466-2935.**

Mahogany Shoals Bar—$

While the term "hole in the wall" does come to mind, it can't do justice to this small (some would say intimate) and down-to-earth bar at the end of Paynes New Harbor Dock. It's the most famous Irish bar in the whole of Rhode Island, and we've been told that it sells more Jamieson's and Irish Mist than anywhere else in the state. Irish songs are the specialty of Walter McDonough, whom you can hear throughout the summer on Wednesday and Sunday evenings. Count on it being fun, loud and crowded. You can ground on the Shoals from the third week of June–mid-Sept. **Payne's Dock, New Harbor.**

Services

Visitor Information

Block Island Tourism Council, P.O. Box 356, Block Island, 02807; (800) 383-BIRI or (401) 466-5200.

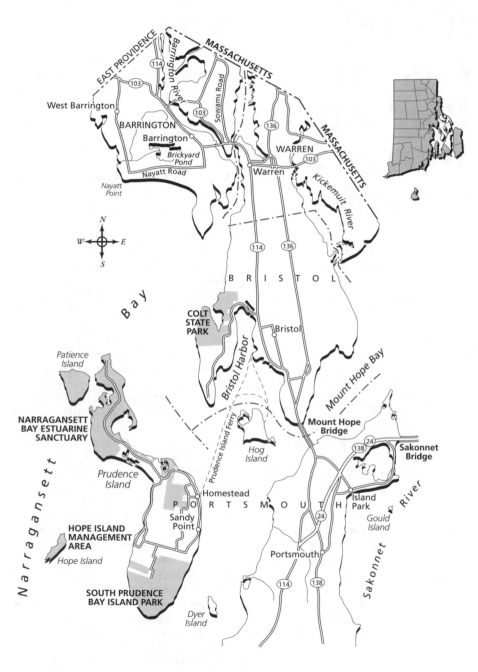

Bristol County

Bristol County: Barrington, Warren and Bristol

Ships were and still are at the heart of life in the almost-island that holds the towns of Bristol, Warren and Barrington. At Barrington's boatyards and marinas are moored both pleasure craft and commercial fishing boats, and the deep water channel that made Warren and Bristol major early trading ports is still busy with boat traffic. Rhode Island's fleet of sightseeing cruise boats is headquartered in Warren, the offspring of Blount's Marine, which has built thousands of ferries and excursion craft in use the world over.

Fine homes of every era line the streets: Colonial center-chimneys, the tiny gambrel-roofed cottages of craftsmen and shipwrights, fine Georgian and Federal mansions of prosperous captains and shipowners, and Victorian homes of whaling captains and the estates of later gentry.

Rte. 114, which connects all these northern towns of the East Bay, is the old Wampanoag Trail, a reminder that these were the lands of Chief Massasoit, who sold the land here to the Plymouth Pilgrims.

Visitors will find more than architecture to interest them here, however. Parks, gardens and nature areas invite walking, one of New England's premier bicycle trails skirts the scenic bay coast and the peaceful wildlands of Prudence Island are as close as the Bristol ferry landing.

History

The Plymouth Colony established the first outpost here in 1632 when it built a trading post close to the Wampanoag settlement, where Chief Massasoit had his headquarters. While the chief was alive, relations with European settlers were cordial, but his son Metacomet, known as King Philip, vowed after the death of his brother, to exterminate all whites. This led to King Philip's War and subsequently to the death of Metacomet, at Mount Hope (now part of Bristol) in 1676.

Bristol was settled soon after this and flourished as the commercial port for the Plymouth Colony under a Massachusetts charter. This explains why Bristol, unlike other Rhode Island towns, was laid out around a central commons with its church.

Bristol ships were active in the China and Triangle Trades, and by the Revolution, Bristol was home port to about 50 ships. During the war, Bristol and much of Warren were sacked and burned by the British. But their deepwater harbors were still valuable assets, so both towns rebuilt, and Bristol soon became wealthy on trade and shipbuilding, with a bit of privateering thrown in. The grand homes that line the streets of these towns today were built on maritime profits. Clipper ships bound for China, whalers and the ships that supplied the California gold rush were all built here.

Nearly everyone in Bristol was in some way connected to the shipping trade: Either they built or outfitted the ships, lent the money to finance them, distilled the rum they carried or loaded and unloaded the cargoes. But the leadership and ownership of the maritime commerce that formed the area's economic base was in the hands of a few families.

Most prominent and successful of the Bristol trading families were the DeWolfs; their empire was begun in the 1700s by the merchant, slaver and privateer Mark Anthony DeWolf. By 1810, his descendant George DeWolf was the richest and most powerful man in town, and he built the home that is still Bristol's best-known landmark: Linden Place. In this three-storied mansion he entertained President Monroe and other luminaries.

Once again, Bristol's prosperity was cut short. In December of 1825 DeWolf was bankrupt, and he and his family left Bristol in the middle of the night for Cuba. The town awoke to find him gone, and with him their investments, their jobs and their futures.

Some Bristol shipping continued, however, and at about this time Warren began to emerge as a whaling town, with 19 active ships. But whale oil for lamps was replaced by kerosene, larger ports edged out those on Narragansett Bay and by 1870 all foreign trade in the area had ended.

By then, however, the railroad had brought new commerce to Bristol, connecting it to Providence and Boston. The line ended there, making Bristol the connecting port for steamers that carried passengers on to New York and to other cities on the bay.

With the advent of steam manufacturing, Bristol, which had no rivers to provide power, could at last turn to manufacturing. Textile and rubber production began and by 1901 were thriving industries. Meanwhile, the Herreshoff brothers had launched their boatbuilding business, which made Bristol once again a name synonymous with shipbuilding.

In 1898 the railroad was extended to Barrington, bringing wealthy families who built estates and summer homes along its shores. Rum Stick Point is still a highly fashionable address, its roads lined with fine mansions built at the turn of the century. The history of this entire area is told in its buildings, which represent one of the finest architectural collections anywhere, with outstanding, often rare examples of every period since the 1600s.

171

Suggested Reading

Historic and Architectural Resources of Bristol, Rhode Island, published in 1990 by the Rhode Island Historical Preservation Commission, is a must for anyone interested in the fine and varied architecture of the area. It not only gives street-by-street listings of Bristol's historic buildings, it shows the most significant of these in high-quality photographs. It is available at Linden Place.

By Force of Arms, by James L. Nelson (Pocket Books, 1996), although fiction, paints a vivid and historically accurate picture of the Bristol-Providence area in the days between the burning of the *Gaspee* and the opening shots of the Revolution. It's also a rollicking good tale of adventure at sea. Bristol has a good bookstore, called, appropriately **Good Books,** at **495 Main St.; (401) 254-0390.**

Getting There

Rtes. 114 and 103 lead south from East Providence and I-95. Rte. 136 approaches the area from I-95 in Massachusetts. The peninsula is joined to Aquidneck Island to its south by the Mount Hope Bridge, from which Rte. 114 continues on to Newport. RIPTA buses connect Bristol with both Providence and Newport on a regular schedule, with several departures each day.

Getting Around

While a car is distinctly useful in seeing some of the more remote corners, the historic sections of these three towns lie along the route of **RIPTA's** buses. They stop hourly in each direction at the corner of Hope and State Sts. in Bristol, at Main and Joyce Sts. in Warren and at the White Church in Barrington. Northbound buses will be marked "Providence," southbound marked "Newport." Buses are less frequent on weekends but always at least one every two hours. Those traveling by bus will find lodging along Rte. 114 to be the most convenient; buses will stop on request at other points, so you are not limited to in-town lodgings. They run until about 10 P.M. on weekends, 11 P.M. on weekdays.

The gardens at Blithewold cover 33 acres overlooking the bay.

Those who enjoy bicycling can reach this area from Providence via the **East Bay Bicycle Path,** which connects the historic centers via a coastal scenic route (see page **174**).

Festivals and Events

Annual Spring Bulb Display
April

Blithewold Mansion and Gardens celebrates spring with thousands of blooming bulbs planted throughout its grounds, which overlook the mouth of Bristol Harbor as it joins Narragansett Bay. More than 50,000 daffodils have naturalized there; **(401) 253-2707.**

Herreshoff Marine Museum Lecture Series
May–October

Throughout the summer and fall, a series of evening lectures may cover subjects from the Vanderbilts to the Herreshoff company's work as a builder of military craft during World War II. These are held at the museum; **(401) 253-5000.**

Civil War Encampment
June

Early in the month, **Colt State Park** hosts a reenactment of the battle of Stone Chapel. Visitors can see the camps of both armies, drills and the battle recreated each day. There is no admission charge beyond the normal park admission; **(401) 253-7482.**

Independence Day Parade
July

The oldest Independence Day parade in the country—it began in 1785—features hundreds of floats and marching bands. To secure a good spot along the parade route (easy to find, since the traditional yellow line in the center of the road is replaced here with red, white and blue stripes), you'll need to arrive before daybreak. Or reserve the best seats in town, on the lawn of Linden Place, as savvy locals do ($25 includes lunch). To avoid traffic (a nightmare, because up to 250,000 people have been known to converge here), although you will be too late for a good parade-route view, arrive on the Vista Jubilee, with reserved bus connections by **Conway Tours** from Woonsocket, Pawtucket, Providence and Warwick. Call Conway at **(800) 888-4661** or **(401) 658-3400; Bay Queen Cruises** at **(800) 439-1350** (from Rhode Island only) or **(401) 245-1350; Linden Place** at **(401) 253-0390.** For parade information, call **(401) 245-0750.**

Warren Quahog Festival
July

Family activities, entertainment, music, crafts, games and plenty of seafood celebrate Rhode Island's native clam; **(401) 247-2188.**

Concerts on the Common
July–August

Free concerts on Thursday evenings bring a variety of music to Bristol's Common, where you'll hear everything from a pops chorale and big band music to jazz, folk and traditional bandstand favorites. Concerts begin at 7 P.M.; **(401) 253-7000.**

Annual Harvest Fair
September

Coggeshall Farm's season culminates in a traditional fair, with demonstrations of early crafts, chowder, jonnycakes, cider, pony rides, hayrides and old-time games and entertainment; **(401) 253-9062.**

House and Garden Tour
September

Homes from four centuries of Bristol's history are open once a year during this one-day tour sponsored by the **Bristol Historic Preserva-**

tion Society. The oldest is the 1698 **Joseph Reynolds House.** A trolley bus cruises the route all day, and box lunches are available. Since nearly all are private homes, this is a rare chance to see the restored interiors of one of New England's finest groups of historic residences; **(401) 253-7223.**

Pumpkin and Corn Sale
October

Coggeshall Farm Museum opens its two-day farmer's market, selling apples, cider, pumpkins and ornamental corn as well as demonstrating old-fashioned harvest skills of cider-making and threshing; **(401) 253-9062.**

Bristol's Grand Illumination
December

On the first weekend in December, Bristol closes its main street to traffic and has an evening of caroling with church choirs, hay-or sleigh rides, and the simultaneous lighting of all the street and tree lights along Hope St. The shop windows are decorated and hot cocoa is sold as everyone turns out to stroll downtown and begin the holiday season; **(401) 253-7000.**

Christmas at Blithewold
December

While the main focus throughout the rest of the year is on the splendid gardens, during the holidays attention turns to the house itself, furnished in early-twentieth-century style and decorated for Christmas; **(401) 253-2707.**

Crafts for Cancer
December

Top craftspeople from all over New England gather to show and sell their work, which includes wooden ware, jewelry, fabric arts, glassware, baskets and more; **(401) 722-8480.**

Homes for the Holiday
December

Linden Place, sparkling at any season, is the centerpiece for a tour of seven Bristol homes in Christmas finery. Like the summer house tour, this is a good chance to look inside some of the town's historic private residences; **(401) 253-0390.**

Outdoor Activities

Parks and Recreation Areas

Colt State Park

The Colt estate overlooks Narragansett Bay from its sloping open fields, and even when Samuel Colt built it in the early 1900s, he welcomed the public to share the grounds. Some areas are forested, and the roads and paths are perfect for walking and bicycling. Ask for a copy of the self-guided walking tour. In the spring the property is filled with blooming bulbs and rhododendron. The remaining architectural highlight is the huge stone barn with its round stone silo, once home to Colt's prize Jersey herd. Picnic sites are in an attractive grove near the bay. A small admission fee is charged during the summer. The park entrance is easily recognized by the two giant bronze bulls that guard the gates on Rte. 114, north of the center of Bristol; **(401) 253-7482.**

Haines Memorial Park

Set along the Providence River, the park is one of the access points for the **East Bay Bicycle Path,** with plenty of parking. It also has a public boat dock and picnic tables (use of which involves a park fee). You can often watch cormorants fishing close to the shore; **(401) 253-7482.**

Veterans Memorial Park

In the early 1900s, this area was the scene of a thriving brick-making industry. Now a park

of more than 200 acres, it has picnic tables, rest rooms and grills. It also has access to the **East Bay Bicycle Path,** and to walking trails through the woods and along the edge of **Brickyard Pond.** During the fall and winter you can see flocks of ring-necked and canvasback ducks that make their winter home here. The park is free and may be reached via West St., which is off Maple Ave. opposite the Barrington Town Hall; **(401) 247-1925.**

Biking

The **East Bay Bicycle Path** is a prototypical recreation corridor, offering cyclists fine views of the shoreline from Providence to Bristol. On its 14.5-mile route it passes through parks, along quiet streets and through the historic centers of Warren and Barrington before ending in Bristol. Salt ponds filled with swans and geese, woodlands and fine views of the upper bay are highlights of the route, which follows an old railway line. This makes it quite flat, but a prevailing afternoon breeze can make it feel as though you were climbing a hill as you head south. For bicycle service and repairs, contact **Bay Path Cycles at 13 State St., Bristol; (401) 254-1277. Prudence Island** also offers flat terrain for bicycling (see page **175**).

Birding

The mild climate of this peninsula makes it a winter habitat for a number of water birds. At **Veterans Memorial Park** in Barrington, for example, you can see canvasback and ring-necked ducks and other waterfowl in the winter. On the pond at **Osamequin Bird Sanctuary** are swans. At the latter you can also see osprey nests on specially built platforms, as well as egrets and terns. Warren's **Touisset Marsh** is another good birding area. Birders wishing to see an unusual sight should go just over the northern border of Barrington into the **Crescent Point section of East Providence.** Go past the carousel and bear left onto **Sabin Point.** In the trees along these residential streets are giant hodgepodge nests, and on branches, telephone wires and other roosts are small green parrots. We don't know why or how they got there.

Fishing

Charter boats are operated out of Bristol by Captain Stan Wilbur aboard the *Endurance*. Bait and tackle are provided; **(401) 53-0370.** The best bluefishing is off **Colt State Park.**

Golf

Bristol Golf Club and **Pocasset Country Club** are the only two courses in the area open to the public. Nine-hole, 34-par Pocasset overlooks Mt. Hope Bridge and the bay and has a lounge and restaurant. It's on Bristol Ferry Rd; **(401) 683-2266.** At the rolling **Bristol Golf Club** (par 71), the back nine is the flattest. It is on Tupelo Rd.; **(401) 253-9844. The Silver Spring Golf Course,** a six-hole course on Pawtucket Ave. in East Providence, is open to the public for a limited number of hours; **(401) 434-9697.**

Hiking and Walking

Osamequin Bird Sanctuary

Marked nature trails cover 42 acres of wetland, tidal marshes and coastal uplands along **Hundred Acre Cove.** This is one of the state's finest estuaries, with a variety of bird and plant habitats. Osprey nests are on platforms specially built to encourage their return. Access the reserve from Rte. 114, at the north end of Barrington. It's free and open year-round; **(401) 247-1920.**

Touisset Marsh Wildlife Refuge

An Audubon Society property, the marsh has a varied habitat of salt marsh, woods, old fields, swamp, cove and tidal river. It is very rich in bird life. In the woods look for the speckled rocks called pudding stones, a sedimentary rock made from smaller pebbles compressed into a softer base that then hardens. From Rte. 103 in Warren, take Long Lane to Barton Ave., then your first right onto Touisset Rd. The

marsh access is from the parking lot beside the fire station; **(401) 949-5454.**

Prudence Island

Lying closer to Portsmouth but most readily reached by ferry out of Bristol, the island is a quiet place. One store, one school, one lighthouse and a lot of protected natural habitat is about all you'll find there. Both ends of the island are preserved as public parkland and were once served by frequent boat service bringing day visitors to the facilities at either end. But the tiny deer tick stopped all that. Because of deer ticks, which carry Lyme disease, you are safer keeping to the island's roads and out of the grass or undergrowth. Or go in the late fall, early spring or winter, when ticks are less common. The cause of the high deer-tick population is the island's dense deer herd, so you may see deer along with other wildlife. In any case, wear long pants, light-colored clothing and a repellent designed for ticks. You can pick up a brochure with precautions and information at nearly any tourist information center or state park, and you should do so.

The island's roads and tracks are perfect for bicycling or walking. On the southern end of the island, which you can explore in a nine-mile loop of roads, you'll find some old navy munitions bunkers and the overgrown remains of a campground. To the north is the **Estuarine Sanctuary** and interpretive signs describing the plantation that once covered the land. The ferry leaves Bristol on a seasonally changing schedule. The fare is $2.85 for adults, one way. The landing is on Thames St.; **(401) 253-9808.**

Rock Collecting

Those who collect rock and mineral specimens will find some interesting beachcombing on Bristol County shores. Especially along the shore of **Mount Hope Bay** and around **Bristol Point and Harbor,** jasper, agate and chalcedony samples, worn and polished by the tides, are found on the beaches. These show up best in the ebbing tide, when they are wet and their colors more pronounced.

175

Sailing

The entire sweep of Narragansett Bay and its tributaries is among the finest sailing venues on the continent. The **Barrington/Newport Sailing School** teaches beginning and advanced sailing; **(401) 246-1595. Constellation Charters** offers sunset and moonlight sails from Bristol; **(401) 254-1310.**

Seal-Watching

On Saturdays and Sundays during the winter, **Bay Queen Cruises** operates four-hour sealwatch trips in the middle of the day. Bring lunch and a pair of binoculars, plus a long camera lens—they don't want to disturb the seals by getting too close; **(401) 245-1350.**

Swimming

Colt State Park has a small but attractive beach with a picnic area and playground. Expect clean water and water-worn pebbles underfoot instead of sand. Out-of-state residents pay a parking fee. **The Warren Town Beach,** on South Water St., is open to nonresidents, but they must park elsewhere (closest is the public parking on Railroad Ave., off Rte. 103 on the other side of Main St.). Lifeguards are on duty here throughout the summer.

Activities for Kids

In Barrington, the **Peck Center Playground** has excellent modern play equipment designed for children under 12 only. It has mazes, slides and swings, many with handicapped access. It's behind the parking lot at Barrington Town Hall on Rte. 114. **Rockwell Park,** at the ferry landing in Bristol, has a playground, as does **Veterans Park** at the north end of Wood St. in Barrington. Herreshoff Museum's **Young Mariner Discovery Center** has hands-on activities: Children can try cranking a winch or hoisting sails in its child-friendly atmosphere (see page **178**). At **Coggeshall Farm** kids can pet the sheep, maybe even help shear them.

There's nearly always something they can try their hands at, often in the company of local 4-H members, who care for the animals. Cows are milked daily at 4 P.M. in winter, 5 P.M. summer. Children will certainly enjoy the highlight of the **Annual Harvest Fair:** the National Pumpkin Seed Spitting Contest (see page **173**). **Linden Place** has **Summer Art Camp** for children ages six to 14 the week after July 4. Each day features activities in art, music, dance and theater. It also holds **American Girl Parties,** with activities appropriate to the period and story of each *American Girls* book (see pages **179–180**).

Seeing and Doing

Cruises

The *Bay Queen,* a 600-passenger cruiser, tours Narragansett Bay from its home port in Warren. Day, night and sunset cruises each show the bay and its shore in a different mood. Throughout the season (Apr.–Dec.) dinner-dance cruises are also scheduled. Reserve early to view Bristol's July 4 fireworks from off shore. Boats leave from **Blount Marine, 461 Water St.; (800) 556-7450 (in Rhode Island only)** or **(401) 245-1350.**

Barrington

Tyler Point Cemetery

A small piece of land extends between the Barrington and Warren Rivers as they flow together. This is the site of one of the state's oldest cemeteries. The first marked stone is from 1702, and you'll see fine examples of early effigy and carved stones here. **Tyler Point Rd., off Rtes. 114 and 103, just south of Barrington.**

Mouseachuck Canal

In the days of Barrington's brick-making industry, this canal was built to transport the finished bricks to the river, where they were loaded onto ships. The barges were pulled by horses, and you can follow the tow path

176

through the woods along the canal. Take Legion Way, off Middle Highway, which you can reach from Maple Ave., opposite the Barrington Town Hall.

Crescent Park Carousel

This neighborhood is really in East Providence, but it lies just over the northern border of Barrington. The Looff carousel, with its original horses, dates from 1895. Its 66 figures are intricately hand-carved and hand-painted. No two are alike, and each is decked out in jeweled trappings. The chariots are the finest in existence, with intertwined serpents, the work of Looff's son. It's not just for children, and rides are so inexpensive that you'll want to climb on, too. This is all that remains of the large amusement park that once stood there. The carousel is a National Historic Landmark, the finest example of these carousels to survive. Even the pavilion that houses the carousel is the finest one still standing. Open Apr.–June and Sept.–mid-Oct., Fri.–Sun. from noon–8 P.M.; July–Aug., Tues.–Sun. daily from noon–9 P.M.. At the **end of Bullock Point Ave. just off Rte. 103; (401) 434-3311.**

Warren

Waterfront Historic District Walking Tour

The streets along Warren's once-busy dock area could be used as a movie set. They still carry the feeling of the busy whaling port and have not been gussied up to hold cute boutiques. Brick, stone and clapboard buildings have been (or are being) restored, not as museums, but as the private homes and businesses of a town that's still very much alive, even though its great whaling and clipper days are history. The best examples are in the streets that run between Water and Main. We suggest beginning at the corner of Water and Liberty Sts. and walking up Liberty to see the two Greek revival–early Victorian homes at the first corner **(37 Liberty St. and 90 Union St.)** The second is the earlier, and pure revival, while the one facing Liberty is more Victorian.

Turn right onto Union St., then left onto Miller St. Opposite the corner of Lewin St., **#33** was built in 1789 and was once home of Joel Abbot, second in command to Matthew Perry on his historic trade mission to Japan. Continue along Miller St. to Main to a landmark of particular interest to those associated with Brown University, the **Warren Baptist Church.** The Gothic-style building was designed by the noted architect Russell Warren (as were a number of other buildings in town) in 1844. It replaces the church and parsonage that were the original home of Rhode Island College, which became Brown University after moving to Providence. Its first commencement was in the old meeting house, which, along with the parsonage, was torched by the British during the Revolution in May of 1778.

Return on Miller St. and take Lewin St. to see the 1796 **Masonic Temple,** whose exterior is remarkable for its elaborate hand-carved woodwork. It is the second-oldest Masonic temple in the country and was built with timbers from British ships sunk during the Revolution. Waste not, want not. The **Firemen's Museum** is opposite (see page **178**).

Return to Water St. to see the **Maxwell House** (see page **178**), between Baker and Church Sts., then walk up Church St. to the **Methodist Church,** one of the oldest in New England, built in 1844. It has its original box pews. A common, where ships once filled their water barrels at the pump, lies between Church and State Sts., faced by the fine federal **Eddy-Cutler House,** built by a captain of the West Indies Trade and later owned by a whaling captain.

Charles W. Greene Museum

Located in the castlelike Victorian library building, the museum concentrates on the finds in a Wampanoag burial ground unearthed at nearby Burr's Hill in 1913. It also has the assortment of local memorabilia that make town museums so interesting. Warren's past as a whaling town gives this collection a maritime turn. Some Peruvian and other South American ethnographic items are shown, too. Although the museum is in the library, it is not open during all library hours, only Wednesday afternoons from 2 to 4. **530 Main St.; (401) 245-7686.**

Firemen's Museum

The old **Fire Station #3** holds a two-century history of fire fighting, its prize possession being an 1802 Little Hero. It was the town's first fire engine, a hand tub, which was a great improvement over previous methods. Other pieces of equipment, including giant megaphones, are displayed in the 1846 building at **38 Baker St.** It is open for special events and by appointment year-round; **(401) 245-7600.**

Maxwell House

The large brick gabled house was built in 1755 by a prominent family of shipowners and traders and is the oldest surviving on the waterfront. The bricks of its exterior are handmade. Inside it is furnished in period pieces and has paneled fireplaces and a central chimney with two ovens. Colonial skills, including hearth and brick oven cooking, are demonstrated often. A period herb garden is in the yard. Open the first Fridays of June, July and August, for special events and at other times by appointment. **59 Church St.; (401) 245-7652.**

Bristol

Coggeshall Farm Museum

The life and work of Rhode Island farm families of two centuries ago is shown here in a hands-on atmosphere. Costumed interpreters explain their tasks as they care for the flock of horned sheep, a working ox team and other livestock, or tend the vegetable and herb gardens. Along with the 1700s farmhouse, you will find a blacksmith shop, carriage house, weaving shed and barns for livestock. Special events and programs highlight seasonal farm activities such as sugaring and cider making. In addition to interpreting the activities of a farm, the museum explores the relationship between farming and Bristol's maritime community.

This re-creation of a working farm is a fitting tribute to Chandler Coggeshall, who was born here and who went on to found the Agricultural School at the University of Rhode Island. Open daily Mar.–Sept. from 10 A.M.–6 P.M., Oct.–Feb. from 10 A.M.–5 P.M. It is located in **Colt State Park,** and can be reached from Rte. 114 in Bristol via Poppasquash Rd; **(401) 253-9062.**

Herreshoff Maritime Museum

The name Herreshoff has been synonymous with racing and cruising yachts for almost a century and a half. Designers and builders of eight America's Cup winners, many contenders and hundreds of premier racing yachts, cruising yachts, torpedo boats and PT boats, Herreshoff Manufacturing Company came to be equated with speed and grace.

On the site of that company's plant from 1863 until its demise in 1945, this museum celebrates the art of boat design by focusing on its leading family and their work. Photographs show the evolution of yachts, and a model of the Herreshoff plant as it was in 1914 shows its 21 buildings, which dominated the waterfront here. Hull plates, sweaters of the *Endeavor* crews, a 1917 triple expansion steam engine built for J. P. Morgan's commuter yacht and early brass steam engines are just a sampling of the memorabilia shown.

The **Hall of Boats** is a candy shop for boat lovers, with more than 45 craft. Herreshoff hulls here show the genius of their designers and the beauty of their creations. Earliest is *Sprite*, built by Charles and John Herreshoff in 1859, based on drawings and figurings by the then eleven-year-old Nathaniel Herreshoff. *Anemone* (1905), *Torch* (1929), the very early fin keeler *Jilt* (1898), Nathaniel Herreshoff's own 35-foot *Cara* (1887), *Thania* (1905) and others, including one of the earliest cruising catamarans, fill the hall. Nat Herreshoff's last design, the 56-foot yawl *Belisarius*, when it is not under sail in the bay, is at anchor in front of the museum.

The **Young Mariners' Discovery Center** offers activities, workshops and hands-on experiences to introduce children to the world of sail. Headed by the grandson of "Captain Nat," the museum is a labor of love. The staff is not

Bristol County: Barrington, Warren and Bristol

only knowledgeable but related through their families to the Herreshoff history. Admission is $3 for individuals, $5 for families. Open May–Oct., Mon.–Fri. from 1–4 P.M., Sat. and Sun. from 11 A.M.–4 P.M. **7 Burnside Street, at the corner of Rte. 114; (401) 253-5000.**

America's Cup Hall of Fame

Across the street from the Herreshoff Maritime Museum, the newly opened exhibits honor the sailors and yachtsmen who have championed not only the competition but yacht design as well, for the world's oldest international competition. In addition to memorabilia (which includes a piece of the keel of the original *America*) are half-hull models of all U.S. America's Cup winners and many of the primary contenders, and plaques with the photographs and contributions of Hall of Famers. Five new members are added each year. Outside, two racing hulls show the design changes of the last 80 years. There, the gracious lines of the 1913 Herreshoff *Spartan* can be contrasted with the modern *Defiance,* at the leading edge of current design. Admission is included in the Herreshoff museum ticket, and the hours are the same.

Haffenreffer Museum of Anthropology

Established on land once occupied by the Wampanoags, the Haffenreffer contains Brown University's outstanding collections of primitive and traditional cultures. Artifacts are from the Americas, Asia, Africa and the Pacific. As we write, the museum is in the process of planning a move to the Old Stone Bank Building in Providence. For information on the status of the collections, call the Mount Hope facility at **(401) 253-8388.**

Mount Hope

The Wampanoag summer camping grounds on the hillside overlooking Mount Hope Bay was both the Fort Sumter and the Appomattox of the 1600s hostilities known as King Philip's War. After two years of intense fighting, which took a heavy toll on both sides and resulted in the burning of Providence and many other towns, King Philip at last retreated to his head-

quarters at Mount Hope, where the war had begun, and was killed. A quartz outcrop on the hillside, which offered a view out over the bay, was his command post, known as King Philip's Seat. A short trail leads there from the parking lot at Brown's Haffenreffer estate.

A far more puzzling rock was first discovered at the shoreline here in 1780 by Ezra Stiles, later President of Yale. The rock had the clear image of a high-sterned boat and inscriptions Stiles recorded. The rock was forgotten until a century later, when it was again found and again recorded. Since then graffiti has been added, but the original inscription is still decipherable by a photographic process and has been the subject of considerable discussion, claims and pooh-poohing in academic circles. Those who are interested in the possibilities of early Celtic, Phoenician and Viking explorations in America should refer to *America B.C.* by Barry Fell, which has a photograph of the inscriptions and a lengthy discussion of their possible meaning. Mount Hope is on the far end of Tower St., reached from Rte. 136 on the east side of Bristol.

Linden Place

General George DeWolf, the man upon whose shipping empire Bristol's fortunes rose—and suddenly fell—built Linden Place in 1810. It was the town's showplace, standing like a three-tiered cake overlooking Hope St. It is once again, but there were long years in between.

The day after DeWolf's bankruptcy and sudden departure for Cuba, the house was stripped by his creditors, a customs man at the door keeping a record of what was taken in exchange for what debt. The silver washbasin set that President Monroe had used went to pay the crew of one of DeWolf's ships. Remaining DeWolfs bought the house and owned it one after another, but when the last of these went bankrupt, his wife (in whose name he had prudently placed the house) was left with a white elephant, which she ended up running as a boardinghouse. The beautiful round conservatory became a barbershop. When she died, the sadly deteriorated house went up for auction.

Linden Place is still the showpiece of downtown Bristol.

Like Bristol itself, Linden Place would bounce back. When General George decamped in 1825, he took with him his wife and six children, one of whom, Theodora, was later sent back to New England to be educated. She married a Colt of the arms manufacturing family and was subsequently left a very wealthy widow. Just when the declining fortunes of Linden Place were at their lowest, her son Edward bought the house for her at the auction. After 40 years she would return to the house where she was born and from which she was taken as a five-year-old. She lavished attention and money on it, buying back some of the furnishings that had been taken by creditors. Like her father, she entertained presidents there.

Today, Linden Place is one of the finest federal-style homes in the Northeast. Its spiral staircase rises unsupported for four stories, crowned by a domed skylight. At Christmas, with tiny lights along its banister garlands, it looks like a chambered nautilus shell alight. The chandelier is from Buckingham Palace, and the mahogany dining table was built from the packing cases used to ship latex to the Colt rubber plant in Bristol. Open for tours Memorial Day–Columbus Day, Thur.–Sat. from 10 A.M.–4 P.M., Sun. from noon–4 P.M. The gift shop, which has an excellent selection of books on Rhode Island history in addition to period home accessories and gifts, has longer hours,

and opens in April. The house opens for tours at Christmas. **500 Hope St. (Rte. 114), in the center of town; (401) 253-0390.**

Bristol Art Museum

The ballroom of Linden Place occupied a separate building that is today used as an art museum. National and local artists are featured in changing exhibits throughout the year. A full Concert in the Ballroom schedule includes a wide range of music, mostly classical. Admission is charged for the concerts, but the art exhibits are free. The entrance is on **Wardell St.; (401) 253-0390.**

Bristol Historical Preservation Society Museum

The old **Bristol County Jail,** which houses the museum, was built in 1828 from ballast stones brought home by Bristol ships. Inside is an assortment of local relics from Bristol's early past and from its days as a thriving merchant and Triangle Trade port: slave papers, ship models and children's toys. One wonders how Benjamin Franklin's writing box ended up in Bristol. Opening times vary. **48 Court St.; (401) 253-7223 or 253-5705.**

Blithewold

This English manor house on 33 acres of arboretum and garden overlooking Narragansett Bay began quite simply as a proper anchorage for a new Herreshoff yacht Mr. Van Wickle bought for his wife. What began as a mooring became a lifelong passion for both his wife and his daughter. The house, built in the style of an English manor, is not furnished to a particular period; Mrs. Van Wickle traveled extensively and bought what she liked, combining antiques, reproductions and contemporary pieces with a fine sense of style. The result is a uniquely livable mansion. Although the house is elegant, the gardens continue to be the primary focus, as they were when Marjorie Van Wickle Lyon lived here. An avid horticulturist, she was more interested in her trees and her perennials than in the house. When she could no longer walk the extensive grounds, she buzzed around them in a golf cart.

Some highlights are the largest giant sequoia in the East, still growing at 90 feet, a bamboo grove and a Japanese water garden. Special events are held seasonally: Daffodil Month in April, Concerts by the Bay all summer, Christmas open house. Guided tours of the mansion and grounds take about 90 minutes. Ask for a map of the grounds and a list of trees for a self-guided tour. Open Apr.–Oct. from 10 A.M.–5 P.M. daily; house tours Tues.–Sun. from 10 A.M.–4 P.M. The mansion reopens for the month of December from 10 A.M.–8 P.M. daily, except for Dec. 24 and 25. The gift shop, which has elegant garden-related items, remains open through Nov. **Ferry Rd, near the Mount Hope Bridge; (401) 253-2707.**

Blithewold is built in the style of an English country house.

Shopping

Warren is known as one of the best centers for antique shopping in New England. Water St. has six blocks almost entirely devoted to antiques, and Main, Miller and Baker Sts. have more. A large group shop, the **Warren Antiques Center,** has over 150 dealers. There are so many of them that it is really pointless to list each one. You can't miss finding them, and whatever you collect, you're sure to find it represented. For a list of shops with addresses and phone numbers, although no description of their specialties, write to the **Historic Warren Merchants Association, P.O. Box 412, Warren, 02885-0412.**

Bristol is also a haven for antique shops, which are mostly on Hope St. (Rte. 114) and State St.

Where to Stay

Rockwell House Inn—$$$

The elegant interior, with inlaid hardwood floors and pocket doors and its charming "courting corner" vies for attention with the spacious backyard, which lures you outdoors to play croquet or sit on the terrace in the shade of Rhode Island's largest and oldest tulip poplar tree. The full-time innkeeper-owners have thought of everything: sherry in the par-

lor, tea on the terrace, turn-down bonbons, fluffy bathrobes. Four guest rooms are furnished in antiques, with hooked rugs and fine decorative detail. King beds or twins—specify when you reserve. Movie buffs will like the collection of autographed movie star and entertainer photos, and everyone will like the full breakfasts. Fresh breads are baked daily, and hot entrees might be Dutch puffed pancakes or a breakfast pudding with cinnamon apples. Children over 12 are welcome, pets are not. The location is a plus, in the historic center of Bristol. You can watch the July 4 parade from the verandah. **610 Hope St., Bristol 02809; (401) 253-0040.**

Joseph Reynolds House— $$ to $$$

Those who value the intense labor that goes into preserving and restoring a historic home will not only appreciate the work that's been done at the Joseph Reynolds House but will not want to miss a chance to see it in progress. This is a unique property, still a bit short of a finished inn, but one of the most significant historic homes in New England. Lafayette didn't just sleep here, he lived here; Washington and Jefferson visited him. This is the earliest three-story wooden structure surviving in New England. Its massive plaster cove cornice is exceedingly rare. But is it a good place to stay? Yes, if you don't expect a cute decorator magazine atmosphere, and don't mind a bit of work going on here and there. Guest rooms now have private baths and the two suites sleep four or five persons. The room in which Lafayette lived is the largest. All rates drop by about 40% in the off-season. The full breakfast is an event in its own right. Ghosts, the underground railroad, the Marquis ... and where else (short of Europe) can you stay in a house built in the 1600s? It's at the northern end of town. **956 Hope St., Bristol 02809; (800) 754-0230 or (401) 254-0230.**

William's Grant Inn—$$$

Peace and quiet reign in this historic neighborhood that is within an easy walk of the waterfront area. Inside, antiques are blended with fine and folk art, creating a charming environment that is never cute or frilly. Painted walls and cabinetwork set the tone for each room: The kitchen has vegetable and herb vignettes painted on the cabinet doors. Rooms on the first floor have private baths, the two upstairs rooms share a bath. The Blithewold room is done in shades of rose, with shuttered windows and hooked rugs. The Middlebury room has a hunt theme; the Garden room is light and bright, filled with original art and soft colors. The Victorian decor is lightened by the lively, often playful touches. Breakfasts could be French toast with fresh strawberries or huevos rancheros, and there are lots of low-fat, modified recipes. "Healthy foods don't have to sacrifice taste," says the owner-innkeeper. There are bicycles for guests use, as well as kayaks. The house is on the parade route, and on July 4 it has a celebration of their own for family and friends, which include inn guests. **154 High St., Bristol 02809; (800) 596-4222 or (401) 253-4222.**

Nathaniel Porter Inn—$$

The original part of this house on Warren's historic waterfront was built in 1750, the front was added in 1795. Along with its restaurant (see page **183**), the inn offers three beautifully restored bedrooms furnished with canopy beds and Oriental rugs. They are decorated in authentic period styles, and each has a fireplace and private bath (a welcome concession to the twentieth century). Elegant detailing and inlaid hardwood floors in the hallways and wide-board floors in the guest rooms are original. A Continental breakfast is served. **125 Water St., Warren 02885; (401) 245-6622.**

King Philip Inn—$$

Rooms here are on the plain side, a cut above the standard roadside hotel, with king-sized beds in second-floor rooms and efficiency kitchenettes in all first-floor rooms. These have outside doors as well as hallway access. Rooms are comfortable and well kept, favored by business travelers and families who appreciate the few-frills approach and the reasonable prices. Hallways are wide, well lighted and newly carpeted. The lobby looks more like that of an apartment building but has a sitting area and a large adjacent game room with a pool table. Continental breakfast is included in the rate, and there is no extra charge for cots and cribs. All rooms have color TV and phones. Rates increase for July 4, as they do elsewhere in town. **400 Metacom Ave., Bristol, 02809; (401) 253-7600 or (800) 253-7610.**

Where to Eat

BREAKFAST AND LUNCH

Newport Creamery—$ to $$

You'll find representatives of this local chain elsewhere in the state, indulging the Rhode Island passion for ice cream with the usual coffee cabinets (see **Cuisine**, page **xi**) and a legendary concoction of their own called an Awful Awful. They are also a reliable stop for lunch or breakfast. Open daily from 7 A.M.–11 P.M. in the summer; Sun.–Thur. from 7 A.M.–10 P.M., Fri–Sat. from 7 A.M.–11 P.M. the rest of the year. Located on **Rte. 114 in Barrington, opposite the town hall; (401) 245-2212.**

T. J. Cinnamon's—$

This bakery is known for its cinnamon rolls, coffee cakes and muffins, but you can get sandwiches and hearty soups, too. Open Mon.–Fri. from 6:30 A.M.–5 P.M., Sat.–Sun from 7 A.M.–5 P.M.. On **Rte. 114 in the village of Barrington; (401) 245-0460.**

Rod's Grill—$

While you can get soups and a grilled chicken sandwich here, everybody comes for the hot wieners, voted best in the state by *Rhode Island Monthly* readers. We've tried them, and they are good, well seasoned, the onions just right. (In case you haven't yet encountered New York System Wieners, see **Cuisine,** page **xi**. These are not to be confused with plain old hot dogs.) Open Mon.–Thur. from 6:30 A.M.–5 P.M., Fri. from 6:30 A.M.–6 P.M., Sat. from 6:30 A.M.–4 P.M. **6 Washington St., Warren; (401) 245-9405.**

Cafe La France—$

Huge sandwiches are served on French bread here from a menu that also includes ice cream, a variety of coffees and teas, breakfast breads and dessert pastries. The roast beef sandwich is mounded with thinly sliced, tender beef (rare, if you specify) on a crusty fresh long loaf. Cheese—generous portions of Brie, Cheddar, boursin or Swiss, are 50 cents extra. Chicken tarragon salad is filled with chunks of tasty chicken. The throaty sounds of Piaf hang in the air and the Parisian mood is extended outdoors in the summer with sidewalk tables lining the street opposite the elegant white facade of Linden Place. Table service and take-out are both available. Open from 7 A.M.–10 P.M. daily. No credit cards, but they do honor the *Rhode Island Monthly* discount card. **483 Hope St., Bristol; (401) 253-0360.**

The Last Word on Weiners

We were once on a bus full of Rhode Islanders (there's bound to be a story here) each of us loudly defending the glories of our own personal favorite place to get hot wieners. Bob Billington, of Blackstone Valley, proclaimed Sparky's in Central Falls, we cried out for Olney, but the man across the aisle was talking into his cellular phone through all this din. As the bus came into Warren, it stopped at the corner of Water St. and the man jumped out. We knew he worked at Blount Marine, so we thought he had an errand to run, and continued our raucous debate. Two minutes later he climbed aboard carrying a huge tray of hot wieners, steaming and redolent of onion. He passed them out, one to each person on the crowded bus. While we'd been arguing, he'd been placing his order at Rod's. Silence fell on the bus; our mouths were too full to talk, and he'd rested his case.

Golden Goose Deli—$

You can eat your custom-designed sandwiches, cakes or Continental pastry at sidewalk tables by windows overlooking the street and a New Orleans–style house opposite. A carillon in the brick bell tower across the street plays at noon. We like the Basically British sandwich—lean roast beef, Cheddar cheese, cole slaw, Bermuda onion and Shedds Sauce. Curried chicken salad with walnuts and grapes is good, too. Espresso and cappuccino. Hours change seasonally. **365 Hope St. (Rte. 114), Bristol; (401) 253-1414.**

DINNER

Nathaniel Porter Inn—$$ to $$$

In a large waterfront house just over 200 years old, this restaurant's elegant dining rooms are set in historically restored rooms with wall murals, stenciling, fireplaces and beamed ceilings. While the atmosphere is authentically early American, the cuisine is new American, using fresh local products in creative ways with influences from all over the world. Trout is encrusted with nuts, shrimp sautéed with tequila, bouillabaisse is seasoned with cilantro and salads are dressed in a tangy raspberry-cantaloupe blend. Desserts, all made in-house, may include chocolate pâté: a fudgelike base with almonds, pistachios and pecans over crème anglaise. Special-occasions dinners include the annual yule log celebration, Cognac Nights and tasting dinners. The menu changes each month. When reserving, specify whether you wish to be seated in the completely separate smoking room. Open Mon.–Fri. from 5:30–9 P.M., Sat. 5–9 P.M. and Sun. from 4–8 P.M. **125 Water St., Warren; (401) 245-6622.**

Tyler Point Grille—$ to $$$

Polished wood tables, rush-seat chairs and a stunning bar keep your attention from being entirely diverted by the harbor view all around you. The menu changes daily and the wine list weekly. Appetizer specialties, which stay on the menu, include crab cakes with Louisiana tartar sauce and fried calamari with hot peppers. Steaks and chops are wood-grilled in the open kitchen. A lunch menu may offer fettucini with grilled vegetables or a Cajun grilled chicken sandwich. Dinner may be grilled swordfish over mesclun or grilled pork chop with peach bourbon sauce. Twelve wines are available by the glass, priced at $3.50 to $5.00. Open Tues.–Fri. from 11 A.M.–2 P.M. and from 5:30–9 P.M.; Sat. and Sun. from 5–9:30 P.M. On **Barton Ave.,** which leaves Rte. 114 between the two bridges just south of Barrington; **(401) 247-0017.**

Redlefsen's—$$ to $$$

With all the ethnic variety of Rhode Island restaurants, it's hard to find any that serve German food. While Redlefsen's isn't a German restaurant, its international menu does include some well-prepared German specialties,

especially if you go in October, when you can get spaetzle and other hard-to-find dishes. Along with the smoked pork chop and bratwurst with sauerkraut, however, you may find seafood cakes, Portuguese-style steamed clams or grilled scallops in a tomato-basil sauce, and a popular appetizer, Boboli pizza. The restaurant is handicapped-accessible. It does not take reservations. Open Tues. –Thur. and Sun. from 5–9:30 P.M., Fri.–Sat. from 5–10 P.M. **425 Hope St. (Rte. 114), in the center of Bristol; (401) 254-1188.**

The Lobster Pot—$$ to $$$$

Readers of *Rhode Island Monthly* already know that this place is famed for more than its sweeping views of Bristol Harbor as it meets Narragansett Bay. They consistently vote it the best seafood restaurant in the state. It's one of the rare places where you can order a clam-bake for one person, and the baked stuffed lobster is excellent. Nonseafood entrees are offered, but it would be a shame to go to this restaurant and miss what it does best. You will need reservations. Open from 11:30 A.M.–3 P.M. and 3:30–10 P.M. Tues.–Sun. Across from the Herreshoff Marine Museum, at **19 Hope St. (Rte. 114), at the south end of Bristol; (401) 253-9100.**

Jack's Family Restaurant— $ to $$

You have to look hard to find anything over $10 on Jack's menu: Even the whopping Godfather Platter, which serves two and includes veal cutlet, chicken, meatballs and sausage, is only $12.50. Fried clams, sole, fried smelts, the spicy seafood zuppa, Portuguese-style pork chops and lots of pasta dishes provide a good value in a casual setting. Look for lobster specials on Mondays and early-bird specials weekdays before 6 P.M. Smoking is allowed. Open Mon., Wed., Thur. from 11:30 A.M.–10 P.M., Fri.–Sat. from 11:30 A.M.–11 P.M., Sun. from noon–10 P.M. **294 Child St. (Rte. 103), Warren; (402) 245-4052.**

Services

Visitor Information

Bristol County Chamber of Commerce, P.O. Box 250, 654 Metacom Ave., Warren 02885; (401) 245-0750.

The Bristol Museums Association has a combined pass for visitors. For information, call **(401) 253-2707.**

Parking

Warren has a public lot on **Railroad Ave.,** which runs parallel to Rte. 114 (Main St.) south of Rte 103. Bristol's public parking is at **Independence Park** on Thames St., at the southern end of the East Bay Bike Path.

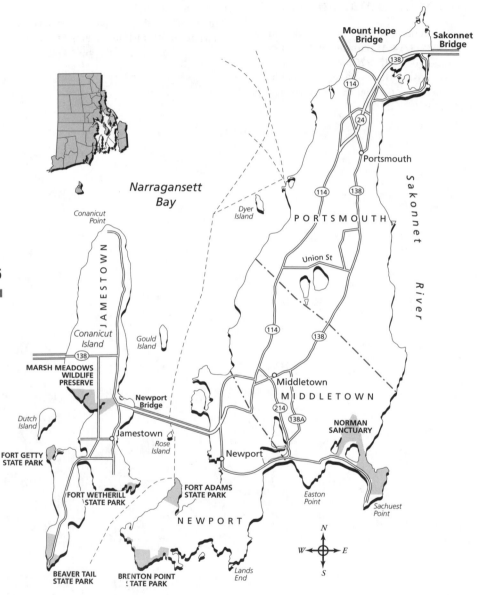

North Aquidneck and Jamestown

North Aquidneck and Jamestown

While Newport dominates the southern part of Aquidneck Island and is certainly its best-known feature, the north is more sparsely settled and rural, with nature preserves and historical sites. It is also larger: The towns of Portsmouth and Middletown each occupy more land area than Newport. And with shoreline on both Narragansett Bay and the Sakonnet River, there is an abundance of waterfront.

Jamestown and Prudence Islands lie west of Aquidneck. Jamestown is the name of the town—the real name of the island (the land mass) on which it lies is Conanicut Island, but since the town covers all its land, nearly everyone refers to it as Jamestown. We have included Jamestown in this chapter, while Prudence Island is discovered in the chapter on Bristol County, since the only public access to it is from the ferry out of Bristol.

History

When Anne Hutchinson and William Coddington were expelled from Massachusetts Bay Colony in 1638, they traveled to the Providence Plantation. Roger Williams took them to his trading post at Cocomcussoc and negotiated the purchase of Aquidneck Island, but once they were settled into the northern part of the island, Coddington and Hutchinson immediately began to argue about leadership. Coddington left, going to the southern tip of Aquidneck to found Newport. The boundary was not precisely drawn, however, and the two towns—Hutchinson's in the north and Coddington's to the south—disputed it constantly.

As Newport developed, the residents of its northern part remained farmers, while in the town itself almost everyone was involved in shipping or commerce. Divisions grew, with the rural north charging that the ruling merchants forbade artisans and skilled workers from living outside the compact part of town, and that farmers were being taxed to pay the poor relief of unemployed sailors. Middletown was created out of northern Newport in 1743, finally establishing the town boundaries on Aquidneck. The area remained agricultural, with some fishing and shipping along the shores.

Saint Columba's Chapel in Middletown has a lych-gate, rare in the United States.

When the British seized and occupied Newport at the outbreak of the Revolution, they also moved into Middletown. It was on the Middletown-Portsmouth line, in 1777, that Colonel Barton of the colonial militia captured the commanding general of the British forces as he lay sleeping in the home of a lady friend. Rhode Island's only major land battle of the war took place in Portsmouth in August of 1778, when Continental troops failed in an attempt to oust the British from Newport and had to leave the island. The battle is notable for the regiment of Black soldiers comprised of former slaves that fought in it.

The war was harsh on Aquidneck farmers, many of whom lost everything they had, but following the war farmers in both towns returned to begin over. In the 1800s, serious efforts were made to use the coal found under Portsmouth. Fishing was an important industry, and a huge complex was built to process porgy (menhaden) oil for paint and varnish manufacture. In the late nineteenth century the U.S. Navy expanded north from Newport and set up a coaling station on the bay shore which was expanded as a fuel station and manufactory of antisubmarine nets during World War II.

Jamestown's fortunes, meanwhile, had pretty much followed those of the Aquidneck towns. Early settlers used it as grazing land, for which it offered two advantages. Because it was a small island, fences were unnecessary. And the Narragansetts had long used it as a summer home, and to clear land for gardening they had burned large areas that had since run to hay. These fields served as ready-made grazing land for sheep. The woodlands that the Narragansetts left were cut during the siege of Newport, when every available splinter within reach was burned for warmth.

Because of its strategic position with clear views over both passages of Narragansett Bay, Jamestown was fortified from pre-Revolutionary times through World War II. During the Gilded Age, while New York society repaired to Newport for the summer, Philadelphians chose the quieter country life of Jamestown and built their more modest cottages there.

Getting There

From Providence, take I-195 east to Rte. 136 south through Bristol to the Mount Hope Bridge. From Fall River, Massachusetts, take Rte. 24 over the Sakonnet River Bridge. On the Portsmouth side, Rte. 138 runs south along the Sakonnet River (east) side of the island, and Rtes. 114 and 24 lead to and along the bay (west) side.

RIPTA buses between Newport and Providence pass through Middletown and Portsmouth hourly or more often on weekdays, hourly on Saturdays. They follow Rte. 114, with scheduled stops in Middletown at Two Mile Corner (the intersection of Rte. 114 and East Main Rd.) and at the Mount Hope Bridge in Portsmouth. A local bus connects Newport and lower Middletown via the beaches. These buses will stop on request. A bus route connects Newport and the University of Rhode Island campuses via Jamestown, providing hourly or more frequent service between Newport and Jamestown. For schedules and information call **(800) 662-5088** or **847-0209.**

Even though a bridge now connects Jamestown with Newport, a ferry service still operates on a regular summer schedule between the two, stopping at Fort Adams, Goat Island and Bannister's Wharf before returning to Conanicut Marina at East Ferry in Jamestown. It runs at two-hour intervals throughout the day, with evening trips on weekends. It will also make stops on request at Rose Island and at the New York Yacht Club. The fare is $7 one way, $10 round-trip; **(401) 423-9900.**

Festivals and Events

Birds and Breakfast
May

This is your chance to get an authentic Rhode Island hearty breakfast and a guided bird walk and feel good about it. On the first Sunday of May the **Norman Bird Sanctuary** hosts a breakfast featuring jonnycakes and other goodies as a fund-raiser. The $10 fee ($8 for members) includes breakfast and a guided tour of one of the trails on the refuge. The tours start at 6 A.M. and breakfast starts at 6:30 A.M., and both continue until noon. See page **192** for access directions; **(401) 846-2577.**

Newport Antiques Festival
June

For a number of years the **Glen Farm** in Portsmouth has been the site of the largest antique show and sale in the state. Over 200 dealers from several states gather here to sell their wares in an outdoor setting close to the Sakonnet River. The festival is held Saturday and Sunday of the first weekend in June from 10 A.M. to 5 P.M. **Glen Farm Recreation Area, Portsmouth** (see **opposite column** for access directions); **(800) 759-7469.**

Historic Walk in Jamestown
September

A member of the Jamestown Historical Society leads a walk through the village, describing how it once looked and telling the history of the buildings that line Narragansett St. Call for dates and particulars; **(401) 423-0784.**

Norman Bird Sanctuary Harvest Fair
October

The large Harvest Fair on sanctuary grounds has become a local favorite, especially with kids, who enjoy pony and hayrides, a mud pit, dunking booth, monkey bridge, bell ringers, children's games and a midway. There are also field games (sack race, tug-o-war, wheelbarrow race, egg toss), a greased pole contest, crafts and gardening exhibits and a country store. Entertainment includes folk and blues music and children's programs hourly starting at 11 A.M. on both days and running until 5 P.M. Admission is $5, $1 for kids. At Norman Bird Sanctuary on Third Beach Rd. See page **192** for directions; **(401) 846-2577.**

189

Outdoor Activities

Parks and Recreation Areas

See also the Hiking and Walking section for information about wildlife preserves, and the Swimming section for beaches.

Glen Farm Recreation Area

Owned by the town of Portsmouth, this area occupies the grounds of an old manor house and has softball, soccer, horseback riding and picnic facilities. A trail leads down to the shore and a beach, then to a seawall and the ruins of the old fishing pier. There is a parking fee. From Rte. 138 in Portsmouth take Glen Rd. (opposite Almy House Antiques) east to a sign for the manor at Frank Coelho Dr. Turn right, passing the school, to the manor. **Town of Portsmouth, Town Hall, East Main Rd., Portsmouth 02871; (401) 683-3255.**

Biking

Bicycling on the main north and south routes, Rtes. 114 (West Main Rd.), 138 (East Main

Rd.), 24 (from Sakonnet Bridge to its junction with Rte. 114) and 138A (Aquidneck Rd.) is extremely dangerous because of the heavy traffic and the large number of drivers trying to figure out how to get to Newport. There are some nice, fairly quiet roads along the east side of the island, in Middletown, Portsmouth near the Norman Bird Sanctuary and north of there, but you still have to be concerned about beach traffic. **Island Windsurfing Sports** rents 18-speed bicycles, along with child seats, trailers and kids' bikes. They can advise you on the best and safest routes. **86 Aquidneck Ave., Middletown 02842; (401) 846-4421.**

Birding

One of the most popular places for bird-watching in the state is the Sachuest Point section of Middletown. Both the **Norman Bird Sanctuary** and the **Sachuest National Wildlife Refuge** provide a large and varied habitat for waterfowl and upland species. Over 250 bird species have been sighted here, and it is a particularly important place for migrating waterfowl and hawks. Black ducks, mergansers, common goldeneyes, red-breasted ducks, buffleheads, harlequin ducks, common loons, horned grebes and geese are here as well as shore and wading birds such as the spotted,

Sachuest Point is now a National Wildlife Refuge, with walking trails and platforms for watching birds.

least and semipalmated sandpipers, piping plovers, great and snowy egrets and the great blue heron. Ospreys, sharp-shinned and Cooper's hawks and peregrine falcons are also seen during migrations. The Norman Sanctuary also has a wide range of native and nesting birds, including pheasant, grouse and woodcock. The Norman maintains a facility to heal and rehabilitate injured birds, and several too injured to return to the wild reside on the grounds. A natural history museum explores the birds and their life cycles. The sanctuary is easy to reach by following the southern shore along the beaches to its outermost point.

Conanicut Island Sanctuary, in Jamestown (see page **192**) provides good sightings of wading birds, including egrets, herons and glossy ibis, during the summer and waterfowl in the winter. Also in the winter, on the west side of **Beavertail State Park,** you can often find songbird species that normally migrate south at this time of year. They live in the bushes along this protected shore.

Canoeing

The Sakonnet River is a popular place for sea kayaking and canoeing as well as for boating. The river in this area is really more a bay than a traditional river. While it lacks the heavy commercial and naval traffic of the west side of Aquidneck, it has all of the dangers of ocean canoeing: tides, currents and weather, which can turn nasty in minutes. Anyone venturing into the water should be prepared to deal with all aspects of ocean canoeing. There is a boat ramp at **Third Beach,** close to **Sachuest National Wildlife Refuge.** The miles of marshland nesting and resting grounds for waterfowl are perfect for canoes.

Diving

Ocean State Dive Charters has night and lobster dives, as well as charters to Rhode Island dive sites. They have an instructor and are located at **East Passage Yachting Center in Portsmouth; (401) 683-3444.**

Fort Wetherill, on Jamestown, has two sheltered south-facing coves and a rocky drop-off that is a popular area for divers, especially in the late summer and fall, when tropical fish species are brought north by the Gulf Stream. The western shore of **Beavertail State Park** is also a popular dive site. **Ocean State Scuba** at the pier in Jamestown will treat you to a free dive if you bring your own gear and show your certification card on a Saturday or Sunday morning at 10 A.M. Call by Thursday afternoon for a reservation; **(800) 933-DIVE** or **(401) 423-1662.**

Fishing

In Middletown the best fishing is off the rocks at the **Sachuest National Wildlife Refuge.** Surf fishing here is likely to yield bluefish, striped bass and tautog. There is also surf fishing nearby off of **Third Beach Rd.** From Hanging Rocks Rd. continue to Third Beach Rd. and turn right. There is a boat ramp at Third Beach. Other popular places are off **Common Fence Point** in the narrows between Aquidneck and Tiverton near the Sakonnet River Bridge, and in the north coast areas around the **Mount Hope Bridge.** You can also fish from the old abutments of the **Old Stone Bridge,** near the new bridge. **St. Mary's Pond** is stocked with rainbow and brook trout and some warmwater species; it is off Union St. between East Main St. (Rte. 138) and West Main Rd. (Rte. 114) in Portsmouth. **Melville Pond** in Melville Park is also stocked with trout. **Beavertail Point,** at the southern end of Jamestown, has excellent surf casting.

Myles Standish Charters

J. C. Standish operates the *Mayflower* on sport- or bottom-fishing trips from Middletown. The boat holds from one to four passengers and supplies all the gear and bait. Bottom fishing is for tautog (blackfish), fluke and scup, and sport fishing is for stripers, bluefish and mackerel. The rate for the six-hour trip is $55 per adult and $45 for a child under 12 for sport fishing, and $35 per adult and $30 per child for bottom fishing. Reservations are required. (The boat is Coast Guard–licensed for up to six passengers.) **J. C. Myles**

Standish, 4 Smithfield Dr., Middletown 02840; (401) 846-7225.

Golf

Montaup Country Club welcomes the public to its 18-hole par-71 course, where golf greats Walter Hagen and Gene Sarazen have played. It offers a dining room and a bar as well as cart rental. On Anthony Rd. at the very tip near the Mount Hope and Tiverton Bridges. Close by, overlooking Mt. Hope Bridge and the bay, the 9-hole par-34 **Poccasset Country Club** has a lounge and restaurant. It's on Bristol Ferry Rd just before the bridge; **(401) 683-2266.**

Green Valley Country Club has 18 holes, par 71, with four par-five holes, the longest of which is 600 yards. You can rent carts, and there is a restaurant and lounge. At **371 Union St.,** between Rtes. 114 and 138 in Portsmouth, not far north of the Middletown line; **(401) 847-9543.**

Jamestown Country Club, is one of the oldest golf courses in the state. It has a snack bar and lounge, and you can rent carts. It's on East Shore Rd., close to the end of the Newport Bridge; **(401) 423-9930.**

Hiking and Walking

Norman Bird Sanctuary

Over 450 acres of a former farm are now a sanctuary for birds and small mammals, as well as a place to preserve native plant and animal communities and the special landforms found here. Over eight miles of trails wind through varied habitats. Four hard-rock ridges run through the property, creating valleys. From the top of the ridge on **Hanging Rock Trail** you can see the ocean, **Gardiner's Pond** and the marshlands. Hardscrabble vegetation on the ridge tops, lush forests in the valleys and wetlands along the ponds attract a wide variety of bird life. Spring and fall bird walks begin at 8 A.M. on Sundays; natural history walks and a nature day camp are operated by the foundation. One arm of the sanctuary extends south between Gardiner Pond and

Nelson Pond, where an old slate quarry has formed a small pond. A trail map is available, and it describes each of the 11 trails, none of which is over a mile and a half long. An interactive natural history museum shows many of the species found here. In winter it's open Tues.–Sun, from 9 A.M.–5 P.M., and it's open daily in summer, remaining open until 9 P.M. on Wednesdays. From Newport take Memorial Blvd. east, and at Easton's Beach take Purgatory Rd. (also called Second Beach Rd.) straight ahead to Paradise Ave. Turn left onto Paradise and almost immediately right onto Hanging Rock Rd. At Third Beach Rd. turn left to the entrance. From the north take Rte. 138 south and turn onto Mitchell's Ln. just after the Middletown–Portsmouth line. It will turn into Third Beach Rd. **583 Third Beach Rd., Middletown 02842; (401) 8846-2577.**

Sachuest Point
National Wildlife Refuge

Sachuest is adjacent to the Norman Sanctuary and occupies the entire end of the peninsula. The point sticks way out into the water, forming the west jaw at the mouth of the Sakonnet River, directly opposite Sakonnet Point. The strategic importance of these two points that controlled the Sakonnet basin made it the site of a naval facility and a fire control point during World War II. Three miles of walking trails cross the refuge. A trail map is posted, showing the routes—some are interior and some are along the coastline. Three raised observation decks help you to see the lay of the land, which is largely high and scrub-covered, with intertidal marshes and shore grasses—a perfect feeding, nesting and resting habitat for migrating waterfowl. Open daily, dawn to dusk. A visitors center is staffed intermittently by volunteers. Follow the directions for the Norman Sanctuary, but from Hanging Rock Rd. turn right onto Sachuest Point Rd. **U.S. Fish and Wildlife Service, c/o Ninigret NWR, Shoreline Plaza, Rte. 1A, P.O. Box 307, Charlestown 02813; (401) 364-9124.**

Melville Nature Preserve

When the navy started downsizing, a lot of land on Aquidneck was abandoned, and the 92 acres of Melville Nature Preserve are a result. The town has built over four miles of trails through the woodlands and down to the shoreline. From the preserve there are views out into the bay and of Hog Island and Prudence Island offshore. It lies to the west of Rte. 114 just south of Cory Rd.

Conanicut Island Sanctuary

Adjoining an Audubon Society preserve and a marsh on Jamestown, this wildlife sanctuary has a loop trail that circles through its fields and woods, with good views over the surrounding marshlands. A number of wading-bird species nest in these marshes, and duck species winter here. The entrance to the area is opposite the Jamestown Police Station, where you can park, close to the end of the Newport Bridge; **(401) 423-7220.**

Horseback Riding

Newport Equestrian Center

The center has a full range of horseback options, from solo rides to lessons, riding camp and pony parties. Especially attractive are beach trail rides along the shore of the Sakonnet River both by daylight and moonlight. Rides are $55 per person for 90 minutes, and two-hour rides are $65 per person. From Rte. 138 take Rte. 138A south (Aquidneck Ave.) and turn left onto Green End Ave. From Newport take Memorial Blvd. to Purgatory Rd. at Easton's Beach, then take a left and a quick right onto Hanging Rocks Rd. At Third Beach Rd. turn left. **287 Third Beach Rd., Middletown 02842; (401) 848-5440** or **(800) 846-7737.**

Swimming

Middletown and Portsmouth offer a lot of choice in beaches, all of them along the Sakonnet River (east) side of the island. Right on Memorial Blvd. just over the Newport line in Middletown is a long, and very popular, beach area with lifeguards and changing rooms. Restaurants and fast-food places are just across the street.

Take Purgatory Rd. (also called Second Beach Rd.) to its end, then take Paradise Rd. a few feet to the left and turn onto Hanging Rock Rd. From this road you can turn right onto Sachuest Point Rd. or continue straight ahead. If you turn right you will end up at **Sachuest Beach** (also called Second Beach), a three-mile-long beach and the only one in the area with real sand dunes. It abuts the Sachuest Wildlife Refuge. There are lifeguards. This is a premier surfing beach. Parking is $5 from Memorial Day to Labor Day, and the lot holds 3,000 cars.

If you don't turn on Hanging Rock Rd. you will come to **Third Beach,** with a nice view of the Sakonnet hills across the water. The main problem with Third Beach is that some of it is private, so you have to be careful to stay in the public areas. There is a boat ramp.

Along the middle of the island, on the Sakonnet side, is **Sandy Point Beach,** in Portsmouth, which is open to nonresidents for a fee. It's a lovely setting, but don't expect sand. Depending on the recent weather, the water can be clean or a little thick. There is usually no lifeguard, and the beach is open from 9 A.M.–6 P.M. from late June to Labor Day. Picnic facilities with cooking grills are available. From Rte. 138 take Sandy Point Rd. east.

Island Park Beach and **Teddy's Beach** are on the north end of the island in Portsmouth, on the Sakonnet River side. Island Park has no lifeguard. Teddy's is just up the road, and although there is no fee, there are lifeguards, picnic sites and fishing. It's right next to the Old Stone Bridge. From Rte. 138 in the north end of the island take Park Ave. east.

Mackerel Cove Beach, on Jamestown, is a half-mile crescent of coarse sand with calm water, but sometimes it is filled with debris. This is due to the narrow cove, which doesn't allow the tides to wash out quite as much as they wash in.

Windsurfing

The most popular areas for windsurfing are off the three beaches at the southern shore of Middletown just described. **Island Wind Surfing Sports** has equipment to buy or rent, as

At Conanicut Point, at the northern tip of Conanicut Island, you can see a house that was once a lighthouse.

well as windsurfing lessons. They give lessons at Fort Adams (Newport) and at Third Beach (Middletown). Lessons are $20 per hour ($90 for six hours) and the rentals are $10 per hour. There is even a land simulator so you don't have to get wet. The shop is at Easton's Beach (First Beach). **86 Aquidneck Ave., Middletown 02842; (401) 846-4421.**

Seeing and Doing

Tours and Cruises

Schooner cruises aboard the gaff-rigged *Legasea* include lunch and dinner cruises and twilight departures. The sailboat is a replica of the coastal trading schooners in use about 100 years ago. Dinner cruises include fresh lobster and leave Jamestown's Conanicut Marina at 5:30 P.M. from Fri.–Sun. in the summer. Luncheon trips begin at 2 P.M. from Fri.–Sun., and twilight cruises set sail at 6 P.M. from Mon.–Thur.; **(401) 789-3904.**

Aquidneck

Prescott Farm

Feel sorry for poor Henry Overing. Henry was a well-off citizen of Newport in the latter part of the 1770s who had a farm in Middletown, at the time very rural. Henry's wife took a shine to General Richard Prescott, the commander of British troops in Newport. The general, reciprocating, moved out to Henry's farm to be with her, moving his headquarters with him. On July 9, 1777, he was in bed (it's not known if she was there too) when he was roused by colonial troops under Colonel William Barton and captured. Henry's wife not only humiliated him, but his own farm still bears the name of the cad who seduced her. The site has the original guardhouse, a country store in a building that served as the ferrymaster's home in Portsmouth before being moved here and a working wind-powered gristmill dating from 1812 (originally in Warren but moved here to replace a similar one). The mill, with its huge fabric-covered arms, still grinds Rhode Island flint corn, which you can buy at the country

The churchyard at Saint Columba's Chapel would be at home in an English village, with its effigy tomb and Celtic crosses.

store. The nearby gambrel-roofed Nichols-Overing house, where the general was captured by Colonial troops, can be seen from the outside. **2009 West Main Rd., Middletown; (401) 849-7300.**

Whitehall Museum House

Introduced at the court of Queen Anne at the age of 28, George Berkley was made Dean of Londonderry, Ireland, in 1724 at age 39. When he proposed to build a college in Bermuda to train sons of colonists and American Indians, George I enthusiastically promised him the funds. His ship, blown off course, landed in Newport in 1729. While waiting for the funds for his new college, funds that never came, he built himself a stunning home in Middletown with a formal facade, hip roof, false double front door and cross central stairway, all features unusual in New England at the time. After three years he gave up and returned to England, where he was appointed Bishop of Cloyne, Ireland. He gave his home to Yale University, and during the Revolution it was a barracks for British officers. It was being used to store hay when it was rescued by three Newport women in 1897. Now furnished in pieces authentic to the period, the house is an exquisite example of a country mansion of a highly placed citizen of the day. Docents interpret the life and times of George Berkley for visitors and discuss the importance of his role in early Newport. Next to the house the **Newport Garden Club** maintains an eighteenth-century garden. Open daily from July 1 to Labor Day from 10 A.M. to 5 P.M., in June and September by appointment. Admission $3. On Berkley Ave.; a sign is posted on Rte. 138. From Newport take Rte. 138A (Memorial Boulevard) east as it turns left and becomes Aquidneck Ave. **311 Berkley Ave., Middletown; (401) 846-3116 or 847-7951.**

Purgatory Chasm

Created when a crack formed in the underlying pudding-stone conglomerate stone, the action of the sea smashing into and out of this cleft over the years has done the rest. The chasm is about 10 feet wide and about 50 feet deep, extending back from the cliff at the shoreline for 75–100 feet. As the water is forced up its ever-narrowing channel during high seas it makes a loud noise. There is a full view of the entire chasm from a bridge at one end: *Don't climb into it,* because it is extremely dangerous. Take Memorial Boulevard from Newport to Easton's Beach and continue onto Purgatory Rd. (also called Second Beach Rd.) to the intersection with Paradise and Tuckerman Rds. Turn right onto Tuckerman Rd., and the parking area will be on the left.

Saint Columba's Chapel

This little stone chapel is one of our favorite places in the state. In 1884, a number of wealthy people who had built substantial homes in this area (many of which remain) built this granite chapel with a small bell tower and a covered side portico. The interior is filled with the warm glow of stained glass by three of the finest workmen in that medium, Louis Tiffany, John La Farge and Maitland Armstrong. A touching memorial incorporates the sword of a West Point cadet who was killed while successfully saving the lives of others; another is a memorial to the actor Edwin Booth. A pyx hangs at the front of the church, and the furnishings are also reminiscent of English village churches. A stone wall encloses a fine late-Victorian cemetery with interesting stones, including one with a ship, an effigy tomb and some fine Celtic crosses with knotwork designs. Services (Episcopal) are 8 A.M. and 10 A.M. Sundays, Eucharist Tuesday and Thursday at noon and Wednesday at 6:30 P.M. Music in the Chapel programs are held occasionally, featuring well-known musicians. These are held at other churches as well; call **(401) 849-7081** for information on the music programs. The chapel is open Mon.–Fri. from 10 A.M.–1 P.M. From Rte. 138 take Mitchell's Lane, continuing to follow it as it becomes Wapping Rd. Take Peckham Ave. to the right, then take Vaucluse to the right. From the south take Purgatory Rd. from Easton's Beach, then go left and take an immediate right on Hanging Rock Rd., then Indian Ave. along the shore to Peckham Rd. Then take Peckham and turn left

Saint Columba contains windows by three of America's greatest stained glass artists.

onto Vaucluse. **Parish Office, 55 Vaucluse Ave., Middletown; (401) 847-5571.**

Newport Vineyards

This winery is unusual in that it is not located at the vineyard where the grapes are grown. It is right along busy East Main Rd., while most of the grapes used are grown at Hopelands Vineyards along the Sakonnet River. Others are brought in from associated vineyards in New York. You can sample the wines in the showroom, and take a free tour explaining the wine-making process. The vineyards make a viking red, three whites made of seyval and vidal blanc grapes, a Riesling and a blush. They can bottle your wine with customized labels. Open May–Oct., Mon.–Sat. from 10 A.M.– 5 P.M., Sun. from noon–5 P.M., with free tours daily at 1 P.M. and 3 P.M. The winery is at Eastgate Mall on Rte. 138 just north of the Rte. 138A intersection. **909 East Main Rd., Middletown; (401) 848-5161** or **(800) 345-1559.**

Butts Hill Fort

On August 29, 1778, Rhode Island's only major battle of the Revolution centered around Butts Hill Fort in Portsmouth. Built by the British in 1777 to protect their northern flank, it was occupied in August of 1778 by about 10,000 American troops who were trying to drive the British off the island. Although the Americans

Green Animals in Middletown is a topiary garden, with shrubbery pruned to animal shapes.

lost the battle and the British retained New-port, this event is known for the cleverness of the retreat. The Continental troops, led by General Sullivan, created the illusion that they had settled in for the night around their camp-fires. Seeing tents pitched and campfires burn-ing, the British did the gentlemanly thing—they went to bed, to resume the battle in the morning. By morning the American troops were gone, having slipped away during the night. All except for Lieutenant John Vial, who was on picket duty in advance of the Con-tinental line and didn't get the word. He was captured, imprisoned, escaped, was captured again and escaped again before the war was ended.

At the time of the U.S. Centennial, and even into the twentieth century, the site of the fort was maintained. A stone wall and a large bronze plaque on a stone monument marked the entrance. At some point, however, this place has been forgotten, neglected and van-dalized. Two big water towers now loom over it, and the grounds, once well kept, are over-grown with weeds as brush and trees reclaim the earthworks. The stone entry is falling apart, and the monument has been toppled. In spite of this desolation it is still a fascinating place. It was in this battle, on the right flank at

the foot of the hill, that the first Black regiment in America ever fought in an engagement. There is a tremendous sense of presence here, of that ragtag bunch of upstarts who dared to challenge the British Army. You can still walk the earthworks, examine the gun emplace-ments, walk the parade ground and try to imagine what it was like for the Continental troops, knowing that the best army in the world was on the other side of those mounds of earth.

The site is unmarked and tricky to find. On the north end of Portsmouth take Sprague St. east from either Rte. 114 or 24. Butts St. and Dyer St., off the south side of Sprague St., both lead up to the fort. Find the old road at the top that leads up to the old main entrance.

The monument to the First Rhode Island Regiment, the "Black Regiment" composed of freed Black and Indian slaves, is on the west side of Rte. 114 north, near its junction with Rte. 24.

Green Animals

Topiary gardens, while not uncommon in En-gland, with its moist, even year-round climate, are rare in North America, especially as far north as Rhode Island. But the sheltered shores of West Passage create a microclimate where the long process of clipping and training has succeeded. The 80 pieces of topiary in the garden include geometric forms, ornamental designs and 21 whimsical animals and birds created from yew, privet and boxwood. Be-tween the sculpted shrubs are parterre flower beds, a rose garden and other plantings that create a colorful setting for the "green ani-mals." Among the animals represented are the boar, camel, donkey, elephant, giraffe, lion, ostrich, reindeer, swan, unicorn and bear. A map and plant list are available at the entrance. The Victorian house adjacent to the gardens has a museum of Victorian toys that features a puppet theater, toy soldiers and a tin Ferris wheel. Open daily (weather permit-ting), May 1–Oct. 31 from 10 A.M.–5 P.M., and for special programs at Christmas. Admission is $6.50. Green Animals is included in the combination ticket with several of the Newport mansions. **Cory's Lane, off Rte. 114; (401) 847-1000.**

Friends Meeting House

The religious tolerance of the founders and settlers of Rhode Island gave Quakers the freedom to worship in their own fashion, a freedom they didn't have in Massachusetts. The sect flourished here; even William Coddington converted before he died. The Friends Society had a congregation here in the seventeenth century, and the Meeting House dates from 1700. It served as billets for British troops in the Revolution and afterward was the home of Moses Brown School before the school moved to Newport in 1819. Near the corner of East Main Rd. and Hedley Ave. It's open for services year-round. **11 Middle Rd., Portsmouth 02871.**

Portsmouth Historical Society– Union Meeting House and School

The Historical Society maintains these two buildings as museums of Portsmouth history, but, like many labors of love such as this, the hours are limited. But even if they are closed you can still see the buildings and look into the windows of the 1716 schoolhouse. The meeting house, once used as a church, is a plain clapboard building with eyebrow lintels over the windows and a double front door surmounted by a round window. Julia Ward Howe, author of *Battle Hymn of the Republic* lectured here on world peace, women's suffrage and women's rights. She lived down the road at 745 Union St. at the time of her death in 1910 at the age of 91. The church is now a museum, displaying costumes, household items and farming tools and implements from the town's more than three centuries. The schoolhouse next door, built in 1716, is also a museum, set up as a school of the period would have looked. One of the initial skirmishes of the Battle of Rhode Island in August 1778 took place on the grounds. Open Sat.– Sun. from 1–4 P.M. Memorial day to Labor Day and by appointment. **East Main Rd. (Rte. 138) at Union Street, Portsmouth; (401) 683-9178.**

Newport International Polo Series

From early June to early September, the polo series plays at Glen Farms in Portsmouth. The **International Series Grand Prix** is held there on the last weekend of August. Matches start at 5 P.M. on Saturdays throughout the summer. Glen Farm, Portsmouth (see page **189**). **(401) 846-0200.**

Jamestown

Jamestown Windmill

The dome of this early shingled windmill turns, so that the huge wooden arms can face the wind. It was built in 1787 and was used regularly for more than a century. The grinding stones on the main floor are over five feet in diameter, and grain was poured in through a trap door on the second floor, above them. You

197

The wooden shingled Jamestown windmill, built in 1787, is now a museum.

can see the interior and learn about its operation mid-June–mid-Sept, Sat.–Sun. from 1–4 P.M. or by appointment. A donation is requested. On **North Rd., between the Newport and Jamestown Bridges; (401) 423-1798.**

Sydney L. Wright Museum

An archaeological dig of an Indian burial site on Jamestown, judged to be over 3,000 years old has yielded a fascinating collection spanning the period from its earliest use until after the arrival of European settlers. This collection, which is very nicely exhibited, has an ancient ax head and other stone implements, the oldest known Narragansett basket (from the 1600s, a long time for a basket to survive under the best of conditions) and some items of English manufacture that were probably received in trade from early settlers. It's free and open all year, Mon.–Sat., in a section of the Jamestown Philomenian Library, at **26 North Rd.; (401) 423-2665.**

Jamestown Museum

The Jamestown Ferry is the main focus of the museum, located in an old schoolhouse. From the 1600s until the bridges replaced them in 1940 and 1969, these boats were the only public access to the mainland. From sail to steam, exhibits follow the ferries with photographs, models, maps and gear. Changing exhibits explore other features of island history. The museum is open late June–Labor Day from Tues.–Sat. A donation is requested. **92 Narragansett Ave.,** south of the bridges and not far from its intersection with North Rd.; **(401) 423-1798.**

Jamestown Fire Museum

An 1894 steam pump engine, which still pumps water, and a hand tub are the centerpieces of this little museum, which also displays other old tools of fire fighting. The most exotic treasure, however is a nozzle from Hitler's Eagle's Nest, his mountaintop retreat near Berchtesgaden, Germany. Undoubtedly the postwar trophy of a local GI, you're thinking. Well, you're close: It was General Dwight Eisenhower, who spent a lot of time in the Newport area and gave the nozzle to the Jamestown fire chief. Open all year, Mon.–Fri. from 9 A.M.–3 P.M., or ask at the fire station at 50 Narragansett Ave., south of the bridges; **(401) 423-0062.**

Fort Wetherill

The earliest earthworks here were taken by the British before the cannons were in place, but defensive positions were completed before the War of 1812 and manned during the Civil War. By the time of the Spanish-American War, a century later, the position was fortified by seven batteries, had 16-foot thick walls, and was hidden in sand and vegetation, with plotting rooms and ammunition storage deep underground. The tracks you see now are from the two world wars. The fort has a picnic area, boat launch and hiking trails that wind along the point, along with splendid views of Newport's waterfront, Fort Adams and Castle Hill light. It was, of course, these unobstructed views of the approaches to the bay that made Fort Wetherill such a defensively strategic site. Open daily all year from 6 A.M.–11 P.M. There is no fee for use of the facilities. **Off East Shore Rd.,** not far south of the Newport Bridge and the village of Jamestown; **(401) 423-9941 in the summer,** or **(401) 884-2010 year-round.**

Captain Kidd's Treasure Cave?

We can't tell you exactly where to find this, but local legends abound (here and on almost every other island along the Atlantic coast). Jamestown does have a Kidd connection, however, since he was a friend of the local privateer, Captain Thomas Paine. So much is historical fact, since Paine's association with Kidd was investigated by the authorities at the time of Kidd's capture and execution at the end of the seventeenth century. All we know is that his cache was reputed to have been hidden in a cave in the vicinity of what is now **Fort Wetherill State Park.** No one has reported seeing his ghost here, however.

Beavertail Lighthouse

The first Beavertail lighthouse was the first lighthouse installed in Rhode Island, and it was burned by the British during the Revolution. The hurricane of 1938 exposed its long-covered foundation, south of the present stone tower, which was built in 1856. The prototype steam fog warnings were tested here. It is still a working lighthouse, and a museum is housed in the old keeper's cottage. The collection features a Fresnel lens and other lighthouse-related artifacts and equipment. The museum is free, as is entrance to the park around it. Open daily mid-June to Labor Day, from 10 A.M.–4 P.M., it can be reached via Beavertail Rd., south of the village and the bridges; **(401) 423-9941.**

Watson Farm

Even before the Watson family began their 200 years of farming this land, the Narragansetts had burned the trees to clear fields for corn and beans. The land, although no longer in the original family, is still a working farm where sheep and cattle are raised commercially, as well as a large vegetable garden. On **Lamb Day,** in the spring, visitors can see the baby lambs and demonstrations of shearing and wool processing. When Rte. 138 was widened, an 1840 farmhouse slated for demolition was moved here. It is being restored and adapted to house a visitor's center with museum exhibit space and a farm shop.

A self-guided tour takes you through the farmyard, hay fields, pastures and woodlands, where you can see the animals, a windmill that pumps the water for watering holes in the pastures and where you can learn how and why stone walls were built and how Indians made wampum. The Watson Farm is open to visitors in June–mid-October on Tues., Thur. and Sun. from 1–5 P.M. Admission is $4. The farm is at **455 North Rd.,** just south of the intersection with Rte. 138; **(401) 423-0005.**

Beavertail State Park

A look at a map shows how Beavertail got its name: The entire piece of land hangs off the end of the main island like a broad round tail.

The original Beavertail Lighthouse was the first one in the state.

At the state park you can learn about the formation of the land here, and that this was once a separate island, later connected by the formation of the sand spit at Mackerel Cove. Naturalist programs at the park explore the geological history and the marine life of the park, as well as the navigation history of the point's many shipwrecks and the lighthouse. One tour explores some of the old military buildings and underground facilities used during World War II. The park covers a rocky peninsula with low vegetation, so views are outstanding, reaching along the mainland coast to Point Judith and across to Brenton Point in Newport. On a good day you can see Block Island just off to the left of Point Judith.

The ruins of former military buildings are still here. Just to the left of the parking lot on the east side of the lighthouse is the sealed-off bunker of Battery Whiting, and beyond it an observation station you can explore. You can see the gun emplacements just outside. Beyond, along the shoreline, look for the large blocks of building stone washed up from a shipwreck in the last century—you may even be able to see the carving on the surface. **(401) 423-9941 in the summer** or **(402) 884-2010 year-round.**

Where to Stay

ACCOMMODATIONS

Out of the high-rent district, several good chain hotels offer attractive, clean and comfortable lodgings outside of Newport, but within minutes of the city. They offer an option to the higher rates and more quickly filled places in town. You will find Budget, Marriott Courtyard, Comfort Inn and Econo Lodge along Rte. 114 (East Main Rd.), the main route into Newport. Howard Johnson and Royal Plaza Inn are on Rte. 138 (West Main Rd.).

Sea Breeze Inn—$$$ to $$$$

Aquidneck Ave. is Rte. 138A, and this 10-unit inn is on the Newport-Middletown line—not an attractive location, but handy. It's on the bus line to Newport and close to First Beach. The inn is family-operated and the people here are helpful and friendly. The second-floor rooms are nonsmoking and have a deck outside each unit. The rooms are attractively decorated and comfortable. Some have a sitting room. All rooms have queen-sized beds, marble floors in the baths, TV and air-conditioning. Complimentary coffee is served from 8 A.M., and a Continental breakfast is included in the rates. The inn will accommodate special diets at breakfast. There is a two-night minimum on in-season weekends, and three nights on holidays. During the winter months the rates include complimentary admission to two Newport mansions. Children under 18 stay free. Handicapped-accessible, no pets. **147 Aquidneck Ave., Middletown 02842; (401) 849-1211.**

Seaview Inn—$$$ to $$$$

Close to First Beach, the inn is only two miles from Newport. Not fancy, but clean and well maintained, it's a good family place with playthings for children, lawns and free use of bicycles, kites and beach equipment. There are 40 rooms, many with views of the ocean and Easton's Beach. The rooms are adequately sized, have two double beds, TV and air-conditioning and are comfortable but not upscale. Rates from Nov.–April are significantly lower. Two-night minimum on weekends in season. **240 Aquidneck Ave., Middletown 02842-5612; (401) 846-5000 or (800) 495-2046.**

The Inn at Shadow Lawn—$$–$$$$

Elegant from the first sight of its grand white facade, this inn is an 1853 Italianate mansion set on large lawns shaded by huge old copper beech trees. The formal first-floor rooms are filled with late-Victorian details—paneling, cornices and moldings—and are lit by large, almost floor-to-ceiling, windows reminiscent of the Old South. There are French crystal chandeliers, and in the paneled library Tiffany lighting. The florid gold mirror in the grand entrance hall is from a Barbary Coast brothel. Upstairs, the guest rooms are less dramatic—some are almost plain. All have private baths and either king, queen or twin beds. Each room also has a refrigerator that comes stocked with a complimentary bottle of wine, which you can enjoy from a wicker chair on the porch overlooking the lawn. Five of the rooms have attached kitchens. Off-season midweek rates are a bargain at $50. The inn provides complimentary scheduled shuttle service daily to downtown Newport. Take Miantonomi Ave. west from Rte. 114 a short distance south of the Rtes. 138 and 114 intersection. **120 Miantonomi Ave., Middletown 02842; (401) 849-1298.**

Founder's Brook Motel—$$$ to $$$$

Although this motel is on the very north end of the island, it is still only a short ride into Newport. Bristol, Warren and Barrington are also within easy reach. There are eight single units here and 25 suites, each with a living room, kitchen-dining area, bedroom and big closets. It's a perfect place for a family, with facilities for cooking breakfast and basic meals. The rooms are carpeted and well kept. There is a full roster of menus of local and Newport restaurants in the small but adequate lobby. On weekends during high season there is a two-night minimum. The motel allows pets. Weekend rates are about $30 to $40 higher than weekday; weekly rates save even more. Immediately after getting off the Mount Hope Bridge, bear left at the intersection onto Boyd's Ln. The motel is just a short distance on the right. **314 Boyd's Ln., Portsmouth 02871; (401) 683-1244 or (800) 334-8765.**

Brown's Bed and Breakfast—$$ to $$$

Wake up in the morning to see sailboats skimming the West Passage, eat breakfast (of homebaked Portuguese breads) overlooking the bay across the sweeping and immaculately tended lawns. A classic bungalow with three guest rooms in the main house and two more in a converted carriage shed, Brown's has just the right balance of elegance and homeyness. Hand-embroidered dresser scarves, color-coordinated linens and well-kept solid furniture from the 1930s and 1940s will remind you of your room at your favorite aunt's house. Little touches show a thoughtful host: pencils and scissors on the desk, a scale in the closet, introductions at breakfast. Baths in the main house are shared. Just south of the Mount Hope Bridge at **502 Bristol Ferry Rd. (Rte. 114), Portsmouth 02871; (401) 683-0155.**

Bay Voyage—$$$$

Stylish modern suites with well-equipped kitchenettes overlook the water, with the Newport skyline and Rose Island on the horizon. The main building is an old inn (with an interesting past—it was floated to Jamestown on a barge), and the suites are in the nicely blended wing. Separate bedrooms, a swimming pool and a program for children make the Bay Voyage popular with families. Rates are by the suite, no matter how many occupy it. The highest-priced suites have balconies and water views. Rates in the off- and shoulder seasons (the inn is open all year) offer excellent bargains, as low as $60 a night in September. A social director arranges activities, at least one per day, including trips to nearby Newport and boat rides. A complimentary Continental breakfast is served. **150 Conanicus Ave., Jamestown, 02845; (401) 423-2100 or (800) 225-3522.**

CAMPGROUNDS

Melville Pond Campground

When the town of Portsmouth took over the former navy land for the Melville Nature Preserve, it built a campground near the pond. There are tent and RV sites with fire rings and hot showers available. It's pretty open and pretty basic but one of the few camping places in this area. On Bradford Ave. off Rtes. 114 and 24 a bit south of their junction. **181 Bradford Rd., Portsmouth 02871; (401) 849-8212.**

201

Where to Eat

Coddington Brewing Company—$ to $$$

We don't know if William Coddington was a drinking man, but he does have a fine brewery named for him. It is combined with a nice restaurant, where you can get a good steak, barbecue chicken or souvlaki, rack of baby back ribs or seafood, including scallops, shrimp, grilled tuna or baked sole. For lighter fare they have a sandwich menu and soups. A hearty chili is under $4. The calamari is cooked just right. The atmosphere is contemporary and casual with touches of the traditional, such as brass rails and plank-top tables at the booths. There are seven regular brews on the menu plus an occasional special. Try the hazelnut porter or the blueberry ale. West on Coddington Hwy. from Rte. 114 between the Rtes. 214 and 138 intersections on the south side of the road. **210 Coddington Hwy., Middletown 02842; (401) 847-6690.**

Andrew's Grill and Pasta— $$ to $$$

This casual and comfortable eating place is right next to Newport Vineyards. Lunches include entrees, pasta, burgers, special sandwiches and regular old sandwiches, mostly in the $5 to $7 range. Dinners offer a big choice of appetizers, from nachos to calamari, crostini and crab cakes. The entrees include a nice selection of pasta dishes, chicken with Dijon crust, prime rib, grilled veal steak Madeira and chicken Portofino. Sandwiches, burgers and salads are also available during the dinner hours. There is an early-dinner special from 5 to 6:30 P.M. Monday through Thursday for under $10, and a sizzling steak special from 3 to 9 P.M. on Sundays for $12.95. Andrew's also has a Sunday brunch from 10 A.M. to 3 P.M. with a big menu and just about everything under $6. Rte. 138 at the Eastgate Mall. **909 East Main Street (Rte. 138), Middletown 02842, (401) 848-5153.**

Hisae's—$$ to $$$

Hisae's advertises "genuine Japanese Food at Reasonable Prices," and that's exactly what you'll get. The menu offers a wide choice, including bento box specials for lunch and for dinner. The bento lunches are mostly under $7 and include miso soup, yakisoba, hyashi-somen noodles and a choice of ten entree items from tempura squid rings to sashimi. Dinner bento runs from $12 to $17 for miso, salad, tempura, potato croquette, shrimp teriyaki and an entree choice. Between the shushi-maki and shushi-nigiri there are 28 choices. Dinner entrees include other specialties, such as tori-katsu and tonkatsu, donburi and sushi-sashimi. **21 Valley Rd. (Rte. 214), Middletown; (401) 848-6263.**

Sea Shai—$$ to $$$

Rhode Island Monthly readers have rated the sushi in this restaurant "best." There is also a broad menu of other Japanese specialties, as well as dishes from Korea. Entrees offered include kushi-yaki, shabu-shabu, nabe, bulgogi, hae mool jun, tempura and sukiyaki. Open from 11:30 A.M.–2:30 P.M. and 5–10 P.M. daily. Take Memorial Boulevard from Newport. Sea Shai is a mile and a half from Easton's Beach on Aquidneck Ave. **747 Aquidneck Ave., Middletown; (401) 848-5180.**

Flo's Drive-In—$ to $$

A basic clam shack, nothing fancy, but when you ask a native about fried clams, this is where they'll send you. Pick up fried clams, or fried whatever you want, from the window and eat them at one of the outdoor tables. The food is good, and the view over the water is great. Take Park Ave. from Rte. 138 toward Island Park. Flo's is on **Park Ave., Portsmouth; no phone.**

15 Point Road Restaurant—$$$

Although seafood reigns here, there are plenty of other offerings. This is in the old Island Park section of Portsmouth, and the area once boasted a large amusement center and casino, now gone. Try the sole serafino, sautéed with mushrooms, tomato, scallions, shrimp and white wine chicken Nanaquaket, sautéed with apple, celery, lingonberries, walnuts and calvados or chicken Normandy, with mushrooms, broccoli and a white-wine pesto sauce served over a bed of pasta. Less exotic dishes include grilled sirloin and baked scallops and shrimp. The view from the dining room is across the Sakonnet to Tiverton, attractive at all times of year, and the dining rooms are light and inviting. No reservations. Open Wed.–Thur. from 5–9 P.M., Fri.–Sat. from 5–10 P.M., Sun. from 2–9 P.M. Closed January. Take Park Ave. east from Rte. 138 on the north end of the island. The restaurant is just past Teddy's Beach. **15 Point Rd., Portsmouth; (401) 683-3138.**

Slice of Heaven—$

This bakery and cafe is well known for its cinnamon buns, chemical-free breads, muffins, calzone and lunch sandwiches. All served with espresso, cappuccino or fresh-ground American coffee. **32 Narragansett Ave, Jamestown; (401) 423-3970.**

Bay Voyage—$$$ to $$$$

The semicircular dining room, decorated with fine stained glass panels, overlooks Jamestown's harbor and the bay. The basically Continental dinner menu has a new American flair, with chicken served with Armagnac and truffles, and grilled salmon with a sauce of champagne, leeks, honey and cream, along with the classic favorites of filet mignon with béarnaise and duck à l'orange. A tavern menu ranging from burgers to beef bourguignon is served from Mon.–Thur. after 5 P.M. Open Mon.–Thur.. from 5:30–9 P.M., Fri.–Sat. 5:30–10 P.M., Sun. 10 A.M.–2 P.M. Just south of Newport Bridge. **150 Conanicus Ave., Jamestown; (401) 423-2100.**

Trattoria Simpatico—$$$ to $$$$

Details make this place: Virgin olive oil with a hint of rosemary accompanies crisp hot bread, Verdi and Puccini arias float in the air, the linens are crisp, the service well informed and the china is chosen for each dish. Of course, it couldn't happen if the food weren't simply smashing, which it is. Grilled asparagus and prosciutto are served over arugula with a currant and chive vinaigrette, grilled shrimp comes with wild-mushroom-and-tomato-herbed risotto, a pan-seared pork chop is topped with a peppercorn ragout. It's a happy blend of fine food and flawless surroundings, well worth a trip to the island if you aren't here already. Several good wines are available by the glass, priced from $3.75. Open daily, April–Jan. from 11:30 A.M.–2:30 P.M. and 5–10 P.M. **13 Narragansett Ave.,** one block from the ferry landing; **(401) 423-3731.**

Jamestown Oyster Bar and Grill—$$

This is not a tony city oyster bar—it's a down-to-earth place, a favorite of fishermen, who know who gets the freshest seafood. The fish and chips is superb, and more innovative dishes are well done. If you haven't tried stuffies yet, you won't get a better sample of this Rhode Island specialty than here. Open for lunch and dinner every day. One block from the ferry landing. **22 Narragansett Ave., Jamestown; (401) 423-2100.**

Services

Visitor Information

Newport County Convention and Visitor's Bureau, 23 America's Cup Ave., Newport 02840; (800) 326-6030 or **(401) 849-8048.**

For information and brochures on Prescott Farm: **Newport Restoration Foundation, 39 Mill Street, Newport 02840; (401) 847-2071.**

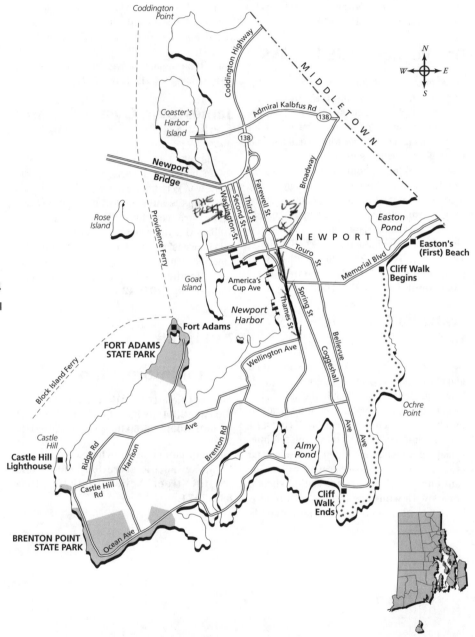

Newport

Newport

Two legacies of Newport's Gilded Age—the mansions and yachting—provide the highlights for most of Newport's visitors. Its charming historic neighborhoods and the busy shops and restaurants on its waterfront are close behind in interest. Newport is perhaps the finest example anywhere of the tasteful blending of historic properties with modern amenities for the traveler. Because the town preserves so many periods so well—it has nine buildings dating from before 1700, and over 100 Greek revival–era buildings in addition to the nineteenth-century mansions—it has a lot to work with. That abundance is a mixed blessing, bringing with it a great responsibility and a tremendous financial burden. But through the work of public-spirited organizations and individuals, Newport has preserved and maintained the treasures of its past and keeps a significant number open for the public to tour. Dozens of other historic buildings line the streets of the Point and the Hill as private homes, creating street after street of pleasant strolling for those visitors who appreciate period architecture.

If history were all, Newport would be a remarkable period piece (or, more accurately, periods piece), but it is *not* all. A lively, upbeat waterfront combines a busy marina for private yachts with stylish shops, restaurants, cafes, small museums and abundant opportunities to view Newport and the bay from the water on sailing ships, cruisers, tour boats and motor launches. Sunset sails on the schooner *Adirondack,* luncheon cruises or transport via launch to Rose Island join a dozen other ways to explore the waters around Newport, waters you may share with the *Bounty* or the sloop *Providence* proceeding under full sail.

Much of the charm of Newport comes from the legacy of the many flamboyant and eccentric people who have summered or resided here. Stories abound, as do local characters—from Beatrice Turner, the eccentric and reclusive artist who painted no subject but herself

205

and who had her mansion painted black after the death of her father, to Mrs. Fish, whose caustic insults were highly prized by her guests, to the host who dressed a monkey in full formal attire and made it guest of honor at a society dinner. Newport was the summer playground of New York's "Four Hundred," a term that originated with the comment of Newport summer resident Ward McAllister that there were only 400 people really worth knowing

Black Heritage in Newport

Long Wharf was the New England center for the Triangle Trade in the colonial era, with ships arriving regularly laden with molasses and slaves from the West Indies. Slave ownership was common among Newporters, as well as among the southern families who moved here with their household servants each summer. **Trinity Church** still has the slave pews at either side of its organ, and in the **Common Ground cemetery** at the corner of Farewell and Warner Sts. (see page **231**), is a section set aside for the graves of slaves at the far northern end, nearest the bridge. The first individual congregation in America to vote that its members could not hold slaves was the **Newport Congregational Church,** on Pelham St., and the first free Black church in America was formed in 1824 by a group of 12 prominent Blacks. They built the **Colored Union Church and Society** at **49 Division St.,** which served as a station on the Underground Railroad before the Civil War. It was replaced by the present church on that site in the 1870s.

History

Early New England settlers were an independent lot, and it was not unusual for a group of them to pull up roots and move on when things didn't go their way. It was such a dissenting group that left the Portsmouth settlement in 1639, packing up and moving farther south on Rhode Island. They chose a site where the East Branch of Narragansett Bay opens into Rhode Island Sound, a location with a good harbor and islands strategically placed for defensive safety.

By the middle of the eighteenth century, Newport had grown into a leading port of the American colonies. Its residents were well educated and sophisticated and even in Europe were known for their elegant and gracious society. Always a city of religious tolerance—its founders left Puritan Massachusetts because of their nonconformism—it attracted large numbers of Jews and Quakers, who prospered here. Newport was the northeast base of the Triangle Trade. More than 50 ships, many of them owned and mastered by Quakers, carried rum to Africa, where slaves were bought and then sold in the Caribbean islands and the ports of Georgia and the Carolinas. The slaves were replaced in the ships' holds by barrels of molasses, which were brought back to Newport and processed into rum. Slave-holding was common, and most of the leading homes were staffed by slaves.

Friendships grew out of business associations between the shippers and the southern aristocracy, and Newport became a favorite place for them to escape the South's summer heat. Today, mansions of the shipowners and their southern friends constitute one of the finest collections of seventeenth- and eighteenth-century architecture in the country.

It was this summer influx of aristocracy from Charleston and other southern ports that lead Newport to call itself "America's First Resort"—and accurately. Newporters also like to quip that when the Italian navigator Verrazano explored the bay and islands in the sixteenth century, he stopped and anchored off Newport for two weeks, making it the scene of

(400 was the capacity of Mrs. Astor's ballroom).

A friend of ours, a longtime Newport resident, remarked that while Newport may not have the really great restaurants you will find in Providence, you won't find a bad one either. That comment was made a few years ago, before the opening of some serious contenders, but her observation stands. You will be well fed in Newport on some of the finest and freshest seafood anywhere. Lodgings are likewise good, ranging from very comfortable to some of New England's finest. A visitor could spend a vacation here without ever seeing "the sights," but just by enjoying the ambiance from the comfort of one of Newport's historic lodgings and choosing a different restaurant each evening.

the first two-week vacation in the New World.

Rising tensions before the Revolution extended to Newport. In 1764, local residents attacked the crew of the British schooner *St. John*, who wisely retreated to their ship for safety. Frustrated, the Newporters fired on the ship, but when royal authorities filed charges against the town, the citizens responded that *they* had officially authorized the action and need not answer to anyone for it. The following year they rioted in opposition to the Stamp Acts.

Newport's glory days as a colonial port collapsed suddenly in December 1776, when British troops occupied the city, ending its trade. During the occupation the city was ravaged by hunger and looting. Many of its citizens slipped through British lines to Providence, which remained in colonial control. When the arrival of the French forced the British to leave Newport, 480 of its 1,200 buildings had been used for firewood by the 6,000 British troops and the 5,000 Newport residents. Commerce never recovered from the siege.

But Newport's harbor was not destined to die. The fresh air and ocean breezes that had attracted visitors before the Revolution began to attract the new kings of American industry about the time of the Civil War. Before them, as early as the 1840s, when Boston intellectual writers and artists—Longfellow, Henry James, Julia Ward Howe, John Singer Sargent and Oliver Wendell Holmes—were attracted to Newport's "quaint rustic simplicity." This rusticity was short-lived. By the end of the century the Astors, Belmonts, Vanderbilts and others had built summer homes inspired by European palaces and manor houses, where they held extravagant dinners, balls and parties on a scale not seen before, or since. Their fondness for sailing and yacht racing made Newport the yachting capital of the Northeast, and home to the America's Cup competition, boatbuilding and the many yachting clubs and marinas that still line the shore of Narragansett Bay.

The Gilded Age ended with World War I, the income tax and the 1915 sinking of the *Lusitania*, in which disaster nearly every major Newport family lost at least one member. But some of the old glamour lingered on, and a 1937 description noted that from mid-July to

Built to replicate a Swiss mountain village, Surprise Valley was a favorite Sunday drive for Newporters.

the beginning of September, "The '400' fill the avenues with gorgeous turnouts, the harbor with yachts, the houses and clubs with elegantly dressed men and women." Even at the rock bottom of the Great Depression, in Newport "Society" was spelled with a capital S.

Newport has had a long and close relationship with the navy since 1775, when the Rhode Island Navy sloop *Katy*—later recommissioned as the *Providence*—engaged in the first naval battle of the Revolution by defeating the British ship, tender *Diana* at the mouth of the bay. In 1884 the Navy Department established The Naval War College as a place for research into "all questions relating to war and to statesmanship connected with war, or to the prevention of war." Here Captain Alfred Thayer Mahan wrote his seminal work on the role of sea power, *The Influence of Sea Power upon History, 1600–1783*, while he was its second president. During World War II Newport was a major center of naval activity, and the War College keeps the U.S. Navy presence alive here today.

Suggested Reading

The Last Resorts, by Cleveland Amory, has an entire chapter on Newport, relating its history and gossip and providing a clear view of its excesses, tragedies and eccentricities.

Newport: A Tour Guide, by Anne Randall and Robert P. Foley (Peregrine Press, 1983), is a very useful little book for anyone interested in architecture. It not only tells the dates and architects for many of the significant buildings but also shows small pictures of each, so you can be sure you are looking at the right one. It is available in bookshops in Newport.

The Arts and Crafts of Newport, Rhode Island, by Ralph Carpenter, published in 1954, has excellent information on the early cabinetmakers, silversmiths and other decorative artists and their work.

Getting There

The most direct path from US 1 on the "mainland" is via Rte. 138 south of Wickford, across the Jamestown Bridge, across Conanicut Island and over the Newport Bridge. Signs from the second bridge lead you straight to the Visitors Center, at 23 America's Cup Ave. If you are traveling on I-95 from Connecticut, you can take Rte. 138 in Hope Valley and follow it to the coast.

Traveling from Providence, or from the north, follow US 1 to Wickford and take Rte. 138, or take I-195 east (in the middle of Providence marked "Cape Cod") and follow Rte. 136

At any time of year, Newport's waterfront is lined with boats.

south through Bristol and over the Mount Hope Bridge to Rte. 114, which leads into Newport, where you will pick up signs to the Visitors Center. From Cape Cod, travel west on I-195 to Rte. 136.

RIPTA (Rhode Island Public Transit Authority) buses connect Newport to Providence and other points in the state on a regular schedule, and **Bonanza Bus Lines** connects to Providence. A RIPTA bus leaves each city at least once an hour on weekdays, every two hours on weekends. The trip takes 55 minutes, and the fare is $2.50. Several buses each day are equipped with wheelchair lifts—all weekend and holiday buses are. (See page **xix** for information on discounted fares for seniors and handicapped passengers.)

Hourly RIPTA service connects the Wakefield Mall and University of Rhode Island campuses with Newport via the bridges, a 50-minute ride. The fare is $2.50. All buses are lift-equipped. For RIPTA schedules and information, call **(401) 781-9400** or **(800) 244-0444.**

Bonanza Bus Lines connects Boston and Newport, with buses leaving every two hours, except that there is no noon bus. The trip takes an hour and 45 minutes; **(401) 751-8800** or **(800) 556-3815.**

Those arriving by air at **T. F. Green Airport** can take **Cozy Cab's** almost hourly shuttle service to Newport; **(401) 846-2500 reservations.**

Getting Around

All buses arrive in Newport at the **Transportation Center,** which adjoins the Visitors Center. A taxi rank is just outside, but be forewarned that taxi rates in Newport are not cheap. Several lodging choices are within walking distance of the terminal. RIPTA also operates buses within Newport, so if you are arriving by bus, ask your hosts if they are close to one of their lines. These run the length of Thames St., along Bellevue Ave. as far as Ochre Point (Salve Regina University) and along Memorial Dr. past Easton's Beach to Middletown. Most

208

operate hourly or half-hourly and the fares are $1.00. In the summer a free shuttle bus runs along the most popular tourist routes every half hour on weekdays, and every 20 minutes on weekends. For RIPTA details, call **(800) 244-0444.** Traffic during the summer is so congested in downtown Newport that you'll get there faster by walking. If this is out of the question, take the RIPTA bus to the mansion area and walk around there, then take it back.

Bicycle rentals are available just north of the Visitors Center, at **Ten Speed Spokes** on America's Cup Ave.; **(401) 847-7238.** Rental cars are available through **International Car Rental at 6 Valley Rd. in Middletown; (401) 847-4600.** They will pick you up at the Visitor's Center. Other car rental agencies include **Avis** at **(800) 331-1212** or **(401) 846-1843,** and **Hertz** at **(800) 654-3131** or **(401) 846-1645.**

Festivals and Events

Few cities of its size have as many festivals as Newport. Although the Jazz Festival and yachting events are legendary, the many others are just as well planned and nicely run. These aren't just made-for-tourists events; local people have just as much fun as visitors. Nearly every festival has a number of free events. Exact dates vary, so we have grouped them by month. This is only a sampling of the larger and more unique festivals and events. For a full schedule, call **(800) 326-6030.**

Newport Winter Festival
January–February

Featuring 10 days of over 150 indoor and outdoor events, this festival has been called New England's largest winter extravaganza. Food and wine tastings, tours, ice skating, hayrides, ice sculpture, music and events for all ages include a contest for local merchants, who decorate their shop fronts. The dogsled races go on whether or not there's snow on the ground. WinterFest is usually held in the last few days of January into the first week of February; **(401) 849-8048** or **(800) 326-6030.**

Irish Heritage Month
March

March is filled with citywide activities celebrating Irish culture and traditions, with folksingers, step dancing and other performers. The Irish presence in Newport predates the Revolution, when numbers of Irish came to work as stonemasons. During the Gilded Age, Irish were sought as servants in the mansions. The Fifth Ward area around lower Thames St. where it joins Wellington Ave., was—and still is—the major Irish neighborhood. During Irish Heritage Month, the street in front of **St. Augustine's Church,** the Irish parish, is painted green. A green stripe marks the route of the spirited St. Patrick's Day parade; **(401) 849-8048** or **(800) 326-6030.**

Religious Heritage Week
April

This week focuses on the history of Newport as a haven for people of all beliefs. The origins of the settlement here are so entwined with the concept of religious freedom and the separation of church and state that they influenced the character of the city from the very beginning. Performances, concerts, lectures, programs and tours at the many historic houses of worship illustrate this theme and explore the many ways in which tolerance has affected Newport.

Maritime Arts Festival and Armed Forces Day Celebration
May

With displays and demonstrations of maritime arts and skills, these celebrations recognize Newport's many ties with the sea, ships and the U.S. Navy. Special events have included a mock naval battle and Gilbert and Sullivan performed on board the sloop *Providence.* **Bowen's Wharf; (401) 849-2243.**

209

Secret Garden Tours
June

On a Friday and Saturday in mid-June, the tours provide a chance to visit 15 to 20 gardens of private residences that are not normally open to the public. They are at their height at this time of year. Sponsored by **Benefactors of the Arts, 33 Washington St.; (401) 847-0514.**

Annual Newport Outdoor Art Festival
June

A judged show of fine art, including oils, pastels, watercolor, graphics, sculpture and photography. In downtown Newport at **Eisenhower Park and Long Wharf; (401) 846-5909.**

Kidsfest and Family Nights
June

These include rides, music, storytelling, hands-on exhibits and food. At the **Newport Yachting Center on Commercial Wharf; (401) 846-1600.**

Chowder Cook-off
June

With all-you-can-eat chowder from 30 of the area's best chefs, this contest is taken seriously, and the title for best chowder is a real feather in any local toque. Crafts and music add to the festivities. Held at the **Newport Yachting Center on Commercial Wharf; (401) 846-1600.**

New York Yacht Club Regatta
June

Races fill the Newport harbor with sails and the town with sailors. Unless you are here for the yachting events, it's a good time to avoid Newport, since it is brimming full; **(401) 846-1000.**

Newport Music Festival
July

Chamber music in the Newport mansions. Hearing these small groups play in these settings is a rare chance to experience chamber music in the venue for which it was composed; **(401) 846-1133.**

Black Ships Festival
July

This festival features Japanese cultural events throughout the city and a colorful kite festival at Brenton Point. Martial arts demonstrations, Japanese brush painting, tea-ceremony and sumo-wrestling demonstrations and workshops are scheduled throughout the weekend. The celebration commemorates Commodore Matthew Perry's historic expedition to Japan, where he succeeded in negotiating a treaty that opened trade with the United States. Perry, a Newport native, landed at Bannister's Wharf on his return. Many events relate to the lively cultural exchange between Newport and its Japanese sister city, Shimoda. **(401) 846-2720; (401) 847-7666, kite festival.**

New England Regional Croquet Championships
August

These are held at the **Tennis Hall of Fame at 194 Bellevue Ave.; (401) 849-3990.**

Ben & Jerry's Newport Folk Festival
August

This festival brings well-known and rising performers to **Fort Adams State Park; (401) 847-3700.**

Newport Jazz Festival
August

This the granddaddy of them all, featuring top-name performers in concert at **Fort Adams State Park.** Tickets go quickly, and lodging is booked solid. Like the big yachting weekends, this is a good time to avoid Newport if you're not coming for the festival; **(401) 847-3700.**

Annual Arts and Crafts Festival
August

In **Touro Park,** this festival features more than 75 craftspeople. It's difficult to imagine a nicer setting than this genteel park on Bellevue Ave; **(401) 847-0287.**

A Weekend of Coaching
August

The weekend features turn-of-the-century coaches drawn by thoroughbred horses along **Bellevue Ave.,** which is closed to motorized traffic. During the heyday of the mansions the street was closed by a gate to prevent the less-privileged from looking in through the fences, so blocking the street has historic precedent. So does the coaching parade, which took place every afternoon during the Newport social season as ladies of the mansions went for their highly ritualized afternoon rides. This event is held only in even-numbered years; **(401) 847-1000.**

Classic Yacht Regatta
September

The regatta features what many boat enthusiasts call the finest assemblage of beautiful craft gathered anywhere. It also gathers some of America's best and most experienced sailors, including the top America's Cup sailors. The **Museum of Yachting** sponsors the event; **(401) 847-1018.**

Irish Music Festival
September

The festival features top performing artists, Irish art, dance, poetry, crafts, foods and storytelling; **(401) 849-2028** or **(800) 326-6030.**

Taste of Rhode Island
September

This is a culinary experience featuring foods of 40 restaurants served in small portions so attendees can sample some of each. Sponsored by Guinness Stout and Bass Ale, the weekend includes cooking demonstrations, live music and an obstacle course for waiters, for some good fun along with the good food, at the **Newport Yachting Center on Commercial Wharf; (401) 846-1600.**

Harvest-by-the-Sea Festival
October

This lasts the entire month, with free hayrides, pumpkin-carving contests, farmers markets and other harvest events; **(401) 849-8048** or **(800) 326-6030.**

Oktoberfest
October

With beer, wine, foods and oom-pah bands, this is an authentic re-creation of German Oktoberfests. Held in the **Newport Yachting Center on Commercial Wharf; (401) 846-1600.**

Festa Italiana
October

This includes exhibits and activities relating to Italian art, culture, food and wine, culminating with a Columbus Day parade. One of the special features is opera bel canto performances; **(401) 849-8048** or **(800) 326-6030.**

Christmas in Newport
November

The festivities begin near the end of November with the decorating of the mansions.

Festival of Trees
December

The Festival of Trees features 60 Christmas trees, each decorated in a theme, displayed

Places to Rest Your Feet and Watch the World Go By

The garden of **Seaman's Church Institute,** America's Cup at Market Sq., is shady and cool in the summer, a tiny oasis in the middle of the busiest part of town. **Patriot's Park** at Touro Synagogue on Touro St. is an open, sunny park with a small garden and benches. At the end of Washington St., in the Point, **John J. Martins Memorial Park** has benches facing the bay and Rose Island—a quiet spot for a picnic and to watch the sunset. **Aquidneck Park,** on Spring St. between Lower Thames and Bellevue Ave., is a large area of green lawns with benches. There are stone benches on the **Cliff Walk,** just south of the Narragansett St. entrance at Forty Steps. The **Ann St. Pier,** off Lower Thames St., is a popular place to sit and watch the boats come and go.

in **Building 80 at the Naval Base; (401) 847-3179.**

Christmas in Newport
December

This is a full program of open houses, crafts, music and decoration; **(401) 849-8048.** Major events include the opening in **Washington Square** with a bonfire and carols, candlelight tours of private homes, a craft show at the **Hotel Viking,** concerts by the navy band, story hours for children, carol sings, a tour of inns, a concert of choral and orchestral music in **Trinity Church** and Christmas music in various other churches. Activities are scheduled every day, with abundant options each weekend. The entire city is decorated in white lights, and shops vie for the best window displays. Many of the events are free or open by optional donation. A complete schedule is available at the Visitors Center or by mail from **Christmas in Newport, P.O. Box 716, Newport 02840; (401) 849-6454.**

Christmas at The Newport Mansions
December

Tours of the mansions in holiday decorations, plus special events, teas, music and children's programs. Mrs. Astor's Beechwood features Christmas trees in each room, and tours highlight seasonal games and pastimes. Call **(401) 847-1000** for activities at Preservation Society properties; call individual mansions for the others.

Opening Night
December

A family-oriented New Year's Eve celebration of the arts, Opening Night features performers throughout the city. Many of the events are designed for children, and fireworks begin at 9:15 P.M. so younger children can attend. Free shuttle buses connect the various venues. A formal Midnight Madness Ball is held at **Belcourt Castle** by reservation; **(401) 846-0669 for the ball, (401) 849-8048 or (800) 326-6030 for all other events.**

Outdoor Activities

Biking

The entire Newport area is perfect for cyclists, offering few hills. In fact, given the traffic in Newport, a bicycle may be a lot faster than taking your car or the shuttles. Ocean Dr. is a beautiful route, and nearly any street offers views of fine mansions or historic homes. The side streets off Bellevue Ave. are particularly interesting, lined with elegant homes and mansions whose yards are often planted with exotic trees and well-kept gardens. A little explored although less level neighborhood of fine homes that would, in any other context, be considered mansions, lies east of the lower section of Bellevue Ave., behind the **Redwood Library.** It extends to the shore of **Easton's Pond,** and is bordered to the south by Memorial Blvd. Remember that many streets are one-way, and that traffic rules apply to bicycles just as they do to automobiles.

Ten Speed Spokes rents all-new road and mountain bicycles by the hour, day or week. Maps, helmets and locks are included in the rate, which begins at $5 an hour or $25 a day. If you have your own bicycle, they offer repair service as well. Their location couldn't be handier—right next to the Visitors Center on America's Cup Ave.; **(401) 847-7238.**

Newport Wheels rents mountain bikes at the same hourly rate from its shop at **436 Thames St.; (401) 849-4400. Firehouse Bicycle Co.** has a full range at competitive prices as well, from **35 Broadway; (401) 847-5700.**

Birding

Rose Island is a significant rookery for several species of wading birds, notably black-crowned night herons, glossy ibis and great white and snowy egrets. These nesting birds should not be disturbed, so birders should observe them at a distance of at least 20 yards offshore from kayaks or canoes until after mid-June.

The **Norman Bird Sanctuary** in Middletown is of particular interest to birders, as is the adjoining **Sachuest Point National Wildlife Refuge,** both described in the North Aquidneck and Jamestown chapter.

Diving

Warm currents, especially in the summer and fall, bring a startling variety of fish to Rhode Island from tropical waters, making this an excellent area for divers. The variety of tropical fish is so great that museum and aquarium staffs come here to collect specimens in the fall, when warm-water species would no longer survive. Waters are very clear and there are interesting shipwrecks, some dating back to the 1700s, as well as ledges and reefs to explore. The rocky shore of **Brenton Point State Park** is particularly popular for diving. **Adventure Sports** (see page **216**) and the **Newport Diving Center** at **550 Thames St.;**

(401) 847-9293 or **(800) DIVING-0,** both offer lessons and diving gear.

Fishing

The waters off Newport attract fishing enthusiasts all summer, but those in the know choose spring and fall, when migrating game fish are closer to shore. Mackerel provide a good fight, but larger game fish are also available, including bluefin tuna and blue marlin. Newport was the scene of early pioneering in saltwater fly fishing around the turn of this century, when local sport-fishing-club members used split bamboo rods. A number of places along the rocky Newport coast offer challenging fishing for bluefish or striped bass, especially in the evening, when these predators move closer to shore. **Brenton Point State Park** is a popular fishing spot, and **Brenton Reef** is considered one of the bay's best sites for striped bass and bluefish.

Local outfitters offer equipment and charter trips for offshore fly casting for marlin, mako shark or tuna. Charter boats will take you game fishing for yellowfin, giant bluefin, blue marlin and albacore tuna, going as far as the continental shelf, nearly 100 miles offshore. No license is needed for saltwater fishing, either from shore or a boat.

A number of ponds near Newport offer freshwater fishing. **Easton and Green End Ponds** are stocked with brook and rainbow trout. Purchase a license at any bait shop or sporting goods store. For daily limits and other regulations, contact the **Division of Fish and Wildlife; (401) 277-3075.**

The Saltwater Edge combines instruction in saltwater fly fishing and guided fishing trips with a full-service retail shop. Half-day guided shore-fishing trips cost about $150 for two people, boat trips cost $250. Located at **559 Thames St.; (401) 842-0062** or **(800) FISH-543.**

Fishin' Off, Inc. offers half-day, full-day or evening fishing trips both on- and offshore aboard a 36-foot cabin cruiser. Board at American Shipyard near the causeway to Goat Island; **(401) 849-9642.**

The Rhode Island Guide

Cliff Walk literally passes through the backyards of some of Newport's finest mansions.

Miles Standish Charters takes up to four passengers on the *Mayflower* for sport and bottom fishing; **(401) 846-7225.**

Beachfront Bait and Tackle rents rods and reels as well as shark and tuna gear, sells baits and can make charter arrangements. Located at **103 Wellington Ave.,** which is reached from lower Thames St.; **(401) 849-HOOK.**

Hiking and Walking

The Cliff Walk

The most elegant of the mansions were built along the rim of a long rock cliff overlooking Rhode Island Sound. Although the real estate at the top of the cliffs belonged to the gentry, a path along the cliffs remained open to public traffic, often to the dismay of the Four Hundred. When one of them built a stone wall across it, locals promptly tore it down. When he rebuilt it, higher and with a broken-glass top, locals took him to court, which decided in their favor. Today, Cliff Walk is one of the most popular places in Newport.

The path extends three miles, from Memorial Blvd. at **Easton's Beach** to **Coggeshall's Ledge,** also called Land's End, near the end of Bellevue Ave. The most popular segment passes the area rich in mansions—although they line the entire walk—from **Forty Steps,** at the end of Narragansett Ave., to **Marble**

House, easy to identify by its red Chinese Tea House almost directly above the path.

The condition and surface of the path vary from neatly laid flat stones and level packed sand to rough, rocky shoreline where you must hop from rock to rock or pick your way along the ledges. The area between Forty Steps and **The Breakers** is the best, having been rebuilt recently with cement retaining walls. But one good storm could change all that. If you decide to take the entire route to Land's End, wear very sturdy shoes and be prepared to perform athletic feats in places. Don't take the lower end of the walk if it is raining or has been recently, for the rough rocks are treacherous when they are wet. The Cliff Walk is open every day, year-round, from 9 A.M.–9 P.M.

If you arrive by car, park at Easton's Beach on Memorial Blvd., or at the end of Narragansett Ave. to begin at Forty Steps. In the summer, spaces are limited in both places, as they are everywhere in Newport. A RIPTA bus route passes the northern end of Cliff Walk hourly on its way to and from the waterfront. Parking is almost nonexistent at the Land's End terminus.

From Memorial Blvd. to Forty Steps, the path winds along the shore with good sea views and little else. The first grand estate is **Ochre Court,** next is The Breakers, which has ornate gates at either end of its section of the walk. After rounding a point, the trail passes several estates including the Tudor-style **Fairholme** and **Ochre Lodge,** a large rambling cottage and an excellent example of the shingle style popular in Victorian summer homes.

Mrs. Astor's **Beechwood** is fully visible through its unattractive chain-link fence. At a sharp point close to Beechwood the path goes around a bunkerlike building that was once the pavilion for an estate. Next is Marble House and its red Chinese Tea House, with fanciful dragons and upswept roof corners. The cliffs are so steeply cut here that the trail goes through a tunnel almost beneath the Tea House. The trail disappears into a shingle beach well below the street level, then farther east facades of more estates appear above,

214

most notably **Rough Point**, an English Tudor-style manor of rough-cut sandstone. Your attention is likely to be diverted here by the necessity of crossing over a deep chasm on a little wooden footbridge (which is occasionally lost in storms and replaced with a new one). At one point the trail is bordered by a rock-strewn area, where large pieces of someone's estate, or its wall, lie about the shore. Fragments of building stone—part of an arch, some dressed granite, a corbel—and bits of brick have been tossed by the tides but are easy to identify. There's quite a lot of clambering over rocks before the walk meets the end of Ledge Road at Land's End. Edith Wharton lived here at her family's estate, **Pencraig** (but she never cared much for what she called the "watering-place mundanities"). On clear days you can see the west shore of Rhode Island, and even Block Island, from the cliffs here.

Instead of retracing your route back along the Cliff Walk, we suggest returning via Ledge Rd. and following Bellevue Ave. and the other streets that parallel the coast. This gives you a front-gate view of many of the same mansions you saw from the ocean side. It's also shorter and easier walking. (To identify some of the homes you will see here, see pages **236–237**.)

The **Cliff Walk Society** offers guided tours of the walk, **(401) 849-7110**, as does the **Historical Society; (401) 846-0813**.

Brenton Point State Park

There's hardly a place on the shore of Narragansett Bay that is not connected to either the coastal defenses or old estates. Brenton Point is connected to both and is the best place to fly kites, picnic, fish and enjoy sea views. There's no beach, but that's about the only seaside attraction it lacks.

A seawall runs along most of the park's shore next to Ocean Ave., and the strip in between makes a smooth walking path from which stone steps descend to the tidal pools. On the far eastern end a path follows along a narrow point. Benches en route face Jamestown, **Beavertail Light** and **Castle Hill**, and placards identify the shapes of the various boats you might see. In the interior of the park,

close to the monuments to the early Portuguese explorers, is the park headquarters, once servants' quarters for the estate that once occupied the point. Beside this building are gardens, from which you can reach (through or around the high stone wall) the old driveway to the large stone stables. You can't go in, but the building is certainly worth seeing. A path on the right leads to the stable yards and on to a round stone tower, with exterior steps sticking out of the masonry like giant spiraling teeth. A safer, but far less aesthetic wooden stairway ascends the rear of the tower. Unfortunately, the tower and stable are favorite spots for vandals with spray paint. The sky above the mowed field in front of the stables is usually bright with swooping kites. They fly here year-round on any weekend day with good weather.

A site for radar and antiaircraft searchlights in World War II, the Point was equipped with antitorpedo boat weapons, and you can still see the wide circular Panama gun mount near the parking lot. The park headquarters has information on the history of the property and a schedule of nature programs. The park is on Ocean Ave., reached by following Bellevue Ave. to its southern end; **(401) 846-8240**.

Horseback Riding

Surprise Valley Farm (see page **228**) offers guided trail rides through its own 47 acres of rolling pasture and along the back roads of Brenton Point, which contains some of Newport's finest private estates. Rides cost about $40. The farm also offers lessons, summer riding camps and carriage rides for weddings and tours. **200 Harrison Ave.; (401) 847-2660**.

Kayaking and Boating

Public boat launch sites are located at the **Elm St. Pier,** off Washington St., at **Third Beach** in Middletown and at **King's Beach Park** on Wellington Ave., reached from the end of Thames St.

Adventure Sports Rentals conducts adventure boating tours and rents sailboats, outboards, kayaks and seacycles. Expect to pay $10 per hour for a one-person kayak, $15 for a canoe, $20 for a seacycle. Next to the Newport Harbor Hotel at **Bowen's Wharf; (401) 849-4820.**

Atlantic Outfitters conducts sea kayaking tours of the harbor and around the shore, following the route of Ocean Dr., but with the view from the water side. No experience is needed, since all tours include instruction. They also rent kayaks at about $30 a day. Located at **152 Bellevue Ave.; (401) 848-2920.**

Kite Flying

Brenton Point is considered the best place for kites. The annual Kite Festival is held here in August during the Black Ships Festival. The almost steady breeze in Newport makes for a good kite lift nearly anywhere. In the off-season the beaches make good kite fields. **High Flyers Flight Co., 492 Thames St.; (401) 846-3262. Flying Colors, Ltd., 468 Thames St.; (401) 846-0418. Blue Sky's Kite Connection, 207 Brick Marketplace; (401) 846-kite.**

Sailing

Sail Newport is a nonprofit organization that rents sailboats, teaches sailing and conducts sailing tours. Rentals begin at $35 for three hours. Boat rentals and instruction are offered during the summer only. Children as young as seven are welcome for sailing instruction. Courses begin at about $80. **The Sailing Center** is inside **Fort Adams State Park** (admission fee charged); **(401) 849-8385.**

Sight Sailing of Newport offers a 10-hour sailing course and half-day crewed charters ($45 per person), as well as one- and two-hour sailing tours ($12.50 to $22.50) from **Bowen's Wharf; (401) 849-3333.**

Womanship offers sailing instruction for women only; **(800) 342-9295.**

Charters

Several brokers represent boats of all types available for charter. One of the most interesting of these belongs to the Philadelphia Maritime Museum. *Principia* is a fully restored classic wooden yacht dating from 1928 and completely rebuilt in 1994. You can entertain your friends on a private cruise or have a party dockside. Its wood-paneled interior is pure class. **Newport Yacht Services; (800) 234-7720.**

The **Tideman Collection** offers charters of five different vintage yachts, each restored to its original condition. They range from 12-meter sloops of the 1930s to 62-foot rumrunners from the teens and twenties; **(401) 847-5007.**

Groups of six (or fewer, but you pay for a minimum of six) can sail on the 36-foot sloop S/V *Big Dipper* for two hours or all day. There is a flexible schedule of sunset cruises, picnic lunches in a secluded cove or a full dinner on board; **(401) 846-3724.**

America's Cup Charters offers classic yachts for charter, including Ted Turner's *American Eagle* and America's Cup winner *Weatherly;* **(401) 849-5868.**

Marinas

In Newport there are state guest moorings on the south shore of **Brenton's Cove**, near Fort Adams. **Banister's Wharf** and **Christie's Landing,** both off Thames St., have guest slips, as do **Goat Island Marina, Newport Harbor Hotel** and **Newport Yachting Center,** which has the most.

Restaurants with moorings include **Christie's, (401) 847-5400), Marina Grille** on Goat Island, **(401) 846-2675, Mooring** on Sayer's Wharf, **(401) 846-2260,** and **Newport Harbor Hotel** on America's Cup Ave., **(401) 847-9000.**

Swimming

Beaches in Newport offer either bay or ocean exposure. The bay beaches are more protected, and those on the ocean side have heavier surf as a general rule.

Easton (or First) Beach

Easton is on Memorial Blvd. and offers parking for over 700 cars ($5 weekdays, $10 weekends). Nonetheless, get there early on a summer day if you want to find a space. The cabana and pavilion are new, replacing the one destroyed by Hurricane Bob in 1993. It's a nice sandy beach, but the surf can be rough if the wind's from the south. Lifeguards are on duty weekends from late May through mid-June, and daily through the summer. Several lodgings in Middletown and Newport are within walking distance of this beach.

Fort Adams State Park

A much smaller beach, with quiet bayside waters. It has picnic and other facilities and is favored by families. The entrance fee is $4. Lifeguards are on duty weekends in early June and daily through the summer.

King Beach Park

On Wellington Ave., King Beach Park has a very small beach, but it is watched over by a lifeguard from mid-June through Labor Day. Parking is streetside on Wellington Ave.

Gooseberry Beach

Gooseberry is on Ocean Dr. and is privately owned but open to the public. It is less well known than Easton's but has good swimming. Parking costs $12 per day.

Wind and Board Surfing

Fort Adams and **Third Beach** in nearby Middletown are the best places for windsurfing. South or southeast onshore winds tend to bring the long rolling breakers surfers seek. Both **First Beach (Easton's Beach)** in Newport and **Second Beach** in Middletown have designated surfing areas. Second Beach is considered one of the best surfing areas in the state. In Rhode Island, tune to 95.5 FM at 8:35 each morning to find out where the tide's up.

    Water Brothers Surf and Sport rents boards at $5 an hour or $25 a day and offers three-day surfing classes in July. Located at **39 Memorial Blvd.; (401) 849-4990.**

    Island Sports offers lessons (with a simulator) and rentals of windsurfer and surfboard equipment from its mobile locations wherever the surf's up, or from the shop at **86 Aquidneck Ave.**, near Easton's (First) Beach; **(401) 846-4421.**

Yachting Events

If you're looking for boat and yacht racing, Newport is the place to be. There is an almost constant event for one class of boat or another throughout the sailing season. The **Museum of Yachting** holds a number of these. Don't miss its **Classic Yacht Festival** in early September. The **Newport Yachting Center** also sponsors several events for boat owners and those who just appreciate the beauty of boats. In late May the **Newport Waterfront Carnival** starts off the summer boating season, followed two weekends later by the **Used Boat Show**. Traditionalists will want to be at the **Wooden Boat Show** on the last weekend of June, when over 200 wooden craft are on display, both in and out of the water. In mid-June the **Newport to Bermuda race** and the **Yachting Block Island Race Week** often coincide. For schedules and details, contact the following: **Newport Yachting Center, America's Cup Ave., P.O. Box 550, Newport 02840; (401) 846-1600. Yachting Block Island Race; (203) 661-6945. Newport to Bermuda Race; (508) 526-8401. Sail Newport Sailing Festival** and **Sail Newport Memorial Day Regatta; (401) 846 1983.** The **Black Ships Festival**, commemorating the Matthew Perry connection with Japan, is in late July. Check with the Yachting Center and the Yachting Museum for special events, such as the frequent visits of tall ships.

Activities for Kids

Family fun is high in Newport's priorities, and the city offers not only attractions to interest

217

children but events timed and planned for the entire family. Beyond the obvious draw of the beaches, Newport offers an **aquarium at Easton's Beach** with hands-on exhibits (see page **231**), the **Fishermen and Whale Museum at the Seaman's Church Institute Building** (see page **226**, parents will want to hang around this one, it's so interesting), the **Thames Science Center** (see page **225**), the impressive fortifications at **Fort Adams** and other forts on nearby Conanicut, (see page **227**) and the **lighthouse on Rose Island** (see page **230**). The two mansions kids seem to like best are Mrs. Astor's **Beechwood** (see page **243**), where costumed performers give them lots of attention, and **Belcourt Castle** (see page **244**), which offers a Thursday evening ghost tour. The wide variety of boat trips are sure kid pleasers, especially **Flyer**

The towers of an early-twentieth-century arcade, a nineteenth-century fire station and Trinity Church, built in the 1700s, are all visible from Thames St.

Sailing Tours (see page **220**), which uses a catamaran where older children can ride right over the water in the nets. Exhibits at the **Museum of Newport History** (see page **221**) make special provisions for children, with a whole set of labels and activities at their eye level. Remember that Newport is a walking city, so even children who normally scorn the stroller may welcome a ride here.

In the summer, **Children's Nights,** every Tues. and Thur. at 6:30 P.M., offers free programs at **Easton's Beach; (401) 847-6875.** The **Newport Yachting Center** hosts a special **KidsFest** in July; **(401) 846-1398.** The **Black Ships Festival** in July includes several children's events, including a sumo workshop for kids, and a kite festival. The season around Halloween offers a number of spooky doings, including a hayride through the "haunted woods" of **Glen Farm** in nearby Portsmouth (see page **189**). **Opening Night** festivities on New Year's Eve are planned early with children in mind: The fireworks begin at 9:15. Throughout December, **Christmas in Newport** has events especially for children, and nearly all the many festivals include storytelling and other children's activities. If you plan to be in the area for two weeks, you can sign up children over age seven for sailing camp. After two weeks, they'll sail circles around you.

Seeing and Doing

The Lay of the Land and Water

Newport is easy to find your way about, since the harbor provides both a focal point and an easy-to-find landmark. In the center of this area is the **Visitors Center**, where most travelers begin by collecting maps, tickets and brochures for all the attractions. It is open seven days a week, year-round, from 9 A.M.–5 P.M. in winter, and through the evening in other seasons. Short-term parking is free here—be sure to bring your ticket to be validated. (A little machine on the wall next to the ticket windows will do it without your having to stand in line.) Along with brochures and maps, you can get tickets here for the mansions and for events and tours.

From this busy center, Thames St. (pronounced, unlike the London river, with the *th* sound and a long *a*) runs south along the shore, and Bellevue Ave. runs almost parallel to it along the hill. One of the most historic neighborhoods lies between these two streets, rising along the slope overlooking the harbor. Its historic buildings and homes include a number that bear the designation "oldest": **Touro Synagogue** (the oldest synagogue in North America, 1763), **Redwood Library and Athenaeum** (oldest continuously used library building in the United States, 1748), **Artillery Company of Newport Armory and Museum** (oldest militia organization in continuous service in America).

Bellevue Ave., whose name is synonymous with mansions, leads toward a long waterbound peninsula lined with shore estates, and Thames continues along the waterfront as the main shopping and restaurant street. (The latter meets Wellington Ave., which follows the shore and leads eventually to Ocean Ave. This continues along the shore, meeting the far end of Bellevue Ave., which completes the circuit by leading back into the downtown area.)

Behind the Visitors Center is the causeway to **Goat Island.** The site of the original gun batteries that protected the harbor, it now hosts a large hotel, a marina and condominium developments. It is the starting point for some harbor tours and a good place for a nice view of the city, especially in the late afternoon light. Before you leave Goat Island, cross to the bay side for an expansive view extending from Rose Island Lighthouse and the Newport Bridge on the north to Fort Adams and the East Passage to the south.

Another of Newport's several historic districts is located just north of the Visitors Center. **The Point** is a collection of authentically restored eighteenth- and nineteenth-century houses, all on their original sites on Washington, Second and Third Sts. Although most are not open, this is a wonderful place for a walking examination of sea captains' and merchants' houses.

Newport on the Silver Screen

The mansions were built more as stage sets than homes, so it's appropriate that they should have been used as the settings for so many movies. Best known is *The Great Gatsby*, which was filmed at Rosecliff in 1974. The kitchen of The Breakers was used for one scene, and the outdoor scenes were filmed at Hammersmith Farm. Rosecliff was also used for *The Betsy,* with Laurence Olivier. *High Society,* the musical version of *The Philadelphia Story,* starring Grace Kelly, Bing Crosby, Frank Sinatra and Louis Armstrong, was filmed at Clarendon Court, and begins with some fine aerial views of Newport and the mansions. *True Lies,* starring Arnold Schwarzenegger, was filmed in 1994 at Ochre Court. *The Bostonians* used the harem-style upstairs sitting room at Chateau-sur-Mer as a setting, as did the recent BBC production of Edith Wharton's *The Buccaneers.* Van Johnson was a Newport native, but none of his movies were filmed here (*Brigadoon,* however, could have been set quite easily in Surprise Valley).

219

The waterfront extends along Thames St. and America's Cup Blvd., filled with restored stores and warehouses that are now shops and restaurants. **Bannister's Wharf** has always been the maritime heart of Newport, hosting Oliver Hazard Perry when he returned victorious in 1813 and Ted Turner when he successfully defended America's Cup in 1977.

Cruises and Ferries

The 78-foot twin-masted schooner *Adirondack* offers sailing cruises of Newport Harbor and the bay almost entirely under canvas. It is just barely off the wharf when it hoists its sails. Our favorite cruise is at sunset, when the sky seems to be a different color every time you look at it and the shoreline sinks into silhouette as the lights blink on all over Newport.

Goat Island sits close to shore in Newport's harbor.

Christened in 1994, the *Adirondack* is a replica of a turn-of-the-century vessel. There are four sailings a day in the summer, three in the spring and fall. The fare is $20, $25 for the sunset cruise and children under 12 are half-fare. There are special senior rates. Make reservations at the kiosk on America's Cup Ave., or call **(401) 846-1600.**

Yankee Boat Peddlers offers a two-hour sailing tour of the harbor and bay on board the 70-foot schooner *Madeleine,* a replica of a nineteenth-century vessel, or on *Rumrunner II,* a restored wooden motor yacht dating from 1929. A tour on the latter includes abundant lore of Prohibition days. *Madeleine* makes four runs a day in the summer, fewer in spring and fall. Fares are $20, and $25 for the sunset cruise. Children under 12 sail at half-price, and there is a 10% senior discount. Fares on *Rumrunner II* are $14 and $18. *Madeleine* sails from **Bannister's Wharf** and *Rumrunner II* from **Ann St. Pier; (401) 849 3033.**

Oldport Marine Harbor Tours has a one-hour narrated harbor tour on the M/V *Amazing Grace* from Oldport Marine on America's Cup Ave. They make four or five trips a day in summer, three on spring and fall weekends and one on weekday afternoons, at a fare of $6.50. Four-hour bay cruises are about $55; **(401) 847 9109.**

Newport Navigation offers a similar tour on board the M/V *Spirit of Newport* six times a day in the summer for $7.50 regular fare, $6.50 for seniors and $3 for children five to 12. They depart from the marina at the **Newport Harbor Hotel at 49 America's Cup Ave.; (401) 849-3575.**

Sail Newport offers two-hour sailing sampler tours of the harbor for $50, during which you can get a quick course in sailing technique, if you like; **(401) 846-1983.**

Viking Tours of Newport has a one-hour tour of Newport and a two-and-a-half-hour tour of the bay area that stops for a visit at Hammersmith Farm. Short tours are $7.50, longer ones $13, with discounts for seniors and less than half-fare for children. M/V *Viking Queen* departs **Goat Island Marina** but can be contacted at **101 Swinburne Ave. in the Brick Marketplace; (401) 847-6921.**

Flyer Sailing Tours, a huge 65-passenger catamaran, sets sail for two-hour cruises daily. With all those passengers it's still not crowded, since many—especially kids—like to sit on nets over the water. The guide is a good one, giving a lively, gossipy narration, not a canned talk. A full bar offers refreshments on board. Four sailings daily from May–Oct. at a fare of $20, $25 for sunset cruises, children under 12 half-fare. Leaving from **The Inn at Long Wharf, 142 Long Wharf; (401) 848-2100.**

Those who prefer smaller vessels can take a harbor tour on the 40-foot motor cruiser *Blue Moon,* leaving four times daily from **Long Wharf Marina; (401) 846-6660.**

If you are headed to Block Island, the **Block Island Ferry,** operated by the Interstate Navigation Company, leaves daily at 10:30 A.M. from **Fort Adams State Park; (401) 783-4613.**

Museums and Historic Buildings and Sites

THE HILL AND HARBOR AREA

Hunter House

One of the dozen finest colonial homes remaining in America, Hunter House was headquarters of the French Admiral de Ternay, commander of the French fleet that relieved Newport of the British. Now a museum, Hunter House has some of the finest examples of the work of the famed Newport cabinetmakers Townsend and Goddard. A particularly fine piece is the marble-topped mahogany mixing table made by John Goddard. Originally, the house's most ornate entrance faced the water, where the owner's ships came and went, engaged in an active trade. The original door, with its polychrome pineapple, disappeared when a porch was added during late-nineteenth-century modernization and was rediscovered on a nearby building on Poplar St. It has since been returned and the other building fitted with a replica, but the elaborate door was placed on the street side of Hunter House this time. The interior decoration in the house is extraordinary, with five rooms fully paneled. The pineapple over the front door is a common motif of welcome in Newport. Originally when a captain returned from a long voyage, he put a fresh pineapple at his door so neighbors and friends would know he was back and receiving. Who but a captain freshly back from the tropics would have a fresh exotic fruit? It became a symbol of welcome throughout the colonies. Gilbert Stuart's first commissioned oil painting, completed when he was only 13, hangs in the house. The garden, accurately restored to the colonial period, overlooks the bay. Open weekends in April and in October and daily from May to the end of Sept. from 10 A.M.–5 P.M. Admission $5 adults, $3 children ages six to 11. **54 Washington St.; (401) 847-1000.**

Friends Meeting House

The oldest religious structure in Newport, dating from 1699, the meeting house was the center of worship for Newport's largest religious community. Like the Jews, the Quakers were drawn here from England and from other colonies by Rhode Island's policy of religious tolerance. The building's present shape and size dates from enlargement around 1800, but recent restoration has uncovered some of its original interior. The meeting house is open by appointment (with one week notice, if pos-

sible), and although there is no fee, donations for upkeep are always welcome. Facing White Horse Tavern, it is on the **corner of Farewell and Marlborough Sts.; (401) 846-0813.**

Museum of Newport History

The Brick Market building is a historical attraction in its own right, the last major work of Peter Harrison, who designed the Redwood Library. The arches on the lower floor were originally open to the street for use as a covered market but were closed when the building was remodeled as the city hall in 1842. It now houses, appropriately, a museum illustrating the entire span of Newport's varied past. It is exceedingly well presented in lively, often interactive displays, which highlight everything from the changing life of a particular neighborhood to a single subject such as the U.S. Navy, or an entire era. The exhibits interweave different elements skillfully, using old photos, art, audio descriptions and contemporary diaries, with artifacts from the Newport Historical Society's vast collections. These may include the neon sign from a sailors' bar and grill or a reading of Anne Hutchinson's words as she speaks in her own defense during her trial for heresy. Especially compelling are the spoken descriptions of the arrival of the British ships that began the occupation and the subsequent flight of a Tory woman and her six children as the French fleet arrived to end it. One popular feature is the **Ocean House Omnibus,** a replica of the one used to carry its guests. Climb aboard for a ten-minute "ride" down Bellevue Ave., with a narrated film. The museum is designed on two levels, with descriptive information at a child's-eye level written by a local sixth grade class. Throughout are printed sheets, which you can take with you, each with a map and text that help you explore an exhibit's subject as you tour Newport. Themes include religious tolerance, the mansion era and Newport's long association with the navy. The purpose is not only to explain Newport but to help visitors follow certain threads through the tremendous variety of historical sites in the city. The museum is open Mon. and Wed.–Sat. from 10 A.M.–5 P.M. and Sunday from 1–5

P.M.; hours are shorter in the winter. Admission is $5 for adults, $4 for seniors and $3 for children. Children under five are admitted free. Located at the foot of **Washington Sq., at Thames St.; (401) 846-0813.**

Colony House

The Old State House, as it is also called, was once the capitol of Rhode Island, the site of the legislature's renunciation of its ties with Great Britain on May 4, 1776, making Rhode Island the first colony to claim independence. From it, Governor Hopkins had ordered the firing upon the British ship *St. John* 12 years earlier, so rebellion was already a tradition. George Washington met with General Rochambeau here to plan the Battle of Yorktown. Today this is one of the finest buildings of the colonial era in America. Here also is one of Rhode Island's two original Gilbert Stuart portraits of George Washington. Open for free tours in July and August, at other times by appointment. Located at the head of parklike Washington Sq. facing the Museum of Newport History; **(401) 846-2980.**

Wanton-Lyman-Hazard House

The peaceful-looking colonial home you see today doesn't give a hint of its tumultuous past. It's the oldest restored dwelling in Newport, dating from 1675, but it's a wonder it survived at all. Home of a close friend of the king's stamp master in prerevolutionary Newport, the house was a target of the hatred locals felt toward the man who enforced such a heavy tax burden. Protesting the Stamp Act in 1765, residents dragged the stamp master's effigy through the streets, then burned it. While the mob was rampaging in the neighborhood, they broke windows in this house, entered and smashed paneling, threw out the owner's law books and carried off his possessions. They even, according to some accounts, threw a rope around the chimney and tried to pull it down. The house was later owned by Joseph Wanton, governor of the colony, whose strong support of the royalist position resulted in the property being confiscated. It is now a museum, furnished in the manner of an upper-

middle-class merchant in colonial times, and a tour of the house gives a good idea of everyday life in that era. The original kitchen fireplace was found behind a wall during restoration, and the winding stairway is especially interesting. The garden has been restored to a colonial-period kitchen garden. Open mid-June–August, Tues.–Sat. from 10 A.M.–5 P.M.; other times by appointment. Admission is $3; children under 12 are admitted free. Located at **15 Broadway,** close to Washington Sq.; **(401) 846-0813.**

Artillery Company of Newport

Although the armory was built in 1835, the artillery company was founded in 1741 under a charter from King George II, making it the oldest continuously active company in the United States. It participated in seven wars, and its collections of uniforms, weapons and military memorabilia is among the best in the country. It contains, among other things, the flag flown by Oliver Hazard Perry at the Battle of Lake Erie. Open June–Sept., Wed.–Sat. from 10 A.M.–4 P.M. and Sun. from noon–4 P.M. Admission is $3 for adults, $1.50 for children. The museum is wheelchair-accessible. **23 Clarke St.; (401) 846-8488.**

Touro Synagogue

The oldest Jewish house of worship in North America, Touro Synagogue was founded in 1763 by Spanish and Portuguese Jews. Home to an active congregation, the synagogue stands today because the sons of its first rabbi, Isaac Touro, left bequests for its maintenance. (One of these sons, Judah, also left money for the restoration of several churches of other denominations.) The congregation chose Peter Harrison to design the new temple, which is considered to be the finest of his works. Inside, a good deal of decorative work is skillfully incorporated into a relatively small space. Around three sides of the sanctuary are balconies supported by 12 finely detailed columns. It is all original and is considered one of the finest interiors of its period in America. It contains the oldest Torah in the United States, dating from the late

1400s. George Washington visited the synagogue twice, and the presentation of his letter of August 21, 1790, guaranteeing Jews religious freedom, is observed each year. A copy of it is on a tablet in the garden of **Patriot's Park.** Open July 4–Labor Day, Sun.–Fri. from 10 A.M.–4 P.M.; in spring and fall it is open Mon.–Fri. from 1–2 P.M. and Sunday from 11 A.M.–3 P.M. In the winter it is open Sundays from 1–3 P.M., or by appointment for weekday tours at 2 P.M. Tours are free during open hours, the last begins 30 minutes before closing. Located on **Touro St. near its intersection with Spring St.; (401) 847-4794.**

Newport Historical Society

Along with its extensive library on local history, the society maintains collections of period decorative arts, ship models, silver and furniture, including a number of pieces by the famous local cabinetmakers Goddard and Townsend. These are shown in changing exhibits. Attached to the society's building is the **Seventh Day Baptist Meeting House,** dating from 1729. Its interior is known for its raised paneling and wainscoting, including a sounding board paneled in the design of the Union Jack. The library is open to researchers. It has the complete records of the oldest Quaker congregation in America, the account books and records of Aaron Lopez and other early Jewish merchants, account books of the slave traders, ship logs and the second largest genealogical library in Rhode Island. Open Tues.–Fri. from 9:30 A.M.–4:30 P.M. and Sat. from 9:30 A.M.– noon year-round. The society's headquarters are at **82 Touro St.; (401) 846-0813.**

Redwood Library

Founded in 1747, The Redwood Library's building was begun the following year, making it the oldest library building in America. It was designed by Peter Harrison, who is thought to have designed the little octagonal gazebo on the grounds, too. Walk along the left side of the building to see a portion of the chain that once extended across the Hudson River at West Point, New York, to block passage by the British Navy. The collections of the library must remain in the building and may be used there; its collections of paintings and decorative arts are also open to the public. Paintings include works by Gilbert Stuart and Rembrandt Peale. It's like stepping into another era: The library smells of leather bindings and varnish. Open Mon.–Sat. from 9:30 A.M.–5:30 P.M., only until 5 P.M. in July and August. At **50 Bellevue Ave.,** next to the Newport Art Museum; **(401) 847-0292.**

Newport Art Museum

A fine example of Victorian domestic architecture in the stick style, this mansion was the work of Richard Morris Hunt, thought by many to be his finest. Now home to the Newport Art Museum, the interior is quite open and bright, despite the use of dark wood. The paneling in the salon is especially fine. Works displayed from the permanent collection of nineteenth- and twentieth-century American art include those of Winslow Homer. Changing exhibitions may focus on any local topic and use art and early photographs to illustrate anything from Looff carousels to lawn croquet. A small shop has a selection of art books, especially those relating to Newport subjects, such as the Vanderbilts, local architecture and the collections of the museum. Some estate jewelry is for sale on consignment. Hours are 10 A.M.–4 P.M. Tues.–Sat. and noon–4 P.M. on Sunday. Admission is $5 for adults and $4 for seniors and students; $4 and $3 when not all galleries are open. Children under 12 are admitted free. Parking is available for museum visitors, and the galleries are handicapped-accessible. Located at **76 Bellevue Ave.,** opposite Touro Park; **(401) 848-8200.**

The Stone Mill

You can tell a real Newporter by his conviction, against any archaeological evidence, that this tower was built by the Vikings. The academic establishment thinks otherwise, but a number of students of the Viking sagas point out that the shores of Narragansett Bay match the descriptions of Vinland. The most commonly held theory is that the mill is a windmill constructed by Benedict Arnold, first governor of

223

Rhode Island, whose written records describe such a mill. (He's not to be confused with the later general of the same name who turned coat in the Revolution.) An analysis of the mortar supports this. Most recently, evidence has supported the theory that the truth may lie somewhere between the Vikings in A.D. 1000 and the governor in the 1650s, placing the tower as the work of early Portuguese explorers of the thirteenth or fourteenth century. Whatever it was, the tower is a fine one, solidly built with stone arches, its walls straight and solid. The number of words written about it, if printed out in single-spaced elite type would fill it to overflowing. Both Longfellow and James Fenimore Cooper have immortalized it in literature. Touro Park is off Bellevue Ave., between Mill and Pelham Sts.

The Casino and International Tennis Hall of Fame

When a friend of *New York Herald* publisher James Gordon Bennet was bounced from the exclusive Newport Reading Room in 1880 for riding his horse inside (members were not allowed so much as a whisper in some of its rooms), Bennet hired McKim, Mead and White to design a new club. He had it built around a spacious lawn with plenty of room for his own favorite, the new sport of lawn tennis. In its day it was the most complete sports resort facility in the country, with racquet courts, croquet lawns and a bowling alley, as well as shops, a theater and a cafe. Unlike the Reading Room, it welcomed both gaiety and ladies and soon became the fashionable place to be seen. But not by just anyone. When President Chester A. Arthur visited, the footman wouldn't even call for his carriage when he left—he had to do it himself.

They're more hospitable now. The building has been fully restored and the International Tennis Hall of Fame has been added, with memorabilia and exhibits, some of them interactive, on tennis and its greatest players. These include everything from a nineteenth-century racquet-bending machine to a collection of comic post and greeting cards featuring tennis themes. You can even stand in the cen-

ter of a famous competition match recreated on two life-sized screens. The casino's grass tennis courts are open to the public—as they most certainly were not when it was new—and lessons are available to both children and adults. The indoor "court tennis" facility, among only nine in the U.S. and 34 in the world, is also open, providing a rare chance to sample the medieval precursor to all our modern racquet games. Amateur and professional tennis tournaments take place there during the summer, but there is almost always a match going on, which you can watch free from the benches that surround the court, or from the cafe tables overlooking it. The Hall of Fame is open May–Sept. from 9:30 A.M.–5 P.M. and Oct.–Apr. from 11 A.M.–4 P.M. Admission is $6 for adults, $3.50 seniors, $3 for children under 16. Located at **194 Bellevue Ave.,** just south of Memorial Blvd.; **(401) 849-3990.**

Newport Congregational Church

One of only two churches in America with a full John La Farge interior (the other is Trinity Church in Boston), the Newport Congregational Church has both the opalescent glass windows for which La Farge is so well known and his colorful painted wall and ceiling decorations. The latter, which adorn even the organ pipes, have an almost Byzantine quality, surprising in a denomination whose churches are known for their New England simplicity. It's an indication of how far Newport was from the Puritans who settled much of the rest of New England. The trick for La Farge was to create monumental murals appropriate for a house of worship without using any of the traditional religious symbols, which were frowned upon by that congregation. Open Tuesday and Thursday mornings from 10 A.M.–noon between Memorial Day and Labor Day, or at other times by appointment. The church is at the **corner of Spring and Pelham Sts.; (401) 849-2238.**

Trinity Church

One of the most graceful of all New England's early churches, Trinity was designed by Richard Munday, who claimed to be only a carpenter. He went on to design another of Newport's outstanding buildings and its first brick one—Colony House. The rounded tops on Trinity's double row of windows relieves its rectangular lines, and its whole shape seems to draw the eye to its beautiful tall steeple. It is the quintessence of New England village church, writ large. Inside, it is every bit as fine—paneled and with box pews, vaulted ceiling and a gallery at either side of the organ, where slaves once worshipped. The most outstanding feature, however, is the rare three-tiered wineglass pulpit and the sounding board suspended above it. These obscure the altar and communion rail, most unusual in an Anglican church. The brass chandeliers, most of which date from 1728, still use candles. Queen Anne gave the bell—thought to be the first one rung in a New England church—and the communion silver.

The bell in Trinity Church may have been the first church bell to ring in New England.

Before the Revolution the interior was further decorated by a painted and gilded lion and unicorn holding the royal arms above the altar, recognizing Trinity's position as the Crown's established church. After the British evacuation it was torn down by a group of patriots and destroyed in a public bonfire. They left the crown over the organ and the one at the top of the steeple, the latter for obvious reasons. They also missed the paneling in the design of the Union Jack in the ceiling of the unusual "nursing pews" in the back of the church.

In the corner pew at the far right of the altar, look for two old prayer books in a glass case, in one of which all references to the Crown have been crossed out or pasted over.

Just as it was the church of prominent families in the colonial era, this was the parish of many of the Four Hundred during the Gilded Age. Vanderbilts and Astors were married here, and families owned private pews. These were upholstered in various colors, and many had comfortable easy chairs in place of benches. The Morgan pew was so elegantly done up that it was known as "Morgan's Parlor Car." Pew number 66, elegant in pale blue velour, belonged to the Vanderbilts.

The organ was the gift of the philosopher, Bishop Berkeley, who lived for a time at

Whitehall in nearby Middletown, and local tradition is that Handel once played it (before it came to the New World). When Queen Elizabeth was in Newport during the U.S. Bicentennial, she sat in the pew in which George Washington had worshipped, just below the pulpit. You can recognize it by the royal and presidential seals on the two needlepoint kneelers.

In the adjoining churchyard are buried Admiral de Ternay, commander of the French Navy, and General Lafayette's aide-de-camp. Because they were Catholic and there was no Catholic parish or cemetery in Newport, a section was specially consecrated for them here. The oldest stone is from 1707, nearly 20 years before the church was built. Open Mon.–Fri. from 10 A.M.–1 P.M. Sunday services are at 8 and 10:30 A.M. year-round, and tours are available immediately following the late service. The church is handicapped-accessible. Trinity is off Thames St., almost opposite Bowen's Wharf, and easy to spot from anywhere along the harbor; **(401) 846-0660.**

Thames Science Center

A small museum designed for children and covering the whole spectrum of sciences and technology, the Science Center is an innovative hands-on experience. Kids have so much fun here that they forget they're learning things. Along with changing exhibits and an interesting feature on using insects as indicators of water quality, the center has a busy schedule of programs in its **Learning Lab,** which require prior registration. It's worth checking ahead if you're bringing children to Newport. The shop is a blend of kits, projects, brainteasers, software and interactive activities. It's open on Mon. and Wed. from 10 A.M.–6 P.M., on Tues., Thur. and Sat. from 10 A.M.–9 P.M. and on Sun. from noon–5 P.M. Admission is $2, $1 for children under 12 and free to those who hold membership in any of 150 affiliated science museums nationwide. Located at **77 Long Wharf; (401) 849-6966.**

Seaman's Church Institute

Founded in 1919 as "a haven for men and women of the sea," the institute includes a well-stocked library, reading room, lunch counter and cafe, a chapel and a garden, as well as public rest rooms, laundry facilities and the only public showers in town. It's a very democratic place, where visiting recreational yachtsmen are just as welcome as the itinerant shiphands and fishermen of its original mission. It was established by members of Trinity Church. A current priority is assisting members of Newport's fishing fleet to meet changes in the maritime economy. You don't have to arrive by boat to use it—lunches and breakfasts here are quite inexpensive (see **St. Elmo's Galley** on page **255**). Be sure to find the 1929 art deco chapel on the second floor, through a door in the left-hand wall of the library. Its stone floor is inlaid with seashells, and on its walls are frescoes of the patron saints of fishermen. The entire chapel is built to be disassembled. According to the terms of the gift, if the mission of the institute is ever changed, the entire room will be literally rolled up and carried off to the Naval War College. Even the faux marble ceiling is painted on fabric. Outside the fine Georgian revival building, a small walled garden in memory of those who "challenged wind and sail in pursuit of a dream" has a model of a fishing boat set into its brick wall. Open daily year-round. No admission is charged, but the institute always welcomes donations to help carry on its work. Located **at Market Square at America's Cup Ave.; (401) 847-4260.**

Rhode Island Fisherman and Whale Museum

Very accessible and low-tech, with nearly every exhibit inviting hands-on participation, this is the kind of museum you wish they'd had when you were a kid. Where else can you actually put your hand into whale blubber (and who but a kid would want to?) or compare yourself bone by bone to a cetacean? A darkened room (entered through a seaweed curtain) simulates the undersea world of Newport Harbor, where the Gulf Stream brings fish from the warm waters of the West Indies, so you can watch fish found in no other New England waters. As the museum's director graphically describes the phenomenon: "The Gulf Stream is like a giant underwater freight train that brings all these tropical fish to Newport, but it's a one-way ticket." Magnifying glasses and microscopes are available for examining minute sea life. Open Wed.–Mon. from 10 A.M.–5 P.M., Fri.–Mon. in the winter. Admission is $2.50 for adults and $1.50 for children aged two to 12. In the **Seaman's Church In-**

Masts and rigging are still part of Newport's busy wharves.

stitute at Market Square on America's Cup Ave.; (401) 849-1340.

Samuel Whitehorne House

Possibly the city's finest example of a federal period–home, and one of the rare remaining merchant homes on the waterfront, this building had once been a tenement housing eight families. Its interior was largely destroyed. But the structure was intact, and enough evidence remained for restorers to work with—fragments of hand-painted silk that had once covered the dining room walls, for example, provided enough of the original design so that new coverings could be reproduced. Much of the actual decoration is, of course, based on educated conjecture, but enough is known of Samuel Whitehorne and his times that the house could be furnished in pieces he certainly would have used.

The furnishings alone make this one of New England's premier museums, featuring well over a dozen pieces made by or attributed to the colonial cabinetmakers Townsend and Goddard, along with silver, pewter and china from the colonial period. The mahogany dining table is one of only two signed Townsend tables known to exist (the other is in the John Brown House in Providence). In the counting room, where shipowner Whitehorne would have met with his returning captains, is an oak Bible box from the 1600s.

So many fine examples of eighteenth-century Rhode Island craftsmanship fill this house that it is hard to single out specific pieces to look for. Of particular architectural interest is the back stairway, which extends three stories from the kitchen to the third-floor servants' quarters. In the back is a beautiful period garden; be sure to look down on it from a second-floor window to appreciate its design. In season you can stroll along its paths.

Tours of the house are individually guided, so don't expect to breeze through here in 10 minutes. Allow at least 45 minutes, longer if you expect to ask questions. Those especially interested in furniture, or other subjects, should tell the guide before beginning the tour, since the docents here are well informed and

have excellent reference material available. The house is open May–Oct., from 1–4 P.M., and Sat.–Mon. from 10 A.M.–4 P.M., including holiday Mondays. The admission is $5. **416 Thames St., (401) 847-2448.**

St. Mary's Church

St. Mary's is the oldest Catholic parish in Rhode Island, although this church was not begun until 1849. It is of brownstone and considered to be one of the finest Victorian Gothic revival buildings in the East. The main altar, which is of Carrara marble, was made in Florence, Italy, as were the two side altars. Senator John F. Kennedy married Jacqueline Bouvier here in 1953, and they attended Mass during his presidency whenever they were in Newport. Open Mon.–Fri., except holidays from 7–11 A.M. Located **on the corner of Memorial Blvd. and Spring St.; (401) 847-0475.**

OCEAN DRIVE

Fort Adams

First built in 1799, Fort Adams was rebuilt and enlarged by the Scottish stonemason Alexander McGregor in 1824. Its massive walls had casement ports for more than 450 guns, and this was among the largest and best-equipped seacoast forts of its day, designed to destroy vessels entering the bay and to withstand cannon fire from the water and assault by land. Steamships and powerful guns developed during the Civil War made it obsolete, so the fort was modernized in 1896, and it was used until after World War II.

Until recently, visitors could not go inside the walls of Fort Adams because of its deteriorating condition, but this massive brick-and-stone defensive position has been shored up, and guided tours are now offered. Along with inspecting its interior, take time to walk around it. Along the bay are very useful interpretive signs, which show the shapes of a wide variety of craft you may see sailing past. The fort is open May–Oct. from 10 A.M.–5 P.M. daily. The park is open sunrise to sunset daily, year-round. Admission is charged in the summer. To reach Fort Adams State Park by car, take

Surprise Valley is one of Newport's most unusual "follies."

Thames St., Wellington Ave. and Harrison Ave. to the entrance gate. Or you can go by boat from the Oldport Launch Service on America's Cup Ave.; **(401) 847-2400.**

Museum of Yachting

The beauty and fascination of yachting from the nineteenth century to the present is preserved in The Museum of Yachting on the grounds of historic Fort Adams State Park. Four galleries illustrate yachting in the heyday of the mansions. They focus on sail- and power boats (including an 1895 Herreshoff sloop), the single sailors who have sailed the oceans of the world and the America's Cup races. The museum also has *Shamrock V*, one of the challengers in the 1930 cup races and one of only three remaining America's Cup J-boats. The reproduction of the Continental sloop *Providence*, the 10-gun sailing ship that was the first command of John Paul Jones, is sometimes moored here. Recently added is the 1885 American yacht *Coronet*, which returned to Newport as the centerpiece of the International Yacht Restoration School located at the museum. The library is a research and archival center, and the museum sponsors a number of sailing events throughout the season. Open daily mid-May–Oct. from 10 A.M.–5 P.M., and in the winter by appointment. Admission is $2.50, $2 for seniors or $5 for an entire family. To get there, take Thames Street, Wellington Ave. and Harrison Ave. to Fort Adams State Park, or go by boat from the Oldport Launch Service on America's Cup Ave.; **(401) 847-1018.**

Surprise Valley

Follies—unusual structures built to decorate the estates of the very wealthy—are more common in England than in America, but a few, such as Mrs. Vanderbilt's Chinese Tea House, were built in Newport. The most ambitious of these was part of the James Estate. Tucked into a little hollow is an entire medieval stone village, complete with houses, outbuildings and a humpback bridge. Built between 1914 and 1916, it was intended to replicate an alpine Swiss village, and the sight of it appearing suddenly out of the pasturelands of Newport is akin to stumbling into Brigadoon. Surprise Valley is a good name for it. There were once nearly 50 buildings, including stables, a pigsty (with separate stalls and yards for each pig, of course) and homes for the full range of farm animals that lived there. Little signs written in verse commented on each building, and locals were invited to drive through on the winding lane that curved down and under the bridge. Longtime Newport natives remember it, but it became overgrown and almost forgotten, its tile roofs and stone walls weathering into a fine patina. Quite recently it has become part of the new **Surprise Valley Farm,** and its charming little barns now house the horses for the farm's riding school and trail rides. The new owners welcome visitors. If you enjoy riding, there is no better way to explore the beautiful rolling pastures and back roads of this area than on one of Surprise Valley Farm's guided trail rides. Look for the sign at the road just past Independence Square, at **200 Harrison Ave.; (401) 847-2660.**

Hammersmith Farm

The last fully operating farm on Aquidneck Island, Hammersmith Farm, the summer home of the Auchincloss family, continues to have some of the finest gardens in the Northeast. It is also the only one of the great estates that is completely livable. It is in fact so pleasant and comfortable that one could picture moving in for the summer. Without the pretense and ostentation of the Bellevue Ave. confections, it is just an overgrown beach cottage furnished in exquisite taste. It has the added appeal of its brief time as the summer White House of the Kennedy Camelot years. When the rising young senator from Massachusetts married Jackie Bouvier (her mother was married to Hugh Auchincloss at the time), the reception was held here under a tent on the lawn that sweeps down to the bay. When the news media called Hammersmith Farm recently to ask what observation would be made of the anniversary of Jackie's death, they were told "We've put fresh flowers in her room." It's the sort of refined understatement one misses in the Bellevue Ave. mansions.

The house is furnished as the family used it: Mrs. Auchincloss's favorite snapshots of the children are still thumbtacked to a bulletin board in her dressing room, but for many visitors the primary interest in the house is its Kennedy association. The Kennedys visited here often, both before and after he became president, at first using Jackie's childhood bedroom on the third floor. But Mrs. Auchincloss thought it less than suitable for the President of the United States and invited them to use the master bedroom instead. On the desk in this room is a plaque listing the bills that were signed into law here, including the one that established the Peace Corps. Look out the window to see the garden—its colors match the suite's wallpaper.

The Auchincloss family commissioned Frederick Law Olmsted to design gardens for the nearly 100-acre farm. This landscape architect, designer of New York's Central Park, was responsible for much of the landscaping in Newport during the mansion-building era, but here he had all the open space he needed, unlike the somewhat cramped backyards of Bellevue Ave. It took 30 gardeners to tend and maintain these ambitious grounds.

The gardens at Hammersmith Farm were designed by Frederick Law Olmsted.

The gardens are still glorious. They spread from the house itself across wide lawns and into more intimate woodland settings, finally emerging into the extensive cutting gardens, a riot of color all summer, providing flowers for the more than two dozen floral arrangements maintained throughout the house.

The background is always the blue bay, usually studded with sails. On the point is a windmill. Several of the outdoor scenes in *The Great Gatsby* were filmed here. Open daily Apr.–mid-Nov. and weekends in Mar. and late Nov. from 10 A.M.–5 P.M., with extended hours until 7 P.M. in the summer. Admission to the house and garden is $8 ($3 for children). Located on Ocean Dr. close to Fort Adams State Park, the house is part of a tour offered by Viking Tours of Newport on board M/V *Viking Queen*, which leaves from the Goat Island Marina; **(401) 847-6921.** Visitors on this cruise arrive as many Auchincloss guests did, by boat at the private landing. Or you can drive or bicycle from downtown Newport by following Thames St., then Wellington Ave.; **(401) 846-0420.**

Castle Hill Coast Guard Station

Although this is an active Coast Guard station protecting the bay and Long Island Sound, its crew members are happy to show travelers how they accomplish their mission. Inside the station, along with a communications room (where all radio transmissions, weather, distress calls and harbor traffic are monitored), are a number of paintings and photos relating to Coast Guard work, as well as a lens from the Warwick Light and a model of the Ida Lewis Lighthouse. A tour here is filled with fascinating information, including how to "translate" the identification numbers on a Coast Guard cutter (the first two numbers are its length in feet, the last three the order in which it was built), and what the symbol of a leaf painted on the boat means (it's been in a successful drug raid). Kids, and adults, will want to see the cutters, one of which is capsize-proof. The boathouse is a short walk from the main station building and contains the boats and the equipment used in search-and-rescue work. It's a one-on-one tour, so you can ask all the questions you like and go aboard the various craft. You do need to call ahead for an appointment, however, in order that someone will be on duty to show you through. Located on Ocean Dr., between Hammersmith Farm and Brenton Point State Park; **(401) 846-3676.**

OTHER LOCATIONS

Rose Island Lighthouse

To fully appreciate Rose Island Lighthouse, and the island itself, you must understand what it's been through. Charlotte Johnson, the director of the foundation that restored the lighthouse, described it as "in the worst shape of any building I've ever seen that anybody thought could be restored." That about sums up the sorry remnants of the 1870 structure that was declared surplus in 1984. What you see now is not a shiny new reconstruction but the original lighthouse restored to its appearance in the 1940s, when it was still active and had a resident keeper. Helping with the restoration was a local man who had spent childhood summers with his grandparents, the lighthouse keepers here.

Close to the lighthouse, and almost overgrown by vegetation, is a set of barracks constructed in 1798, when the island's fortification and earthworks—first built by the British, then taken over by the French during the Revolution—were expanded as Fort Hamilton. Because nearly all the other First System Fortifications (the nation's oldest coastal defensive positions) have been lost or seriously altered, Rose Island is an important historical site, especially since the barracks are in such good structural condition. When the island was used later as an storage point for explosives, because the TNT and black powder stored here became unstable when damp, the roofs on the old barracks were carefully maintained.

One of the many exciting things about the restoration of the lighthouse is the decision to tie the island's historical attractions to the environment. The lighthouse uses a wind-generation system, and there are programs on birdlife, plants and other features of the island's natural history. In the spring, flowering bulbs bloom around the lighthouse.

Those with private boats can visit the island any time except Apr. 1–July 15, when access is controlled because of nesting birds. Anchor south of the island near the lighthouse landing to beach dinghies, or put passengers ashore at the float, but you cannot tie up there. Access by launch is provided from Newport by **Oldport Marine; (401) 847-9109;** and from Jamestown by **Conanicut Marina; (401) 423-1556.** Call first to be sure of the schedule.

Tours to the island cost $7 and include the ride there on the launch—well worth the entire tour price just for the views of the harbor and island. The launch runs between 11 A.M. and 2 P.M. on weekdays, with an 11 A.M. tour of the lighthouse, keeper's cottage and Revolutionary-era barracks; you can bring a picnic lunch, as Newporters did in the nineteenth century. You can also sign up to be lighthouse keeper for a week or stay overnight in the lighthouse, a cozy and secluded B&B (see page **248**). The island sits off Newport Harbor south of the Newport Bridge, and the Rose Island Lighthouse Foundation's offices are in the Newport Harbor Center at **365 Thames St.; (401) 847-4242.**

Newport Aquarium

All the creatures at the aquarium, from the lumpfish to the starfish, are native Narragansett Bay residents, or visitors who rode there on the Gulf Stream. A big touch tank has hermit crabs and a live shark—kids are surprised to find that most varieties are gentle and harmless. There's no dolphin show, just a lot of interesting local sea life kids can really get to know, like squids hatching and growing up. The big event is the **Setting Free Party,** at the end of September, when kids come with buckets and take all the fish back to the bay. The emphasis here, as in the Fisherman and Whale Museum, is on learning, not collecting, so everything caught for the aquarium all summer is put back in the fall. Open Memorial Day to Labor Day from 10 A.M.–5 P.M. daily. Admission is $3.50 for adults and $2.50 for children. Located **at Easton's Beach (First Beach) on Memorial Blvd.; (401) 849-1340.**

Naval War College Museum

Its alliance with the sea has given Newport a long and close relationship with the navy. Along with the history of the navy in Narragansett Bay, the museum examines the art and science of naval warfare from strategic, legal and foreign-policy perspectives. Its exhibits include World War II photos, a torpedo collection, and large-scale ship models: a five-foot model of HMS *Victory,* one of the sloop *Providence,* and a beautiful model of the HMS *Rose,* the ship sent to Rhode Island to enforce the Navigation Act.

The **Naval Education and Training Center** has awards and pass-in-review ceremonies that are open to the public, as well as ship tours on weekends May–Sept., Sat. and Sun. from 1–3 P.M. For information on ceremonies or ship tours, call **(401) 841-3538.** Open Mon.– Fri. from 10 A.M.–4 P.M., and on weekends June–Sept. from noon–4 P.M. Handicapped-accessible. The Naval War College Museum is in Founders Hall on Coasters Island. The access road is north of the Newport Bridge. Follow the signs from downtown, enter through Gate 1 and stop at the gatehouse to get a visitor's pass; **(401) 841-4052 or 841-1317.**

Restored as a museum, Rose Island Lighthouse is now a unique bed and breakfast.

Cemeteries

The oldest public burying ground in Newport is also one of the first sites a visitor passes upon entering the city from Newport Bridge. The **Common Ground** was laid out in the 1660s, and its oldest section, with slate headstones, is in the back. Many of the stones lie flat on the ground, and several are memorials to those lost at sea. Fine examples of early memorials were done by Newport's best stone carvers, the Stevens family. Their shop, now run by only the second family to have owned it since colonial times, provided the memorial for John F. Kennedy's grave. At the far end, nearest the bridge, is the section for the many slaves owned by Newport families. Among these is a signed Stevens stone. Few New England cemeteries have as fine a collection of early stonework, including winged little moon-faced cherubs, grinning skulls and long inscriptions listing the manifold virtues of the departed. The Common Ground lies along Farewell St., an example of Newport's several descriptive street names, just north of its intersection with Thames St. in the historic section known as the Point.

Next to the Common Ground, up Warner St., is **Island Cemetery,** begun in 1836 and filled with grander stones of granite and marble. Both Oliver Hazard Perry and Matthew Perry are buried here. A large standing angel monument is the work of the noted sculptor Augustus Saint-Gaudens, another of whose works can be found in the Unitarian Church on Pelham St. Farther south (toward the center of town) on Farewell St. is the small **Coddington Cemetery**, with the graves of several of the colony's early governors, including William Coddington, who was Newport's first settler.

Touro Cemetery, with the graves of early Jewish families, is on Bellevue Ave. across from the Hotel Viking, and several of the churches, most notably Trinity, have small churchyards (see pages **224–225**).

Just down the hill from Touro Park, on Pelham St., a tiny burying ground lies between two houses. In it are the graves of colonial Governor Benedict Arnold and members of his family, including several of his children, who died at ages ranging from 17 days to 11 years. The tiny slate markers are a touching reminder of how difficult life was in early Newport. At the southwest corner are two particularly good slate stones with winged skulls.

At the **Clifton Burial Ground** are the tombs of more early governors, the Wantons and Walter Clarke. Although small, it contains some good slate stones and some with skulls and angel heads, most from the late 1600s. Also believed to be buried here is Roger Williams's daughter, Mary. This small lot is on Golden Hill St., which runs up the hill from Spring St., south of Memorial Blvd.

Nightlife

For the latest on what's happening in Newport, be sure to pick up copies of the newspaper called *Newport Traveler*, the magazine-sized *Newport This Week* and the glossy annual *Newport Magazine*. Each of these is free and presents different information, so it's worth settling into a cafe for an hour or so and looking through all of them to find those activities that interest you. Nightlife information is also included in the **Hospitality Hotline**, a 24-hour phone information service at **(401) 846-2366.** Expect most places with music to be geared to the college and younger crowd in the summer, and to be crowded and a little crazy.

The Newport Playhouse and Cabaret Restaurant

The playhouse presents dinner theater, with a good buffet, followed by a live stage performance, then cabaret. The dinner and theater is about $35; there is no extra charge for the cabaret. Theater tickets without dinner are $17.50. Open year-round with performances on Fridays and Saturdays at 8:30 P.M. and Sundays at 7:30 P.M. Dinner is served two hours before curtain time. **102 Connell Hwy.,** just off the traffic circle on Rte. 138, north of town; **(401) 848-PLAY.**

Jane Pickens Theater

Built in 1836 as Zion Episcopal Church, the theater became a burlesque house in the early twenties, then a movie theater when the talkies replaced burlesque. The screen is huge, as screens once were; the sound system is new and state-of-the-art. On Washington Sq.; **(401) 846-5252.**

Star Clipper Dinner Train

Serves a five-course dinner during a three-hour train ride along the bay to Portsmouth and back. The cost is $40 and the train leaves from the station next to the Visitors Center on America's Cup Ave.; **(800) 834-1556 in Rhode Island, (800) 462-7452 elsewhere.** It's a good idea to reserve spaces before arriving in Newport.

Newport Blues Cafe

The cafe offers live blues and jazz on Thur.–Sun. beginning at 9 P.M. **286 Thames St.,** opposite the wharves; **(401) 848-2105.**

Christie's

Located at **Christie's Landing,** this is an informal place to sit outdoors and hear live bands on Fri. and Sat. evenings; **(401) 847-5400.**

Waverly's

In the **Newport Harbor Hotel** on America's Cup Ave., Waverly's has entertainment on Fri. and Sat. evenings and Sun. afternoon; **(401) 847-9000.**

232

Newport Harbor Hotel and Marina

You'll find live dance music on Friday and Saturday evenings from 8 P.M. and Sundays from 2–6 P.M., with no cover charge. **49 America's Cup Ave.; (401) 847-9000.**

The Red Parrot

Located **on the corner of Thames St. and Memorial Blvd.,** with live jazz every weekend, year-round; **(401) 847-3140.**

Shopping

The waterfront, which extends along Thames St. and America's Cup Blvd., is filled with restored stores and warehouses that now house shops and restaurants. **Brick Marketplace,** at the intersection of the two streets, has a number of small specialty shops in restored nineteenth- and twentieth-century stores. The early warehouses and maritime buildings on **Bowen's and Bannister's Wharves** are filled with specialty shops poised above the sea. Many of the shops in these three markets, and in others along Thames St., sell maritime art and antiques, scrimshaw, maps and charts, books on boating, ship brasses and other nautical objects. Farther up the hill, parallel to Thames St., **Spring St.** is dedicated almost entirely to antiques and crafts; above that, **Bellevue Ave.** has several fine shops as well.

Franklin St., which runs up the hill from Thames St. opposite Commercial Wharf, has a heavy concentration of antique shops, as does Spring St., especially in the block north of its intersection with Touro, right behind Old Colony House, on Washington Sq. In one block, beyond Muriel's Restaurant, are **Renaissance Antiques,** with nineteenth-century furniture (they do restoration, too), **and Lamp Lighter Antiques Emporium,** with glass, china and old radios and Victrolas and several others.

Many shops are open in the evenings during the summer, some as late as 10 P.M. Browsing before or after dinner is a favorite Newport pastime.

THAMES ST.

Army Navy Store

One of the few of its genre left, this is the real thing, dating to before World War II. Look here for nostalgia items, flight jackets, costume makings, camping gear or just good, sturdy warm clothes. The shop is not undiscovered—*Vogue* has mentioned it at least once. **262 Thames St.; (401) 847-3073.**

The Spectrum of American Artists and Craftsmen

The display window is enough to stop you in your tracks—filled with art glass in colors and designs as fresh as the bay breeze. Some pottery and stained glass, as well, but it's the glass you'll notice. **306 Thames St.,** opposite the Newport Blues Cafe.

JT's Ship Chandlery

Opened in 1907, this shop remains the genuine article, selling nautical instruments, foul-weather gear, boat shoes, marine hardware, charts, nautical books and a sprinkling of giftware. **364 Thames St.; (401) 846-7256.**

Euphoria!

This store specializes in estate jewelry, amber set in sterling silver or 14-carat gold and unusual gold and silver work from all over the world. Music-box collectors should stop in. **411 Thames St.; (401) 846-2290.**

Norton's Oriental Gallery

The gallery restores and conserves antique Oriental textiles, so if you have a treasured piece, bring it here for museum-quality attention. Or shop here for Asian art, especially textiles, including full-silk kimonos, fans and embroidery. **415 Thames St.; (401) 849-4468.**

The Doll Museum and Museum Toy Shop

Featuring a collection of antique and modern dolls as well as miniatures and stuffed toys, the shop also repairs dolls. **520 Thames St.; (401) 849-0405.**

Bowen's Wharf is now lined with boutiques and trendy shops.

The Armchair Sailor

A bookstore designed for travelers, it is especially for those who go by water. We have trouble getting out of this place without a full duffel bag. Look here for books on sailing, the sea, New England, travel and maritime history, as well as children's books. The owners invite you to browse, and provide you with a cup of tea while you do. **543 Thames St.; (401) 847-4252.**

THE WHARVES

The Museum Store

This is a branch of the shops run by the Preservation Society of Newport County at The Breakers and their other properties. Look here for books on all subjects related to Newport history, the sea and American decorative arts, along with fine replicas of classic export and other china styles. Household decorative items, jewelry and a variety of reproductions at reasonable prices are the first reason to shop here. Knowing that the profit from the things you buy will go to help preserve Newport's many historic properties is another. **1 Bannister's Wharf; (401) 849-9900.**

Over Narragansett Bay and Beyond

An unusual photographic art gallery specializing in aerial views of New England, many of which are of the Newport and Narragansett Bay area. Tall ships from every angle, the mansions from above and some more traditional perspectives of city and village streets fill the small shop. Unlike many of the other shops, this one remains open Friday and Saturday evenings in the winter and until 10 P.M. every night in the summer. **5 Bowen's Wharf; (401) 848-9191.**

Newport Scrimshanders

The store carries, as you would guess, scrimshaw, much of it created by the owner. In case you wonder about the use of ivory, be assured that modern scrimshaw is done on legally obtained material. The results are delicate, lovely and a nice reminder of the many arts of yesterday's sailors. The shop carries ivory antiques, Nantucket Lightship baskets and a few other related items, including the exceedingly rare sailors' Valentines by James Chase. **14 Bowen's Wharf; (401) 849-5680 or (800) 635-5234.**

Roger King Gallery of Fine Art

Offering the crème de la crème in art of the nineteenth and early twentieth centuries, Roger King's collection often includes Newport subjects, but you may find anything here, from a Mary Hazelton portrait to yachting scenes. **21 Bowen's Wharf; (401) 847-4359.**

Thames Glass

No longer on Thames St., the gallery features art glass designed by Matthew Buechner, who creates perfume bottles, paperweights, delicate bowls and fragile Christmas tree ornaments. **Bowen's Wharf; (401) 846-0576.**

The Scribe's Perch Bookstore

The place to look for out-of-print books on any subject but especially local and New England history and life. There are new children's books, as well, and the shop is known among bibliophiles for its monthly auctions of rare books. The owner is an entertaining auctioneer. If you have out-of-print or rare books to sell, ask about consigning here. It is a bright, pleasant place to browse, at **69–73 Long Wharf; (401) 849-8426.**

THE HILL

Lily's of the Alley

Lily's has a changing assortment of clothing and discontinued boutique items at less-than-boutique prices. You never know what you'll find here. **64 Spring St.; (401) 846-7545.**

Nautical Nook

This nook is for those who love the sea—as its owner surely does. Half hulls and models of ships, maritime antiques, charts and other things related to the sea fill the shop. If you have nautical antiques or ship models in need of restoration or custom-built display cases, this is the place to go. The owner has a B&B here, too, decorated by things nautical. **86 Spring St.; (401) 846-6810.**

J. H. Breakell, Silversmith

Many of the original designs in sterling silver and 14-carat gold jewelry here are inspired by the sea. The workshop is at **132 Spring St.; (401) 849-3522.**

Macdowell Pottery

Combining a studio with a retail shop, MacDowell's sells the work of several local potters, plus other gifts, including glassware. **140 Spring St.; (401) 846-6313.**

Patriots' Shop

Located in the 1880s parish hall of the Newport Congregational Church on the corner of Spring and Pelham Sts., this shop sells china, glassware and other antiques and collectibles on consignment. You may find anything here, from Asian art pottery to fine handmade linens. Open Fri. from 1–4 P.M. and Sat. from 10 A.M.–1 P.M.

The Griffon Shop

Located in the Newport Art Museum, this is a consignment shop of Newport treasures, especially estate jewelry, small antiques and collectibles. Open museum hours only: Tues.–Sat. from 10 A.M.– 4 P.M. **76 Bellevue Ave.; (401) 848-8200.**

Newport Books

Specializing in works on Rhode Island, Americana and military history. This shop carries rare and unusual volumes, along with prints. If you're looking for anything hard to find, check here. **116 Bellevue Ave.; (401) 847-3700.**

Cadeaux du Monde

This could pass easily for a museum of ethnography, except that the tags all have prices on them. Traditional artwork and folk crafts from Africa, Asia, South and Central America fill the shop, where browsers are welcome. **140 Bellevue Ave.; (401) 848-0550.**

Spectator Sports

Baseball

For a taste of what baseball used to be like before the megateams, attend a game at **Cardines Field**, the small, early-twentieth-century stadium close to the Visitors Center on Marlborough St. Local Sunset League teams play, as they have since 1919, supported noisily by their fans. The games are free and you'll meet the locals; **(401) 847-1398.**

Tours

Anyone interested in the early history of Newport will want to explore it on foot. While you can do this on your own, you'll learn a lot more in the company of Anita Raphael, of **Newport on Foot**. A Newport historian whose knowledge of the city's past has no rival, she provides lively insights that only a dedicated historian could offer. In a walk through a 10-block area she brings colonial Newport to life: You begin to see those streets as they were more than two centuries ago, busy with carts and wagons instead of automobiles. Along with the schedule of regular tours, Anita offers tours on specialized subjects, such as the Newport cabinetmakers and craftsmen, tav-

235

erns and a ghost and graveyard tour at Halloween. Most walking tours cost $7. **P.O. Box 1042, Newport 02840; (401) 846-5391.** Tours leave from the Visitors Center or from the White Horse Tavern, and reservations are essential for some, suggested for all. Anita is also the curator of the **White Horse Tavern** and hosts tavern talks there on Friday mornings at 10:30 from Memorial Day to Columbus Day weekends. One, called "Merchants, Mariners and Molasses" deals with the Triangle Trade. The modest $5 charge includes morning coffee and refreshments in the tavern. Dinner lectures are accompanied by a dinner based on an appropriate theme, such as ingredients available in colonial Newport.

The **Newport Historical Society** offers tours of the historic district every Friday and Saturday morning at 10 A.M. from mid-June–Sept.; **(401) 846-0813.**

Viking Tours departs from the Visitors Center and travels by bus past the mansions and other landmarks with a narration. Longer tours include admission to one of the mansions. Three different bus tours are offered each day in the spring and fall, five from mid-June to Labor Day. Each has several departure times, at prices ranging from $14 to $29.50 for adults and $8 to $15 for children aged five to 11. Tours leave from the Visitors Center; **(401) 847-6921.**

Field Trip Photo offers unique tours for those who want to find the best photography sites and get some professional tips to make their photos better. Field Trip knows the most photogenic places and the best times of day to shoot them; **(401) 842-0555.**

Old Colony Newport Scenic Railway leaves from the little depot next to the Visitors Center for a scenic ride along the bay. Choose an open-platform coach or an elegant parlor car, hauled by a vintage diesel. The rail line is eight miles long and leads to **Green Animals** topiary garden in Portsmouth (see page **196**); **(401) 849-0546.**

Secret Gardens is a once-a-year tour, in late June, of 16 private gardens in the historic Point area that are not otherwise open to the public. Tickets are available by advanced reservation, usually for $12, or on tour days (when they cost more); **(401) 847-0514.**

A **Candlelight House Tour** of eighteenth- and nineteenth-century homes decorated for the holidays is held the week following Christmas as part of the **Christmas in Newport** events. Admission is $3 per house; **(401) 849-6454.**

Kayak tours of Newport's coast are offered by **Atlantic Outfitters** for $39, single, and $72, double (see page **216**); **(401) 848-2920.**

For a self-guided **driving tour**, rent the 90-minute audiotape of history enlivened by music and sound effects available at the Visitors Center.

Neighborhood Walks

Southern Bellevue Avenue

While the **Cliff Walk** gives the best view of some of the estates, others are better seen through their front gates. This route, combined with Cliff Walk, makes a nice circuit and avoids the necessity of retracing the outer shore route. Because many readers will use it in combination with Cliff Walk, we have begun this neighborhood walk at the southern end of Bellevue Ave., where it meets Ledge Rd. The neighborhood is a showcase of the work of the most important architects of their time, freed of budget restraints and able to indulge their imaginations and talents.

Several nineteenth-century houses face the intersection of Ledge Rd. and Bellevue Ave., followed by one of the several unique gatehouses along the street. This one, part of the long-gone Rockhurst estate, is almost hidden by an unattractive fence. **Rough Point** sits behind its matching red sandstone wall, at the point where Bellevue Ave. turns sharply to the left. **Belcourt Castle** (see page **244**), and **Miramar** sit almost opposite each other. Miramar was the last of the palatial estates built in Newport, completed in 1914.

Clarendon Court and **Beaulieu** sit side by side, each with an interesting past. Clarendon was the setting for the Bing Crosby–Grace Kelly film *High Society,* and Beaulieu was a Vanderbilt estate, where Alice Roosevelt, daughter of President Theodore Roosevelt, is reported to have scandalized Newport by dancing the hootchie-kootchie atop its mansard roof.

Marble House and **Beechwood** (see pages **244** and **243**), belonging respectively to the Vanderbilts and the Astors, are next, on the ocean side of the street. Opposite is **Champ Soleil,** the French provincial built in 1929. **Rosecliff** (see page **247**) follows on the ocean side, faced by **Sherwood**, a huge colonial revival with Palladian windows. **Ivy Tower,** also on the west side, combines a stone first floor with half-timbered upper stories. At the corner of Ruggles Ave., **Fairlawn** represents the Elizabethan revival popular in the 1870s, using brick and brownstone.

Past Ruggles Ave. (which you should follow to the right if you wish to stay closer to the shore and the mansions you saw from the Cliff Walk), Bellevue Ave. continues this gallery of mixed styles and fashions. **Vernon Court,** on the right, is a turn-of-the-century reproduction of a French chateau. Beyond is **Chateau-sur-Mer** (see page **242**), and opposite is **Swanhurst,** on the corner of Webster St., both from the early 1850s. At Narragansett St., **Rockry Hall's** Gothic stone-and-shingle facade faces the former **St. Catherine Academy,** of heavy rough-cut granite. On weekdays you can see the downstairs interior of the academy building, now the Newport Preservation Society. Stop to look at its rose gardens, as well. The turreted and gabled Gothic **De la Salle** on the right contrasts with the classical lines of **The Elms** (see page **246**), across the street. Several homes of the 1880s follow. **Berkeley Villa,** the only colonial revival in this area, faces the early Gothic gem, **Kingscote** (see page **242**). Opposite Jones Ave. is the remarkable **Audrain Building,** in Moorish style with high arched windows over each of its storefront bays, and decorated by ornamental tiles and terra-cotta scrolls. Southern Bellevue Ave. ends at Memorial Blvd. with the **Casino's** long shingled facade (see page **224**), and the half-timbered **Travers Block,** designed by Richard Morris Hunt.

Northern Bellevue Avenue

This short section at "the other end" of Bellevue Ave. is almost completely separated, historically and architecturally, from the streets immediately to its west, which form the heart of colonial Newport. It is a showcase of the early and experimental works of several of the foremost American designers, including the best of them, Peter Harrison. You don't have to be in the mood for a serious investigation of either architecture or history to enjoy this end of Bellevue. You can mix shopping, sight-seeing and even a stop for a little bit of something as you stroll.

Begin at the intersection of Bellevue and Memorial Blvd., opposite the Travers Block, and go north. (For those to whom compass points are akin to Sanskrit, when you're facing north, Memorial Blvd. goes downhill to your left, toward the waterfront.) In the first block are two art galleries. Look along Downing St., which ends in the strikingly well-restored art deco facade of **Villa Liberte** (see page **251**).

On the left, at the corner of Pelham St. is the white **Elks Home,** surrounded by an ornate porch. During the Civil War, the U.S. Naval Academy left Annapolis, a little too close to Confederate Virginia for safety, and moved to the Atlantic House (from 1861–1865), which stood here. Midshipmen used to parade in **Touro Park** just opposite, where one of Newport's best known (and least understood) landmarks stands. Called variously the Old Stone Mill, the Stone Tower and the Viking Tower (see page **223**), and also variously attributed to the Vikings, the Portuguese and to Governor Benedict Arnold (not the Revolutionary War general), it is lighted at night and makes Touro Park a nice place to visit on a summer evening. The park was a gift to the city from Judah Touro, son of Newport's first rabbi. A statue of William Ellery Channing, the Newport native who founded Unitarianism in America, faces the granite church named for him. It was a meeting place for artists, writers and intellectuals and is known for its two stained glass windows by John La Farge, who lived only a few blocks away, and for a memorial by the sculptor Augustus Saint-Gaudens.

237

The Rhode Island Guide

Back on Bellevue, the **Newport Art Museum** (see page **223**) stands in the open setting of its wide lawns, one of Richard Morris Hunt's finest—some say *the* finest—works, in the half-timbered stick style ("sticks" refer to the exposed supporting timbers that fill the larger spaces). Here you might want to detour onto Old Beach Rd. to see two good examples of work by McKim, Mead and White (Stanford White's firm) and by George Champlin Mason, on either corner of Sunnyside Place. The **Redwood Library** (see page **223**), next along Bellevue, is an earlier work, built in 1748 and designed by Peter Harrison. When you first look at the building it seems to be made of stone, but a closer look shows it to be wood that has been grooved and textured to look like stone.

Directly opposite is an ornate little cottage covered in octagonal patterned slate. **Bird's Nest Cottage** is a confection of fretwork, porches, finials and turrets, topped by a slate roof. It was built in 1872, and although there is no proof that Richard Morris Hunt designed it, it *does* have a lot in common with his home nearby, at **33 Greenough Place.**

The two-tiered porches of the building on the corner of Church St. look as though they have been transplanted from a gracious southern city. The building on the corner across Bellevue Ave. was one of Newport's most fashionable Victorian hotels, a favorite of Henry James and other literary figures. The brick **Hotel Viking** was once owned by Mrs. Vanderbilt, who needed a place to put her houseguests (Marble House has only one guest bedroom).

Across from the Hotel Viking is the **Jewish Cemetery,** dating from 1677. Some of its stones are so old that there is no evidence of any inscription. The writing on others is in Hebrew, Portuguese, Spanish, English and Latin. A block farther down Touro St. is the **Touro Synagogue,** the oldest surviving synagogue in America, dating from 1763. Founded by Jews from Spain and Portugal, the worship there still adheres to the Sephardic rite. Peter Harrison designed it, and it is considered to be his finest work (see page **222**). In

Patriot's Park, which adjoins the synagogue, is a tablet with a replica of George Washington's famous 1790 letter reassuring the Hebrew congregation of Newport that Rhode Island's religious toleration would be the policy of the new republic, and that it would give "bigotry no sanction."

The Hill

Bounded by Bellevue Ave. and the harbor on the east and west, the Hill is filled with outstanding examples of American architecture, from the late-seventeenth-century **Wanton-Lyman-Hazard House** to those from the early twentieth century. Richest in historic buildings, and the streets that look most like they did before the Revolution, are Clark, Spring, Mill and Pelham Sts.

Begin this walk on Clarke St. as it meets Touro at Washington Square, where you are immediately surrounded by mid-eighteenth-century Newport. On the left side are private residences, including that of Ezra Stiles, minister of the church across the street, who left Newport to become president of Yale. Next to the church is a later armory, built by the same man who did the stonework at Fort Adams. Be sure to see the handsome eagle arms in the pediment. Several homes in this area have been enlarged by raising them and adding a lower story; you can see this clearly in the one at number 11. **Vernon House**, at the end of the street on the left, was used during the French occupation of Newport as the headquarters of the French commander-in-chief, Count Rochambeau.

Turn left at Vernon House, then right onto Spring St., a patchwork of styles and eras. Next to the 1775 shop on the corner is a fancy shingled Queen Anne built almost a century later. The house on the facing corner was built 70 years earlier. Among the homes from the early 1800s are two with gambrel roofs. One, next to the **Pilgrim Inn,** has a brick end and a fine doorway, while the other, at the corner of Church St., has been converted into a shop by the addition of Palladian windows on the street level. **Trinity Church** (see page **224**) faces the harbor; the angel faces on its early slate gravestones look out at Spring St. A short excursion down Mill St. to the right takes you to a unique little 1880s brick fire station.

Back on Spring St., turn right, noting particularly the two gambrel-roofed houses at **#175** and **#181,** which sit in characteristic style of the late 1700s, with their ends to the street. Opposite these are two Queen Anne homes with decorative shingles and unique windows with stained glass. Turn left onto Pelham St., passing the **Newport Congregational Church** on the far corner (see page **224**) and, on the near corner, the home of John Bannister (of Bannister's Wharf), where General Prescott lived during the British occupation. You can't miss the imposing pillars of the **Augustus Littlefield House** in the same block. Beside the house is the burial place of Benedict Arnold, first governor of Rhode Island, along with the graves of several of his children. As you continue up Pelham St. to Touro Park, houses become more and more Victorian in their style.

The Point

Just north of the waterfront businesses and the Visitors Center, the Point was the residential district for colonial merchants. Washington St. was lined with docks and fine homes of shipowners, captains and traders. Close by were the homes and shops of the craftsmen, cabinetmakers, sail makers, shipbuilders and others whose goods outfitted their Newport ships. Washington St. had the finest homes in the colonies. Then came the Revolution, and British occupation. Trade stopped and never came back, even when the French arrived after the British left. Newport would not regain its trade, and the War of 1812 ended what little was left. Later, when other areas of Newport began to attract summer visitors, the Point languished in obscurity, its fine houses run down and decaying. Now many of the homes have been carefully restored and others are being restored. One, the **Hunter House,** is a museum, and the others can be enjoyed from the outside. Occasionally some of these private homes are opened for charity tours, as they are during **Christmas in Newport,** and

gardens are open in June during the **Secret Gardens Tour.**

Begin at the corner of Marsh and Washington Sts., at the end of the Goat Island Causeway. The first block of Washington St. has several buildings from the mid-1700s, including the **Brenton Counting House** at **#39.** Hunter House, on the waterfront side of the street and built in 1748, is one of the finest colonial homes still standing in America. Following the British occupation, it was headquarters for Admiral de Ternay, commander of the French Navy in Newport. Follow Elm St. to the water's edge next to Hunter House to see the shore facades of the Washington St. houses, and imagine the scene when each of them had its own wharf, and sailing ships docked there.

An even earlier house at **#64,** dates from 1725 and is still owned by descendants of the family that bought it in 1760. One of the rare Victorian houses here, it has an exaggerated mansard roof and corner porch. Formerly a museum, the **Sanford-Covell Villa** is now a B&B, but visitors are welcome to see its remarkable Arts and Crafts period stenciling (see page **254**). Facing the end of Walnut St. is a gambrel-roofed captain's house from the mid-1700s. On the far corner of Chestnut St., the small gambrel-roofed cottage from the early 1700s was brought here from Providence piece by piece.

Take Chestnut St. to the right, then right again onto Second St. On your left, at the corner of Walnut St., is the house where Matthew Perry, who opened trade with Japan, was born. Opposite each other in the next block are two fine early-eighteenth-century buildings, one with a center chimney and gambrel roof, the other with an asymmetrical gambrel. In the next block, at **#42,** is a style typical of the early 1700s, with the door set to one side of center, directly under one of the four upper-story windows. At the corner, on the left, notice the unusual chimney on the **John Frye House,** and on the side facing Poplar St., the original beaded clapboards.

Poplar St., to the right, is lined with colonial architecture, including a fine 1740 gambrel on the left, another opposite it with its end to the street, and a Greek revival at **#63.** One of the finest homes in the area is next door, built in the early 1740s with a balustrade on the rooftop and an elegant doorway, which is a replica of the one on Hunter House.

The Wharves

The waterfront, from the Visitors Center to the intersection of America's Cup Ave., Memorial Dr. and Thames St., is not very long, but it could take all day to make your way through it. Wharves extend out into the harbor side by side in long rows, several of them lined with small shops and cafes. From nearly any of these you can get a view of the maritime activity of the harbor, especially in the summer, when the water is filled with yachts and the sky with masts.

From **Goat Island,** reached by a causeway behind the Visitors Center, you can get a good

Rose Island still has buildings from the time of the Revolution.

perspective on the harbor and the wharves. From here the view extends to the bridge, with tiny **Rose Island** and its lighthouse in the bay almost at its feet, along the shore of **Conanicut Island (Jamestown),** to the narrows guarded by the hulk of **Fort Adams,** and along the entire Newport waterfront, with the town rising behind it. A looming hotel building interrupts the scene in the foreground, but it replaced a none too scenic torpedo station. From the causeway there is a nice waterside view of the Washington St. houses, showing the facades that were originally used as front entrances. A little lighthouse of whitewashed stone marks the northern tip of Goat Island.

Long Wharf, the first as you walk south from the Visitors Center, was a trading center in the early colonial era; it shows on an 1685 map. The center of Newport's thriving Triangle Trade, as well as a loading point for lumber, tar, candles and foods bound for England, it was also a butcher-shop-on-the-hoof. Where live steers once were brought and shoppers could chalk off their cut, you're now likely to see lobster traps and boats.

Bowen's Wharf was built early in the 1700s, and at least two structures—a chandlery and a three-story building—remain from the early days of the wharf. **Bannister's Wharf** is next, opposite the end of Pelham St. A fishing wharf, it was the scene of a lively market where the catch was sold directly by the fishermen. The **Clarke Cooke House** was moved from Thames St. and restored as a restaurant.

Sayer's and Commercial Wharves are the center of yachting activity, port to several harbor cruises and the **Newport Yachting Center.** The end of America's Cup Ave. is punctuated with the striking granite **Perry Mill Building,** built as a textile mill in 1835 by the builder of the Armory on Clarke St. and Fort Adams. The textile industry never caught on here, and it is now a handsome hotel, the **Newport Bay Club** (see page **249**). In the center of the wide sidewalk at this intersection is the striking sculpture, *The Wave.* A five-foot ocean wave rises in a graceful curve and from it extend two human feet. They've grown shiny from the hands that rub them in passing, and in cold weather it is common to see them neatly clad in warm socks. *The Wave* is the work of Kay Worde, and one of the most appealing public sculptures we've seen anywhere.

If you continue up Thames St., a right turn brings you to **Ann Street Pier,** a nice place from which to watch the boats come and go. The imposing three-story mansion on the "inland" side of the street is the **Francis Malbone House,** the only eighteenth-century merchant house of its size remaining on the waterfront. It is now beautifully restored as a B&B (see page **249**). Several other buildings on that side of the street are notable, including the **Samuel Whitehorne House** (see page **227**), an outstanding example of a federal mansion, built in 1811. It is open to the public, fully restored and furnished with some fine Newport pieces.

The Mansions

From Kingscote to Belcourt Castle Bellevue Ave. has America's most fabled assembly of palaces. It was once so exclusive that commoners were not allowed to use Bellevue, and there were no street numbers. Everyone knew who lived where. Perhaps the best description of the wild architectural variety of these summer retreats was written by Cleveland Amory in his book, *The Last Resorts.* In the vocabulary of racehorse breeding: "Here, side by side, in extraordinary proportions, in an extremely small area ... are represented every kind of architectural crossbreeding from a weird Queen Anne gingerbread sired by an errant Florentine palazzo to a medieval marble blockbuster out of Versailles by the Grand Central Station."

The grandest mansions have been restored to their original opulence and are open to visitors. Of these, The Breakers, Kingscote, Chateau-sur-Mer, Rosecliff, The Elms and Marble House are in the hands of the Preservation Society. Beechwood is privately owned, and Belcourt Castle is still a family residence, although it is open to visitors on a regular basis. The Preservation Society properties can be visited separately or on a combined ticket.

Frederick Law Olmsted, the foremost landscape architect at the turn of the century, designed formal flower beds for The Breakers' lawns.

It's not a good idea to plan too many mansion visits in too short a time. One or two in a day, or up to three in a single weekend are quite enough; after that you lose perspective. Although it is a purely personal choice, and one you will be able to make better after reading the characteristics of each, we would choose Marble House and Chateau-sur-Mer if we were limited to two. Most choose The Breakers first, and because it's the largest and most famous of the mansions, this is justified. Each has its own stories and unique features, so you could choose at random and not go wrong.

The fabled life of the very wealthy families in the highest echelons of New York's Social Register reached new heights at Newport fetes and dinners. On one occasion an entire ballroom was filled with butterflies. One hostess decorated her dining table in nothing but American Beauty roses, another covered hers in beach sand in which was buried gemstones and gave each guest a sterling sandpail and shovel to uncover them. Today we can only imagine these gala, often ludicrous, shows as we tour the palaces. It is their final irony that these estates, once so carefully guarded from prying eyes, should now be open to the paying public. The following mansions are listed in chronological order to better follow the architectural and social history they tell.

241

Kingscote

The earliest of the mansions, built in 1841, before ostentation and grandeur were the standards, Kingscote began the movement that later put Newport on the social map. Society was not the goal of its Savannah builder, who chose the hilltop location to get away from the center of town. Newport's summer pleasures were simple outdoor ones, and many of its summer residents were southerners.

The atmosphere in Newport began to change with the arrival of Boston intellectuals, many of them fierce abolitionists. The southern gentry felt less and less comfortable, until, with the beginning of the Civil War, they sold their Newport homes to avoid having them confiscated. Kingscote was sold in 1863 to the King family, who lived there until the 1970s. One of its most remarkable features is this continuity of ownership, which preserved the house and its mid-nineteenth-century furnishings. It is a museum not only of architectural styles but of the treasures collected by a major family in the China Trade, including possibly the finest private collection of Chinese paintings in America.

The King family hired Stanford White to design an addition, which added the home's best-known feature, its ballroom-sized dining room. It blends styles with a delicate screen of carved spindles, a cork ceiling and an entire wall of Tiffany glass bricks and tiles.

The overall effect is quite livable, different from most of the mansions that followed. It shows the transition between postrevolutionary Newport and the Gilded Age. Open daily May–Sept., from 10 A.M.–5 P.M., and weekends in October and April. Admission is $6.50 ($3 for children), or by combination ticket. Located on **Bellevue Ave. at the corner of Bowrey St.**, next to the shopping center; **(401) 847-1000.**

Edward King House

Restored as the Senior Citizens Center, this 1846 villa was designed by Richard Upjohn shortly after nearby Kingscote was built. It is Gothic-style brownstone and brick, and features Italianate trim and balconies. Tours are sometimes available, but visitors are always welcome to see the interior and its outstanding central hall. On Spring St. you can see the small home that was originally the gatehouse for this mansion. Open weekdays from 9 A.M.–4 P.M. year-round. Wheelchair-accessible. Located **in Aquidneck Park, off King St.** (one block off Bellevue at the end of Jones Ave.); **(401) 846-7426.**

Chateau-sur-Mer

Under an impressive porte cochere that faces an immense weeping beech tree, the entrance to Chateau-sur-Mer is part of a later addition. The house, in fact, underwent so many reconstructions since its 1852 origins that it is an outstanding example of the major Victorian architectural styles.

The Wetmores, another China Trade family, built their retreat in the days when Newport was preferred by people of intellect and culture. It was massive, the most costly home of its day in Newport. The son of the original owner hired Richard Morris Hunt to renovate and enlarge the house. Hunt cut his architectural teeth transforming the Chateau into an American showcase of the geometric Eastlake style. Cutting through three floors for a soaring great hall (as tall as the one he would later design for The Breakers, but not nearly so large), he increased the impression of height by widening the balconies of each subsequent floor to make the distance between them seem greater.

The Wetmores, who lived in Europe for 10 years, wanted to incorporate the designs of William Morris's Arts and Crafts Movement into the upstairs decor. The wall coverings in Wetmore's bedroom are original Morris paper, and the upstairs sitting room is Turkish-inspired—any Victorian house worth its salt had a room with an exotic Oriental theme. (The movie *The Bostonians* used this room as a setting, as did the recent BBC production of Edith Wharton's *The Buccaneers*.)

A bedroom suite of Eastlake in butternut, all original, has been in the house since the 1860s. Be sure to note the outstanding ceiling frieze in the Butternut Room using nature

242

motifs and a geometric knot pattern in the corners.

By contrast to the designs of Eastlake and Morris, the library and dining room are ornately Italian, designed by Luigi Frullini, with deeply carved furniture and an ornate ceiling, walls covered in stamped and gilded leather and intricate patterns of inlaid wood.

It is an altogether charming house, as well as a virtual museum of nineteenth-century decorative styles. Adding to its attraction are articulate, good-humored guides who can bring both the human and the architectural history to life. Open daily from 10 A.M.–5 P.M. from May through September. Open weekends in January, February, March, October and November from 10 A.M.–4 P.M., and the same hours daily in December (except Dec. 24 and 25). Admission is $6.50 (children $3), or by combination ticket. **Bellevue Ave. between Leroy and Shepard Aves.; (401) 847-1000.**

The Astors' Beechwood

The Mrs. Astor, doyenne of New York Society at the close of the nineteenth century, was married to the grandson of John Jacob Astor and was the arbiter of who made it socially and who did not. She ruled Newport Society with an iron hand. Her cottage, Beechwood, was not the grandest of the lot, nor the largest, but an invitation to it was Newport's highest prize.

Today it is the only mansion inhabited by a cast of performers who re-create in a spontaneous and often interactive theater the social world of Newport's Gilded Age. A lady's maid, valet or perhaps one of the Astor children greets and welcomes each visitor into the somewhat severe entry, watched over by a gigantic full-length portrait of Mrs. Astor. She is pictured ready to receive, in a Paris gown trimmed in jewel-encrusted lace.

A visiting "prince" may join you and suggest a parlor game as you wait for other guests. A tour of the house follows, guided by a gossipy maid or valet who illuminates the lives of both The Four Hundred and their servants. No ropes bar the rooms: you can poke into the closets and see what visiting debutantes will be wearing this season, or hear what outrageous dishes will be served at dinner. There will often be an entertainment in the ballroom as houseguests practice for an amateur show or invite you to join in singing Christmas carols.

Along with the regular tours are special events such as teas, murder mystery tours, tea dances and seasonal activities. Although the house is not sumptuously furnished, the interior is well kept; it is also the only one of the mansions where you get a look at the backstairs beyond the kitchen. At Christmas the house is decorated, and activities include a festive dinner (at $60 per person) with dancing and a tour. Open year-round daily from 10 A.M.–4 P.M.; other times for special events by reservation. Tours are $8, $6 for children, seniors and those unable to climb to the second floor. Special programs are $10.50 to $12. Combination tickets are available for Beechwood, Belcourt Castle and the Tennis Hall of Fame. The mansion is located on **Bellevue Ave. between Rosecliff and Marble House; (401) 846-3772.**

Ochre Court

The first of the grander mansions, Ochre Court is in a late Gothic French chateau style with an incomparable setting overlooking the sea. Although it is not a museum, it is open to the public as the administration building of Salve Regina University. Much of the preservation in the Ochre Point area is due to the university's use of the buildings for dormitories, classrooms and other facilities. The interiors of some have been adapted, but the exteriors and grounds remain much as they did in their heyday.

Richard Morris Hunt's three-story great hall moves from the rather plain marble first floor to the more highly decorated upper reaches. Apart from the architecture, the most outstanding feature is the stained glass from the Spitzen collection. If the building is closed—as it is on weekends—go around to the ocean-side terrace and look in the large windows to see the stained glass. Late afternoon is a good time, when the sun is shining through the west windows on the opposite side

243

of the building. If it is open, ask at the reception desk for the free leaflet describing the building and its art treasures.

Look up as you pass the south side of the building to notice the sundial on the chimney. Open free of charge Mon.–Fri, from 9 A.M.–4 P.M., year-round, except holidays. Inquire about guided tours during the summer. Located at **100 Ochre Point Ave.**

Marble House

Not the largest but the most tastefully opulent of the mansions, Marble House was built by the early yachting enthusiast William K. Vanderbilt as a 39th birthday present for his wife, Alva Smith Vanderbilt. Marble House was the work of Richard Morris Hunt and was completed in 1892, a year before he began The Breakers. It shows Hunt's Paris training and reflects the design of the Petit Trianon at Versailles. Its neoclassical white marble exterior gives little clue to the exuberant riches of its interior.

Its ballroom, inspired by the Hall of Mirrors at Versailles, is almost entirely encrusted in gold. Here and elsewhere in the house the sunburst masks of Apollo, symbol of Louis XIV, are prominent. The room is grander than its counterparts in nearly any European royal palace. The elegant dining room, an almost exact reproduction of a salon at Versailles, is in pink Numidian marble. The custom-made dining chairs are solid bronze, weighing 75 and 100 pounds each, so heavy that footmen were required to move them so guests could sit or rise.

The woodwork in Alva's bedroom reaches a crescendo of rococo swirls and doodads, matched in an elaborate bed. Through the house runs the sad story of her daughter, Consuelo, forced to marry the ninth Duke of Marlborough. (Mama later recanted, the marriage was annulled and Consuelo married a French aviator.)

Three years after the birthday for which Vanderbilt gave his wife Marble House, she divorced him to marry Oliver Hazard Perry Belmont, moving to Belcourt Castle, where we shall meet her again. She kept Marble House,

however, and later used it for Women's Suffrage meetings and conferences.

Many years after she had left to summer at Belcourt, she added to Marble House the Chinese Tea House, which every walker spots from the Cliff Walk. It originally sat about 75 feet closer to the sea, but the deterioration of the cliffs threatened, so it was moved and restored. Illuminated in lantern light and approached by a similarly lighted pathway over a Chinese bridge, the bright red walls and green-tiled upswept roof of the Tea House must have made a stunning impression on the guests at the ball Alva gave to introduce it in 1914.

Throughout the house are memorabilia of Mrs. Vanderbilt and the Gilded Age. "Votes for Women" ironstone is in the scullery; in the small guest sitting room, pause to read the *Nautical Dictionary* in the case to the left of the door, in which a bustle is described as a "small outrigger over the stern." Open daily late Mar.–Oct. from 10 A.M.–5 P.M., and weekends January–Mar. from 10 A.M.–4 P.M. Admission is $6.50, $3 for children or by combination ticket. **Bellevue Ave. just north of Yznaga Ave.; (401) 847-1000.**

Belcourt Castle

Oliver Hazard Perry Belmont's mother had been among the first of the grand dames to bring New York high society to Newport, and in 1891 the 36-year-old bachelor built a home to fit his position in society—and his considerable fortune. It took four years, during which time the front lawn became a workshop for more than 300 stonemasons, wood carvers and other European artisans. Its interior design is more like a castle than a palace, and Belmont furnished and decorated it with his collections of medieval armor. In the windows of the French Gothic–style ballroom is America's finest collection of thirteenth-century stained glass.

Belmont lived as a king, and in an era known for its excesses, his were legendary. His stables housed 30 of the finest carriage horses in America, and they slept on pure white linen sheets embroidered with the family crest (his, not theirs). When they drew his ornate carriages, they were decked in equipment that varied with the time of day. Liveried footmen in knee breeches and powdered hair attended Belmont and his guests, standing at six-step intervals along the grand staircase, each holding a fully lit candelabra as guests proceeded to the second-floor ballroom.

Shortly after the completion of Belcourt, society queen Alva Smith Vanderbilt left Marble House and her husband to marry Belmont. No other member of society could have carried it off and kept her throne, but no one of consequence dared to drop Alva from their guest list. Besides, it was *Alva's* guest list that mattered.

This is the only one of the grand mansions still used as a private family residence (although not by the Belmonts), and the only one where you can explore at your own speed to read the placards and admire or pass by pieces as you wish, with the help of an eight-page descriptive brochure. The collections throughout the castle come from the Tuileries (the portrait of Louis XIV was cut from its frame as the palace burned), the Vatican, the Doge's Palace in Venice, Versailles, the Imperial Palace in Peking and the Temple of Amenhotep. A full gold-lined porcelain tea set was carried into battle by Napoleon (speaking of excesses). The oldest piece in the house is a tenth-century sacristy chest in the chapel. The collections range from the historic (a suit of Samurai armor presented to Belmont's grandfather, Commodore Oliver Hazard Perry, by the emperor of Japan) to the curious (a mummified crocodile) to the fascinating (a Japanese cabinet for the storage of ancestral ashes) and make Belcourt Castle well worth seeing as a museum in addition to its interest as a mansion.

Although you are not required to go in a group, tours are offered hourly from 9:30 A.M. until 4:30 P.M. in the summer, three times a day the rest of the year. Theme tours and programs focus on ghosts and on French art and culture; candlelight tours highlight the Winter Festival and the Christmas season. The castle is open from 9 A.M.–5 P.M. daily June–mid-Oct, from 10 A.M.–5 P.M. daily in Apr. and May and from 10 A.M.–4 P.M. late Oct., Nov., Feb. and Mar. It is closed in Jan. Admission is $6.50 for adults, $5.50 for seniors and college students, $4.00 for ages 13 to 18 and $2.00 for children ages six to 12. Guided tours are $1.00 extra, and for $10.00 you can have a private tour for as many as nine people. Theme tours are $12.50, and both these and the private tours include refreshments and a slide presentation. Belcourt Castle is at the southern end of Bellevue Ave; **(401) 846-0669.**

The Breakers

Commodore Vanderbilt built his family's wealth on steamships, the fur trade in the Northwest and railroads. His grandson, Cornelius, built this summer place in 1893–1895, the largest, grandest and most expensive of the mansions, although its cost was a closely guarded secret at the time. They didn't want it to become the standard; no one should be able to say that their cottage cost more than the Vanderbilts'. But no expense was spared. The cottage Richard Morris Hunt designed for the clifftop setting had 70 rooms, 33 of them just to house the staff, most of whom traveled from New York with the family each summer.

Its sheer size and opulence are so overwhelming that it's almost easy to miss the wealth of decorative detail that has been lavished on almost every surface. Guided tours point out the highlights and give some family

245

Cornelius Vanderbilt spared no expense in building The Breakers.

history but can't possibly describe all the house's features. The most spectacular room is the Great Hall, with its fantastic cornice, grand staircase and glass wall with ocean views through the two-story loggia. The formal dining room is so ornately embellished that the eye can find no place to rest.

While these rooms may be the most impressive, more endearing are some of the less ornate family rooms and some of the smaller gemlike rooms, such as the ladies' reception room adjoining the front entrance. Its carved and gilt paneling was commissioned by Marie Antoinette for the Paris home of her godchild. The only glimpse we get backstairs is the enormous kitchen, with its copper pans and giant central table set on a floor of terra-cotta tile. The stove is a marvel. This, and the nearby pantries, are as fascinating as the house itself.

Stroll in the grounds, designed by the firm of Frederick Law Olmsted, and to the Queen Anne playhouse between the house and the side gate. The mansion has an elevator to the second floor—those with impaired mobility should call ahead; **(401) 847-6543.** Open from the end of March through the end of October daily from 10 A.M.–5 P.M. In the summer it is open until 6 P.M. on Saturdays. In November it is open only on weekends, Veteran's Day and the Friday following Thanksgiving Day from 10 A.M.–4 P.M. In December it is decorated for Christmas and open daily from 10 A.M.–4

The Elms has three grand doorways, spaced to allow three carriages to deliver passengers simultaneously.

P.M., except for December 24 and 25, when it is closed. Admission is $10 for adults, $3.50 for children ages six to 11. Combination tickets with other mansions range from $12.50 for any two buildings to $35.50 for all eight Preservation Society properties. Admission to The Breakers includes the stables. **Ochre Point Ave. at Ruggles Ave.; (401) 847-1000.**

The Breakers Stable

The brick stable and carriage house is a mile from the mansion, on Coggeshall Ave. It not only housed the coaches and 28 horses but their grooms as well. Displayed here are about 30 vehicles, including the famous Vanderbilt coach "Venture," livery equipment and a collection of memorabilia related to the Vanderbilt family. The stable is open daily from late May until Labor Day from 10 A.M.–5 P.M. Admission is included in the price of The Breakers; separately it is $3.50. **Coggeshall Ave. at Bateman Ave.; (401) 847-1000.**

The Elms

Designed by the architect who later created Harvard's monumental Widener Library, The Elms has a classical balanced design, with three grand doorways spaced so that three carriages could arrive and discharge passengers simultaneously.

An elegant main stairway rises on columns and supports of dramatically veined Breccia marble, whose lacy effect is echoed in the delicate scrollwork of the wrought-iron railing. The ballroom, like much of the rest of the house, is bright and light, with white-on-off-white decor and rounded corners.

The grounds and gardens of The Elms are filled with exotic trees (labeled for the botanically inclined), which include ginkgo, linden and weeping beeches, but not the handsome elms for which it was named. Throughout are fountains and statuary, and two small tea houses flank the entrance to a formal sunken begonia garden with patterned boxwood hedges. Open daily May–Oct. from 10 A.M.–5 P.M., weekends only in Jan.–Apr. and Nov. In December the mansion is decorated for Christmas and open daily except on Dec. 24 and 25.

An elevator provides access to the second floor but is too narrow for some wheelchairs. Admission is $7.50 (children $3), or by combination ticket. Located **on Bellevue Ave between Dixon St. and Bellevue Ct.; (401) 847-1000.**

Rosecliff

One of Newport's most legendary hostesses and characters was Tessie Oelrichs, from San Francisco. Her father had made his fortune from the Comstock Lode, and with this inheritance Tessie became one of the triumvirate of Newport women who shared another sort of legacy—that of Mrs. Astor's rule on society. Tessie Oelrichs reigned from Rosecliff, one of the later, and most livable, of the mansions. Like Marble House, it was modeled on Versailles, this time on the Grand Trianon at Versailles, but this was the work of Stanford White, the most fashionable architect at the turn of the century.

The house was designed for entertaining and had Newport's largest ballroom, which is still used for formal occasions, such as the Gatsby Ball in mid-July. Along with the largest ballroom, Rosecliff has Newport's most gracefully elegant grand staircase. It rises in sweeping baroque curves, its steps narrowing as they rise to a landing where they divide and continue their long flowing curve to the floor above. The Preservation Society has wisely chosen *not* to decorate this open airy space as Mrs. Oelrichs did, with masses of potted palms and large flowering plants.

On the south side of the house, one of the many rose gardens that once surrounded it has been restored with tea roses and climbing everblooming varieties. The house was used in the filming of *The Great Gatsby*. Open late Mar.–Oct., daily from 10 A.M.–5 P.M. Admission is $6.50 ($3 children), or by combination ticket. **Bellevue Ave at Marine Ave.; (401) 847-1000.**

Scenic Drive

Whether for commerce or recreation, it is the ocean that has always drawn people to Newport, and for a continuing series of sea views, as well as a look at some of the shore estates,

The sunporch at Hammersmith Farm overlooks Narragansett Bay.

make the circuit around the southern tip of Aquidneck Island along Ocean Dr. Begin at the harbor, where America's Cup Ave. joins Thames St. Follow Thames to Wellington Ave. and turn right. In a short distance the **Ida Lewis Yacht Club** (named for its heroic lighthouse keeper) can be seen on its tiny island, connected to the shore by a long bridge. After the road turns inland, turn right again, along Harrison Ave. Just to the left of the entrance to **Fort Adams State Park,** a large house sits alone on a rise. This is **Eisenhower House,** the summer White House during his presidency. Coincidentally, the next public entrance is to **Hammersmith Farm,** also on the right (see page **228**), the summer White House during the administration following Eisenhower's. This whole area was part of an enormous farm owned by Colonial Governor William Brenton, site of the orchards where the Rhode Island Greening apple was developed.

Just beyond Hammersmith Farm, the well-marked route turns onto Ridge Rd., past the twin-towered **Oceancliff,** one of the first mansions built on Ocean Drive during the Gilded Age, and the **Castle Hill Coast Guard Station** (see page **229**). You can park at the station to follow the path to **Castle Hill Light,** which gets its name from the site of the first fortifications built to defend the bay.

Brenton Point Park is a good place to stop for easy access to the wave-battered, rocky shore. Ocean Ave., which the Ocean Dr. has now become, continues along small bays, across inlets and past oceanside mansions, beginning with **Wildacre** on the right. This estate was designed by a California firm just after the turn of the century for Albert Olmsted, the landscape architect. The difference between its lines and those of contemporary eastern architects' works is quite noticeable. A series of "cottages" on the ocean side follow one another almost too quickly to see by car—a good reason for doing this route by bicycle—ranging from a playhouse built among the rocks (part of a long-gone estate), a French provincial–style estate entered through an arched gate and several English- and French-style manor houses. On the left, past the pond, is **Crossways,** the colonial revival mansion built by Stanford White's firm for Mrs. Stuyvesant Fish, who shared the throne of Newport's elite with Tessie Oelrichs and Alva Belmont (formerly Vanderbilt) following Mrs. Astor. The Crossways ballroom, already enormous, could be extended by opening nearly the entire first floor. The Harvest Festival Ball held here ended the social season each fall.

After Bailey's Beach, Ocean Ave. turns sharply right and then left, as it joins Newport's best known street, Bellevue Ave., past the most glittering of the mansions and back into the harbor area.

Where to Stay

Accommodations in Newport are scarce during the summer and on weekends year-round, really scarce on summer weekends and virtually unavailable during big event weekends in the summer. In other words, plan ahead a little at any time of year, and a lot at the busiest times. And don't limit yourself to rooms right in Newport; Middletown and Portsmouth offer lodgings that are close by and often less expensive. The rates we mention in the dollar-sign codes may be confusing, since they will show a tremendous price range. This is because the prices drop dramatically in the winter and are always higher on weekends. So when you see

$$–$$$$, expect rates in the lower range to be midweek in the off-season (usually November through April) and the higher to be for weekends May through October. Most Newport inns have a minimum stay of two nights on weekends, some have three nights on holiday weekends. But you should always ask. In the winter, several establishments join in a Newport Getaways program, with rates that include extras, such as admission to one of the mansions; call the **Visitors Bureau** at **(800) 326-6030 for details.**

Unless you know exactly where you want to stay, you might consider the very useful services of **Taylor-Made,** a reservation service representing over 125 lodgings, from the simplest B&Bs and motels to luxury hotels, inns and condo rentals. Karen Taylor has built a highly respected business on helping visitors find exactly the right room in the right price range, often on very short notice and at very busy seasons. She can save you hours (and dollars) worth of phone calls, because she already knows who's full and who has rooms. This lodging service costs the traveler nothing. Karen will also make dinner reservations and advise you on events and which mansions will be open. **(800) 848-8848** or **(401) 847-6820.**

Wherever you stay, you will find Newport innkeepers among the most genial and hospitable anywhere. At all but the big hotels, you'll almost immediately feel like a house guest staying with old friends.

THE WATERFRONT

Rose Island Lighthouse— $$$ to $$$$

Surely the most romantic of all Newport lodgings is on lonely Rose Island, owned by the Rose Island Lighthouse Foundation, which saved the historic light from demolition and preserved it as a museum-cum-bed-and-breakfast. The only habitable building on the island—without television or other reminders of the modern world—the keeper's cottage attached to the light tower is straight out of the

248

1920s. This is the real thing, much as it was when the last family kept the light there (see page **230** for more about its history). The wind howls around the tower and shakes the windowpanes in the winter, but inside the cottage is cozy, with a woodstove in the kitchen and the light of gas lamps. Pack a basket of food from one of Newport's several emporia, a bottle of good wine and chocolates for dessert and spend a romantic evening before snuggling into the brass bed under a real patchwork quilt. Contact the **Rose Island Lighthouse Foundation, P.O. Box 1419, Newport 02840; (401) 847-4242.** The island is reached by launch from **Oldport Marine, (401) 847-9109,** or from Jamestown's **Conanicut Marina, (401) 423-1556.** Dinghies and canoes may be beached except between April 1 and July 15, when they would disturb nesting areas. If lighthouse life appeals to you after you've stayed a night, sign on as keeper for a week. You'll be responsible for about an hour a day of work; pay is $600 per week (plus transportation to the island) in the winter, more in the summer.

Admiral Fitzroy Inn—$$$ to $$$$

The location couldn't be more convenient, on Lower Thames St. facing the harbor, amid a row of popular restaurants and shops. Unlike many of the other fine area inns, the Fitzroy welcomes children. Each guest room has a refrigerator, TV, air-conditioning, hair dryer, electric teakettle and tea selection, as well as a bathtub and beautiful hand-painted designs decorating the walls. We like rooms 18 and 19, on the fourth floor, which reward the exercise of getting there with a private deck overlooking the bay. Another deck is shared by all the guests. The inn's elevator (rare in a historic building) goes as far as the third floor. One room is fully wheelchair-accessible. Breakfasts in the bright first-floor dining room include a hot dish each morning. **398 Thames St.; (401) 848-8000 or (800) 343-2863.**

The Francis Malbone House—$$$$ to $$$$$

This is as close as you will get to living in a museum—a meticulously restored 1760 colonial mansion, carefully maintained. One of only two (the other one *is* a museum) remaining of the shipowners' mansions that once lined Lower Thames St., the Francis Malbone House is adjoined by an 1860 counting house—now a charming suite attached by a corridor—and a new addition in the back, which adds new rooms without sacrificing historic integrity. Homes along here—this one included—were equipped with underground passages from the docks, where contraband could be unloaded out of sight of the revenue men. Today things are quieter, with two drawing rooms for comfortable relaxation where guests find books, games, magazines and helpful information on local activities. Guest rooms are individually decorated in the uncluttered elegance characteristic of the federal and colonial eras, with period antiques and fine reproductions. Fireplaces work: There are few greater treats in life than returning here on a snowy evening and curling up amid the exquisite bed linens and comforters in the flickering light of a fire. Full breakfasts served in the formal dining room include the often hilarious and lively conversation of the innkeepers, who give the inn its personal warmth. It's not the least expensive place in town but an experience few can match. In the winter, three nights are the price of two—bringing the rate as low as $65 a night per couple, an extraordinary bargain for a historic property. The new addition has whirlpool tubs and a fully wheelchair-accessible room, plus a room with a kitchenette. **392 Thames St.; (401) 846-0392.**

Newport Bay Club and Hotel—$$$ to $$$$

The historic stone mill building, built by the same man who constructed Fort Adams, has been nicely renovated into a comfortable all-suite hotel. No location is more central than this waterfront corner where Memorial Blvd.

meets Thames St. and America's Cup Ave. Below are the shops of Perry Mill Market, but guest rooms are quiet and the larger townhouse suites have balconies overlooking the bay. Marble baths have large whirlpool tubs. Cable and HBO are included, as is Continental breakfast. Matched pine furnishings add warmth to the good-sized rooms. Townhouse suites are large, with spiral staircases connecting the two levels.

On the back, overlooking the bay, a public deck gives guests a place to watch the sunset. On Monday evenings there is a cocktail reception for all guests. Day permits to a local health club are available for $5. Off-season packages include extras such as meals at local restaurants or on board the *Star Clipper* dinner train. The lobby is on the first floor, off the Perry Mill Market, at **337 Thames St.; (401) 849-8600.**

250 Newport Harbor Hotel and Marina—$$$ to $$$$

A good location right on the waterfront in the midst of all the harbor activity, and a staff whose hospitality would credit a small luxury inn are the main draws of this large (133 rooms) hotel. Its casual restaurant and heated indoor pool overlooking the bay make it popular for families with children. A 60-slip marina provides dockage for guests arriving by boat. Rooms have coffeemakers, hair dryers, movies and direct-dial phones, which are convertible to modem. A few refrigerators are available. Rooms are fairly standard: pleasantly decorated and bright, all newly renovated. **49 America's Cup Ave.; (401) 847-9000** or **(800) 955-2558.**

THE MANSION AND CLIFF WALK AREA

The Victorian Ladies—$$$ to $$$$

When you mention this traditional bed and breakfast to anyone in Newport, the first thing they say is "You should see their gardens!" And indeed you should, but the pleasures of The Victorian Ladies do not end with the carefully tended grounds. Rooms are decorated in rich Victorian colors—forest greens and warm burgundy red—but are restrained in their furnishings, with four-poster beds, sumptuous pillows, gold-framed prints and enough decorative touches to lighten the atmosphere but remain far short of frilly. We like room 2, with its burgundy on burgundy wide-striped wallpaper, rose carpet, high-canopied bed and sitting-room alcove. Most rooms have queen-sized beds and all are decorated differently. Framed antique linens decorate walls and others are used in guest rooms. Breakfast includes hot dishes as well as homebaked breads. Gardeners—and anyone who loves flowers—will want to come in the spring and summer, when the surrounding gardens are at their peak. Located at **63 Memorial Blvd.** between Bellevue Ave. and Easton's Beach, the inn is three blocks from the start of the cliff walk and from the beach (saving the hefty $10 parking fee there in the height of summer); **(401) 849-9960.**

Elm Tree Cottage—$$$$

Perhaps it's better not to see all the rooms in this magnificently restored summer "cottage" designed by William Ralph Emerson, since each is so different and so attractive that a choice could become impossible. The Library, for example, on the first floor, has a masculine decor, large windows and overlooks the garden. The Tiffany Suite has a bathroom the size of most hotel rooms, a fully furnished vanity, antique linens and two sitting areas. Throughout the inn are custom-made, hand-carved Louis XV beds, working fireplaces, fine antiques and stained glass windows (the owners are preeminent stained glass artists), as well as an aura of sunlight and cheerful hospitality. This is the Gilded Age at its best, and we had difficulty resisting the temptation to curl up in the sun-filled morning room and forget about sight-seeing. Breakfast is served on pink china and includes a hot entree along with home-baked breads. The inn is closed in January. In a quiet neighborhood overlooking Easton's Pond, and two blocks from the beach, at **336 Gibbs Ave; (401) 849-1610** or **(800) 882-3ELM.**

Ivy Lodge—$$$ to $$$$

One of the few lodgings in the center of the mansion district, Ivy Lodge was designed by Stanford White, and in it you will see the same attention to architectural detail that characterized his work on the more famous "cottages" in the neighborhood. Upstairs hallways form balconies overlooking the tall oak-paneled entry hall. Room 1 has a striking oak bed and a fireplace, room 4 a mahogany sleigh bed and an adjoining smaller room ideal for families. A full breakfast is served in the formal dining room, amid crystal and silver service. Thoughtful touches for guests include beach towels and chairs, bicycles and fresh flowers in the rooms. Movie fans should know that Arnold Schwarzenegger stayed here while filming *True Lies*. A block from both Bellevue and Narragansett Aves. at **12 Clay St.; (401) 849-6865.**

Cliffside Inn—$$$$ to $$$$$

The history of this elegantly appointed mansion, close to Cliff Walk and downtown Newport, is hanging on every wall. Built by a governor of Maryland, the house was for many years the home of the eccentric heiress Beatrice Turner, who painted extraordinary self-portraits without formal training. (Her father made her drop out of art school when he discovered they used live nude models). The owners have collected a number of her paintings and information on this unusual artist, which they love to share with guests. Victorian throughout, but not heavy or dark, each room is entirely different in character and furnishings: Some have skylights, one a steam bath, one a double marble shower, some VCRs and all are furnished in antiques. For a romantic retreat for two, ask for the Tower Suite in its own separate little building, one room per

floor. Fresh fruit, complimentary soda, sherry and appetizers are all included in the not-in-considerable price. An off-season special offers three midweek nights for the price of two. Located just off Memorial Blvd. a short walk from Easton's Beach and overlooking the Cliff Walk at 2 **Seaview Ave.; (401) 847-1811** or **(800) 845-1811.**

THE HILL

Villa Liberte—$$$$

In a town full of Victorian and colonial buildings, this beautifully restored art deco inn is a breath of fresh air. The villa's checkered past—it was a tearoom for fashionable ladies by day and a "retreat" for their husbands after dark—only makes staying here more fun. The decor is stylishly flamboyant (but never gaudy), with an emphasis on comfort. Bold black-and-white tile walls surround sinks set in arched alcoves in some of the rooms. Each floor has a bright sitting room and access to a secluded terrace behind the inn. Rooms are large: Some are suites with separate sitting rooms and small refrigerators. The location could hardly be better—on a quiet street one block from Bellevue Ave. The full concierge service is especially welcome in a city where dinner reservations are hard to get, and we've found the host's advice on restaurants to be golden. **22 Liberty St.; (401) 846-7444** or **(800) 392-3717.**

The Pilgrim House—$$ to $$$$

Spring St., only a short walk up the hill from the busy waterfront, is lined with colonial and Victorian homes interspersed with antique shops and small craft studios—a perfect location for this casual, hospitable inn. A fire welcomes guests to the Victorian parlor in the cold months, a pleasant gathering place where lemonade or sherry and shortbread is offered in the late afternoon. Rooms are comfortably furnished, airy and bright, with tasteful, understated decor. The third-floor breakfast room adjoins a deck with cafe tables that overlooks the waterfront and sunsets. A vivacious innkeeper puts guests instantly at ease and is usually busy planning some special package weekend, which may include a Victorian Christmas celebration with carolers on the stairs, a romantic getaway or a seminar with an artist or writer. Two of the 11 rooms share a bath; all others are private. **123 Spring St.; (401) 846-0040 or (800) 525-8373.**

Hydrangea House—$$$ to $$$$

Six beautifully decorated rooms, some overlooking Bellevue Ave. and one with a private deck in the garden, are in a restored 1876 townhouse five minutes from the first in the row of mansions. Fine antiques add the finishing touches to each room—a spinet writing desk in one, a cameo chair in another—and works by Rhode Island artists decorate the walls. In fact, the first floor is an art gallery where breakfast is served in the winter; in the summer guests relax over the full buffet served on the verandah overlooking the flower gardens. Raspberry pancakes are among the specialties. Prices vary, with one quite small room well below the prices of the others: $55 in the winter and $89 in summer. The newest room has a separate entrance from the garden and is suitable for children. **16 Bellevue Ave.; (401) 846-4435 or (800) 945-4667.**

Mill Street Inn—$$$ to $$$$

The transformation of this nineteenth-century mill building into a stylish, comfortable all-suite hotel, is remarkable. What could easily have been barlike spaces with impossibly high ceilings have become spacious and inviting contemporary suites by the judicious use of partitions, ample track lighting, large artwork and oversized sofas. Brick walls, huge windows and wooden beams have been retained to relieve the expanses of white walls, and in the townhouse suites spiral staircases connect

the two levels. Some suites have refrigerators and microwaves, one is fully handicapped-accessible. Continental breakfast, TV with HBO and afternoon tea are included. The use of a nearby fitness facility is available at a small extra charge. Special off-season and midweek packages include dinner at top Newport restaurants. **75 Mill St., (401) 849-9500 or (800) 392-1316.**

Admiral Farragut Inn—$$ to $$$$

The owner of the Admiral Farragut is a talented painter, and the whimsical side of her work is displayed in the wall paintings here. In room 4, for example, a tree grows in the closet. This historic house, where General Rochambeau's aides-de-camp were quartered during the Revolution, sits in the center of one of the city's most historic—and centrally located—neighborhoods. Furnished in simple colonial styles, with a combination of antiques and handmade furnishings, the rooms are restful, bright and very comfortable. Shaker pieces complement the fine antique architectural features, which include 12-over-12 windows. In-room phones and full air-conditioning bring the comforts up to date, but the atmosphere is well preserved. A Continental breakfast is served buffet-style. **31 Clarke St.; (401) 848-8000 or (800) 343-2863.**

Admiral Benbow Inn—$$ to $$$

High on its hill, between Bellevue Ave. and the waterfront, Admiral Benbow Inn occupies the former home of a prosperous sea captain of the mid-1800s. The decor hints at the house's past, with marine art and a collection of old barometers. Rooms are spacious, furnished with comfortable wing chairs, four-poster beds and fine fabrics. Our favorite is the west-facing room 5, with its fainting couch and bay of four Palladian windows, although the third-floor room with its own deck and waterfront sunset view is a contender, especially in the summer. A buffet breakfast is included, served in the bright cafe-style common room on the ground floor. Afternoon tea is served, and there is concierge service. Although homes on the Hill catch the pleasant summer breezes off Narragansett Bay, the inn is fully air-conditioned. **93 Pelham St.,** just below Touro Park; **(401) 848-80000** or **(800) 343-2863.**

The Inntowne—$$$$

Larger than an inn, but too personal and warm to seem like a hotel, The Inntowne has the best features of each: afternoon tea, breakfast amid antiques and the personal attention of a professional staff. Beautifully decorated rooms range from bright floral prints to understated deep colors, with four-poster beds, coordinated linens and quality colonial reproductions. The TV in the guest lounge has a movie library, and in good weather guests can enjoy a rooftop deck with lounge chairs and cafe tables. In November, December and January, when Newport is alive with Christmas and winter festivals, the inn offers special packages with substantial savings. The main drawback here is the $10 a day fee for parking. Right in the center of town at busy **Thames and Mary Sts.; (401) 846-9200.**

The Hotel Viking—$$ to $$$$

This classic brick hotel was built in the 1920s to accommodate out-of-town guests of the mansion-owners. The lobby still rings of that white-paneled grace, with original chandeliers and woodwork and a wonderful brass mail chute beside the elevators. Although this atmosphere may sound a bit formal, the staff is friendly and helpful. Rooms in the original building are smaller than those in the newer wing, but they have more character. Decor in both is attractive, with floral wallpapers and linens. Dataports and refrigerators are available, and the roomy suites have hair dryers and VCRs. The pool and exercise room are in a bright greenhouselike area with large windows. Off-season rates are among the lowest in Newport, as low as $39 midweek. The address is fashionable, at **One Bellevue Ave.; (401) 847-3300** or **(800) 556-7126.**

The Melville House—$$ to $$$$

On one of Newport's quietest intown streets, only a block off busy Thames, this 1750s inn quartered the French troops of General Rochambeau during the Revolution and retains the simple understated charm of the colonial period. Rooms with both shared and private baths are tastefully decorated, and guest services include afternoon tea (with homemade soup on cold days), sherry and bicycles for loan. Breakfasts may include hot cornbread, buttermilk biscuits, sourdough pancakes with fresh fruit, scones and even traditional Rhode Island jonnycakes (which are very hard to find), as well as stuffed French toast and homemade granola. In the winter only a fireplace suite comes complete with champagne, after-dinner drinks, breakfast in bed and, of course, a warming fire to come home to. Located at **39 Clarke St.; (401) 847-0640.**

THE POINT

The Willows of Newport—$$$ to $$$$

This place isn't for everyone. It's for couples only—no kids, no singles. Its owner has designed it to be unabashedly romantic. If little stuffed bunny rabbits in adorable poses, seven pillows, layers of frills and breakfast in bed delivered by a woman in top hat and tails (after a rather incongruous wake-up call of piped-in music and a Newport history lesson) strike you as perfect for your anniversary, this is the place. It's highly recommended in various lists of romantic inns. The garden is a lovely oasis with a heart-shaped pool; fresh flowers decorate the rooms year-round. The very accommodating owner has one of the best concierge services in town. **8 Willow St, in the Point; (401) 846-5486.**

253

Sanford-Covell Villa Marina—$$$ to $$$$$

While the Francis Malbone House gives guests a chance to live in a museum-quality colonial home, the Sanford-Covell House actually was a museum, owned by the Society for the Preservation of New England Antiquities. One of the finest examples anywhere of the decorative styles of the 1870s that influenced Richard Morris Hunt, the house was sold back to the Covell family under a stewardship program that protects it and allows its use as a B&B. A 35-foot-high entrance hall, its fine wood details highlighted by painted decoration, is heightened visually with projecting balconies, but the hall pales beside the house's most outstanding feature—the painted and stenciled dining room ceiling. How guests can concentrate on their breakfast coffee under such a glorious canopy is beyond us. Speaking of coffee, it is made here on a 1710 Dutch lowboy, one of the house's 90 pieces of historically significant furniture. Rooms vary greatly both in decor and the state of their restoration, but all retain the original feel of the Victorian family cottage. Some, such as the Covell Room, are large, bright, beautifully decorated and have full ocean views in two directions (the house sits on the water), while others are smaller, less opulent and somewhat dark. Our favorite, The Playroom, is one of the smallest, and with a shared bath, but snuggles into a gable, with its own balcony overlooking the front hall. For anyone who loves nineteenth century decorative arts and antiques and wants to live among them, this house is a dream. The innkeeper is more than willing to show all the available rooms, so we suggest stopping by in advance to select one you like. A swimming pool overlooks the bay and sunset. Located in the Point just north of the Visitors Center, at **72 Washington St. (401) 847-0206.**

Stella Maris Inn—$$$ to $$$$

Large rooms are decorated in French Victorian style with bold flowered fabrics and light, airy colors. The red-stone mansion was built in the 1850s as a summer home. Its broad front porch offers a good view of the sun setting over the bay. Continental breakfast includes homemade breads and fresh fruit. Conveniently located for those arriving from the Jamestown bridge, at **91 Washington St.; (401) 849-2862.**

Where to Eat

Newport restaurants follow the enlightened Continental custom of posting the day's menu outside. As a result, menu browsing is a popular pastime beginning late in the afternoon and continuing through the evening. On weekends in the summer, however, you would be wise to browse early and call for a reservation at the restaurant of your choice. A number of the more popular places do not accept reservations, but if you are staying at an inn or hotel, ask your host to call for you. Knowing the right people still works wonders in Newport.

BREAKFAST OR LUNCH AND CAFES

For breakfast, see also Asterix and Obelix (page **259**) and Muriel's (page **256**).

Franklin Spa—$

Diner food featuring hot muffins and home-style soups is served in a bright corner storefront, a local favorite. Breakfast is served all day, which makes sense, since the fruit-pancake plates are big enough for lunch. Open Mon.–Sat. from 6:30 A.M.–3:00 P.M., Sun. until 2 P.M. **229 Spring St. at Franklin St.; (401) 847-3540.**

Cappuccino's—$

An upscale breakfast spot with white linens and a patio of wrought-iron garden furniture, Cappuccino's serves French pastries, gigantic sandwiches and Sunday brunch dishes such as

254

stuffed French toast. Like most other cafe-style breakfast spots, it's open for afternoon coffee stops as well and is especially known for its tortes. Open Tues.–Sat. from 7:30 A.M.–9 P.M., Sun. from 8 A.M.–5 P.M. and Mon. from 7:30 A.M.–5 P.M., with brunch served until 2 P.M. on Sun. **92 Williams St., just off Bellevue Ave. opposite the Casino; (401) 846-7145.**

The Wharf Pub and Restaurant—$

Booths and tables in a publike atmosphere inside, umbrella-topped tables on a balcony outdoors, The Wharf draws a young crowd for its wide selection of beers and ales, which include specials from more than 10 micro-breweries. The sandwiches—club, Monte Cristo, roast beef, pastrami, veggie pockets—are big, and the chili is hearty, spicy and filled with meat. Expect a wait here at lunchtime on a summer day—it's also a popular spot for a beer and nachos after a long day at the mansions. It's open from 11:30–A.M.–10 P.M. daily. **On Bowen's Wharf; (401) 846-9233.**

St. Elmo's Galley—$

Fresh-baked muffins, homestyle soups, chowder, chili and other old favorites are served at the lunch counter in the lobby of the Seaman's Church Institute and in the plain, bright dining room. Hearty sandwiches of hand-carved roast beef, turkey or ham are $4.75, ham and egg breakfast sandwiches are $2.75. Open daily from 7 A.M.–3 P.M. from 8 A.M.–4 P.M. in the winter, the Galley is a good value with substantial servings at low prices. In the **Institute Building at Market Sq. at Bowen's Wharf; (401) 847-4260.**

Espresso Yourself Cafe—$

Lots of coffee flows here, brewed from a variety of beans and in about every way imaginable, from macchiato to mocha. It's the place for a Continental breakfast, with muffins, bagels, cinnamon rolls and scones to go with the coffee, or an afternoon break for carrot cake and other sweets. In the **Perry Mill Market, at the corner of Thames St. and America's Cup Ave.,** at the foot of Memorial Blvd.

Via Via—$

Brick oven pizza with toppings that range from fresh tomatoes and sausage to artichoke hearts and wild mushrooms is the big draw in this informal pizzeria. It's a good lunch or snack value at $2.70 a slice, and always good quality. Along with the take-out section, there's a traditional dining room where you can order sandwiches (Italian sausage in a rich marinara sauce is a favorite), pasta dishes and standard seafood offerings. It hardly seems to close at all—open daily from 6 A.M. until 2 A.M. **372 Lower Thames St., at the corner of Ann St.; (401) 848-0830.**

Gary's Handy Lunch—$

Now in a shiny new red-and-chrome-diner atmosphere, Gary's still opens at 5 A.M. and serves breakfast until its 3 P.M. closing. At lunch it's standard burgers and sandwiches fare. In the summer Gary's stays open Fri.–Sun. evenings with dinner specials. **462 Thames St.; (401) 847-8381.**

DINNER

White Horse Tavern—$$$$ to $$$$$

Not only the oldest place to dine in Newport but quite possibly the country, this is the oldest operating tavern in the United States opened prior to 1673. Local story has it that the location of the Colony House, once Rhode Island's capitol, was chosen so as to be within easy distance of this tavern. It offers a real New England experience in an authentic setting. There's nothing stodgy about the menu, and the favorites of its colonial past are served with style and interesting touches. Roast pork, for example, has become roasted three peppercorn pork loin accompanied by garlic

255

The Rhode Island Guide

Ships of all kinds put in for repairs at Newport's shipyards.

256

mashed potatoes and baby vegetables on a roasted shallot reduction. Beef Wellington and rack of lamb done to a turn bring locals back time after time; this is the preferred spot for very special occasions.

An extensive wine list includes a wide variety of imports along with domestic choices. Decor is largely original dark tavern wood lit only by candlelight, but elegant with crisp linens and fine professional service. It is handicapped-accessible. Open for lunch, dinner and Sunday brunch. Proper dress is required at dinner. **Marlborough St. at Farewell, near the northern end of Thames St. and the Visitor's Center; (401) 849-3600.**

The Place at Yesterday's— $$$ to $$$$

The presentation of each dish here is flawless, as are the subtle and often surprising blends of flavors. Impeccably fresh ingredients are blended with an eye to the overall effect. Crab ravioli includes ginger and chèvre, grilled quail is served on a corn pudding with a marmalade of Vidalia onions. Fresh halibut is pan-seared and served on a creamy sweet red pepper risotto in a fennel and tomato broth with littlenecks. This is accompanied by a single skewer of shrimp and scallop kabob, grilled andouille sausage and asparagus. Grilled beef tender-

loin is served over black bean chili with sweet potato puree. We dream about the signature dish, lamb roasted in a pecan crust, which adds crunch and flavor to each bite. Presentation is a highlight.

The atmosphere is upbeat and lively, with a wine bar and dining areas on split levels. Service is both smooth and very well informed. They offer 19 wines by the glass; the full wine list has well over 50 choices. Open for dinner only from 5:30–10 P.M. (10:30 on weekends); closed Mon. year-round and Sun. in the winter. We advise reservations. The restaurant is wheelchair-accessible. **28 Washington Sq., close to the Brick Market; (401) 847-0166.**

Tucker's—$$

A slightly funky decor of mixed mega-art on red walls, bistro-paper-over-linen table covers and unmatched table lighting sets the tone for the unexpected here, but the menu offers few surprises. Beef Bourguignon is pleasantly topped with a saffron pastry, flank steak is grilled with lemon pepper, salmon is glazed with sweet dilled mustard. The grilled breast of chicken is tasty in a creamy sauce of jalapeño and cilantro. Try taking your own glasses and corkscrew. Desserts are an interesting variety: banana bread pudding, strawberry-kiwi custard tart, profiteroles. The espresso arrives hot. **150 Broadway, a short walk from Washington Square; (401) 846-3449.**

Muriel's—$

From stuffed peppers to roasted quahogs, Muriel's serves comfortable dishes everyone likes, including a chowder that's been a consistent winner in Newport's Chowder Cook-off. It's a popular spot to meet in the afternoon for a coffee or tea with bread pudding, cheesecake or carrot cake, and it's where other restaurant owners come for chicken and mushroom crepes, huevos rancheros or omelets. Breakfast is served Mon.–Sat. from 8:30–11 A.M., lunch Mon.–Sat. from noon–5 P.M., dinner Sun.–Thur. from 5–9 P.M. and Fri.–Sat. until 10, Sunday brunch from 9 A.M.–2 P.M. They offer a dinner theater special with the Jane Pickens across the street: Dinner and movie is $11.95. If you're in by 6 P.M. you'll be out in time for the 7 P.M. show, in before 8 P.M. and you'll make the 9:30. Fully handicapped-accessible. **Spring and Touro Sts.; (401) 849-7780.**

Salvation Cafe—$ to $$

The funky decor here looks as though it has been put together from garage sales, but it works. The food is good, a blend of different cuisines and fresh ingredients: the jerked chicken is nicely spiced and served with a fruit sauce for contrast. A courtyard is open in the summer; bring your own wine. Open Tues.–Thur. from 5:30–10 P.M., Fri.– Sat. from 5:30–10:30 P.M., Sun. from 5–9:30 P.M., Sat. and Sun. brunch from 9 A.M.–2 P.M. **140 Broadway; (401) 847-2620.**

Vanderbilt's—$$ to $$$

A classic hotel dining room, but far from stodgy, with dishes such as filet of sole stuffed with lobster and scallops and baked in a piquant buerre blanc. Begin with artichoke hearts filled with Boursin and simmered in white wine. The menu is heavy on beef, with some chicken as well as seafood. A wine list includes about 30 selections from France, Italy and Australia. Open Mon.–Thur. from 5–9 P.M., Sat. and Sun. from 5–10 P.M. Open weekends only Nov.–Apr. In the **Hotel Viking at One Bellevue Ave.; (401) 847-3300.**

Pizza Lucia—$ to $$, Zia Lionella—$$

Overlooking the busy wharf area of Thames St., Pizza Lucia and its adjoining restaurant, Zia Lionella, serve Bolognese specialties, including a fried pizza called crescentina. We go for their "Piatto Unico," a full country-style dinner of penne in a vegetable sauce, chicken breast sautéed with Marsala and sage, roasted potatoes and fresh cheese—a plateful indeed for $16.50. Vegetables are very good here; we suggest ordering the appetizer of three of their vegetable side dishes—your choice—as an accompaniment to dinner. The chef goes easy on cholesterol without sacrificing any of the fine Bolognese flavors.

The setting is bright and upbeat, with green-tinted wood and sunflower wallpaper in the pizzeria and red-and-white check in the restaurant. Flowers decorate the walls and tables. Genial proprietors from Bologna add to the friendly atmosphere. Bring wine to either place. Open Tues. and Wed for lunch from noon until 3:30 P.M., Tues.–Fri. from 5:50 until 10 P.M., Sat. from noon–10 P.M. and Sun. from 11 A.M.–10 P.M. Closed Mon. except holidays. **190 Thames St.; (401) 847-6355.**

Newport Blues Cafe—$$ to $$$

The striking decor will knock your socks off, with its cobalt blue carpet and banquette upholstery, dark wood and brass appointments, fireplace and grand staircase. Happily, the food is good, too. Appetizers are generous: The pan-fried crab cakes with fresh melon salsa are ample for lunch. Shellfish is cooked perfectly. A good variety of the more than 60 wines on their list are available by the glass, priced from $3.50. There is a large selection of ales. The bar is spectacular—even those who balk at sitting at bars will be tempted by this gleaming wood beauty. In keeping with Newport's long jazz tradition, they offer blues and jazz Thur.–Sun. after 9 P.M. The restaurant has full wheelchair access from the parking lot beside it. Open for both lunch and dinner (11:30 A.M.–10 P.M., and until 10:30 on weekends) seven days a week. Reservations are suggested, especially in summer. **286 Thames St. opposite the wharves; (401) 848-2105.**

Puerini's—$$ to $$$

The pasta here, which is what everyone comes for, is made in the restaurant's own factory in nearby Fall River, Massachusetts, so you can be sure of the best pasta around, at its freshest. Pasta is the basis for every entree, or is at

257

least served in generous portions with it. Chicken breast is stirred with artichoke hearts over spinach fettuccine, shrimp is sautéed in butter over linguini, and ten different entrees combine pasta with vegetables at $9 or $10 each. Bring your own wine, and expect a wait—Puerini's, like many other places in town, doesn't take reservations. Also no credit cards or smoking. Open Sun. and Tues–Thur. from 5–9 P.M., Sat. from 5–10 P.M. Closed in January. **24 Memorial Blvd.; (401) 847-5506.**

Dry Dock Seafood—$

You wouldn't choose this very plain little restaurant for its decor or ambiance, but it is a good choice for fresh fish prepared in a straightforward way. Flounder stuffed with spinach and served with hollandaise is about as fancy as it gets. The sardines are a favorite here, but you can get fish and chips, baked stuffed shrimp, pasta dishes with seafood, a fish platter or chicken—fried, grilled or baked and stuffed. No reservations. Bring your own wine and be prepared to pay cash. Luckily, dinner or lunch (open from 11 A.M.–10 P.M., to 11 P.M. on Fri. and Sat.) won't cost a lot. **Located on lower Thames, at the corner of Howard St.; (401) 847-3974.**

Pronto—$$ to $$$

Mediterranean cooking styles predominate at this eclectic and popular Thames St. restaurant. The elegant interior is candlelit, with crisp linens and flowers on each table, but the formality is moderated by the open kitchen. Grilled striped bass is served with marinated scallops, strip steak is blackened and served with Gorgonzola and port wine butter and half a chicken is roasted with herbs and served with a roasted corn risotto. Pasta dishes run $10 to $15. The wine list includes more than 25 choices—domestic, French and Italian. Reservations are accepted, a rarity on fashionable lower Thames St. Open Mon.–Sat. from 11:30 A.M.–4 P.M. for lunch, Sun.–Thur. from 5–10:30 P.M., Fri. and Sat. from 5–11 P.M. and

Sun. from 10 A.M.–4 P.M. for brunch. **464 Thames St.; (401) 847-5251.**

Restaurant Bouchard— $$$$

Elegant, with good lighting and well-spaced tables, Bouchard looks so inviting as you pass its window that you want to walk right in even before you scan the menu posted outside. (We appreciated the thoughtful gesture of providing menus inside the separate foyer on frosty nights so we didn't have to shiver in the wind as we read the one outdoors.) The menu uses classic French preparation to present a slightly wider range of ingredients, such as roasted free-range hen with Oriental vegetables or salmon in a mushroom puree wrapped in phyllo. Most dishes are pure France—baby pheasant in truffle sauce, wild baby boar in a spicy brown sauce, sweetbreads in tarragon. Begin with escargot or asparagus with morels.

The owners have not tried to turn the fine old interior of the Thames St. building into a French bistro or cafe, as so many would have done—the elegant decor is just right for the location and for the haute taste menu. They accept reservations, but you should call early, as the restaurant gets a lot of attention from the Providence foodies. Open Wed.–Mon from 6–10 P.M. **505 Thames St.; (401) 846-0123.**

Cafe Zelda—$$

The most difficult part of eating dinner at Zelda is making your way through the lively, always crowded bar to get to the quieter dining room. It's hard to resist the appetizer menu—nachos, kabobs with wasabi dipping sauce, calamari with pepperoncini, crab and shrimp cakes, Gorgonzola bread and steamed mussels. Basically Italian enlivened by a few other influences, the menu offers entrees such as blackened tuna, tricolor ravioli in a sauce of sun-dried tomatoes, penne with shrimp and artichoke hearts, honey-roasted chicken with herbs and a confetti of shellfish in garlic tomato sauce. A good-sized wine list includes

Australian and Chilean wines along with domestic, Italian and French selections. Reservations are accepted (bless them), and there is live entertainment Wednesday through Friday nights. Open every day for lunch (in the high season) and dinner, opening at noon on Sunday for a popular brunch menu. **528 Lower Thames St.; (401) 849-4002.**

Scales & Shells —$$ to $$$

Always crowded and noisy, with few frills, a youngish crowd and impeccably fresh seafood, Scales is as popular with locals as with visitors. The day's catch is prepared without artifice, most notably over mesquite on the grill that takes up one end of the dining room. Specials fill the oversized blackboard on the back wall. Fish and chips, shrimp or scallop piccata, calamari vinaigrette and scallops Marsala are other popular items on the regular menu.

The tiny bar is far too small to accommodate all the people waiting for tables, as is the only other corner of the room where they can wait, so the line usually trails down the street. No smoking, no credit cards (although they'll take your out-of-town check if you have identification) and no reservations. The second-floor counterpart, **Up Scales**, does take reservations and has the same menu and casual atmosphere. It closes from Oct. 12 until spring. **527 Thames St.; (401) 846-FISH.**

Asterix and Obelix Cafe Restaurant—$$ to $$$

While a refurbished garage may not seem like an ideal venue for a restaurant, this one has been redecorated in softened primary colors, and its roll-up front doors have been converted to glass. They open up in the summer to let the breezes in and connect the dining room, European-style, to the sidewalk cafe in front. Mediterranean and Asian cuisines blend in such entrees as farfalle with salmon, and asparagus in a tomato cream sauce or sautéed swordfish with roasted macadamia nuts in a Thai curry lobster sauce with Chinese greens. Orvieto

chicken is savory with black olives, roasted potatoes and rosemary. Begin with the not-quite-crumbly pâté, perfectly laced with cognac. Vegetables are respected, properly cooked and not treated as a garnish; the crisp green beans are so small they fall between the tines of a fork. Service is amiable and well informed as well as good humored.

The restaurant is fully wheelchair-accessible. Ask about the Monday evening cooking classes. Open for lunch in the summer only, for dinner until 10 P.M. Sun.–Thur. and until 11 P.M. on Fri. and Sat. Reservations are a must on weekends and in the summer. **599 Lower Thames St.; (401) 841-8833.**

The West Deck—$$$

Not just another waterfront eatery, The West Deck has made a big splash in the dining scene with both seafood and meats. The signature fillet mignon with Stilton is excellent, as almost any variation on this rare-red-meat and blue-veined cheese with Port theme is bound to be. The seafood is beautifully prepared and delivered, seared to just the right point and sauced with bright flavors that offer contrast without overpowering the main event. Look for sea bass in a black-olive crust with fennel sauce, or a grilled shrimp and sea scallop brochette with chipotle pepper. Most popular on the dessert menu are the fondant au chocolat and the rum-raisin bread pudding. In nice weather you can have a drink at the outdoor bar and watch the boats come and go. Open Wed.–Sun. from 6–10 P.M., and Oct.–May, Sun. from noon–3 P.M. **One Waites Wharf (off Lower Thames St.), Newport; (401) 847-3610.**

Elizabeth's Cafe—$$$

In a cozy, eclectic atmosphere of unmatched furniture and rich dark paisley tablecovers, Elizabeth's serves prodigious quantities of well-prepared food. It's not the place to go with someone who doesn't like the same dishes you do—everything is served in platters for two. But it's hard not to like the bouillabaisse

259

served in a sour dough loaf "bowl" or the lobster paella. Bring your own wine. Elizabeth serves a splendid afternoon tea, but call first for the day's exact time. Open Tues.–Sun., noon–3:30 P.M. and 5:30–10 P.M. **404 Thames St.; (401) 846-6862.**

Mama Luisa—$ to $$

The informal family-run taverna atmosphere is the right counterpoint to a hearty but sophisticated cuisine of Italian dishes. Special attention is paid to vegetables; side orders include carrots in Marsala and roasted onions. The gnocchi, which are a specialty, are tender and light, never oversauced. No need to bring your own wine, as in the past; Mama Luisa now has a license and a list of 30 or so wines from Italy. They wisely accept reservations, since they are a bit removed from the restaurant "shopping" zone, way down **lower Thames St.; (401) 848-5257.**

La Petite Auberge—$$$ to $$$$

Not so long ago, a classic French restaurant was the only place to go for a really fine meal. The dining revolution has changed that but has not diminished the appeal of a finely tuned French dinner. Happily, Chef Roger Putier has not forsaken his culinary heritage, and at his restaurant, in the historic home of the naval hero Stephen Decatur, he serves its finest dishes: chicken paired with morels, tournedos Rossini, snails with ceps, goose liver and country pâtés, lobster tails with truffles, frog legs and tenderloin Wellington. An impressive list of specials each night may include an appetizer of chèvre over mesclun or an entree of venison medallions in a richly flavored Marchand de Vin sauce. The list of dessert specials outnumbers the nine on the menu; the wait staff is highly knowledgeable and can describe each in mouth-watering detail and perform tableside shows with flamed dishes. Jackets are de rigueur in this atmosphere of lace tablecloths and candlelight. A cafe menu, served in the pleasant courtyard in the sum-

mer or the informal cafe in the winter, is less expensive: roasted quail with caramelized onion, duck with bourbon and green peppercorn sauce, or a Brie horseradish burger. Open Mon.–Sat. from 6–10 P.M., Sun. 5–9 P.M. **19 Charles St., off Washington Sq.; (401) 849-6669.**

Picnic Foods

Several of the cafes listed above will pack sandwiches to go, and most offer bottled drinks as well.

The Market

The Market names its sandwiches after the Bellevue Ave. mansions—Chateau-sur-Mer is a fresh-baked croissant filled with rosemary chicken salad, dried apricots and almonds—and they are just as stylish. You can have them packed as a box lunch with potato salad, fruit and a cookie for $8 or with a fancier combination for $10. The gourmet box lunch of Brie and grapes, chicken breast with blue cheese on a baguette, vegetable salad and cheesecake is $15. **43 Memorial Blvd.; (401) 848-2600.**

Services

Visitor Information

Newport Convention and Visitors Bureau, 23 America's Cup Ave., Newport 02840; (401) 849-8048 or **(800) 326-6030.**

International visitors can find assistance at **Newport Council for International Visitors, P.O. Box 3032, Newport 02840; (401) 846-0222.** Foreign currency may be exchanged at **Citizens Bank, 8 Washington Square; (401) 847-4411.**

In an emergency, dial 911. **The Newport Hospital, on Friendship St.,** has an emergency room; **(401) 846-6400.**

Public rest rooms are located in the **Visitor's Center, the Mary Street Parking Lot** (open only in the summer) and the **Seaman's Church Institute.** Public showers, of particular interest to boaters, are in the

Seaman's Church Institute on America's Cup Ave. at Market Sq. ($2 on the honor system). The Institute also has laundry facilities.

Taxis

Cozy Transportation Services operates taxis and airport shuttles (about $15); (401) 846-2500.

Access for the Disabled

The Newport Convention and Visitors Bureau offers a brochure listing lodgings, shops, eating places and attractions with varying degrees of accessibility; (401) 849-8048 or (800) 326-6030. The Visitors Center itself is fully accessible. Belcourt Castle, The Breakers and The Elms have elevator access to upper floors, although the width of the elevator at The Elms may not accommodate some wheelchairs. In each case you should call first. The Naval War College Museum, the Newport Yachting Center, Newport Art Museum and Green Animals are accessible, although the latter two do not have accessible rest rooms. The same is true of the Block Island Ferry, although harbor tours by Oldport Marine use fully accessible boats. The chain hotels all offer at least two specially designed rooms. Mill Street Inn and Francis Malbone House both have wheelchair-accessible rooms. A number of restaurants have access, including Muriel's, Christie's and Yesterday's. Most of the churches, among them historic Trinity Church, are accessible.

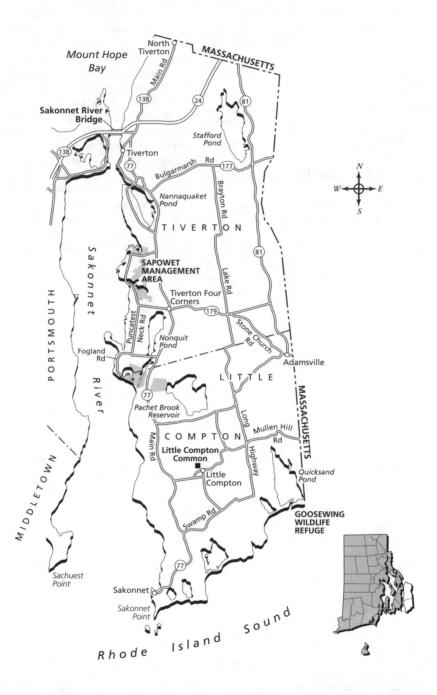

Mount Hope
Bay

North
Tiverton

MASSACHUSETTS

Main Rd

138

24

81

Sakonnet River
Bridge

Stafford
Pond

138

Tiverton

77

Bulgarmarsh   Rd   177

Brayton Rd

Nannaquaket
Pond

TIVERTON

81

Sakonnet

River

SAPOWET
MANAGEMENT
AREA

PORTSMOUTH

Tiverton Four
Corners

Lake Rd

179

Stone Church Rd

Puncatest   Neck Rd

Nonquit
Pond

Fogland
Rd

Adamsville

LITTLE

77

Pachet Brook
Reservoir

MASSACHUSETTS

MIDDLETOWN

COMPTON

Mullen Hill
Rd

Main Rd

Little Compton
Common

Long   Highway

Quicksand
Pond

Little
Compton

Swamp Rd

GOOSEWING
WILDLIFE
REFUGE

77

Sachuest
Point

Sakonnet

77

Sakonnet
Point

R h o d e   I s l a n d   S o u n d

N

W   E

S

East of the Sakonnet: Tiverton and Little Compton

Tiverton and Little Compton are rather like an island off on the east side of Narragansett Bay and connected to the rest of the state only by the Sakonnet River Bridge. They are bounded on the west and south by the Sakonnet River and Rhode Island Sound and on the east and north by Massachusetts. The region is much like the adjoining area of Massachusetts, with a gentle climate and gently rolling countryside. The area and its Massachusetts neighbor are largely agricultural, and the mild climate makes each home to an outstanding New England vintner.

History

These eastern towns were settled by people from the Plymouth Plantation, in Massachusetts, in the 1660s. While the Rhode Island colony had reason to claim them, the Plymouth claim was validated by early settlement and by the building of the Great Road into the area. (see page **265**). King Philip's War extended to these remote towns across the bay, which were attacked. Fogland Beach in Tiverton was the scene of a 1675 attack, and the following year a Quaker minister was killed and dismembered. After the war the citizen farmers found alliance with Rhode Island more to their liking, not only because of similar views on religious tolerance but also because the Newport markets were closer and easier to reach.

The towns resisted Massachusetts control. Tiverton, for example, refused to appoint a minister to be paid with tax money, and when it was forced to do so in 1702 it appointed a Quaker to spite the Puritans of Boston. Matters finally came to a head, and in 1740 Rhode Island asked the colonial board of trade to appoint a commission to decide the issue. Five men, drawn from New York, New Jersey and Nova Scotia met and recommended a boundary line. Massachusetts appealed to London, but Rhode Island won.

During the Revolution, area men prevented the British from using the Sakonnet River to attack Providence and Bristol, both important ports and places of refuge after the British took Newport. In 1792, Captain Robert Gray from Tiverton set sail in his vessel *Columbia* to explore the Northwest coast and discovered the river that now bears the name of his ship. His discovery gave the United States a basis for its claim to Oregon.

Farming and fishing remained for many years primary occupations in the area, with some shipbuilding along the shores of Nannaquaket Pond in the area opposite the intersections of Rtes. 77 and 177. The 1800s, as in the rest of the state, saw the coming of manufacturing, although not on the scale found elsewhere. The largest complex was the Bourne Mill, with five buildings erected in 1881 at the north end of Tiverton. It had 2,640 looms and 1,000 employees and operated until 1961.

Getting There

From Newport take Rte. 138 or 24 north and cross the Sakonnet River Bridge, taking Rte. 77 south on the east end of the bridge. From Providence and I-95 take I-195 east to Fall River, Massachusetts, then take Rte. 24 south to Rte. 77 before the Sakonnet River Bridge. Rte. 77 continues the length of the area, ending at Sakonnet Point.

Outdoor Activities

Biking

There is some wonderful cycling in this part of the state, fairly level touring through quiet countryside without heavy traffic. The following route is not only attractive but passes many of the highlights of this chapter. Start at Tiverton Four Corners and head south on Rte. 77. On the left after about a mile and a quarter there is a side trip to **Fogland Beach** (see page **267**). In just under two miles you will pass **Sakonnet Vineyards** (see page **270**) and Peckham Rd., continuing on to Meetinghouse Lane on the left, about a mile and three-quarters farther. (If you continue south on Rte. 77

about two and a half miles you can take Sakonnet Rd. about a mile and a half farther to Sakonnet Point). Follow Meetinghouse Rd. east to Little Compton Common. Take Willow Ave. north, then take Simmons Rd. east just north of the library. At the T, go left on East Main Rd. and continue straight ahead onto Snell Rd. when East Main makes a sharp left. When Snell intersects with Long Hwy., go left. This road will take you to Colebrook Rd. (also called Adamsville Rd.) on the right, which you should take to Rte. 179. To the right a short distance is the village of **Adamsville** with its chicken monument and historic buildings (see page **269**). From Adamsville take Rte. 179 (Stone Church Rd., which will become East Rd. when you pass Lake Rd.) back to Tiverton Four Corners, where you should reward yourself with a coffee cabinet or ice cream at **Gray's Ice Cream.**

For a side trip, at Meetinghouse Rd. you can continue down Rte. 77. You will pass **Wilbour House** (see page **268**), and at about two and a half miles you will come to Sakonnet Point Rd. A bit over a mile down this road you will come to **Sakonnet Point.** You can either retrace your path back to Meetinghouse Rd. or to Swamp Rd. and take it and Brownell Rd. east just over a mile to South Shore Rd., on the right. This will bring you to **South Shore Beach** (the town beach) and the **Goosewing Wildlife Refuge on Quicksand Pond.** Return up South Shore Rd., turning right onto John Sisson Rd. It will intersect with Long Hwy., which you take to the left (north). On the left you will pass the Snell Rd. intersection and return to the path of the main tour.

Birding

The best bird-watching is in the **Emilie Ruecker Wildlife Refuge** and the **Sapowet Marsh Management Area.** You can find pheasants, rails, ruffed grouse, screech owls, mourning doves, goldfinches, white-eyed vireos, great and little blue herons, cattle egrets and snowy and great egrets, glossy ibis, black-crowned night herons, yellow-rumped and yellow warblers, redstarts, yellowthroats, quail, mockingbirds, thrashers, orioles, bitterns, sandpipers and, during migrations, many varieties of ducks and other waterfowl. There is a short white blazed trail from the yellow trail that leads to an observation blind on a small pond. On the circular section at the end of the yellow trail take one of the narrow paths to the shore and look around on the north shore for tiny fiddler crabs, with one oversized claw, bustling about their business. The best viewing of shore birds is at the end of the blue trail. See the Hiking and Walking section on page **266** for directions.

One of the best places to see the rare piping plover and the equally rare least tern is at **Goosewing Beach Preserve.** The beach forms a barrier between the sea and **Quicksand Pond,** which opens to the sea through a breach. The pond is a breeding ground for shellfish that provide the food for the birds and their young. The area is owned by The Nature Conservancy, which gives guided tours in the summer. Take Rte. 77 south through Tiverton to Swamp Rd. east in Little Compton. Go 1.7 mile to South Shore Rd. and to the town beach, where the entrance is. A $5 beach parking fee is charged during beach season; **(401) 331-7110.** Not far away, **Sakonnet Point** is a good place to spot gulls, loons and mergansers. During the fall it is a good place to see migrating hawks. Take Rte. 77 to its end, then take Sakonnet Point Rd.

Canoeing

Sapowet Marsh Management Area offers boating and canoeing in the marsh channels, noted for their bird life. The area is situated on the east shore of the Sakonnet River, a large estuary that lies between Aquidneck Island and the eastern townships of Rhode Island and runs from Rhode Island Sound to Fall River, Massachusetts. The channels pass through a grassy intertidal marsh zone that is heavily used by migrating waterfowl. From Sapowet Ave., the road turns south and becomes Puncatest Neck Rd. where there is an unimproved ramp. Some maps show this section of road as a continuation of Sapowet Ave.

Fishing

One of the favorite places for shore fishing is the **Stone Bridge at Grinnell's Beach** in Tiverton and south from there along the shore of **Nannaquaket Pond.** It's on Rte. 77 at the Stone Bridge. Farther south along Rte. 77 there is good fishing from the shore at **Sapowet Point** at **Sapowet Marsh Wildlife Preserve** and from boats in the marsh channels. The Sakonnet River off of **Fogland** and from **Gould's Island off Nannaquaket Pond** are both good for boat fishing. For freshwater fishing try **Dundery Brook** in the **Wilbour Woods,** which is well stocked with trout. From Rte. 77 in Little Compton take Swamp Rd. east 0.3-mile to the entrance on the left. You can fish from the rocks at Sakonnet Point, where there is also a boat put-in.

Hiking and Walking

Weetamoo Woods

You begin this hike on a part of the **Great Road** built in the middle of the 1600s from Plymouth Plantation to its distant settlers. This is a long and at times difficult hike, but it's through beautiful and varied environments showing nature's ability to heal itself after intrusive human activity. There are trail maps at the parking lot (sometimes). Close to the beginning of the trail you pass over a stone-slab bridge believed to date from the time of the construction of the road, certainly one of the oldest bridges in the United States. Following the **Red Trail,** you will come across the ruins of an old water-powered up-and-down sawmill with its huge stone-and-earth dam over 10 feet tall and raceway 50 feet long. Another stone slab bridge from the 1750s is close by. When the Red Trail comes to the gasline easement, go to the far side and find the trail into the woods that is lined with parallel logs. The trail goes through laurels a short way to the foundations of an old farm. Return to the gas easement and follow it to the right (if you went to the old farm) to a dirt road that is just past a collapsed shack on the left side of the easement and just before a new house. In a short distance the trail comes out on Lafayette Rd. Follow it to the left to a sign for **Wildcat Rock,** where you can follow the yellow-blazed trail to the top of Wildcat Rock, around to the base of the cliff, and through a huge jumble of rocks before returning to the road. In a short distance follow the yellow blazes again, on the left side of the road, along the **Weetamoo Indian Trail.** You pass through rock jumbles and along stone walls, reminders that this was once farmland. There is another section of laurel in this area. Be sure to follow the yellow blazes as the trail leaves an old woods road. The trail will then turn left onto a woods road and follow the stone wall. A short blue-blazed side trail will take you to **High Rock,** with glacial striations and a view at the top. Return to the Blue Trail and continue on to the intersection with the Red Trail, which you retrace to the parking lot.

To get to Weetamoo Woods, take Rte. 77 (Main Rd.) south to East Rd. (Rte. 179) and follow it about a half mile to the entrance on the left. Weetamoo is owned and operated by the Town of Tiverton Open Space Commission. Maps are also available on weekdays at **Town Hall, Highland Rd., Tiverton 02878.**

Emilie Ruecker Wildlife Refuge—Sapowet Marsh Management Area

During the 1920s, Newport-born artist Emilie Ruecker won acclaim in Paris for her light landscapes inspired by the scenes around her Tiverton farm. To preserve the land that was so special to her, she donated it to the Audubon Society of Rhode Island as a wildlife refuge. The state has also acquired approximately 300 adjacent acres for the marsh management area on the south side of the refuge, to protect the marsh channels. Note that the management area is called "Sapowet" but that the name on the street sign is "Seapowet."

Two of the three walking trails begin at the parking lot. The third is an optional extension of one of them. The **Red Trail** wanders through woods, passing an exposed outcrop of the conglomerate rock that underlies this part of the state. Close by is an open area surrounded by

vine-draped trees where woodcock perform their mating dance in early spring. The trail then joins the **Yellow Trail,** and you return to the parking lot by going left. The Yellow Trail from the parking lot passes through pine and spruce with bittersweet vines. Close to the freshwater pond you can find frogs, toads, salamanders and swallows and eastern phoebes. The **Blue Trail** begins a short way past some blueberry fields and, a bit farther, the Red Trail enters from the right. The trail then circles around the edge of the marsh before returning to the intersection with the Red Trail. If you follow the Blue Trail, it will take you onto a small peninsula that overlooks a marsh with a variety of shore- and seabirds wading and feeding in its waters. The viewing is best at low tide. In the marshes are cordgrass, spike grass, seaside plantain, saltmeadow grass, rushes and bayberry. These walks are short and easy—all three can easily be completed in a morning or afternoon without rushing. Mosquitoes are a problem here, so be sure to bring repellent. A trail map is usually available on-site. Fishing and hunting are permitted in the management area, and there is a canoe put-in. From Rte. 24, take Rte. 77 south past Nannaquaket Pond. Turn right onto Seapowet Ave.; the refuge will be about a half mile on the right. (The entrance is hard to see.) **Rhode Island Division of Fish & Wildlife, Government Center, Tower Hill Rd., Wakefield 02879; (401) 789-3094; Audubon Society of Rhode Island, 12 Sanderson Rd., Smithfield 02917; (401) 231-6444.**

Fort Barton

The town of Tiverton has set up a nature trail at Fort Barton (see page **267**), a pleasant walk along trails where many of the trees are labeled. Start at the top of the fort and take the gravel path to the stairs that descend into a deep ravine. The blazes on the main trail are red, with blue blazes marking side loops. The trail climbs out of the ravine and will pass by outcroppings of conglomerate stone called pudding stone. Passing along a hollow, the trail crosses a brook on a log bridge and runs along the edges of a pond. A small river you will cross is called **Sin and Flesh Brook,** so named for the Quaker minister who was slaughtered near the stream during King Philip's War. His body was thrown into it, turning the water red. Despite the gruesome origins of its name, this is a beautiful and peaceful place. To get there from Rte. 77, take Lawton Ave. uphill to Highland Rd. Parking is across the street from the intersection. At the **Tiverton Town Hall** across the street, open weekdays, you can get a trail map.

Wilbour Woods

This 75-acre reserve is noted particularly for stands of American holly at the northern edge of its range; only the proximity of the warm bay waters allow the plant to survive this far north. Several dirt roads through the area provide easy walking access, and fishing is permitted in the brook. In the park, a stone monument remembers the seventeenth-century female sachem Awashonks, who kept her Sakonnet tribe from joining the Wampanoag Indians in King Philip's War. From Rte. 77 in Little Compton take Swamp Rd. east 0.3-mile to the entrance on the left. **Town of Little Compton, Commons, Little Compton 02837; (401) 635-4000.**

Horseback Riding

Roseland Acres Equestrian Center

Horseback riding is pleasant and easy here, with the weather moderated in spring and fall by the bay. This family-owned equestrian center offers both English and western styles for novice through advanced riders. There are one- and two-hour trail rides, special beach rides and horseback outings on miles of wooded bridle paths. In addition to trail rides, they have a staff of trained instructors who offer training in hunt seat, cross-country, dressage, gymkhana and pleasure riding. Four 11-day camp sessions are available during the summer. **594 East Rd., Tiverton 02878; (401) 624-8866.**

Swimming

Grinnell's Beach is right at the old abutments to the Stone Bridge in the village of Tiverton, with lifeguards, changing rooms and rest rooms. The old bridge approach and abutments are popular fishing places, and there are swings for kids. Just past the Emilie Ruecker Wildlife Refuge **Jack's Beach,** the entrance is at the end of Seapowet Ave., where the road turns south. Farther down Rte. 77, near the Little Compton line, is another beach at the **Fogland peninsula.** Scene of an Indian attack on colonial troops and their rescue, the area is more peaceful now. It has lifeguards, rest rooms, picnic tables and swings. There is a fee. From Rte. 77 take Pond Bridge Rd. west, and at the T go left and then immediately right onto Fogland Rd. and High Hill Rd.

Seeing and Doing

Historical Sites

Fort Barton

At the beginning of the American Revolution, colonial leaders built **Tiverton Heights Fort** on a high hill overlooking the Sakonnet River to protect Providence and Bristol from attack by British forces. From its commanding position they could see to Rhode Island Sound and across to Aquidneck Island, so no vessels could get by this point without being discovered. In 1777 the fort commander, Lieutenant Colonel William Barton, took 40 men across to Portsmouth, where they discovered and overcame the headquarters of the British commander, General Richard Prescott (see page **193**).

The following year the fort was a headquarters for the 10,000-man colonial army that gathered for the Battle of Rhode Island under the command of Generals Sullivan, Varnum, Glover, Lafayette and Greene. Never directly attacked, the fort played a vital role in the American War of Independence. From the top of the observation tower inside the breastworks of the fort it is easy to see how important this site was. The earthworks are still visible. The fort is above the harbor, opposite the Tiverton Town Hall.

Tiverton Historical Road Tour

In 1994, for the tricentennial of the town, a little booklet was published with a road tour of the town's historic sites. We point out the highlights here, but if you can, get a copy of the booklet at the town hall (take Lawton Ave. opposite Stone Bridge and at the top of the hill at Highland Rd. it's on the right) or from **Paul's Press, 7 Main Rd. (Rte. 77) Tiverton 02878; (401) 624-2297.**

Start the tour at the town beach at High Hill, **Fogland Beach,** where Indians attacked colonials in 1675, then go back toward Rte. 77 (noting the fish ladder where the road crosses over Almy's Creek) and turn left at Main Rd. Go to East St. (Rte. 179) and turn right. On your left you will go by **Weetamoo Woods Refuge,** and eventually East Rd. becomes Stone Church Rd. The sides of the road are lined with eighteenth-century stone walls, and it leads to the **Old Stone Church.** If you continue on you will come to Adamsville in Little Compton (see page **269**).

Return via Stone Church/East Rd. to Rte. 77 (noticing the alpaca farm on the right). The **Four Corners** (at Gray's Ice Cream) was, until 1812, the site of the town whipping post, where miscreants were publicly flogged. The women of the town, offended by the practice, joined together in 1812 and toppled the post, so ending public flogging in town. On the opposite corner the beautiful building is the **Soule-Seabury mansion** (1770/1809). Just south of Gray's is the **Chase-Cory House,** built in 1730 and now the home of the Tiverton Historical Society. **Tiverton Four Corners** is the historic center of town. Down Main Rd. at the millpond is an old gristmill, and on the west side of the street the preserved **Tripp's Wheelwright Shop.**

North of the intersection you pass the **Union Library** (1820), the 1832 **Parsonage** and the **Amicable Congregational Church** (1811/1846). Just beyond the church (at **3622 Main Rd.**) is the **home of Captain Robert Gray,** master of the *Columbia*. On the right past Seapowet Ave. at **3118 Main Rd.,** is the **house used by General Lafayette** before the Battle of Rhode Island in 1788. Turn left onto Nannaquaket Rd. along the shore of Nannaquaket Pond, and at the end turn right back to Main Rd. **St. James Convent** was once the home of a wealthy fisherman, Nathaniel Church. Continue north on Main Rd. to **Grinnell's Beach** and **Stone Bridge.** Originally ferries ran from here to Portsmouth across the Sakonnet. Finally a bridge was built, but it was destroyed by storms so often that in 1957 it was replaced by the Sakonnet Bridge upstream. Note the "Doughboy," a World War I memorial. Go up Lawton St. to **Fort Barton** (see page **267**) and look out over the town, river and Narragansett Bay.

Chace-Cory House

This venerable house sits on the east side of Main Rd. in the historic district of Tiverton. Built about 1730, little change has been made over the years. The kitchen still has its huge fireplace, built for heat and cooking, as well as its original paneling. In the parlor is a chocolate pot given to the original owners of the house by Captain Robert Gray, the master of the ship *Columbia*. Fully furnished with items from the original period through the Victorian era, it is a snapshot of life in this area from early times until the turn of the twentieth century. Today it is the home of the Tiverton Historical Society and is open June–Sept. on Sun. from 2–4:30 P.M. It is just south of the intersection of East Rd. (Rte. 179) and Main Rd. (Rte. 77).

Wilbour House

If this isn't the oldest house in the area, it's close. Originally smaller than it is now, consisting of the kitchen and the great room above, it was enlarged by succeeding generations of the same family, who lived here from 1680 until 1925. Restoration took over two years and is still going on. While most of the original detail of the house is still there, any missing or severely damaged items, such as doors, were replaced with pieces from other houses of the period that were being demolished. This is a community project, with many of the items in the house on loan by families who have been in this town since its beginning. Each part of the house is true to the era when it was built, so that it represents the change in style and affluence of its inhabitants from the seventeenth through the nineteenth centuries. The original kitchen is dominated by the huge fireplace, once the center of family life, and is furnished from the period 1690 through 1740. During the eighteenth century the family fared well and added a formal federal-style parlor and a new kitchen with a smaller fireplace and baking oven. A century later, in 1860, another new kitchen was built, again with the latest advantages, including a woodstove. Each of the three kitchens is equipped with the implements and dishware appropriate to its period. Be sure to see the understairs area, where all of the fireplaces join back to back. A large barn houses antique farming equipment and Indian artifacts. By the door of the house is a fine walled herb garden. Open late-June–mid-Sept. Wed.–Sun. from 2–5 P.M. There is a $4 entry fee. **Little Compton Historical Society, P.O. Box 577, Little Compton 02837.**

Little Compton Common

Very few Rhode Island towns have a town common, as most other New England towns do. Tiverton and Little Compton, however, were settled by the Puritan colony of Plymouth Plantation, and the first thing done in these settlements was to lay out common land with the official church prominent within it. The first important buildings of these communities were erected around the common. This triangular common is a fine example. A fine white Congregational church (showing the Puritan influence) was built in 1832 and modernized by the Victorians in 1872. Its graveyard (dating from 1675) has old slate stones and the grave of Elizabeth Pabodie, who was married to the first town clerk and who was the daughter of John Alden and Priscilla Mullins. Also look for the grave of Elizabeth Mortimer, who died in 1776. Her inscription says she "should have been the wife of Simeon Palmer." They were married, but apparently he was so disagree-

able that they lived apart, and she did nothing more than cook and keep house for him.

Adamsville

The village of Adamsville is a small settlement of eighteenth- and nineteenth-century buildings on the Massachusetts border in the northeast corner of town. It is probably best known for the world's only monument to a chicken. The chicken so honored was first developed here as the first bird bred for *both* meat and egg production. At the height of its popularity the breed was the predominant one in the country. Across the street look for the strange wooden tower. It's called the **Spite Tower.** It seems that the sister of Abraham Manchester, who ran a store and inn across the way, would signal him when dinner was ready by hanging a lantern in the window of the house. After Abraham argued with his neighbor, the neighbor built the tower so that Abraham could no longer see the lantern. The fine collection of buildings here includes **Gray's General Store** (see page **270**), and the gristmill beyond. There has been a gristmill here since 1675, and the current one (1877) operates Saturdays and Sundays. The village gives a real sense of life to the New England countryside of a century ago.

Sakonnet Point and Lighthouse

The southernmost part of this area, Sakonnet Point, is on Rhode Island Sound, opposite Sachuest Point National Wildlife Refuge in Newport. The point is a big granite outcrop that forms a small natural harbor, home to a small, still active, fishing fleet. This is a popular place to put in a boat for fishing in the sound and in the Sakonnet River. It is also a good place to see Sakonnet Light, restored but no longer active. During spring and fall you can see migrating waterfowl and hawk here. Follow Rte. 77 south to its end and take Sakonnet Point Rd.

Shopping

Tiverton Four Corners

A number of small shops cluster here. Start at **Provender** (see page **271**), with its line of gourmet foods, both fresh and packaged. **Provender Garden** has unusual garden items, such as fine imported English garden tools. Between the two stores is a pleasant garden where you can eat your picnic or just look around. Down the street a short walk, just beyond the Chace-Cory House, **The Millpond** shops include **Willow Farm Herbs,** which has a wide variety of herbs and related products. **Country Corner** has antiques, quilts and English reproductions, and the **Windmill** also has home-decorating accessories. These shops are in a setting of attractive gardens, herbs and exotic trees.

Sakonnet Vineyards

For more than 20 years the vintners of Sakonnet have been producing quality wines from grapes grown in Little Compton. Now found in stores outside the area, the wine has gained a faithful following in New England. The vintners produce three dry whites, a chardonnay, an estate chardonnay and America's Cup white, as well as a semi-dry Spinnaker white. The reds include an estate pinot noir, America's Cup red, a claret and Rhode Island red. For those who like a blush wine there is Eye of the Storm, the most popular wine. Sakonnet Vineyards offers tastings, vineyard tours and a map, so you can find the vines that produce the grapes for your favorite wine. The tours are on the hour and take about 45 minutes. There is a slide show and a tour of the facilities. In the store you can buy picnic packs, baguettes and goat cheese, Camembert and New England cheddars. A variety of events are held throughout the summer and fall including **Picnic in Paradise,** combining top Rhode Island chefs with wine and music in late June, another special wine and food celebration in mid-July, a harvest festival in early October, also with restaurant food specialties, and **Celebrate Crush** on the second weekend of October, when there is a farmer's market, outdoor concert and wine events. **162 West Main Rd., Little Compton 02837; (401) 635-8486.** (Wine enthusiasts will want to continue into Massachusetts to the nearby Westport Vineyards.)

DeLucia's Berry Farm

The DeLucias operate a small berry farm close to the Sakonnet Vineyards where they raise their own berries and make them into delicious jams, jellies, marmalades and vinegars: Raspberry, blackberry, gooseberry, blueberry, strawberry and peach flavors are sold, as well as combinations. This isn't a big production, but it's nice to find good, fresh local products where you can meet the people who made them. They also sell their preserves by mail. Take Peckham Rd. just south of the vineyard and then turn right onto Willow Ave. DeLucia's will be on the left side of the street. **96 Willow Ave., Little Compton 02837; (401) 635-2698.**

Gray's Gristmill and General Store

Gray's Store has been operating in this spot in this building since 1788. This isn't one of those old-time stores gussied up for the tourists. The town's first post office was here, and you can peek into the postmaster's room, which looks like he stepped out for a minute a hundred years ago and never came back. On the shelves in the back are sold jonnycake, pancake and muffin mix and whole-wheat and rye flours ground at the mill next door, and in a corner in the front there is a small section of antique china, dishes, glassware and do-dads for sale. High on the shelves are unopened packages of food products that haven't been seen for decades, but they're not for sale. Cold drinks, snacks, sandwiches and candy are for sale along with a few antiques. The old heating stove, soda fountain and candy and tobacco cases are real and still used. Never modernized, this is what all the other country stores try to look like. Open Thur.–Sun. from 10 A.M.– 4 P.M. **4 Main St., Little Compton (Adamsville) 02837; (401) 635-4566**

Where to Stay

The Tiverton–Little Compton area is a very rural region with few places to stay. Its proximity to Aquidneck, however, makes available ample lodging within a 45-minute drive of the area.

Where to Eat

Gray's Ice Cream—$

This is the kind of ice cream place people come to from miles around, especially on a hot summer day, but we've waited in line here in December. Gray's is famed for its coffee cabinets and the best chocolate malted we've had in years. The ice cream is rich and creamy. They also have sandwiches and burgers, plus a convenience store around the corner of the building. At the corner of Main St. **16 East Rd., Tiverton 02878; (401) 624-4500.**

Four Corners Grille—$ to $$

While the menu is good anytime, filled with interesting dishes that include crabcakes and hickory-smoked meats, if you go on Tuesday evening, you get an added bonus. The good food stays the same, but the already reasonable price drops to unbeatable: A choice of any two entrees and a bottle of wine (not a carafe of cheap house red, but a bottle of the good stuff from Sakonnet Vineyards) total less than $25. Open Mon.–Sat. from 7 A.M.–9 P.M., Sun. from 7 A.M.–8 P.M. **3841 Main Rd., Tiverton; (401) 624-1510.**

Provender—$ to $$

In a large, nicely restored French Second Empire building at Tiverton Four Corners, across from Gray's Ice Cream, Provender has everything you need for a gourmet picnic. In addition to canned and packaged foods it has a good deli counter, and Provender sells its own homemade soups, salads and sandwiches.

The bakery has a bakery with goodies from croissants to chocolate-frosted brownies, bread and oversized cookies. Open Wed.–Mon. from 9 A.M.–6 P.M. **3883 Main Rd., Tiverton 02878; (401) 624-8096.**

Commons Restaurant—$ to $$

While you know when you enter that this is not likely to be a gourmet find, it is a good lunch or breakfast stop near the Sakonnet Vineyards and the walking trails. New England and Rhode Island dishes are the specialty, including quahog chowder, quahog pie and jonnycake and the general New England fare of meat loaf, liver and onions, clam cakes, baked beans, fried clams, lobster, shepherd's pie, baked scrod and chicken croquettes. They also have soups, sandwiches and salads. During summer there is an outdoor patio. A big breakfast menu is served all day. Open 5 A.M.–8 P.M. daily. No credit cards. From Rte. 77 in Little Compton, take Meetinghouse Ln. east. **The Common, Little Compton 02837; (401) 635-2350.**

The Barn—$ to $$

Rhode Island Monthly readers once voted The Barn the best place for breakfast, so who are we to argue? Open from 6:30–11:30 A.M. weekdays, 6:30 A.M.–noon on weekends. **Main St., Little Compton (Adamsville) 02837; (401) 635-2985.**

Abraham Manchester Tavern—$ to $$$

Next door to The Barn, Abraham Manchester Tavern serves old favorites like roast beef with gravy, but also pork chops Portugal and three-pepper peppered catfish. Fish and chips is only $6.95, and the stuffed mushroom caps are a specialty. Of course Sakonnet wines are served. Open from 11:30 A.M.–10 P.M. **Main St., Little Compton (Adamsville) 02837; (401) 635-2985.**

Services

Visitor Information

Newport County Convention and Visitor's Bureau, 23 America's Cup Ave., Newport 02840; (800) 326-6030 or **(401) 849-8048.**

271

Index

Index

275

The Rhode Island Guide

276

278

About the Authors

Barbara Radcliffe Rogers and Stillman Rogers are natives who have hiked, bicycled, sailed, skied and driven through all corners of New England since childhood. Their particular fondness for Rhode Island shows in every page, as they explore it now through travelers' eyes, stopping to investigate its tiniest museums, hike its trails, sleep in its B&Bs and eat in its abundance of fine restaurants. They bring to their writing about Rhode Island the same humor, gusto and curiosity for the details of human and natural history that have brought other destinations alive in their books.

The authors of a number of books on New England and two on Europe, they are regular contributors to *Yankee Magazine's Guide to New England* and have written travel columns and articles for several magazines and newspapers, including the *Los Angeles Times, The London Free Press, Yankee* and *New England Living.*